PERGAMON POLICY STUDIES

ON BUSINESS AND ECONOMICS

TAXATION, TECHNOLOGY AND THE US ECONOMY

Ralph Landau
N. Bruce Hannay
Guest Editors

A Special Issue of *Technology In Society*

George Bugliarello
A. George Schillinger
Editors

Martha Miller Willett
Managing Editor

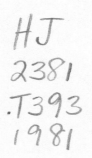

Pergamon Press

NEW YORK • OXFORD • TORONTO • PARIS • FRANKFURT • SYDNEY

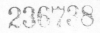

Pergamon Press Offices:

U.S.A.	Pergamon Press Inc., Maxwell House, Fairview Park, Elmsford, New York 10523, U.S.A.
U.K.	Pergamon Press Ltd., Headington Hill Hall, Oxford OX3 0BW, England
CANADA	Pergamon Press Canada Ltd., Suite 104, 150 Consumers Road, Willowdale, Ontario M2J 1P9, Canada
AUSTRALIA	Pergamon Press (Aust.) Pty. Ltd., P.O. Box 544, Potts Point, NSW 2011, Australia
FRANCE	Pergamon Press SARL, 24 rue des Ecoles, 75240 Paris, Cedex 05, France
FEDERAL REPUBLIC OF GERMANY	Pergamon Press GmbH, Hammerweg 6, Postfach 1305, 6242 Kronberg/Taunus, Federal Republic of Germany

Library of Congress Cataloging in Publication Data

Main entry under title:

Taxation, technology, and the U.S. economy.

(Pergamon policy studies on business and
economics)
"A special issue of Technology in society."
1. Taxation--United States--Addresses, essays,
lectures. 2. Technological innovations--United
States--Addresses, essays, lectures. 3. Fiscal
policy--United States--Addresses, essays, lectures.
I. Landau, Ralph. II. Hannay, N.B. (Norman
Bruce), 1921-   . III. Technology in society.
IV. Series.
HJ2381.T393   1981   338'.06   81-8540
ISBN 0-08-027564-8   AACR2
ISSN 0160-791X

Published as Volume 3, Numbers 1 and 2 of *Technology In Society* and
supplied to subscribers as part of their subscriptions. Also available to non-
subscribers.

Printed in the United States of America

Volume 3
Numbers 1 and 2
1981

Technology In Society

An International Journal

Contents

SPECIAL ISSUE

Taxation, Technology and the US Economy

(Continued on next page)

(Continued from previous page)

ISBN 0-08-027564-8   ISSN 0160-791X

Technology In Society, Vol. 3, Nos. 1 and 2 (1981)
Printed in the USA. All rights reserved.

Acknowledgment

Few issues facing the United States today inspire as much commentary and debate among people in government, industry, and various segments of the academic world and the public as the tax policy that has been outlined by the new Administration.

And few sectors of the economy could be affected by this tax policy as crucially as research and development in science and engineering which, in turn, affect the rate of development of new US technological innovation and its diffusion at home and abroad.

Months ago, long before Presidential tax policies became a popular topic of speculation and concern — indeed, even before anyone knew who the President of the United States would be in the year 1981 — two friends of *Technology In Society* inspired this issue and began to stimulate the thinking of bright, aware and informed economists, corporate executives and government figures on how governmental tax laws could — and should — affect corporations, universities and government agencies which are critical in encouraging technological innovation.

Ralph Landau, Chairman and Chief Executive Officer of Halcon International, Inc., is a self-made man, engineer, corporate chairman and entrepreneur with a first-hand knowledge of the effects of taxation on corporations and corporate decision-making. N. Bruce Hannay, Vice President for Research of Bell Laboratories, is not only a renowned scientist with a deep understanding of the economics, organization and management of R&D, but also serves in important leadership positions linking science, technology and the public interest.

Together Ralph Landau and Bruce Hannay have assembled an outstanding group of carefully considered articles for this Special Issue of *Technology In Society* which deals with *Taxation, Technology and the US Economy*.

It is their hope, and the hope of the editors of the journal, that the ideas, insights and suggestions offered in this issue will play some significant part in the development of US tax policies and, in turn, help to turn around troubled areas in the US economy and contribute to worldwide economic and social stabilization.

The editors express their deep gratitude to these distinguished guest editors for their significant contribution to *Technology In Society*.

Patrick E. Haggerty

1914 — 1980

The death of Pat Haggerty leaves a void on the Advisory Board of *Technology In Society* that will not be easy to fill. His brilliance, his enthusiasm and his unstinting willingness to help made him an invaluable adviser to the journal.

Patrick Eugene Haggerty lived the American dream — from his modest beginnings in North Dakota to Chairman of a large corporation, which he was instrumental in building. But he never lost touch with his fellow men in all walks of life, and he never said "no" to a legitimate request for assistance. His activities in professional, academic, and philanthropic areas were phenomenal; his admirers were legion.

The editors of *Technology In Society* and his fellow board members will miss Pat Haggerty as adviser, author, and — most of all — friend.

Technology In Society, Vol. 3, pp. 1–19 (1981)
Printed in the USA. All rights reserved.

Taxation, Technology and the US Economy: Introduction and Overview — The Guest Editors' Perspectives

In the past two years a great deal of national attention has been paid to innovation and its significance for the economy of the United States. Many studies have been completed — by various private and semi-public groups — culminating perhaps in the Presidential Policy Review of President Carter which engaged many levels of government as well as numerous private citizens. This review (the recommendations of which were made public on October 31, 1979) did not contain a section on tax policy, despite the strong recommendations from the various private groups — who in fact *do* the innovating — that tax policy should be the centerpiece in any systematic governmental approach to improving the climate for innovation. In 1980 the Carter administration submitted a tax bill which was never acted upon, and which made no special reference to technological innovation.

Yet it has been widely considered that innovation, and particularly technological innovation, are not as healthy as they once were, and that they are indispensable to the revival of American productivity and economic growth, particularly in an era of high energy costs and growing scarcities of raw materials, as well as increased international competition to American products. Therefore, the editors of *Technology In Society* asked us as guest editors to undertake this special issue, recognizing our involvement in this whole area for a number of years (particularly through the National Academy of Engineering). It was a particularly challenging assigment to combine for the first time in one volume an intensive study of the interrelationships between technology, taxation, and the economy. Although individual writers and witnesses before Congressional Committees (including the guest editors) have contributed isolated discussions, no overall picture has previously emerged. It is the purpose of this issue to provide such a unifying discussion.

Selection of Authors

The task of assembling the present volume was commenced in August 1980 and, of course, was begun within the reality of a Presidential election campaign of more than ordinary significance, but before the outcome was known. Hence, selection of the authors had to be made with the aim of political as well as perhaps ideological and economic balance; such an ideal can not ever be achieved in practice. We urged our prospective contributors to prepare their papers for delivery by early 1981, so as to bring this issue out in time for appropriate con-

1

sideration by the newly elected administration, whichever it might be. The intensity of the campaign itself co-opted some of the authors we might have wished to add as contributors, and also slowed down some of those who did contribute. No matter; we are delighted with those contributions that were eventually received and, with the cooperation of Pergamon Press, are hoping to have the issue out in time for serious consideration by the new Administration and Congress, as well as by various private groups. As it happens, new tax bills are before Congress at this time, and it is our hope that this special issue will be a constructive contribution to its deliberations.

No collection of authorities is ever all inclusive, of course. There are indeed, for example, experts on taxation *per se* who have no special perception or acquaintance with technological issues. We sought, rather, those who could combine both areas. For contrast, we specifically searched for authors from among the private sector who may not be noted as experts on tax policy, but who are at least expert in paying taxes and in the effects thereof on technological innovation and decision-making.

The responsibility for author selection is entirely ours. The responsibility for the contents of the individual papers is entirely that of the authors, of course, and not of any organizations with which they are affiliated.We cannot thank these busy people enough for the efforts they have made in contributing to this issue.

Comparison of the Different Approaches

The Economists

Any groupings of the papers contained herein are bound to be somewhat arbitrary. For greater clarity, we offer in the first group of papers those of the economists. An introduction to this group is the paper by **Joseph Cordes** of George Washington University, which summarizes the various private group reports that have recently been made with regard to technology and tax policy. It is a very useful introduction to this issue, and should be read as such.

Then we have a paper by the 1980 Nobel Prize Winner in Economics, **Lawrence Klein** of the University of Pennsylvania, which refers to some findings of the Wharton Econometric Model, which is his creation and which is one of the three principal private models of the US economy. Dr. Klein points out that limited personal income tax cuts (including further capital gains reduction) should not be neglected when targeting incentives for investment which would improve the *after-tax* rate of return. "Higher investment rates lead to better productivity growth and therefore lower inflation rates. This is fundamental; it is the *real* way to combat inflation, reducing it gradually over time through basic improvements in the economy." These, he points out, should be established on a longer-term basis than heretofore: "steady and long term — those should be the main characteristics of new thrusts in this area of tax policy." He singles out investment tax credits and accelerated depreciation. Klein's concise paper is a distillation of much of current econometric work, and is difficult to summarize any further herein; reference should be made to the complete paper, as is indeed true of all the papers in this issue.

Another of the prominent models of the economy is that of Data Resources, Inc. We have been fortunate in obtaining a paper by **Roger Brinner,** vice president of that firm, which employs some findings from their model. The first section of Dr. Brinner's paper emphasizes from his researches how powerful strong research and development spending is as an anti-inflation force. He shows how industries which have a high index of research effort (IRE) are those which generate innovative, internationally competitive products, hire more labor, contribute to price stability, raise productivity, and provide a high private and social rate of return, the combined total having been estimated to be as high as 35%. The recent decline in R&D spending is therefore ominous for employment, productivity, and inflation, and our society as a whole.

Then Dr. Brinner turns to the role of fixed capital, which does not have so large an anti-inflation leverage because it has been less neglected, but the social rate of return is still close to 12%. However, capital taxation is "perversely, accidentally severe when prices are increasing rapidly [inflation]. Finally, the greater the level of fixed-capital investment, the more rapidly new technology from R&D can be embodied in production processes." He therefore attributes the weak labor productivity growth over the past decade to exceedingly weak fixed- and R&D-capital-spending, and says that a reversal will require enhanced incentives. "While fixed-capital expansion may have comparatively limited leverage on inflation in contrast to R&D, its magnitude dictates it to be the fundamental determinant of labor productivity and hence per capita living standards."

Dr. Brinner thus argues for "a combination of strong tax incentives to support technology development and a tight-fiscal/low interest rate policy stance to raise the investment share of GNP." He concludes that "there is room for a range of expanded traditional investment incentives — fixed investment, tax credits, accelerated depreciation, corporate rate cuts — plus a strong R&D tax initiative," such as a 25% tax credit for R&D costs of all kinds. Data are also given opposing the Reagan Administration's large personal income tax rate cut proposals.

Another very well-known authority on capital formation is **Dale Jorgenson** of Harvard University. His paper is a major contribution to the theoretical basis of this issue, embodying a great deal of very recent macroeconomic data from a sophisticated historical model of the US economy on a disaggregated basis.

Here, too, the contents are so packed with "meat" that full reference to the paper has to be made. A primary conclusion of this study is that "the future development of technology should be the primary focus of efforts to stimulate future US economic growth." Furthermore, Jorgenson's data show that "declines in rates of technical change for the individual industrial sectors of the US economy must bear the full burden of explaining the slowdown in the rate of technical change for the economy as a whole." Therefore, "the major focus for economic policy should be to stimulate the development of new technology for all industries." Proceeding to policy then, he says, "To offset the drag on the development of new technology for the US economy as a whole . . . it is important to take immediate steps to reduce the effective rate of taxation on capital." In his view this could be a particular form of accelerated depreciation which he designates as the Auerbach-Jorgenson approach, and is described further in the paper.

A quite different approach to economic insights is offered by the distinguished scholar **Burton Klein** of the California Institute of Technology. "An engineer by close association," he has looked at the dynamic (feedback) effects of economics, particularly at the microeconomic level of individual and firms' decision-making. He is especially concerned in his paper with the decline in productivity gains of the US economy in the past 15 years, a consequent worsening inability to compete effectively in international markets, and "the reemergence of a business cycle in which declines in the rate of productivity growth anticipate downturns." In his view, these effects reflect "a worsening of the dynamic performance of the US economy brought about by a preoccupation with both short-term profits and short-term stability." His studies indicate to him that "the time has come to make a US goal the adoption of measures aimed at gradually pushing up the average rate of productivity gains in manufacturing to 5% a year — and keeping them there" — a somewhat breathtaking aspiration for the economy!

Dr. Klein introduces some material from a forthcoming book, "The Hidden Foot," which gives a dynamic model of the economy designed "to predict accelerations and decelerations in the rate of progress as well as cyclical movements in productivity." These considerations lead him to develop a new and quite novel tax proposal which rewards firms "on the basis of improvement of their own price performance relative to the industry's average performance during the preceding year," thus stimulating productivity advances and constraining wage increases. In his view, a tax so designed would encourage more rapid productivity gains by providing substantial tax benefits for risk-taking. Its impact on progress should be the same as economic rivalry ("as distinct from static economists' concept of competition"). Such rivalry leads to a "positive sum" game: "In brief, the basic purpose of the proposed tax is to drive the economy to a point at which it can achieve better results than in a zero-sum game." He admits considerable practical difficulty in designing such a tax, which appears to be a type of TIP (tax-based incomes policy), especially since it must be designed to have a minimum distorting effect on the marketplace operations, and yet reward firms and individuals on the basis of performance. Despite these difficulties, Dr. Klein's conclusion is that this is a "terribly important question . . . because all . . . other ways for dealing with our present economic predicament might be far worse."

Michael J. Boskin of Stanford University, a foremost authority on taxation, presents a philosophical paper on the relationship between taxation, innovation, and economic growth. He differs from the preceding author in attempting direct and non-technical answers to some very deep questions which might well be summarized from these sentences in his introduction: "The relationship between technical change and economic growth combines with the recent abysmal growth performance of the US economy to focus attention on the economic incentives surrounding innovative activity. Is it the case that a variety of economic policies and/or changes in the economy have reduced the returns or increased the risks to undertaking such activity, and, if so, has this in turn led to a decrease in our rate of technical change and economic growth? Is there a case for changing current economic policies with respect to innovation and technical change?"

Based on his extensive academic and research experience, as embodied in many articles and other research writings, as well as many contacts with the real world, Dr. Boskin presents in this paper a distillation of numerous personal opinions, judgments, and conjectures on some of the key issues. Indeed, he refers to some of the very papers in this special issue for further technical details and information needed to understand his frame of reference. In commenting on the poor economic performance of the US, he stresses that "very modest changes in annual rates of growth, when compounded over long periods of time, can make an enormous difference in the nature of a society and its relationship to the rest of the world" — a point also made by Landau. He then traces the role of innovation in economic growth and, after reviewing the complexity of measurement of the various factors involved, concludes that technological change accounts for approximately one-third of American economic growth. As a result Dr. Boskin says, "Therefore, there are both analytical and empirical bases for believing that the rate of technical change and innovation in a society is a primary vehicle for generating rising standards of living for its population over time."

From these fundamental considerations he turns to the tax system and its effects on innovation, capital formation, and economic growth. He stresses that inflation which "adds considerably to risk in the economy and combined with an unindexed tax system reduces the after tax, after inflation return to capital is closely linked to monetary policy. . . ." He gives as his personal opinion that in the advanced economies today "the bulk of technological advance comes from decisions made in response to potential economic incentives."

In reviewing tax policy Boskin emphasizes that there are many features of our current tax law, including the corporate and capital gains tax, which lead to a reduction in risk-taking and possible over-all investment. The interactions are very complex, and he simply touches on some of them to emphasize this point. He says, "Therefore, for any given response of investment in R&D expenditures to the tax system, the 1970s were a period where effective tax rates appeared to increase and, hence, to decrease after tax returns and reduce the incentive to invest and innovate."

Dr. Boskin, like many of the other authors, also draws the distinction between investment in R&D expenditures and other types of investment and how tax law affects these. He emphasizes that tax law is biased against investment which must be depreciated over a long period of time as opposed to R&D expenditures, but that the expected returns on R&D are often affected by the effective rates of taxation on the longer-term investment which follows R&D and that this probably more than offsets benefits from any differential taxation of R&D. As a result, the bias toward short-term investments has become more pronounced, with a probable decrease in R&D expenditure and technological advance. "Continuing this pattern into the future will seriously threaten future productivity increases and the potential for increased standards of living over long periods of time. . . ." After noting that various features of the tax system partially mitigate effective corporate tax rates, he still concludes that the overall effect of such a tax has been to reduce the rate of capital formation and innovation.

Turning to the capital gains tax, Dr. Boskin says, "The perception of most non-

economists is that the capital gains tax obviously reduces risk-taking in society."
He points out that being unindexed it therefore taxes a nominal portion of capital
gains when realized and that the US is one of the few advanced economies which
imposes a capital gains tax at all. He discusses in some detail the disincentive effects of US capital gains taxation. With regard to structural revisions in tax policy,
he would favor a gradual change away from taxing income to taxing spending or
consumption, thus removing the double taxation of saving and capital income inherent in the present system. Ultimately, this would lead to a complete integration of the corporate and personal income tax, ultimate elimination of the capital
gains tax, and gradual increase in the number of vehicles and amounts available
for tax-free saving and investment.

Realizing perhaps that such a goal may be some time away from realization
politically, Dr. Boskin would, as a next best solution, complete the direct indexation of the tax system so that only real income — including real capital gains and
real interest — is taxed, and he would also favor integration of the corporate and
personal tax system. These two proposals are also to be found in other papers in
this symposium, particularly in Landau's.

Alvin Jay Harman of the International Institute for Applied Systems Analysis
and the Rand Corporation takes a microeconomic view of a tax policy needed to
stimulate industrial innovation. In particular, he focuses his attention on the key
role of individuals "with special talents, vision, and zeal." He urges direct encouragement to such individuals engaged in innovative activity and "the indirect
support of their enterprises." He, too, looks at the dynamics of innovation, and
especially of infant companies and industries. He concentrates "on the special
aspects of the personnel needed by the firm in a new industry, and on a public
policy designed to encourage such labor and to indirectly subsidize such firms." In
his view, it is insufficient by itself to simply subsidize R&D, because the technology and the market place must be highly interactive. He associates himself
with Burton Klein's views of the dynamic economy, and therefore the activities of
risk-takers are necessarily critical to understanding. His proposal is stated thus:
"Grant a temporary personal income tax credit on wages and salaries earned by individuals employed by highly R&D-intensive, for-profit firms." He discusses this
and alternate strategies to accomplish the same purpose, as well as some practical
difficulties.

Business-Technical Contributions

The second group of papers is that of the business-technical contributors, all at
senior levels in firms which are of importance in the national economic scene. It is
a representative selection that covers the major parameters of the subject as seen
by such active participants.

The paper by **Boyd J. McKelvain** and **Arthur M. Bueche** of the General Electric
Company presents an authoritative view of tax policy as seen from the vantage
point of a major, widely diversified technological company with an outstanding
record of innovation. The authors look with concern at our declining productivity
growth and international competitiveness. They present many macroeconomic in-

dicators of innovation as a function of time and country. They stress its importance and say "the central conclusion that can be gleaned from all the reports is that the US is experiencing a very poor environment for longer-term risky investments in product and process innovation." In examining the need for improved Federal policies, they say "one cannot expect to overcome all the barriers and added costs of innovation that are being imposed by inflation, regulation and other constraints. Tax system modifications, however, can quickly offset these biases, restore a healthy balance between risks and rewards for innovation, and help break the inflationary spiral."

Bueche and McKelvain favor removing the current bias toward consumption and investment in quick payback and nonproductive "hedging" assets, while allowing the market system to guide investment choices without attempting to "target" the tax system to "favor specific technologies, industrial sectors, or types of firms." Hence, they deem it most urgent to bring "capital recovery allowances [depreciation] more in line with replacement costs" for new plant and equipment, and emphasize the importance of this to the cash flow of companies needing to make investments in R&D and plants and the diffusion of technology. Other tax proposals, such as R&D, capital gains, etc., are discussed, but as of lower priority. They note important previous contributions by two of the authors in this issue, Brinner and Zschau, who stress the value of high-technology companies to the whole economy. And they emphasize *feedback effects* to the economy of increased innovation at all levels.

Robert F. Dee is Chairman and Chief Executive Officer of the SmithKline Corp., a pharmaceutical company, which, like most companies in its industry, is a very heavy spender of R&D money and which has enjoyed a spectacular growth during recent years. He views the innovative process as an erratic event "until a critical mass and a subsequent insight produce the creative event." Thus, his attention turns to consideration of which aspects of the creative process can be deliberately encouraged, and which can not. Referring to the work of the Joint Economic Committee of the Congress, he also stresses that capital investment is the key to new innovation, consistent with the thesis of critical mass (a threshold of size, or level of capital accrual, necessary for completion of succesful endeavors). In examining the history of US innovation, he states that the cooperative effort of industry, government, and universities made great strides in computer, agriculture, and space technologies, but that this cooperation has been rare during the past two decades, with resulting damage to American technological leadership and productivity gains. Negative attitudes toward savings, regulation, and taxation are cited, the latter especially for ventures involving a high rate of expenditure for R&D. He, too, refers to President Carter's task force on innovation and its omission of tax and capital formation incentive policies for stimulating innovation while endorsing non-fiscal policies, and it is his opinion that "the real critical mass of American research is one of capital-building."

Mr. Dee analyzes other governments' tax and subsidy policies to encourage R&D, and attendant capital formation. He also draws attention to a particularly unfavorable development in US practice under a new regulation within Section 861 of the Internal Revenue Code, which basically offers a strong disincentive for a US parent company to perform R&D in the US, but rather encourages it to shift it to its offshore subsidiaries. His tax policy recommendations include extension of the investment tax credit to widen coverage of R&D expenditures, exemptions on capital gains taxes from sale of venture capital stock if reinvested in new R&D-oriented businesses, raising the limits on permitted capital loss deductions in such businesses, more Federal support for academic research and facilities, encouragement of personal savings by excluding more interest income from taxation and decreasing the capital gains tax, and changes in Section 861 regulations.

J. Peter Grace has been Chief Executive Officer of W. R. Grace & Company for almost the entire post-World War II era during which period it has proved to be a highly entrepreneurial company, changing its character from the well-known shipping line to a company with substantial chemical, resource, and consumer products interests. He opens his paper by discussing the dynamic or feedback effects of tax changes. His concern is that neglect of this factor in recent years has caused an erosion of the American technological position relative to other countries; he cites statistics which bear on this concern. He, too, emphasizes the stimulative potential of targeted tax cuts, in particular with regard to the role of capital formation.

Comparative data on the tax policies of other governments are presented, such as the capital gains tax, which is higher in the US than in most other countries, with attendant deleterious results on the relative performance of the US economy. Mr. Grace emphasizes that these same countries are even more dependent on OPEC oil than is the US, so that this "myth" of dependence on foreign oil obviously is not an explanation of the poorer American performance. This leads him back to a discussion in greater depth of the capital gains tax, including its primary concentration among lower income tax payers (*i.e.*, with adjusted gross incomes of $25,000 or less). He also analyzes the effect of inflation on the real return on an investment after the average holding period of 7.2 years with varying capital gains tax rates. This analysis shows that such taxes in fact convert an apparent gain into a real (inflation-adjusted) loss. The effect of high capital gains taxes is also shown to be adverse on equity capital raised by small companies, which create the new jobs, according to statistics he presents. From these considerations, he feels that the capital gains tax should be eliminated completely.

Thomas A. Vanderslice is President of General Telephone and Electronics Corporation, a high-technology company, and prior to that was a senior officer of the General Electric Company, giving him unusual breadth of experience in technological innovation. His paper in part stems from his work with the Committee for Economic Development, which completed an extensive study of the innovative process in the US early in 1980. He makes a number of quantitative observations about the US economic performance, from which he concludes, "Of particular importance in enabling US industry to replace its capital stock in a period of high inflation and rapid technological advance is accelerated depreciation." One of the consequences of the absence of such provision in the tax code, he points out, is the reluctance of industry to close down obsolete plants to make way for newer technology. A significant effect of this trend has been that "as a combined result of inflation and inadequate capital formation, Department of

Commerce figures badly overstate effective capital stock growth in the 1970s because of a lack of information about depreciation and obsolescence. One indication of this is the *market* valuation of the nonfinancial corporations in the economy. In 1979, . . . these corporations were valued at only 65% of the computed replacement cost of their assets." Thus, the capital formation problem of the 1980s seems to him to require focusing on inadequate capital recovery and inflation as the most serious long-term problems.

Dr. Vanderslice cites CED studies which concluded that raising the level of investment in plant and equipment will raise the rate of diffusion of new technology; hence the highest priority should be given to changes in the tax laws to create greater investment incentives. The CED productivity study of September 1, 1980, urging more rapid recovery allowances, emphasizes that this is not an unconditional tax reduction for business but rather a tax *deferral,* which may be extended so long as the firm maintains an accelerated rate of new capital investment so as to match the higher level of tax-deductible annual depreciation charges. More rapid capital recovery, he points out, is essential to all industry but crucial to the rapidly emerging computer/telecommunications, word processing, automation, and information processing industries, which are just beginning a revolutionary period of technological change. While approving of accelerated depreciation — not necessarily the 10-5-3 proposal, which he asserts favors buildings excessively — he also urges specific depreciation practice changes of urgent need by the telephone industry, which is the third-largest user of capital in the US.

The Government Sector

A third major grouping of contributors to this issue might loosely be termed as coming from the governmental or political sector, although in some cases this refers more to past than present experience. The first paper is by **Senator Lloyd Bentsen,** a Democrat from Texas, and a senior member of the Senate Finance Committee, who has also recently completed a two-year term as Chairman of the Joint Economic Committee of the Congress. During this period the committee produced some remarkable consensus reports from a very wide spectrum of political opinion which in many ways heralded the political changes that have taken place in the country and in economic opinion generally (*i.e.,* expressing greater concern over declining American innovation, competitiveness and productivity gains, and urging a shift in national priorities away from — among other things — tax and other policies favoring consumption toward those favoring innovation and production). These reports were in fact followed by a nearly unanimous and bipartisan tax bill approved by the Senate Finance Committee late in the summer of 1980 (quite different from later Administration proposals).

Senator Bentsen refers to these events and conclusions in his paper, *e.g.,* "Industrial innovation is at the core of the well-being of the United States and is a major contributor to economic growth. Innovation influences inflation, and stimulates productivity, employment, and the ability of US products to compete both in domestic and world markets." Drawing on his Senatorial experience, including testimony of numerous witnesses, he illustrates his thesis with examples, and provides a useful review as well of some of the economic and theoretical framework, which examines "the links between both R&D expenditures and general productivity growth, and between taxation and R&D activity." Under the former topic, he discusses macroeconomic policies, regulations, and the Federal Productivity Center.

The last part of Senator Bentsen's paper deals with tax policies, which he considers to be at the heart of options for increasing investment and savings, especially by comparison with other industrial countries. He proposes a 2-4-7-10 accelerated depreciation program, improvement in corporate tax marginal rates particularly for smaller corporations, increased investment credits, revision of estate taxes to ease the burden on smaller family-owned businesses so as to encourage continuity of ownership, reduction to 50% of the top 70% "unearned income" marginal tax rate, reduction of personal income taxes, and revision of the capital gains tax by allowing for "rollovers" on a reinvestment basis, plus lower capital gains taxes as well. He also treats a number of targeted tax proposals on the R&D process itself, rather than the more general phenomena of savings and investment described above. In all these he stresses the need to consider the *after-tax* rate of return.

Senator Bentsen concludes by endorsing the Senate Finance Committee proposals of 1980, featuring the 2-4-7-10 capital recovery plan, reduction of the capital gains tax to 20%, a 2% reduction in the corporate tax, and a number of other provisions. He stresses the urgency and gravity of the national condition.

In contrast, but an interesting complement to the foregoing, is the paper on tax policy as it relates to R&D by **George N. Carlson,** an international economist in the Office of International Tax Affairs of the Treasury Department. He gives an extensive literature survey of previous economic findings regarding the relation of R&D and productivity, including comparisons with other countries, as well as the history of changes in those countries, and in their tax policies. He recognizes that "reduced R&D spending [since 1966] is responsible for only about 15% of the overall decline [in US growth rate]. Weak capital formation is a more important source of the productivity decline . . . a problem widely shared by other countries." Despite this, he focuses primarily on the R&D spending and incentive side, and surveys the literature.

Carlson treats the taxation of R&D in depth, on an international comparison basis. In his concluding section, he examines the question of whether additional incentives for R&D are needed, and some of the problems associated with such incentives. His principal policy recommendation would be "an R&D tax credit for privately funded R&D expenditures on wages and equipment. The credit should be taxable and non-refundable."

Gary Clyde Hufbauer's paper may have had somewhat similar origins in that he was Deputy Assistant Secretary for Trade and Investment Policy at the Treasury Department, and Director of the International Tax Staff prior to becoming Deputy Director of the International Law Institute at the Georgetown University Law Center and resuming the private practice of tax law. He addresses tax policy change directly as it influences the generation and implementation of technology. First, under the topic of "Implementation of New Technology," he says, "the most expensive step in translating new ideas into greater productivity is to embody them in new processes in the factory and new products in the marketplace." He goes on to say that "tax policies are not really suitable for reducing regulatory law and overcoming restrictive labor practices. But fiscal policy and broad tax structure policy can make plant and equipment investment more attractive relative both to consumption and to inflation-proof (but also productivity-proof) investments in bricks and mortar," *i.e.,* "faster implementation speeds." In Dr. Hufbauer's view, "individual and corporate savings behavior are . . . highly responsive to after-tax real rates of return." He illustrates this with some numerical examples to underline the debilitating effects of taxation and inflation on the real rates of return. He goes on to say, "to enhance productivity, the tax structure should favor savings and disfavor consumption," and that this favors sales, excise and value-added taxes (not including capital goods), while discouraging high marginal tax rates on personal income "whether 'earned' or 'unearned,' taxes on corporate profits, and capital gains and wealth taxes." He claims that —despite the conventional wisdom which says this kind of pro-savings tilt is politically difficult — in fact, "the post-1950 history of the US tax structure is really a history of pro-savings features," which he enumerates. "At a time when the nation is concerned about productivity, there is no reason why further chapters in this history cannot be written."

Dr. Hufbauer then goes on to treat R&D expenditures. Here he draws attention to the oft-quoted finding that the social rate of return on R&D is much greater than the private rate, so that government tax policy to encourage R&D spending has a legitimate public justification. Here he seeks "to reward not expense, but success," which leads him to a consideration of the R&D success rate, where he considers that "effective management — highly attuned to the commercial potential — can make an enormous difference in R&D results." For accomplishing this, he proposes that patent and know-how income not be taxed at all.

Dr. Hufbauer concludes by giving "two cheers" for President Reagan's tax program, which he says it deserves from the "productivity buffs. It should reduce inflation and the consequent inflationary bias against productive investment. And it should directly stimulate private savings, private investment, and thus the implementation of technology . . . The author's own third cheer is reserved for a tax-free royalty provision."

The last paper in this informal grouping is by **Kenneth McLennan,** Vice President and Director of Industrial Studies of the Committee for Economic Development, and **Charls E. Walker,** chairman of the consulting firm of Charls E. Walker Associates, Inc., and former Deputy Secretary of the Treasury under President Nixon. Like the other papers, they review the relatively poorer performance of the US economy with regard to productivity and innovation. They, too, refer to the fact that "many studies attribute between one-third and one-half of the growth of real income to technological change." They state that "tax policies are of special significance, for such policies can significantly affect the incentive to save and invest, and motivate industry to innovate."

Drs. McLennan and Walker therefore proceed to discuss the concepts of capital formation, innovation, and the distribution of capital stock. They point out the difficulty of measuring the benefits attributable to quantity (capital deepening) and quality changes in capital inputs, the latter resulting in innovations or technological change. Here they have cited some of the recent work of Jorgenson as well as others. In their view, both make significant contributions to productivity improvement, but that, for qualitative or technological change, R&D is a necessary prerequisite.

These authors favor a tax system "which is not biased in favor of investment of some types of capital assets and against others," but admit that no practical system exists which is completely neutral; for example, public policy has encouraged home ownership, and in a period of rapid inflation the incentives are for individuals to invest in residential capital. This has led to a flow of investment away from non-residential capital, thus retarding productivity growth. First they consider "indirect incentives to investment," such as reduction of the marginal tax rate on investment ("unearned") income, in personal income tax rates, to increase incentives for saving, in capital gains and corporate income taxes, "rollover" provisions on reinvestment of capital gains, dividends, etc.

Drs. Walker and McLennan then undertake to review direct tax incentives to increase R&D expenditures. They would extend Section 174 of the Revenue Code to include plant and equipment used in R&D. Next, they discuss direct incentives to increase investment in new plant and equipment, underlining also the effects of inflation and taxes on the *real* return on investment. "The average real economic rate of return on capital investment has declined from its high of 10% in 1964 to about 5% in 1978. It is therefore not surprising that, in general, new plant and equipment is not a particularly attractive type of investment." Hence, they recommend accelerated depreciation of the 10-5-3 or related character, although they give due consideration to the Auerbach-Jorgenson First Year Capital Recovery proposal which they deem to be an inadequate stimulus for innovation.

In conclusion, the authors seek to select the major components of a tax strategy by emphasizing accelerated depreciation (10-5-3 or 2-4-7-10) and showing in diagrammatic form the feedback effects of more rapid capital recovery on R&D, productivity, employment, and tax revenue. They feel that this has a much more important priority than any policy to stimulate R&D, useful though that may be. They consider the case of firms with insufficient profits to benefit from such more favorable treatment (*e.g.,* steel, automobiles, airlines, and railroads), and suggest the "banking" of unused investment tax credits to be "cashable" at a later time, rather than refundable investment tax credits. They also underline the unreliability of published government estimates of the costs of various tax reduction proposals because they "are almost always expressed on a static basis without taking into account the increased tax revenue generated by the income growth stimulated by the investment. Consequently, the revenue costs tend to be overestimated."

McLennan and Walker conclude by saying that "minor tinkering with tax rates to deal with tax bracket creep will be insufficient for the task of stimulating innovation in the 1980s. A sustained increase in the rate of innovation requires a much more fundamental revision of the incentive to innovate through capital investment and an increase in productive work effort." For this they strongly recommend a phased introduction of "10-5-3" accelerated depreciation, and tax relief for individual wage earners assured over the next several years.

The Entrepreneurs

The fourth category of papers which the editors have included is one that might be labeled "entrepreneurs." The first of these is by **Ralph Landau,** Chairman of The Halcon SD Group, and a recognized prominent technological innovator in the chemical industry, as exemplified by his receipt of both the Perkin and the Chemical Industry Medals (the first time for an individual to receive both in 35 years). Dr. Landau has participated extensively in the five-year-long studies of the National Academy of Engineering/National Research Council dealing with innovation, and presented that body's tax policy findings at an Academy of Engineering colloquium entitled "Industrial Innovation and Public Policy Options" (published in October 1980), which reviewed all the recent inquiries on innovation. Dr. Landau takes the viewpoint of an active multiple participant in the innovative decision-making process, as an individual and also as a corporate executive and director, all of which roles he has experienced directly. His views track many of those cited above, for example, as to the urgency of paying attention to America's declining competitiveness, productivity and innovation, and the key role which tax policy and incentives would play in improving the situation, particularly in establishing an improved climate for innovation. He, too, presents comparative international data, including the aging of the US industrial plant. He presents an agenda for practical results, founded on the viewpoint of decision-makers, the actual participants in the innovation process.

Although Dr. Landau touches on many theoretical aspects of these matters, he seeks to present a balanced view of new approaches without calling for major reforms in the present code. One of his points is that tax policy changes have been made much too frequently in the past decade, and that no risk-taker, or innovator, can plan for the longer term without being assured that policy will not be consistent and benign. He presents a broad picture of how long-range capital is provided and used in the US, so as to demonstrate the complex interrelationships among the different sectors, and, therefore, of the effect of proposed tax policy changes. Individuals and corporations are shown to have their different, but vital, places in the capital formation and risk-taking process.

From these, and his own experiences, Dr. Landau proceeds to analyze the motivations first of the individual investor, and then of the corporate investor. For each, he presents sample calculations which show how they arrive at investment decisions, and why, stressing — as do some of the other authors — that *after-tax* real return is the name of the game. Tax policy in recent years has often operated, and especially in an inflationary era, he says, to widen the gap between real and apparent returns, leading to short-term investment decisions and reduced risk-taking: as a result, innovation is discouraged. Both individual and corporate investments are vital to the innovation process; there is room and need for all, he says; only the specific incentives vary. For these, it is necessary to recognize "what

all decision-makers know: that they react to the rules of the game by trying to optimize their own results, and that if enough do so, the macro-results are different
from what would have been predicted from a static model of the economy. As an
engineer, the author is all too aware of the meaning of feedback, which is what
has been described here . . . Fundamentally, of course, this phenomenon of feedback is what is currently being described under the rubric of supply-side
economics, but it has existed for years!"

For the individual risk-taking investor, Dr. Landau emphasizes that the high
marginal rate on investment income (70% Federal tax, plus state taxes) "means
that the governments . . . get three dollars for every dollar [the investor] keeps as
net income." No wonder, he says, that tax shelters (some of doubtful economic
utility) of all kinds have flourished for all classes of investors; he cites particularly
the middle-class utilization of housing investment, which draws off risk-capital
from industry and technology. Dr. Landau does not mention the cash or "illegal"
economy which provides the lower income taxpayer with another form of
"shelter," as *The New York Times* has recently pointed out. He stresses the need
for reduction in the capital gains tax in order to minimize such effects, particularly with length of holding, the reduction of the marginal maximum personal tax
rate from 70% to at least 50%, an increase in the capital loss deduction allowed
from ordinary income, and more favorable treatment for stock options.

For the corporate investors, the inflation problem has led to a low real return on
capital (as McLennan and Walker also point out). The tax measures he recommends are some form of accelerated depreciation (the effect of which he illustrates
quantitatively, as does Hufbauer), an increased investment tax credit, easing of
the "at risk" rules, and, most fundamentally, perhaps, the deductibility of
dividends. The latter, he says, is important to equate debt with equity, making
the choice neutral, and helping improve the liquidity of American corporations
which have been taking on too much debt. He also treats R&D as worthy of
special tax consideration, even though it is a smaller part of the problem, and for
the same reason as Hufbauer and Carlson, *i.e.,* the social rate of return on R&D is
higher than the private rate; "today's R&D porfolio may become tomorrow's
capital budget."

Dr. Landau favors investment tax credits for new R&D, and also for university-
based fundamental R&D sponsored by industry, giving some quantitative
estimates of the effect this latter proposal might have. Landau's conclusion starts
with "This is how it is out in the real world." He looks at the possible costs of his
proposals, but feels in the end that "despite the apparent boldness of the totality
of the measures proposed in this paper, the costs would be very small and the
potential dynamic benefits very large indeed."

The second paper is by **Edwin V. W. Zschau,** Chairman and President of
Systems Industries, an entrepreneur of recognized standing in the electronics industry; he headed a study of the American Electronics Association in 1978 which
was very influential in Congressional consideration of the capital gains reform embodied in the Revenue Act of 1978. Like many of the other authors, he stresses
the economic impact of technology on growth, productivity gain, and interna-

tional competitiveness. Dr. Zschau also discusses the importance of technology for defense, a timely reminder of the new Administration's priorities in this direction, which will require continuing technological superiority (as does Harman). He likewise presents comparative international data on our position, which shows a relative decline. While the needs are urgent, he stresses that "Innovation can't be *forced;* it can only be *fostered.*" This requires a favorable climate and incentives. "Massive government R&D programs aren't the answer. Innovation doesn't thrive in bureaucracies." He emphasizes the key role of individuals or small groups in creating the "breakthrough" innovations, such as in genetics or semiconductors.

In Dr. Zschau's view, tax policy is the most powerful instrument for stimulating investment, entrepreneurship and technical education and research, especially among the young innovative firms which also create most of the new jobs (Landau and Grace point this out also). For these firms, risk capital is essential to start-up and growth. He documents the favorable results that have flowed since 1978 when the capital gains tax was reduced from 49% to 28%. Therefore, he proposes that tax policy embrace a further ultimate reduction in tax on capital gains, which really should not be taxed at all (as Grace also says), in this respect aligning us with Japan and West Germany; the reinstatement of restricted stock options to encourage technologists to join young companies, and a 25% tax credit for contribution to technical education programs and R&D at universities. He refers to the data also included by Brinner regarding the favorable impact of such R&D tax credits.

Venture Capital

The fifth and last category is that of the venture capitalist and is exemplified by the paper of **Reid W. Dennis,** a veteran participant in this field with the Fireman's Fund Insurance Company and the American Express Company, as well as his own firm; he is a past president of the National Venture Capital Association.

Mr. Dennis stresses the history of venture capital and points out that the earliest participants were primarily wealthy individuals and that the institutionalization of the industry began only after World War II. It was not, however, until 1958 with the passing of the Small Business Investment Act that banks and insurance companies began to participate in a meaningful way. Subsequently, because of various difficulties, a number of new private venture capital firms were formed which did not require governmental approval and — by avoiding attendant regulations — were able to operate in a more entrepreneurial fashion. These represent the core of today's venture capital industry. Mr. Dennis breaks down the capital provided by category and shows that, as of the end of 1980, $4.5 billion had been committed to the organized venture capital industry. Although rates of return of many venture capital groups have been quite satisfactory, they do involve a long-term investment (four to eight years being typical) and have little liquidity. As a result, the venture investor is often involved in providing advice to the management of the firms he supports. He points out that "the most meaningful incentive for investors . . . has been the existence of substantial *differential* between the maximum tax rate on realized long-term capital gains and the maximum rate on ordinary income."

Mr. Dennis presents data for the last 17 years to show how this differential has varied, and underlines what several of the other authors in this issue have stressed: that the high capital gains taxation prevalent in the 1976 to 1978 era made venture capital very risky and therefore forced investors to shift from emphasis on venture capital toward the generation of current income while the nation emphasized consumption rather than production. He then takes up the effect of the change in the capital gains tax in 1978, as do several of the other authors in this issue, and states "the change in rates enacted in 1978, more than any other single factor, has had a dramatic impact on the venture capital industry"; in addition, despite the somber predictions by the Treasury, actual capital gains tax receipts in 1979 appear to have been higher than in 1978, demonstrating true dynamic feedback effects.

Mr. Dennis shows how the private capital committed since then has increased greatly and predicts that this high level of investment will ultimately result "in the creation of many of the nation's most rapidly growing enterprises during the decade of the 1980s and beyond." He also shows how the climate for initial offering of securities of small companies has improved during the recent years since the capital gains tax was reduced, but points out that this is still a very risky area for investors.

Throughout, his emphasis is clearly on the significance of incentives for what is now being called by others "supply-side economics." However, Dennis says there are still enormous disincentives to investment and risk taking such as the 70% tax rate on investment income, the double taxation of dividends, the partial limitations on the deductibility of capital losses and business interest expense, and the punitive treatment of stock options. He proposes revisions in all of these to have a beneficial effect; they are quite similar to those proposed by Landau and by Boskin. He urges that the tax rate on long-term capital gains be reduced.

Some Themes That Emerge from the Papers

Despite the great diversity of personal experiences and viewpoints which the authors have brought to this fascinating array of papers, nevertheless it is possible to extract at least a few common conclusions and opinions that stand out in our opinion:

1. There is an extraordinary degree of unanimity as to the urgency of the United States condition. The unsatisfactory economic performance of the country is thoroughly discussed from many angles; it is recognized that there is something rotten in the state of the economy.

2. The recent multiple studies on technological innovation have raised the national consciousness about the subject, and its close relationship to the perceived economic faltering.

3. Many experts have attributed a significant portion of the growth of the US

economy in the past to technological change. In a major paper included in this issue, Jorgenson produces fresh detailed evidence that "declines in rates of technical change for the individual industrial sectors of the US economy must bear the full burden of explaining the slowdown in the . . . economy as a whole," and urges that "the future development of technology should be the primary focus of efforts to stimulate future US economic growth." Boskin makes much the same argument.

4. Foremost among remedial measures is tax policy. There is little difference of opinion on this point, although policy recommendations vary, depending on the author's perceptions.

5. Furthermore, a number of the authors, such as Lawrence Klein, Boskin, Bentsen, Hufbauer, McLennan and Walker, McKelvain and Bueche, Dee, Grace and Landau, emphasize that investors seek *real after-tax* rates of return (corrected for taxes and inflation), and Grace, Hufbauer, Vanderslice, and Landau give some mathematical examples of how these factors affect investment decisions. Other authors implicitly also recognize these relationships.

6. The majority of policy recommendations therefore are in the capital formation and investment area, and the most widely mentioned is clearly some form of accelerated depreciation. Capital gains tax improvements are also specifically favored by a large number (Hufbauer, Bentsen, McLennan and Walker, Lawrence Klein, Boskin, Landau, Dee, Grace, Dennis and Zschau). Investment credits are also referred to in various papers. What is interesting here is the substantial bipartisan political support evinced, as well as support from all five of the groupings of authors listed in this introductory section.

7. R&D tax concessions also receive a wide consensus (Brinner, Bentsen, Carlson, Hufbauer, McLennan and Walker, McKelvain and Bueche, Dee, Landau and Zschau), although it is recognized that without concomitant capital formation these will not have the most profound beneficial impact on the economy.

8. The most visible cleavage comes in the matter of general personal income tax rate reductions. Some of these, in more or less limited amount, are favored by Lawrence Klein, Bentsen, Hufbauer, Boskin, McLennan and Walker, Dee, Dennis and Landau, with a particular mention from many that the *high marginal tax rate on investment income (70%) should be reduced*. This would lead to a reduction in the capital gains tax also. Those who express the most caution, such as Lawrence Klein and Brinner, are concerned about the magnitude of personal income tax cuts of a general nature, particularly if they extend over three years (as in the Kemp-Roth proposal), on the grounds that this would necessitate severe budget cuts and tight monetary (high interest rate) policy which is itself adverse to capital formation. Here one glimpses the nature of the current national debate between the two schools of economic thought, the "main stream" and the "supply siders." It should be noted that no specifically identifiable supply-side economists were included in this issue, but their views are reflected indirectly in the feedback or dynamic approaches of many of the authors. Many of them stress that tax cuts and their effects

must not be viewed on a static basis, but in the context of a dynamic feed-back economy which is at the heart of supply-side arguments (Harman, Burton Klein, Boskin, McLennan and Walker, McKelvain and Bueche, Dee, Grace, Landau, Dennis and Zschau explicitly; some of the others implicitly.) A strong recent confirmation of the reality of this argument is seen by a number of authors in the unexpectedly high actual tax realizations after the capital gains tax cut of 1978, coupled with a number of very beneficial effects to the economy.

It is thus not at all surprising that the active participants in the economy, including the technological innovators, largely agree on this broad concept; the economists who must provide the measurements of results have great difficulty in quantifying such effects or in embodying them in their theoretical framework (as discussed particularly by Burton Klein); the government and political authors do recognize the existence of such dynamic effects but are not sure of the quantitative relationships.

9. Flowing from such considerations, there is substantial qualitative support for the idea that the specific business and investment tax improvements discussed by the authors would really not cost very much in revenues in the longer run. The accelerated depreciation relief, which has a broad constituency, might be expected to have a large revenue loss on a static basis, but — as Vanderslice points out — this is really a deferral, not a loss of tax, unless industry really *accelerates* its rate of investment, in which case the gain to the economy would clearly outweigh the loss of tax revenues. From such considerations, for example, McLennan and Walker concluded that "minor tinkering with tax rates to deal with tax bracket creep will be insufficient for the task of stimulating innovation in the 1980s. A sustained increase in the rate of innovation requires a much more fundamental revision of the incentive to innovate through capital investment and an increase in productive work effort."

10. In essence, then, our intuition is that there is a widespread consensus on the need for far-reaching business and investment tax measures to stimulate R&D and capital formation. This view extends to tax reduction on capital gains and present high marginal rates on investment income. There is no real agreement on the extent of general personal income tax rate cuts, probably because the impact on technology and innovation is less direct. If our interpretation of what the authors are saying is correct, however, policy makers have a right to assume that *extensive business and pro-investment personal cuts* — even of the broadest kinds envisioned by the authors — will really cost the economy very little in static terms, but that it may gain a great deal in dynamic terms as the economy grows and productivity increases. Hence, the largest tax cuts currently under national consideration really come down to the general across-the-board individual tax rate reductions and their dynamic effects on saving, on work, and on numerous other psychological and political factors which are largely outside the scope of this special issue. What the authors are saying, in our opinion, to the policy makers in this volume is nevertheless clear: *You are justified in making — indeed, obliged*

to make in view of the national urgency — extensive business-oriented and pro-investment personal tax cuts. It is better to include a very broad mix, all at once rather than piecemeal, as a real business stimulus to investors; the bigger general across-the-board personal tax cuts must involve additional considerations, some of which are discussed herein.

11. A few of the authors have produced some innovative tax suggestions, based on performance rather than costs (Burton Klein, Hufbauer, Harman). Whether these are practical, in some form, remains to be seen, but they are welcome as examples of fresh thinking always needed. Boskin has proposed that the real solution to the distressing current situation would be to shift altogether from taxing income to taxing expenditure or consumption, and describes how this might be achieved. Burton Klein's paper attempts to build a theoretical framework for other such efforts.

12. It is to be hoped that the current national discussion on this whole subject will soon produce concrete results, and if the papers herein are of any assistance in this regard, the labors of the authors will be amply justified.

The guest editors would like to express their special appreciation to Martha Miller Willett, Managing Editor, for her constant support and expert assistance throughout the preparation of this volume, which, because of the time stringency, has had to be prepared under exceptionally difficult conditions.

Ralph Landau
N. Bruce Hannay

Technology In Society

New York / Oxford / Toronto / PERGAMON PRESS / Paris / Frankfurt / Sydney

Technology In Society, Vol. 3, pp. 21–33 (1981)
Printed in the USA. All rights reserved.

Taxation, Research and Development

Lloyd Bentsen

American ingenuity has done more than anything else to shape the quality of the entire world economy and especially of life in the United States. Technological in-novation has paved the way for unparalleled progress: creating jobs, advancing productivity and prompting gains in real income and the rise of the US to a premier position in international markets.

This country has a remarkable record of success when it has set priorities and worked toward their achievement. The United States—with contributions from industry, government and universities—leads the world in agriculture and has made impressive advances in many other areas, such as the development of the computer. National enthusiasm for progress enabled the US to put a man on the moon within less than a decade after making the commitment to do so.

During the author's chairmanship of the Joint Economic Committee, the group emphasized that today's commitment to research is tomorrow's realization of a better life, and that from ideas come practical developments which can spawn benefits across the nation. A theme of this chairmanship was that the American people need a rededication to the successes of America's creative genius.

There are many examples of US progress resulting from research and develop-ment, but agriculture is perhaps the best, since government initiative in this field is well documented and dates back to the Civil War period when land-grant col-leges were established.

At that time, a farmer could feed himself and two or three others. But, by World War II, the farmer had increased his output four to six times. The 1980 farmer feeds about 65 people at home and abroad. In a 10-hour day, 250 people used to pick by hand the same amount of corn which one modern, self-propelled combine can harvest and shell today.

Lloyd Bentsen is in his second term in the US Senate and was recently chairman of the Joint Economic Committee of the Congress. A bomber pilot with 50 missions over Europe during World War II, he first came to Washington in 1948 as a Congressman from South Texas. He declined to seek re-election in 1954, moving instead to Houston to go into business. Sixteen years later, when he went back into public service by winning election as a Senator, he had established himself as a successful businessman. In addition to his work on the Joint Economic Committee of Congress, Bentsen is a member of three key Senate Committees: Finance, Environment, and Public Works and Intelligence.

The US role in space and its positive effects are sources of national pride. From space exploration has come improved communications, agriculture and weather forecasting. In 1965, when the first communication satellite was launched, it could carry 240 telephone calls at the same time. By the late 1970s, improved satellites could handle 6,250 calls simultaneously. The next generation of satellites will each be capable of transmitting 12,000 to 14,000 telephone calls at once. Satellites provide information which helps management of existing natural resources and the discovery of new sources of minerals and energy.

Industrial innovation is at the core of the economic well being of the United States and is a major contributor to economic growth. Innovation helps combat inflation. It stimulates productivity, employment and the ability of US products to compete both in domestic and world markets.

Without R&D, there can be little advancement in productivity, and, without rising productivity, there can be no real economic health. Rising productivity means an increased standard of living for the average American. But America today neither enjoys the economic health nor the increasing standard of living experienced in other years. The prime cause is the erosion of productivity.

What Is Productivity?

What is productivity?

In 1903, when Henry Ford founded his company, it took 13 hours to produce one car. By 1913, it took one hour. By 1980, 60 cars could be produced in that single hour. That is productivity growth.

Today, using hybrid seed, American farmers can produce at least 20% more corn on 25% fewer acres than was the case in 1930. That is productivity growth.

Today, hand-held calculators pack as much computational ability as room-sized computers of the 1940s. Many more people have access to these calculators and, when they use them, they save time. That is productivity growth.

American industry—through technological innovation—maintained for decades a steady flow of new and better products and services to the world marketplace. Ever larger numbers of people were employed and the United States dominated the international markets with its technologically superior products. In fact, 30% to 40% of the economic growth in the United States during the past three decades has been attributed to industrial innovation. The computer has had much to do with this success (and whoever would have believed it?).

Predictions of the 1940s foresaw a need for no more than 1,000 computers in the world by the year 2000, but today—two decades before the turn of the century—there are millions of computers ranging from large conventional models through minicomputers, microprocessors and computers-on-a-chip.

Forecasters did not expect the computer would be out of the laboratory and into industry by the early 1960s or that, by the late 1960s, the computers would begin to shrink in size and grow in speed. Computer development in industry has come so far that, in 1981, computers enable robots to perform routine, repetitious work on assembly lines. Efforts to make computer components smaller have been so successful that the intricacies of 45,000 transistors can be crammed on a tiny chip the size of a contact lens. Computer technology has advanced so rapidly that the modern pocket calculator is more powerful than the first bulky, room-size computers which were owned primarily by the Federal government.

Computer technology advanced because computers were improved, prices were lowered, and enterprising people found widespread and diversified uses for them. The history of one vital component of computers—semiconductors—shows how the financial support of both government and private industry spurred progress. During an 18-year period, industry spent $1.7 billion on semiconductor work and the Federal government contributed $702 million. Industry provided marketing, production, and technical know-how, while the government promised to be a large-volume customer for the resulting products.

The role of the government as a buyer is often a stimulus to innovation because the certainty of contract purchases lessens the risk in the evolution of fledgling technologies. The contribution of universities to semiconductors and other technology development is critical, too, both in basic research and in the education of personnel. Often it is government's relationship with universities through funding which enables universities to provide the environment for such training.

While the United States government stimulated the demand for computer technology through contracts and purchases, it played a more direct and primary role in agriculture and space technologies, both areas in which the government has long-term national commitments. The government put its powerful shoulder to the wheel of those technologies and pushed for their development through contributions of money, people and support.

To reach the present point in computer development took the joining together of electronics, optics, crystallography, plasma physics and polymer chemistry. In more recent years, surface physics and chemistry have become important along with work in miniaturization, plasma etching and superconductivity. Applications for computer technology have increased many-fold since the first big computer was used to count the population of the United States in the 1950 Census. Computer history, however, is no different from that of any other scientific breakthrough, major innovation, or technological advancement. Work in basic and applied research was followed by the development phase, and during all three stages there was sufficient investment to allow the work to progress in an encouraging, future-oriented environment.

Innovation

Through investment, inventive individuals—working independently or for a company—obtain the financial backing which enables them to pursue their research and development. Investment provides the facilities not only for actual research work but also for the plants and tools to transform the innovative idea into a marketable product. And it is investment through education which equips individuals with the knowledge and skills to engage in R&D work.

Today's investments in research and innovation will help forge tomorrow's economic and social course. Industrial innovation is at the core of the economic well being of the United States and is a major contributor to economic growth.

Innovation influences inflation and stimulates productivity, employment, and the ability of US products to compete both in domestic and world markets.

Innovation and technological progress are woven into the fabric of United States history. Because of technological developments, America has changed the focus of its worklife from agriculture to industry to services and is now on the brink of the information age. During the early years of US history, the country's resources—workers and funds—were invested in farming. In contrast, by 1980, about 72% of employment was in the service sector.

It is significant that, while the bulk of the labor force is concentrated in service employment, the 3.5% of US workers in agriculture supply enough food to feed more than 220 million Americans and to lead the world food market. Mechanization and other innovations enabled farms to produce more food with fewer employees and changed the nature of the society of the US—from rural farmers to urban industrial workers. Through the years, society profited from the technological changes, but often at the expense of displaced workers. Society's challenge is not to denounce change because it is change, but rather to share the responsibility and benefits of such technological changes with the individual workers through training programs and policies aimed at easing the transitions.

Even with all this evidence regarding the relationship of R&D and productivity, there are still doubters. It is a relationship that the Senate Finance Committee, for example, in drawing up tax legislation, has had difficulty quantifying. As a result, this paper will explore this relationship by examining the links between both R&D expenditures and general productivity growth, and between taxation and R&D activity. It will conclude with a review of some policy prescriptions which the author believes are necessary to restore a healthy rate of productivity growth to our economy.

The Link Between R&D and Productivity

It has been only recently that public interest has focused on productivity growth as the panacea to stagflation. The vacuum in economic literature created by this lack of public focus is increasingly being filled by new and better research. But, there is a small number of scholars who have been exalting productivity all along, and who must be viewed as the forerunners in this field. Professor John Kendrick is one, and on June 13, 1978, he minced no words in testimony before the Joint Economic Committee (JEC) regarding the role of R&D in productivity growth.

With respect to the proximate determinants of productivity increase, the fountainhead of advancing technological knowledge, the most important source of productivity, is research and development (R&D). In recent decades, it has been formal R&D outlays that have accounted for most of the increase in the stock of technological knowledge applied to productive processes.

Kendrick and other like-minded scholars form the nucleus of one camp of thought on the linkage between R&D and productivity—a camp which believes there is a strong causal relationship between R&D and productivity.

In his first comprehensive work on productivity, *Productivity Trends in the U.S.,* Kendrick briefly explains the effects of R&D on productivity this way.

Although we cannot measure it precisely, research and development activity is our best indication of the investment in scientific and technological advance that sooner or later results in productivity growth. We should not forget, however, that the volume and relative trend of this type of intangible investment depends on fundamental social values and institutions. The effect on productivity also depends partly on the rate at which cost-reducing innovations spread.

In a later work, *Postwar Productivity Trends in the U.S.,* Kendrick derives estimates of productivity change by industry, and from these performs quantitative analyses of the causal factors behind these changes.

In his latest book, Kendrick, along with Elliot Grossman, devotes an entire chapter to causal analysis. The data base consisted of 20 manufacturing industries, and R&D data were utilized from 1958 to 1976. The results indicate a strong, positive relationship between privately funded applied R&D and productivity changes.

Similar findings, have been made by Nestor Terleckyj of the National Planning Association. Terleckyj's work, *Effects of R&D on the Productivity Growth of Industries: An Exploratory Study,* was one of the first to closely examine the productivity-R&D relationship. This extensive study examined the relationship between total factor productivity and various measures of R&D, proportion of total industry sales which were sold to nongovernment customers, unionization rate of industry workers, and cyclical costability of industry output. As Terleckyj notes (p. 37), "The statistical results are definitely consistent with the existence of positive effects of the company-financed R&D conducted in individual industries on the productivity growth of those industries. . . ."

In a more recent article, Terleckyj updates this study, replacing the total factor productivity figures of Kendrick with those estimated by Frank Gollop and Dale Jorgensen. Terleckyj introduces a variable designed to capture the effect of productivity returns to human capital, as well. The results include a strengthened R&D-productivity relationship, a stronger effect on productivity of purchased R&D, and a strong statistical relationship between productivity and human capital, something that would intuitively be expected.

The Basic Relationships

Zvi Griliches of Harvard University has also conducted important analytical work on the R&D-productivity linkage. In an early work (*Research Expenditures and Growth Accounting*), in fact, Griliches derived the basic model which many other researchers have utilized in their analyses. In a recent work, *Returns to Research and Development Expenditures in the Private Sector,* Griliches analyzes the productivity-R&D relationship in detail and finds a statistically significant relationship to exist. This study is of particular interest for several reasons: (1) the data base used is relatively large (because of access to Bureau of Census data, Griliches was able to utilize expenditure and employee histories from over 800 R&D-performing manufacturing companies); (2) the data are broken down into six broad industry groupings, which enabled him to compare R&D "success" by industry grouping; and (3) Griliches concludes, similar to Terleckyj, that rates of return on R&D are lower where more Federal involvement exists.

The work by these authors, as well as others, suggests that a statistical relationship exists between R&D expenditures and productivity growth. There is another body of literature, however, which indicates that little or no relationship exists between R&D and productivity. This group is best represented by the work of Edward Denison, formerly of Brookings Institution, and now at the Department of Commerce.

Denison's classic work, *Accounting for United States Economic Growth, 1929–1969,* was one of the first comprehensive studies of the factors influencing economic growth. In a more recent work, *Explanations of Declining Productivity Growth,* Denison examined the decline in his measure of productivity, "National Income Per Person Employed." The results are summarized in Table 1.

Denison feels that the factor having the greatest impact on productivity decline or advance is what he terms "advances in knowledge and miscellaneous determinants." This variable includes not only technological knowledge from R&D, but organizational and managerial knowledge as well. This factor also is used as a residual for those identified variables whose effects have been estimated to be zero or not quantifiable. Regarding R&D, Denison says, ". . . organized R&D conducted in the United States, as measured by the National Science Foundation, is responsible for only a small fraction of the contribution of advances in knowledge—my estimates suggest less than one-fourth in 1948–1973."* He feels R&D adds little to advances in knowledge, and thus to productivity growth.

In short, the professional literature suggests that a relationship exists, but of uncertain strength, between R&D and productivity growth. In light of this obvious linkage, what can be done to spur productivity growth through R&D growth? Since productivity is the efficiency with which goods and services are created from inputs, policies to spur productivity must be directed at enhancing the usefulness of factor inputs, or the processes by which these inputs are converted into final products. These policies can be both of a general and of a more targeted nature focusing on tax changes.

General Policies

Macroeconomic Policies

On the most basic level, those policies which improve the predictability, stability, and growth of our economy also improve the atmosphere for more R&D and, hence, for productivity growth. Because a large and significant portion of R&D is performed by the private sector, it follows that one should closely scrutinize those factors affecting business investment decisions.

Such decisions, including the magnitude of R&D outlays, are especially sensitive to the business cycle. In a recession, for example, immediate needs to trim outlays to maintain traditional margins squeeze R&D programs. In addition, smaller firms have a more difficult time obtaining funds in cyclical downturns, including those which are capital intensive, based on high-technology R&D.

---

*Edward F. Denison, "Discussion," *American Economic Review,* Vol. 70, no. 2 (May 1980), p. 355.

TABLE 1. National Income Per Person Employed in Nonresidential Business: Growth Rate and Sources of Growth, 1948–73 and 1973–76

	1948–73	1973–76	Change
Growth rate (%)	2.43	−0.54	−2.97
	Contributions to Growth Rate (%)		
Total factor input:			
Changes in workers' hours and attributes:			
Hours	−0.24	−0.54	−0.30
Age–sex composition	−0.17	−0.25	−0.08
Education	0.52	0.88	0.36
Changes in capital and land per person employed:			
Inventories	0.10	0.02	−0.08
Nonresidential structures and equipment	0.29	0.25	−0.04
Land	−0.04	−0.03	0.01
Output per unit of input:[a]			
Improved allocation of resources[b]	0.37	−0.01	−0.38
Changes in the legal and human environment[c]	−0.04	−0.44	−0.40
Economies of scale	0.41	0.24	−0.17
Irregular factors	−0.18	0.09	0.27
Advances in knowledge and miscellaneous determinants[d]	1.41	−0.75	−2.16

Source: Edward F. Denison, *Accounting for Slower Economic Growth: The United States in the 1970s*, The Brookings Institution 1979, Table 7-3.

[a]Contributions to the growth rate shown in subsequent lines are restricted to effects upon output per unit of input.
[b]Includes only gains resulting from the reallocation of labor out of farming and out of self-employment and unpaid family labor in small nonfarm enterprises.
[c]Includes only the effects on output per unit of input of costs incurred to protect the physical environment and the safety and health of workers, and of costs of dishonesty and crime.
[d]Obtained as a residual.

Inflation affects investment decisions, as well. If inflation is fully anticipated, it would presumably have no significant effect upon spending and income expectations and, therefore, on the intracorporate allocation of resources to R&D and competing investment programs. However, the US scarcely enjoys such certainty regarding inflation which, in recent years, has become the major destabilizing influence in its economy. The effect on investment decisions for firms of uncertain expectations regarding inflation is to shorten their horizon with respect to these investments. Firms raise the required rate of return threshold for investments, and shorten time periods in which payback must be attained. They become reluctant to tie up capital in long-term investments, which R&D programs usually are, because inflation alters relative rates of return on different investments.

Clearly, macroeconomic policies which dampen cyclical fluctuations and inflation are desirable to stimulate R&D expenditures and the related pace of industrial innovation and productivity.

Regulations

The Federal government can affect private investment decisions in more direct ways, as well. For example, its rules and regulations have a far-reaching and, many would argue, debilitating influence on R&D. Regulations are government-imposed constraints on private-sector behavior and products designed to increase or maximize social welfare, reduce negative externalities, or increase equity defined in some fashion or other. To achieve these purposes, regulations purposefully distort market resources allocations. Whenever a regulation is placed on a market, industry, or firm, the market equilibrium dictated by supply and demand forces is altered, generally with an adverse effect upon economic efficiency.

Regulations frequently divert factor inputs from R&D or the production of goods and services to other tasks and, hence, increase inefficiency and reduce factor productivity—a regulatory cost only now coming to be recognized in Washington. In fact, an update of a report prepared for the Joint Economic Committee by the Chairman of the President's Council of Economic Advisers, Professor Murray Weidenbaum, estimated the total costs of complying with Federal regulations at $98 billion in 1979.

The regulatory impact of R&D is multifaceted. Regulation may extend the waiting time for a given return to be earned on an investment. This is perhaps most obvious for drug and medical products which must pass lengthy government safety and effectiveness tests prior to release for the market; the longer the time lag needed to recapture the investment in an inflationary environment, the lower the real rate of return. In addition, regulation increases uncertainty. Firms are at the mercy of regulators who may have the capability to change regulations *ex post,* after firms have decided on a product or process mix, and after the optimal mix of inputs has been determined. Finally, as already noted, regulations distort resource allocations away from R&D and all other traditional investments toward the direction of tasks dictated by regulators.

The growing sensitivity to the hidden, debilitating impact of some Federal rules and regulations on R&D has sparked a number of proposals to provide for the weighing of costs and benefits associated with regulations before their promulgation. The Regulatory Budget Concept, first introduced by the author in 1979, is one useful approach to this problem in which a cap or ceiling on the economic impact of all Federal regulations agency-by-agency would be established by Congress.

Federal Productivity Center

Of course, there are many positive options the Federal government can pursue to spur R&D, options involving more than simply boosting outlays for R&D.

Perhaps the most fundamental one involves a Federal program to reinforce and supplement private-sector productivity efforts by creation of a robust National Productivity Center. Federal concern with the declining state of US innovation began as early as 1963 with President Kennedy's Civilian Technology Program designed to upgrade production technologies utilized by small and medium-sized companies. An initial focus of this program, administered by the National Bureau of Standards, was the textile and apparel industry which received Federal assistance through 1969. In 1965, the State Technical Services program was established within the Department of Commerce to improve the dissemination and utilization of technical information to the private sector. It was terminated in 1970.

In 1971, the Nixon Administration established the New Technological Opportunities Program to spotlight Federal incentives capable of accelerating innovation. This dual-objective program, designed to increase the competitiveness of US exporters and to reduce unemployment among scientists and engineers, survives today on a shoestring budget.

In early 1978, President Carter called for a comprehensive review by a joint public-private sector task force of steps appropriate to ensure continued world leadership in innovation. The results were released in October 1979 and constitute the most aggressive Federal plan of attack yet proposed on the declining rate of innovation. It sparked widespread public discussion by groups as diverse as the National Academy of Engineering and the Massachusetts Institute of Technology. This effort resulted in the promising establishment by the Department of Commerce of a Center for the Utilization of Federal Technology and of Cooperative Generic Technology Centers.

The Reagan Administration, in light of its commitment to productivity growth, may continue this useful Federal thrust and, most importantly, to add badly needed R&D-oriented tax features which were not addressed by the Carter Administration.

Tax Policies

Tax policies designed to stimulate savings and investment will yield R&D advances which promote productivity growth as well. As Kendrick noted before the JEC,

Policies to promote tangible investment and, thus, the rate of growth of real stocks and inputs of structures, equipment, inventories, and developed natural resources would obviously accelerate the growth or real product per unit of labor input and per capita. Real product growth would be favorably affected by the faster rate of diffusion of new technology, reflected in a declining average age of the fixed capital stock.

Thus, if investment levels in general can be raised, they will increase output in addition to expanding R&D and productivity.

Perhaps at the heart of options for increasing investment and savings is the issue of taxation. The US tax system is more biased against capital formation than the system of any other industrialized nation except Britain. Income taxes reduce disposable income and, hence, consumption and savings. Yet, investment into which savings flow are heavily taxed, as well, lowering the present value of these investments and rendering them relatively less attractive than consumption. Thus, the tax system bears at least some responsibility for the notably low level of savings in the US. The most recent five-year average savings rate was 6.7% of disposable income, for example, compared to 14.1% in Great Britain, 15.2% in West Germany, 17.3% in France, and a high 24.9% in Japan. US society does not make anywhere near the relative amount of loanable funds available that its international trading competitors do for investment.

Congress is acting to remedy this dismal savings rate. A provision sponsored by the author became effective this past January which allows individuals to exclude from gross income up to $100 of interest received from a savings account; married couples filing a joint return may exclude up to $200. This is a small step, but it is a long-overdue first step in the right direction to bring about a needed increase in the savings rate.

The tax system can be modified to stimulate R&D investment in other ways, as well. And there is certainly no dearth of opinion on what taxes should be cut to spur savings and investment in R&D, or by how much. The more prominent, current concepts include:

Reducing effective corporate income tax rates by one or more of the following measures:

- Shorten depreciation periods for tax purposes. Under current law, an increase in the inflation rate results in a heavier tax burden on all assets. Moreover, tax law imposes a greater relative tax burden on long-lived assets. The author has proposed what has become known as the "2-4-7-10" capital recovery or depreciation schedule program. This accelerated depreciation proposal would counteract inflation's debilitating effect on historical costs, making long-term investments characteristic of R&D programs more attractive compared to short-term investments than they are presently.

- Decrease marginal tax rates, further graduate the present tax bracket schedule, raise the surtax exemption threshold above the present $100,000 or lower the top rate from 46%. Any of these steps would act to ameliorate the impact of bracket creep, thereby improving the after-tax rate of return on investment in general.

- Increase the eligibility amount for tax credits on used equipment, and increase (expand) coverage of the investment tax credit on new equipment. These steps would increase the incentive for firms to initiate investment *per se.*

- Revise estate taxes to ease the tax burden on smaller, family-owned businesses to encourage the continuity of family ownership and longer-term investments by such businesses.

Options for stimulating savings:

- Extension of the 50% maximum marginal rate on "earned" income to property or capital income as well, to encourage investment.

- Reduce general personal income rates, and stretch out the graduation of marginal rates to counteract the effect of bracket creep and thereby facilitate personal savings.

Revision of the capital gains tax:

• Allow capital gains to be treated on a "rollover" basis. This would defer the taxing of capital gains if the proceeds from the sale of the asset were fully reinvested. Lower capital gains tax rates would encourage more reinvestment, as well.

These and other concepts have been proposed by groups ranging from the Senate Finance Committee, the House Ways and Means Committee, the Committee for Economic Development, and the National Research Council to the New York and American Stock Exchanges. These groups share the concern that the level of investment and savings in the United States is too low, and must be increased to yield distinctly positive effects on R&D investment and productivity.

A variety of targeted tax and other steps have been suggested which are sharply focused on the R&D process itself, rather than on the more general phenomena of savings and investment. The justification for utilizing public resources for narrowly focused R&D activity rests largely on the presence of externalities. These are R&D benefits or spin-offs which specific firms do not capture, but which accrue rather to the benefit of an entire industry or even unrelated industries. Perhaps the classic and still valid example of such externalities is early Federal work on computer and silicon chip technology.

Among the more attractive targeted R&D options are these:

• Permit firms to double-dip by expensing a portion of their capital investments for R&D activity in the year incurred.

• Permit R&D investments resulting in award of a patent to be depreciated rapidly rather than over 17 years.

• Extend the loss carry-forward period for new firms heavily involved in R&D activity.

• Increase the tax credit applicable to R&D investments.

Each of these options would have the effect of increasing the after-tax rate of return to firms for R&D investments or activity. One warning: while these steps would tend to increase the rate of such investment, it would be done largely at the expense of other, less-favored capital investments. That, in turn, may yield a decline in private-sector activities designed to raise productivity in the near term. In effect, these targeted R&D fiscal policies could increase long-term productivity growth at the expense of near-term growth. For that reason, any taxation revision targeted explicitly at R&D should be accompanied by other actions designed to increase the return for all forms of investment and savings as well.

Other options are available to spark R&D expenditures which do not involve the tax system. Obviously, Federal outlays for R&D programs, including better information dissemination or a boost in sagging real Federal R&D outlays (Table 2) will eventually be reflected in productivity statistics. Labor training and, especially, higher education programs will yield beneficial effects in future years. And a host of other options, such as revised antitrust, patent or Federal procurement policies or reduced Federal red tape, can increase the pool of resources available for private-sector investment without requiring an increase in public outlays.

The full range of such options should be mobilized, for a variety of explicit indicators suggest that R&D activity here relative to that of the nation's trading partners is either declining or stagnant. Such indicators as R&D as a ratio of GNP, industrial R&D as a ratio of value-added in manufacturing, and R&D engineers

TABLE 2. Federal R&D and R&D Plant Outlays 1965–1980*
(Dollars in Millions)

Year	R&D and R&D Plant Outlays	R&D and R&D Plant Outlays as a Percent of Total Federal Budget Outlays
1965	$15,756	12.6
1966	16,479	11.9
1967	16,859	10.7
1968	16,362	9.5
1969	14,889	8.9
1970	13,531	8.0
1971	13,168	7.6
1972	13,351	7.2
1973	13,140	7.1
1974	12,391	6.8
1975	12,132	6.0
1976	12,335	5.7
1977	12,888	5.8
1978	13,155	5.7
1979 (est.)	13,342	5.9
1980 (est.)	12,750	5.8

*In constant (1967) dollars.
Source: *Federal Funds for Research and Development,* Volume XXVIII, National Science Foundation, 1980.

and scientists per 10,000 workers all show the nation lagging in comparison to other countries, especially Japan and West Germany. Recent indicators of the fruits of R&D, such as patent filings, show a declining or stagnating pattern compared to past years. In fact, the only bright spot is found in data on the level of resources being committed to R&D. Indices, for example, such as the absolute number of R&D scientists and engineers, the level of national R&D spending, and the number of public offerings by smaller technical companies are rebounding after an extended period of stagnation or decline through much of the last decade. Still, the longer-term prospects for productivity growth are not bright.

Policy Suggestions

The far-from-rosy outlook for productivity growth is mirrored by poor prospects for a marked shift in national resources toward R&D investment. With inflation predicted by many analysts to persist at close to double-digit rates, private-sector investment time horizons will continue to shrink. Traditional contractionary monetary policies will continue to price loanable funds well above levels conducive to R&D investments. The very likely continuation of slow or no real economic or market growth will hamper private-sector efforts and abilities to meet more than the most pressing internal or government regulatory investment requirements. And the continuing squeeze on real disposable consumer incomes, which began in early 1979, will reinforce the sagging rate of personal savings.

It is a grim picture, but one that the US will be facing for years to come if inflation cannot be checked. The traditional anti-inflation policy prescriptions have proved less than helpful in the face of staggering food and OPEC price rises and a growing inflationary psychology that encourages investment in resort housing over corporate debentures. Keynesian demand management of inflation can scarcely be relied upon by policymakers confronting 12% inflation and capacity utilization rates below 80%.

The necessary prescription for this malaise was set in place in March 1980 when the US Senate specified that any tax cut be equally divided between individuals and productivity incentives. The Reagan electoral sweep—with its focus on reduced Federal spending to accompany a tax cut—added a further component. A reduction in 1981 in individual income taxes which exceeds any spending reduction will go a long way toward boosting real growth and savings.

At the same time, a comparable reduction during 1981 in business taxes would help establish the foundation for renewed productivity growth and reduced inflation in the future. The tax package thoughtfully pieced together by the Senate Finance Committee in 1980, but not enacted into law, constitutes one possible parameter for such a cut. It included the author's 2-4-7-10 capital recovery plan to replace the unrealistic and complicated Accelerated Depreciation Range schedule now used to determine plant and equipment depreciation. Other provisions included a reduction in the capital gains tax rate to 20% from the current 28%, a 2% reduction in the top corporate income tax rate, the termination of midyear issuance of W-2 forms, an increase in the permissible number of Subchapter S stockholders to 25, an increase in eligibility for the investment tax credit on used equipment to $150,000 and a host of similar steps. Taken together, they would remove a portion of the present tax bias against investment. But more should be done, particularly to target incentives for R&D investment. Provisions to permit immediate expensing of such investments and increased tax credits on such investments are certainly appropriate, in this regard.

To conclude on a sobering note, this nation is now one year into a very difficult decade, one likely to feature energy supply disruptions, spiraling food prices, continued economic malaise in the Third World, and stagflation here at home. Some of those events are not readily amenable to resolution. But the nation certainly has the capability to deal with stagflation, to regain robust economic growth without soaring inflation or unemployment. It is long past the time when the US should begin to restore to its economy that sense of equilibrium which is brought about only by rising productivity.

The package of investment-oriented tax proposals developed and passed by the Senate Finance Committee in 1980 is the first step along that path, and inclusion of that package in any 1981 tax cut is imperative. Equally important, however, are tax provisions to bias corporate decisions toward long-term R&D investments. For without a renewed commitment to rising R&D investments, any public program to spur productivity will prove to be only a band-aid, dealing with the symptom of a sagging economy rather than the weakening foundations itself.

Technology In Society

New York / Oxford / Toronto / PERGAMON PRESS / Paris / Frankfurt / Sydney

Technology In Society, Vol. 3, pp. 35–44 (1981)
Printed in the USA. All rights reserved.

0160-791X/81/010035-10$02.00/0
Copyright © 1981 Pergamon Press Ltd

Taxation, Innovation and Economic Growth

Michael J. Boskin

There are many reasons to be concerned about the level and allocation of innovative activity in society. Some people may value an inquisitive society *per se;* others may oppose change and favor stability and continuity of tradition. More important, most people tend to associate innovation and technical change with solving particular — often pressing — problems: important examples today involve finding cures for different types of cancer and alternative energy technologies.

Historically, technological change is often associated with the most obvious major breakthroughs made by mankind — from changes in crop rotation systems centuries ago through the steam engine to modern computers. While each of these may be addressed to solving a particular problem, they and a myriad of less noted but collectively extremely important technical changes in techniques of production, product lines, etc., have been a major vehicle for promoting general increases in the standard of living of the world's population. The relationship between technical change and economic growth combines with the recent abysmal growth performance of the US economy to focus attention on the economic incentives surrounding innovative activity.

Is it the case that a variety of economic policies and/or changes in the economy have reduced the returns or increased the risks to undertaking such activity, and, if so, has this in turn led to a decrease in the rate of technical change and economic growth? Is there a case for changing current economic policies with respect to innovation and technical change?

The purpose of this paper is to present a variety of issues involved in analyzing these questions in as direct and nontechnical a manner as possible. The author will also present a variety of his own opinions, judgments and conjectures on some of the key issues involved. The purpose is to raise these questions and present opinions, not to exhaustively evaluate available evidence on each of the major

Michael J. Boskin is Professor of Economics at Stanford University and Research Associate of the National Bureau of Economic Research, Inc. He is the author of approximately 40 articles and editor of five volumes of essays on the subject of taxation, fiscal policy, capital formation, labor markets and related subjects. Dr. Boskin has been a consultant and frequent witness to the committees of Congress dealing with economic policy and to the Treasury Department. He was a member of several of President Reagan's economic policy task forces.

links in the argument; a variety of the other papers in this volume present more
detailed technical information on some of these points and numerous references
thereto.

In the next section the recent economic growth performance in the United
States will be discussed briefly, followed, in the third section, by a discussion of a
variety of different issues concerning the relationship between innovation or
technical progress and economic growth and, in the fourth section, discussion of
some of the major features of tax policy which potentially affect innovation,
capital formation, and economic growth. Finally, there will be a brief discussion
of some of the author's preferred policy options which would, in his opinion, increase the rate of technical change and economic growth toward their long-run
historical level and thereby restore steady progress in the standard of living of US
citizens.

The Recent Growth Performance

Rapid economic growth over long periods is a relatively recent phenomenon for
mankind. Usually traced to the Industrial Revolution or to the period immediately preceding it, the minor annual gains in living standards throughout the world
accelerated substantially in many countries in the last two or three centuries.
While this progress has not spread uniformly across all individuals within a country nor evenly across countries, by historical standards the growth performance of
what are now called the advanced economies over the last 200 years is indeed impressive.

While there are difficulties in comparability, as near as one can tell, real income
per person in the United States grew at almost 2% per year over the last century,
and about at that rate in France and Germany. The United Kingdom, which was
the wealthiest society on earth a century ago, has grown about one percentage
point per year more slowly than the United States since then and is now a relatively poor member of the Common Market. Thus, very modest changes in annual
rates of growth, when compounded over long periods of time, can make an enormous difference in the nature of a society and its relationship to the rest of the
world. At a growth rate of 2% per year, standards of living will almost double
between generations, and the economic and social environment created with that
rate of economic progress is vastly different from that of a slowly growing
economy where tensions over the division of a stagnant output are greatly
magnified.

In the period between the end of World War II and the early 1970s, the United
States grew at slightly more than its historic rate on average. However, since the
early 1970s, like most other advanced economies, its rate of economic growth has
slowed markedly. Measured as the annual rate of growth in real Gross National
Product (GNP) per employed worker, the US growth rate since 1973 has been
0.1%; *i.e.,* it has not grown at all. Virtually all gains in GNP have been accomplished by the massive influx of extra workers into the labor force in the last
decade. While the growth performance of Japan, Germany, France and other

countries has also declined in this period, they have not fared nearly as poorly as the United States. The three countries just named, for example, averaged annual growth rates since 1973 of approximately 3%. If such differences continue for substantial periods of time, the United States will be following the course of the United Kingdom.

The Role of Innovation in Economic Growth

There are several basic ways in which an economy can improve the standard of living for its population. First, the available labor force can be made more productive by providing it with more capital per worker. For example, the average annual increase in this so-called capital/labor ratio in the United States economy from roughly the end of World War II to the early 1970s was about 2.5%; since 1973 there has been no increase whatsoever in this ratio. This implies not only that workers are not getting more capital with which to work, it also implies that production methods are changing more slowly.

A second major method to promote economic growth involves improving the knowledge and skills of the labor force itself, so-called human capital. While difficult to measure, it is clear that in advanced economies, especially in the United States, a substantial fraction of total income is spent on such investment — whether in the most traditional formal higher education or in expenditures on health, nutrition, mobility and experience and training on the job. A much higher fraction of US income is spent on advanced education than in most other societies, and the most recent studies have suggested (see Kendrick 1976) that investment in human capital is about as large as investment in ordinary capital in the United States.

A third potential vehicle for promoting economic growth is technological change. Technological change means improvements in techniques of production, development of new product lines, etc., which enable the *existing* labor force and capital stock to produce more goods and services broadly defined. Technological change may be of a variety of sorts which are discussed in detail elsewhere in this volume.

One of the major issues with respect to the relationship between technological change and economic growth is whether the new technology is embodied solely in new capital or in the entire capital stock. That is, it may be impossible — or at least extremely costly — to convert the existing capital stock to take advantage of the new technology. The same may also be true of the existing labor force, given its knowledge, skill and training. Thus, technological improvements which have the potential for augmenting existing labor force and/or capital stock productivity may have all or a disproportional share of this potential channeled into new investment or newly trained and educated members of the labor force. If a substantial amount of technical change is of the embodied (as opposed to disembodied) type, there is an extremely important link between the rate of innovation and the rate of investment. Even if there is a high rate of technical change, a low rate of investment (labor force growth) coupled with the fact that the new technology is primarily embodied in new capital (or labor) implies a very slow rate of diffusion of this technology over the entire capital stock (labor force) and a slower rate of improvement in productivity.

While it is extremely difficult to say anything empirical about the embodiment conjecture, it does have substantial anecdotal appeal. Therefore, many economists believe that the relatively low rates of investment in the United States — about two-thirds of that in Western Europe and only one-half of that in Japan — mean that even when the US develops new technology, it tends to embody it in its capital stock at a slower rate than do its major competitors.

A second link between development of new technology and the rate of investment in the growth process concerns another conjecture which economists call "learning by doing." This refers to the fact that the investment process itself may lead to — as a by-product — opportunities for new types of investment, further lowering production costs, and freeing resources for other purposes. Once again, if there is a substantial amount of learning-by-doing, the rate of investment feeds back on the rate of technological advance and the low rate of capital formation in the United States may in the long-run reduce the rate of technological change.

While other factors may influence growth over short periods of time, these are the three major sources of economic growth. There are numerous debates concerning the relative contribution of each to the historical — and potential — growth of the US economy. Perhaps the most widely quoted study is that of Denison (1974). In the post-war period, through 1969, Denison attributes about half of an adjusted growth rate of 2.6% to advances in knowledge and about half to changes in capital and land per person employed, to improved resource allocation, and to the economies of scale of larger markets. While attributing approximately half of this growth to advances in knowledge may not seem unreasonable on *a priori* grounds, a variety of attacks on Denison's work has appeared and the relative contributions of capital deepening, human investment and technical change in the growth process continues to be an important research topic. The author's tentative conclusion (see Boskin, 1978a) is that technological change accounts for approximately one-third of US economic growth, capital deepening for perhaps one-third, and human investment for a substantial amount of the rest.

Therefore, there are both analytical and empirical bases for believing that the rate of technical change and innovation in a society is a primary vehicle for generating rising standards of living for its population over time. As the rate of economic growth has slowed markedly in recent years and accelerating the growth rate is now an important concern of policymakers, the effects of a variety of economic policies on innovation and capital formation, especially tax, monetary and regulatory policy, have once again come to the fore. A discussion of some potential avenues by which the tax system can affect innovation, capital formation and economic growth follows.

Taxation, Innovation and Capital Formation

There are many types of government policies which affect the potential rate of innovation and capital formation in US society. For example, the government — at the local, state and, especially, Federal levels — engages in a variety of types of direct research and development activities. Hence, the share of society's resources devoted to governmental research and development can have important impacts directly on the rate of technical change and indirectly through the generation of basic knowledge and research which has spin-off effects in the private sector. Further, the share of resources diverted from private activity to government activity can influence the share of private activity devoted to research and development as well.

Obviously, a variety of types of regulatory activities influence the potential costs and returns and risks involved in engaging in technological research and development and/or investment. Further, inflation — which adds considerably to risk in the economy and combined with an unindexed tax system reduces the after-tax, after-inflation return to capital — is closely linked to monetary policy, although there is not enough space here to discuss economists' disagreement on this issue or the author's personal opinions.

Suffice it to say that a monetary policy which creates, or at least accommodates, a high and fluctuating rate of inflation and hence, nominal interest rates, tends to make long-term investment — including long-term research and development potential payoffs — riskier and less remunerative. It is the author's opinion that, in the advanced economies today, the bulk of technological advance comes from decisions made in response to potential economic incentives. He does not believe that the day of the independent, low-budget, creative genius has passed; only that, of the total potential for research and development, a very large percentage of the highest priority projects must be financed with accumulations of substantial amounts of capital and that the amount of such capital forthcoming to finance risky investment, including R&D, is highly sensitive to expected net returns and perceived risks. While monetary and regulatory policies affect this economic environment, the focus here for a moment is on some of the aspects of US tax laws which potentially impact R&D expenditures and investment decisions.

There is a common perception that a variety of features of the current tax law — including features of the corporate income tax, the capital gains tax, etc. — lead to a reduction in risk-taking and — possibly — overall investment in our society. The different taxes on the potential returns to investment, including investment in R&D, interact in a myriad of ways and have a series of provisions which potentially impact the risk and/or potential return to such activity. Some of the more important include the failure to index the corporation income tax, and, therefore, to base depreciation allowances on historic costs; the taxation and deductibility of nominal interest payments and collections; the non-integration of the corporate and personal income tax; the capital gains tax; the features of the personal income tax which tax the returns to certain types of personal saving a second time at the personal level, etc. Feldstein and Summers (1978) document the substantial increase in the effective tax rates on income from capital in the 1970s, caused primarily by the interaction of inflation and the unindexed tax system. Therefore, for any given response of investment and R&D expenditures to the tax system, the 1970s were a period where effective tax rates appeared to increase and, hence, to decrease after-tax returns and reduce the incentive to invest and innovate.

US tax law draws an important distinction between expenditures on R&D investment and other types of investment. Expenditures on research and development are expensed in the year made, rather than depreciated by a formula which relates to the possible useful life of the asset. Therefore, R&D investment is taxed less heavily than investment, say, in plant and equipment. In fact, the fact that R&D expenditures are expensed should, ignoring other features of the tax system for a moment, not affect the number and composition of R&D projects undertaken privately. A value-maximizing firm will invest to the point where the last project yields a net real return equal to the net real cost of capital, a present discounted value of zero. Since the R&D expenditures are deductible when made, the present value of the depreciation deduction equals the expected present value of future tax liabilities and the net tax rate of return on the R&D investment is not affected by a corporate tax which allows expensing.

Of course, other features of the tax law interact with the treatment of R&D, and R&D expenditures interact with general investment expenditures which are heavily taxed. This will be discussed further. Further, the precise definition of what is a R&D expenditure and what is general investment to be depreciated over a longer span of time than the year made is a non-obvious one and one which can certainly vary through time given the nature of R&D and investment in general. For example, should expenses of commercializing product lines be included as R&D expenditures or not? The point here is that the simple accounting definition of where to draw the line can have a substantial impact on the incentives to invest in research and development or other types of capital formation, or to consume.

Important Links

Since there are important links between technological change and investment for the aggregate economy if either learning-by-doing or embodiment is important, one should also be interested in whether there are important links in the taxation of general investment and R&D expenditures at the level of the individual firm. That is, while R&D expenditures may be expensed, increasing and high rates of effective taxation on the new technology — imbedded in the firm's capital stock and hence reducing its production costs and/or otherwise increasing its profitability — must be considered. Unfortunately, not a lot is known for most sectors of the economy about this link. Indeed, the exact relationship between the R&D expenditures and new innovation and technological advances is also a subject of dispute.

The point here is that US tax law is biased against investment which must be depreciated over a longer period of time as opposed to R&D expenditures; however, the expected returns on the latter are probably often affected by the effective rates of taxation on the former. It is the author's considered opinion that the increasing effective tax rates on investment income in general probably more than offsets the differential taxation of R&D expenditures relative to general capital formation. He also tentatively accepts the embodiment and learning-by-doing conjectures, and, therefore, believes that the increase in effective tax rates on investment income in the economy not only has decreased the rate of capital formation from what it otherwise would have been, but has also biased it towards shorter term investments, and has probably fed back to decrease the rate of R&D expenditures and technological advance. Continuing this pattern into the future will seriously threaten future productivity increases and the potential for increased standards of living over long periods of time for US citizens. It is important to note that there are a variety of features of the tax system which mitigate in part the effective tax rates embodied in the corporate income tax itself. The deductibility of interest and the availability of debt financing at the margin for many types of projects, investment tax credits, accelerated depreciation, etc., at least partially mitigate the impact of the corporate tax rate itself on the overall incentive to invest in US society.[1]

However, even considering these features, it is the author's opinion that a substantial amount of investment has been deterred by the rise in effective tax rates, that not all new innovation and investment can be financed by borrowing and deducting the interest against already accumulating profits from other activities, and that the overall impact of the corporate income tax has been to reduce the rate of capital formation and innovation.

The Capital Gains Tax

The capital gains tax — which currently includes 40% of long-term realized capital gains as taxable income — has been a subject of much dispute among academic economists concerning its effects on investment and risk-taking in society. The perception of most non-economists is that the capital gains tax obviously reduces risk-taking in society. It can do so in a variety of ways, including the so-called "lock-in" effect, whereby individuals are deterred from moving current investment with accrued capital gains to higher productivity and potentially riskier return investment because they would realize capital gains and be subject to tax.

The capital gains tax is also unindexed and, therefore, taxes a nominal portion of capital gains when realized. The US has one of the few advanced economies which imposes a capital gains tax, and there is growing concern over its potential disincentive effects in a variety of important high technology sectors of the economy which finance the large number of very risky potential innovations by so-called venture capital. Spreading the risk over a large number of such projects is common practice, but the available pool of capital forthcoming from households and/or financial intermediaries on behalf of households in order to undertake such potentially risky investments as those concerned in R&D expenditures may be highly sensitive to its return (see Feldstein and Yitzhaki, 1978). That is, it may well be that the country has not only misallocated its investment by locking some of it in via the capital gains tax to potentially lower productivity uses, but also reduced the supply of long-term risk-taking venture capital by its presence. Unfortunately, available empirical information on these effects is only beginning to be developed, and is nowhere as complete or convincing as the longer series and more developed series of studies of the impact of taxation on plant and equipment investment.

The author thinks that the notion that the capital gains tax has very little impact on the available supply of funds for risk-taking is badly mistaken, but it is important to realize that there is a long way to go before this conjecture is convincingly documented.

Again, the failure to integrate the corporate and personal income taxes means that investment income is eventually taxed again at the personal level, either through capital gains eventually realized on retained earnings or on dividends beyond a very modest exclusion allowed in personal income tax. Nominal interest is also taxed at the personal level, even though in recent years households have been paying billions of dollars of taxes on negative *real* interest receipts. Once again, there is growing evidence that the overall taxation of the return to saving originally generated by households and/or corporations on their behalf is more sensitive to effective real net tax rates than previously believed (see Boskin, 1978a).

The overall conclusion, therefore, is that the supply of domestic saving (a pool of capital available for long-term investment and very risky investment) and overall saving (investment and research and development expenditures) have been reduced by a substantial increase in effective marginal tax rates adjusting for inflation in the 1970s. To restore the historic rates of capital formation and innovation, let alone to increase them to higher levels that many deem desirable, will require substantial structural revisions in the tax system.

Policy Options and Conclusion

In brief summary, the author has tried to develop the following argument: the long-run real growth rate depends heavily upon the rate of technological change; this in turn is affected in a variety of ways, including direct government policies and indirectly by embodiment and/or learning-by-doing via the rate of investment. The high and rising effective tax rates on capital income have reduced the rate of saving and investment below what they would otherwise have been, and probably also reduced the rate of R&D expenditures below what it otherwise would have been.

In addition to general inflation, which has increased risks substantially in our society in the 1970s, the pernicious interaction between inflation and a variety of features of the tax system has combined to reduce the returns and probably increased the risks to different types of long-term investment. As a result, too little is being invested in plant and equipment, and also in research and development. This, in turn, may be an important part of the short-term slowdown in the real growth rate and undoing these problems assumes a high priority in restoring the historical rate of economic growth and the continuous increases in the standard of living so necessary to an orderly functioning of the US economy and society. While other policy options are important — including changing the different kinds of regulation and stabilizing the growth of regulatory activity, the author believes that decreasing inflation by a slower and more predictable rate of monetary expansion and reforming the taxation of capital income are the two most important keys to increasing the rate of investment and technological progress in the 1980s and beyond.

The structural revisions in tax policy favored here have been discussed in detail elsewhere (see Boskin, 1978b). The main conclusion is that the focus of our tax system should be gradually changed from taxing income to taxing spending or consumption, thereby removing the double taxation of saving and capital income inherent in the current system of taxation.

The ultimate goal would be complete integration of the corporate and personal income tax, gradual reduction and elimination of the capital gains tax, and gradual increasing of the number of vehicles and amounts available for tax-free saving and investment in the new tax system. Ultimately, then, households would be taxed on their income minus their saving, *i.e.,* on their expenditure. This would be accomplished in a personal tax which could allow for variations in circumstances across households.

Most of the Western European economies rely much more heavily on taxes on consumption than the US does; the US tax system, while collecting a slightly smaller percentage of GNP than do most of the economies of Western Europe, relies about twice as heavily on taxes on investment income as do the Western Europeans. The author does not personally favor a value-added tax as the first best solution, but rather the personal expenditure tax described above.[2]

The author believes that the US must move to such a program gradually, but steadily, in the years ahead, or see the already damaging consequences of its rising effective tax rates on investment in plant and equipment and innovation deteriorate further. Restoring a long-term rate of economic growth is of the utmost importance. Technical change and capital deepening are two extremely important determinants of a long-term growth rate. The process by which spending as opposed to investment, saving and long-term R&D expenditures is encouraged in the tax system should be reversed; it should be made as neutral as possible via shifting from taxing corporate and personal income to taxing expenditure at the household level.

If such a tax policy proves totally impossible to implement politically (note that there have been several moves in this direction recently through the establishment of IRA and Keogh accounts, etc.), perhaps the next best solution would be to complete direct indexation of the tax system, so that only real income — including real capital gains and real interest — is taxed, and integration of the corporate and personal tax system. Once again, this should be thought of as a second best policy to a determined effort to reduce the rate of inflation back down to low single digit levels where the level and fluctuation of inflation and nominal interest rates have much less potential impact on risks and returns in the innovation and investment process.

The deterioration of incentives faced by risky long-term innovation and capital formation projects can be reversed via sensible gradually phased-in revisions in tax and monetary policy. The policy targets announced recently by the Federal Reserve are designed to gradually bring inflation under control. It is time a consensus of the importance of capital formation and innovation in US society was developed for the future living standards of our population, and a series of phased-in reforms of taxation of capital income was gradually implemented to remove the biases currently inhibiting such activity.

Notes

1. See Feldstein and Summers (1978) for a discussion of various features and effective tax rates.
2. Implementation of such changes has been the subject of much debate, and the interested reader is referred to the US Treasury Department's *Blueprints for Basic Tax Reform* (1977) for a detailed discussion of such implementation.

References

M. Boskin, "Taxation, Saving and the Rate of Interest," *Journal of Political Economy,* April 1978a.

M. Boskin, ed., *Federal Tax Reform* (San Francisco: Institute for Contemporary Studies, 1978b).

E. F. Denison, *Accounting for US Economic Growth 1929–1969* (Washington, D.C.: The Brookings Institution, 1974).

M. Feldstein and L. Summers, "Inflation and the Taxation of Corporate Income," *Brookings Papers on Economic Activity,* no. 1, 1978.

M. Feldstein and S. Yitzhaki, "The Effects of Taxation on the Selling and Switching of Common Stock," *Journal of Public Economics,* February 1978.

J. Kendrick, *The Formation and Stocks of Total Capital* (New York: National Bureau of Economic Research, 1976).

Technology In Society, Vol. 3, pp. 45–62 (1981)
Printed in the USA. All rights reserved.

The Proper Medicine for Stagflation

Roger E. Brinner

Inflation is the undisputed entry at the top of the list of national economic problems. Indeed, the other possible contender — high unemployment — is fundamentally due to the current need for a low-pressure economy to cool off inflation. The overwhelming consensus prescription to reverse the upward ratcheting inflation of the 1970s is strong capital spending, and Democrats and Republicans were headed toward a "supply-side" tax cut skewed toward direct business investment stimulus until the Reagan Administration initiatives surfaced. Now confrontation is possible in two areas. The first conflict looms between the consensus view just described and the *new* "supply-siders" who hope for productivity gains born of greater work effort and personal savings in response to tax cuts skewed toward personal, not business, taxation.

The second threatened conflict is between fiscal and monetary policy. The Reagan proposal for a three-year sequence of large-scale tax cuts could not be matched with equivalent expenditure cuts. The resultant fiscal stimulus would create income and hence credit growth beyond the bounds sought by the Federal Reserve, yielding a credit crunch with a pronounced negative impact on investment. The two dimensions of the emerging conflict are thus the composition of the tax cut — focusing on business versus personal tax reduction — and the size of the tax cut.

Perhaps the Reagan-team enthusiasm for the radical personal tax cuts can be traced to an almost desperate desire to try something different to bring the economy out of its nagging stagflation. This essay will argue that a sharp change of tactics is in fact necessary, but that the proper strategy is a combination of strong tax incentives to support technology development and a tight-fiscal/low-interest-rate policy stance to raise the investment share of GNP. The technology initiative proposed here — a large tax credit for Research and Development (R&D) — is the only option which can simultaneously cut inflation and promote

Roger E. Brinner is Vice President and Group Director of the International and Energy Division of Data Resources, Inc. He has been Assistant Professor of Economics at Harvard University and Senior Staff Economist responsible for macroeconomic analysis at the Council of Economic Advisers and has directed Data Resources' long-term economic analysis. Dr. Brinner has had numerous essays and articles published in the areas of capital formation, tax policy, inflation, and general macroeconomic forecasting.

employment. Given the Federal Reserve's conservative money growth targets, tight fiscal policy is a necessity to keep interest rates low and credit available to finance business fixed capital.

The Necessity of Strong Research and Development Spending

R&D is the only possible way to generate the knowledge and flexibility required for a business, or indeed a national economy, to progress and to stay competitive. This postulate has been inadequately recognized in the past by business and government, but the failure of US enterprises to cope fully with the shocks of the 1970s has led to analysis which should generate the necessary awareness of the role of R&D. US labor productivity growth has collapsed. The country's share of international trade has fallen as its reputation for product leadership has been successfully challenged in automobiles, electronics and elsewhere. These problems will not solve themselves. They will get progressively worse in a world where the US' major competitors already recognize the need to shift resources rapidly out of lagging sectors and into developing, high-technology sectors. Japan, Germany and France are subsidizing and sponsoring this transformation process within their countries. The US cannot afford to lag behind, or a weak dollar and declining living standards relative to the industrial world will ensue. The US can afford to provide strong tax incentives to boost research. In the short run, these must be provided at the expense of otherwise desirable personal tax cuts; in the long run, these tax incentives will prove to be a solid investment.

The Impact of Technology on Industrial Performance

An analysis of output, employment, and price behavior in manufacturing industries over the past three decades indicates that "high-technology" industries have surpassed "low-technology" industries according to all meaningful aggregate economic indicators. The score reads:

- *Real Growth:* High-technology industries expanded at a 5.6% compound rate from 1950 to 1978 versus 2.7% for low-technology industries. This growth differential has moved the high technology sector from 42% of the output of the low technology sector to 91%.
- *Productivity:* Over the same time-span, output per employee hour increased 3.3% in advanced industries, only 2.3% in traditional activities.
- *Inflation:* The favorable labor productivity record is mirrored in the price record: 2.5% annual inflation in high-technology versus 3.4% in low technology firms.
- *Employment:* The gains in output per worker were not at the expense of employment. The employee hour gains of rapidly modernizing industries surpassed their conservative counterparts by a six-fold margin: 2.3% versus 0.4%. The enhanced domestic and international competitive posture generated more than enough demand to expand employment at a fast pace.

Figure 1 and Table 1 compare the employment growth rates of the high- and low-technology sectors.[1] The high-technology sector has a clear margin of superiority over the low-technology industries. These results are confirmed for the

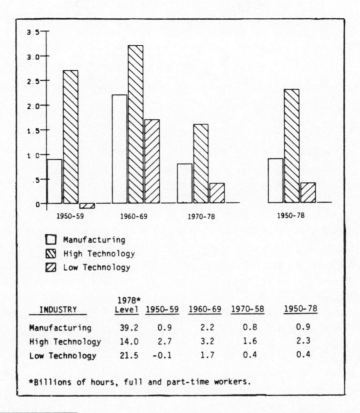

INDUSTRY	1978* Level	1950-59	1960-69	1970-58	1950-78
Manufacturing	39.2	0.9	2.2	0.8	0.9
High Technology	14.0	2.7	3.2	1.6	2.3
Low Technology	21.5	-0.1	1.7	0.4	0.4

*Billions of hours, full and part-time workers.

*In Charts 1 through 4 and the accompanying supplementary tables the growth rates for the sub-intervals may not appear to be consistent with the full interval in selected cases. In fact, they are fully consistent. The sub-interval for 1950-59 presents the rate of increase from the 1950 level to the 1959 level and the sub-interval for 1960-69 from the 1960 level to the 1969 level. Thus, the 1959-60 and 1969-70 individual years are not captured in the sub-intervals but are included in the full 1950-1978 interval.

FIGURE 1. Compound Annual Growth Rate of Employee Hours.

shorter subintervals, and when the disaggregation is extended further to the three-digit, SIC-code level. The contrasts are equally clear when labor productivity increases are examined (Figure 2 and Table 2). The trend rate of increase in real output per employee of 2.5% per year for all manufacturing was led by 3.3% per year in high-technology industries. The manufacturing average was substantially depressed by the 2.3% improvement in labor productivity in industries with low research efforts.

The aggregate effect of increases in employment and productivity is reflected, by definition, in the rate of real growth of high-technology industries (Figure 3 and Table 3). The new products of advanced research have a ready market at home and abroad. For example, capital equipment embodying advanced technology is a leading US export sector, permitting the US to import necessary raw materials to enhance the living standard of its trading partners and itself.

TABLE 1. Supplementary Detail 1: Compound Annual Growth Rate of Employee Hours

	Average Growth Rates				
	1978 Level*	1950–59	1960–69	1970–78	1950–78
Manufacturing	39.2	0.9	2.2	0.8	0.9
High Technology					
Professional and Scientific Instruments	2.1	2.8	2.6	0.8	2.0
Electrical Equipment (incl. Communications Equip.)	4.6	1.8	3.8	2.2	2.2
Communications Services	3.8	3.9	3.2	1.2	2.5
Chemicals	1.2	4.3	3.2	2.8	3.0
Nonelectrical Machinery (incl. Computers)	2.3	1.6	2.7	1.1	2.0
Low Technology					
Rubber and Plastic Products	0.9	2.5	−0.6	6.4	2.0
Petroleum Refining	1.5	2.3	5.4	2.6	2.9
Petroleum Extraction	0.9	−0.6	1.3	0.4	0.2
Stone, Clay and Glass	3.3	−0.3	0.1	−0.7	−0.3
Paper and Allied Products	1.8	−2.9	1.3	−1.0	−1.2
Primary Metals	2.4	0.2	1.7	−0.1	0.3
Fabricated Metal Products	1.5	−1.8	0.9	1.1	−0.3
Food and Kindred Products	1.0	−0.1	2.7	1.6	0.9
Textiles	1.4	1.9	2.1	−0.1	1.1
Apparel	1.4	1.1	1.1	0.7	0.8
Lumber and Wood Products	2.3	−0.5	1.5	−0.2	0.0
Furniture and Fixtures	3.2	1.3	3.5	0.8	1.4
Memo: Other Sectors and Categories					
Durable Manufactures	23.6	1.5	2.7	1.2	1.4
Motor Vehicles	2.0	−2.0	2.6	3.3	0.7
Aerospace & Misc. Transportation Equip.	1.9	9.7	2.5	−0.5	2.7
Nondurable Manufactures	15.6	0.2	1.5	0.1	0.4
Mining	1.8	−2.2	−0.7	4.3	0.2
Service	28.4	2.3	3.2	3.3	2.9
Finance, Insurance, Real Estate	8.4	3.4	3.2	3.1	3.2

*Billions of hours worked by full and part-time employees.

Finally, an examination of the sectors also yields strong evidence that high-technology industries have shown increases in employment while curbing inflation (Figure 4 and Table 4). High-technology industries generated inflation averaging only 2.5% per year, while prices in the low sector increased at a 3.4% pace for the entire 1950–1978 timespan. The margin of superiority increased in each decade.

To classify industries into technological strata, an "index of research effort" (IRE) was created, equal to the average ratio of research and development expenditures to gross product originating in the industry. A natural grouping suggested

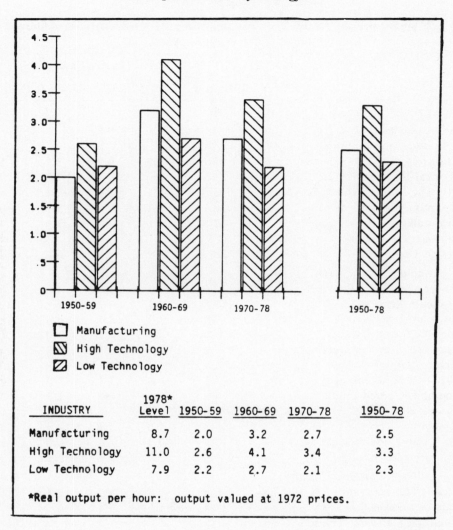

INDUSTRY	1978* Level	1950-59	1960-69	1970-78	1950-78
Manufacturing	8.7	2.0	3.2	2.7	2.5
High Technology	11.0	2.6	4.1	3.4	3.3
Low Technology	7.9	2.2	2.7	2.1	2.3

*Real output per hour: output valued at 1972 prices.

FIGURE 2. Compound Annual Growth Rate of Real Output Per Employee Hour (1972 Prices).

itself such that industries with an IRE of .06 or better were termed "high technology"; those industries with an IRE below 0.6 were designated as "low technology."

National Science Foundation (NSF) data are available at a reasonable level of disaggregation for total research and development spending by industry, and the Bureau of Economic Analysis provides corresponding data on real and nominal product, prices, and employment. Table 5 presents the index of effort by industries at a two-digit, SIC-code level of disaggregation. Examination of these ratios suggested the indicated breakdown into "high" and "low" technology. The line between high and low technology was defined to be .06, slightly below the .07 average ratio of research and development expenditures to output for all of manufacturing.[2]

TABLE 2. Supplementary Detail 2: Compound Annual Growth Rate of Real Output Per Employee Hour (1972 Prices)

		Average Growth Rates			
	1978 Level*	1950–59	1960–69	1970–78	1950–78
Manufacturing	8.7	2.0	3.2	2.7	2.5
High Technology					
Professional and Scientific Instruments	12.1	3.5	4.8	3.1	3.5
Electrical Equipment (incl. Communications Equip.)	8.3	1.1	1.9	1.1	1.5
Communications Services	8.7	3.1	5.8	3.3	4.0
Chemicals	7.8	2.6	4.0	1.3	2.4
Nonelectrical Machinery (incl. Computers)	20.7	5.2	4.9	6.8	5.4
Low Technology					
Rubber and Plastic Products	14.9	1.3	3.7	−4.8	0.6
Petroleum Refining	7.8	2.1	3.2	2.3	2.2
Petroleum Extraction	7.2	3.5	2.7	4.4	3.2
Stone, Clay and Glass	9.8	3.0	3.1	3.3	3.1
Paper and Allied Products	5.6	4.4	5.4	3.3	4.5
Primary Metals	5.1	1.4	1.8	4.7	2.6
Fabricated Metal Products	7.1	3.0	5.4	1.2	3.4
Food and Kindred Products	5.2	1.6	2.0	2.3	1.6
Textiles	9.0	0.8	3.0	4.0	2.1
Apparel	8.1	1.8	2.2	2.3	1.8
Lumber and Wood Products	8.5	0.3	1.6	0.0	0.5
Furniture and Fixtures	7.3	1.9	2.3	1.6	1.8
Memo: Other Sectors and Categories					
Durable Manufactures	8.6	1.4	3.1	2.3	2.1
Motor Vehicles	17.4	1.5	4.4	6.6	3.5
Aerospace & Misc. Transportation Equip.	7.1	1.0	3.0	−0.9	1.5
Nondurable Manufactures	8.8	2.9	3.2	3.2	3.0
Mining	11.6	4.5	3.7	−3.0	1.9
Service	6.0	1.1	1.2	0.5	0.9
Finance, Insurance, Real Estate	25.8	1.4	1.1	1.3	1.2

*Dollars of real output per employee hour, 1972 prices.

In theory, monetary and fiscal policy should be able to keep the economy on a relatively full-employment path, buffering outside shocks to keep long-run employment growth approximately equal to expansion in the labor force. If reality followed theory, the creation and adoption of high technology would have no impact on aggregate job creation: the sole role of new technology would be the enhancement of per capita living standards. However, even casual observation of economic history suggests substantial employment benefits from new products and processes.

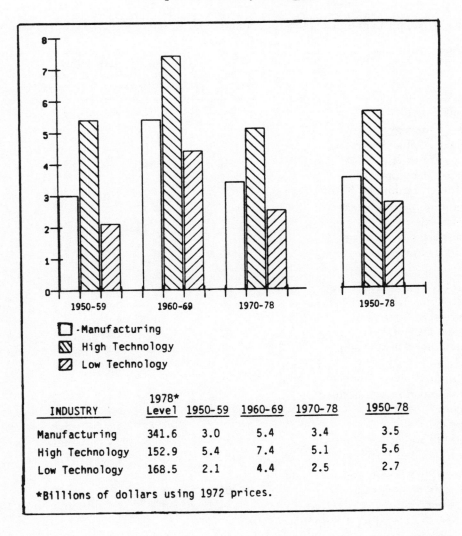

INDUSTRY	1978* Level	1950-59	1960-69	1970-78	1950-78
Manufacturing	341.6	3.0	5.4	3.4	3.5
High Technology	152.9	5.4	7.4	5.1	5.6
Low Technology	168.5	2.1	4.4	2.5	2.7

*Billions of dollars using 1972 prices.

FIGURE 3. Compound Annual Rate of Growth Of Real Output (1972 Prices).

Advanced industries generate innovative products for which there are high-growth markets at home *and* abroad. This product demand leads these firms to attract workers from other sectors of the economy, employing them in more productive occupations. If the economy is near full employment, high-technology industries primarily perform the function of reallocating labor to more effective uses, rather than expanding national employment; if slack does exist in the job market, the growth industries can be expected to increase domestic employment.

Second, high-technology industries can be argued to have a significant, additional impact on employment due to their contribution to price stability. It is unquestionably easier for macro policymakers to counter recessionary shocks if they are not simultaneously challenged to curb inflation. As noted earlier, the price record of industries with strong research and development effort is clearly superior to those with weak research efforts. Thus, indirect cyclical benefits enhance the more obvious long-run gains.

Roger E. Brinner

TABLE 3. Supplementary Detail 3: Compound Annual Rate of Growth Of Real Output (1972 Prices)

	Average Growth Rates				
	1978 Level*	1950–59	1960–69	1970–78	1950–78
Manufacturing	341.6	3.0	5.4	3.4	3.5
High Technology					
Professional and Scientific Instruments	25.5	6.3	7.5	3.9	5.6
Electrical Equipment (incl. Communications Equip.)	37.7	3.0	5.9	3.4	3.8
Communications Services	32.6	7.1	9.3	4.6	6.5
Chemicals	9.7	7.0	7.3	4.1	5.5
Nonelectrical Machinery (incl. Computers)	47.4	6.9	7.7	8.0	7.5
Low Technology					
Rubber and Plastic Products	13.5	3.8	3.1	1.2	2.6
Petroleum Refining	11.4	4.4	8.8	4.9	5.2
Petroleum Extraction	6.2	2.9	4.0	4.9	3.4
Stone, Clay and Glass	32.3	2.7	3.2	2.6	2.8
Paper and Allied Products	10.1	1.4	6.8	2.2	3.3
Primary Metals	12.3	1.7	3.6	4.6	3.0
Fabricated Metal Products	10.6	1.1	6.4	2.3	3.0
Food and Kindred Products	5.0	1·5	4.8	3.8	2.5
Textiles	12.5	2.7	5.2	3.9	3.3
Apparel	11.2	2.9	3.3	3.1	2.6
Lumber and Wood Products	20.0	−0.2	3.2	−0.2	0.5
Furniture and Fixtures	23.5	3.1	5.8	2.4	3.2
Memo: Other Sectors and Categories					
Durable Manufactures	203.8	2.9	5.8	3.5	3.5
Motor Vehicles	34.2	−0.5	7.1	10.1	4.2
Aerospace & Misc. Transportation Equip.	13.2	10.8	5.6	−1.3	4.2
Nondurable Manufactures	137.8	3.1	4.8	3.3	3.5
Mining	20.8	2.1	3.0	1.1	2.1
Service	169.1	3.4	4.4	3.9	3.8
Finance, Insurance, Real Estate	216.1	4.8	4.3	4.4	4.4

*Billions of dollars of real output, 1972 prices.

Quantifying the R&D Impact on Overall Activity

It is important to recognize that the favorable price behavior of high-technology industries is *not* an inevitable result of rapid increases in *labor* productivity: costs for fixed capital and R&D expenses must also be met. However, the rate of return has clearly been sufficiently large to keep total cost increases at a minimum and thus hold price increases to very low annual rates in industries sustaining their investment and development activities.

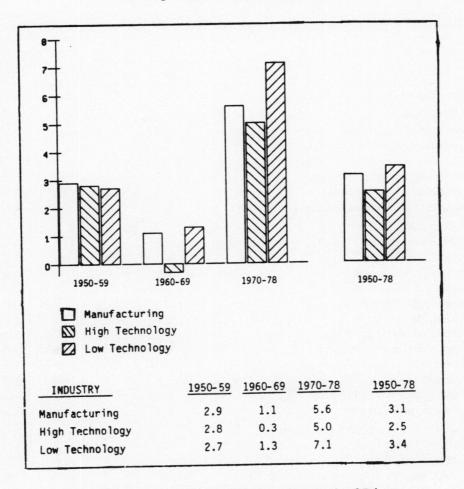

FIGURE 4. Compound Annual Rate of Growth of Prices.

Numerous economists have sought to quantify the rate of return to research and development expenditures. A small data base and the absence of an observable "capital stock" of accumulated knowledge have precluded precise estimation, but a consensus appears to exist on the following points:[3]

• The private rate of profit derived from R&D expenditures is substantially above the return on traditional investments. Conceptual and data limitations make any precise estimate hazardous, but a "ball park" figure near 15 to 20% emerges from investments. Each of these returns is the *real* return beyond coverage of ongoing inflation.

• The private return to the firm initially sponsoring the research is only a fraction — perhaps one-third to two-thirds — of the total return received by the economy. The extra social return is the signal that tax initiatives are needed to bring R&D activity up to an optimal level.

Through further analysis at the macroeconomic level, the social plus private rate of return has been estimated to be as high as 35%.[4] The margin between the total

TABLE 4. Supplementary Detail 4: Compound Annual Rate of Growth of Prices

	Average Growth Rates			
	1950–59	1960–69	1970–78	1950–78
Manufacturing	2.9	1.1	5.6	3.1
High Technology				
Professional and Scientific Instruments	1.3	−1.2	5.3	1.6
Electrical Equipment				
(incl. Communications Equip.)	4.0	2.3	6.7	4.1
Communications Services	1.7	−1.5	5.2	1.6
Chemicals	4.0	1.2	4.9	3.2
Nonelectrical Machinery (incl. Computers)	1.9	0.6	3.1	1.8
Low Technology				
Rubber and Plastic Products	1.8	0.0	15.2	4.7
Petroleum Refining	3.7	0.5	4.8	2.9
Petroleum Extraction	1.0	1.3	5.0	2.3
Stone, Clay and Glass	2.0	1.4	4.0	2.4
Paper and Allied Products	−1.1	−0.4	4.4	0.8
Primary Metals	1.7	2.7	2.2	2.2
Fabricated Metal Products	1.4	1.0	10.3	3.3
Food and Kindred Products	3.0	2.4	4.6	3.4
Textiles	3.7	1.0	5.7	3.5
Apparel	3.8	1.4	6.8	3.7
Lumber and Wood Products	5.6	1.8	9.8	5.4
Furniture and Fixtures	2.4	2.1	7.5	3.8
Memo: Other Sectors and Categories				
Durable Manufactures	3.6	1.2	6.3	3.5
Motor Vehicles	3.9	0.0	2.0	2.0
Aerospace & Misc. Transportation Equip.	4.0	1.8	7.0	4.0
Nondurable Manufactures	2.0	0.9	4.7	2.5
Mining	1.1	−0.1	14.2	4.4
Service	4.1	4.2	7.2	5.0
Finance, Insurance, Real Estate	3.7	2.7	5.3	3.8

return and the private return reflects the spillover benefits not appropriable by the sponsoring firm. Patents and licensing agreements are imperfect, and some research needs further development which the initial firm does not choose to pursue, yet which is followed up by other firms.

The relatively high return implies that the sharply declining share of GNP devoted to R&D from the mid-1960s until recently has had, and will continue to have, a serious negative impact on aggregate productivity growth and inflation. During the past two decades, R&D has contributed 0.3% per year to full-employment, capacity growth. Unfortunately, a 0.2% deterioration has been apparent in each successive five-year interval, such that the contribution has fallen from 0.63% in the 1955–1960 interval to 0.05% in the 1970–1975 interval. Table 6 presents the historical record on R&D spending and its contribution to growth.

TABLE 5. Research Effort by Industry

Class	Industry Activity		Index of Research Effort (IRE)
High	Professional and Scientific Instruments	(SIC 38)	.106
	Electrical Equipment	(SIC 36, 48)	.097
	Chemicals	(SIC 28)	.093
	Nonelectrical Machinery (incl. Computers)	(SIC 35)	.060
Low	Rubber and Plastic Products	(SIC 30)	.032
	Petroleum Refining and Extraction	(SIC 39, 13)	.025
	Stone, Clay and Glass	(SIC 32)	.018
	Paper and Allied Products	(SIC 26)	.016
	Primary Metals	(SIC 33)	.013
	Fabricated Metal Products	(SIC 34)	.012
	Food and Kindred Products	(SIC 20)	.008
	Textiles and Apparel	(SIC 22, 23)	.003
	Lumber, Wood Products and Furniture	(SIC 24, 25)	.003

TABLE 6. R&D Contribution to Growth: 1955–1975*

	% 1955–60	% 1960–65	% 1965–70	% 1970–75
Annual Growth Rates				
Real R&D Spending	9.3	5.5	1.1	−1.4
Real R&D Capital	10.2	7.1	4.1	0.8
Contribution of R&D to Real Output Growth Rates**	0.63	0.44	0.25	0.05

*The historical data are drawn from John Kendrick's compilation of R&D data in *The Formation and Stocks of Total Capital,* National Bureau of Economic Research, New York, 1976. The data on R&D investment and capital used are drawn from Tables B-5, B-23 and C-3. Kendrick's applied R&D net capital stock for 1955–1969 was extended through 1973 based on Table C-3 investment data for an estimated, econometric relation between the earlier investment and capital data. Kendrick's basic research investment series was used to construct a corresponding capital stock by arbitrarily assuming a 10% proportional depreciation rate. Kendrick assumes no depreciation or obsolescence in his series. The total stock equals the sum of Kendrick's applied R&D stock plus the adjusted basic research stock.

**The real output contribution equals the growth of the R&D "stock" multiplied by the estimated output elasticity, .062.

To highlight the future implications of research activities, three alternative forecasts were made of R&D spending for the 1982 through 1995 period.[5] The baseline is approximately equal to NSF projections of 3% real growth in R&D spending each year through 1990.[6] The pessimistic scenario assumes real R&D spending as constant. In the optimistic case, real R&D spending expands sharply to regain its 1964 peak share of real output. Growth is then sustained at 3% from 1988–1995 to match real GNP growth and thus to maintain this share. Table 7 presents the R&D contibution to growth under each of these alternatives.

The baseline future projection implies an average contribution of 0.13% per

TABLE 7. The R&D Contribution to Growth: Alternative Forecasts to 1990

Annual Growth Rates	%1980–1985	%1985–1990	%1990–1995
R&D Spending (The Current Flow)			
Baseline	3.4	3.0	3.0
Optimistic	9.0	5.9	3.0
Pessimistic	1.0	0.0	0.0
R&D Capital (The Accumulated Stock of Past Spending)			
Baseline	1.0	2.4	2.9
Optimistic	2.9	6.7	4.7
Pessimistic	0.2	0.2	0.05
Contribution of R&D to Potential Output Growth Rate:*			
Baseline	0.06	0.15	0.18
Optimistic	0.18	0.42	0.30
Pessimistic	0.01	0.01	0.003

Definitions of Alternative Forecasts: *Baseline:* 3% real growth in R&D each year from 1981 through 1990; *Optimistic:* Real R&D spending grows at 10% from 1981–1987, and then at 3.0% through 1995; *Pessimistic:* Real R&D spending is constant from 1981 through 1995.

*The real potential output contribution equals the growth of the R&D stock multiplied by the estimated output elasticity, .062.

year, close to the record of the past decade but well below the 1955–1965 experience. An even more pessimistic view is generated under the assumption that real R&D spending will continue to stagnate as it has for the past eight years. In this case, current spending will do little more than compensate for the obsolescence of past programs. *Net* investment will be virtually nil, and so will be the contribution to real growth.

In contrast, if a resurgence occurs to push R&D investment back to its peak, mid-1960s' share of GNP by 1983, and then to sustain this share, the potential growth of the economy will be 0.3% per year higher.

These differences are far from trivial. By 1995, a 4.2% output differential exists between the optimistic and pessimistic patterns, which translates into a $663 per capita difference (at 1980 prices). To put this in perspective, the average differential over the next decade would be more than sufficient to pay the interest on the Federal debt. Table 8 shows the cumulative impact of the alternative R&D spending patterns on potential output.

The R&D cure for stagflation will not produce overnight miracles. The macroeconometric model simulations give some indication of the length of time it takes for the alternative R&D spending pattern to impact productivity and, subsequently, prices. There is a two-to-three-year lag before there is any noticeable impact on productivity, and prices do not begin to respond until the fourth year. However, the inflation impacts are greater than the productivity effects because the 1970s' price spiral is encouraged to unwind: better price behavior yields better wage behavior, in turn generating further inflation moderation gains. *R&D investments do reduce, in fact, the total cost of producing output:* the savings in labor and fixed capital costs exceed the research expense because of the high rate

TABLE 8. The Cumulative Potential GNP Impact of Alternative Research and Development Patterns

	1985	1990	1995
I. Percentage Increase Relative to Baseline			
Optimistic	0.6	1.9	2.4
Pessimistic	−0.2	−0.9	−1.8
Differences	0.8	2.8	4.2
II. Absolute Increase Relative to Baseline (Billions of Dollars at 1980 Prices)			
Optimistic	18.0	65.1	91.5
Pessimistic	−6.0	−30.8	−68.6
Differences	24.0	95.9	160.1
III. Per Capita Increase Relative to Baseline (Dollars at 1980 Prices)			
Optimistic	77	267	362
Pessimistic	−26	−126	−271
Differences	103	393	633

of return. The performance margin which is very clear in the industry results would be replicated in the national performance.

The Role of Fixed Capital

Greater investment in fixed capital cannot be expected to have equal anti-inflation leverage on a dollar-for-dollar basis simply because it has been less neglected. The social rate of return is close to 12%[7] far below the 20–35% range estimated for R&D, hence the total cost savings are necessarily lower. However, a strong case can still be made for fixed capital incentives on several grounds. First, a 12% real return is probably more than the appropriate public discount rate: most people would opt for $1.12 next year at the expense of $1 this year (particularly when the $1.12 is indexed to the intervening inflation). Second, it has been well documented by this author and many other economists that capital taxation is, perversely, accidentally severe when prices are increasing rapidly. Finally, the greater the level of fixed-capital investment, the more rapidly new technology from R&D can be embodied in production processes.

The source of weak growth in labor productivity is exceedingly weak fixed and R&D capital spending over the past decade. Only a partial reversal is to be expected without enhanced incentives in the 1980s (Table 9). While fixed capital expansion may have comparatively limited leverage on inflation in contrast to R&D, its magnitude dictates it to be the fundamental determinant of labor productivity and hence per capita living standards.

Specific Policy Prescriptions

The biggest inflation-control bang-for-the-buck can be obtained from strong tax

TABLE 9. Sources of Labor Productivity Growth
(Real GNP Per Worker Adjusted for Transitory Cyclical Movements)

	History					Baseline Forecast	
Contributing Factors	1955–60	1960–65	1965–70	1970–75	1975–80	1980–85	1985–90
Business Fixed Capital Expansion	.95	.88	.84	.05	.58	.57	.47
Additional Capital per Worker	.50	.51	.57	.34	.17	.44	.47
Modernization	.45	.37	.27	−.29	.41	.13	—
R&D Activities	.63	.44	.25	.05	.09	.22	.22
Energy Inputs per Worker	.05	.10	.11	.05	.05	.04	.04
Residual	.76	.74	.59	.60	.53	.70	.70
Total	2.39	2.16	1.79	0.76	1.25	1.53	1.43

Derived from *Technology, Labor and Economic Potential*, p. 88 (see Note 3).

incentives for research and development. If the total return is, in fact, twice the private return to the initial investor, *a 25% tax credit for R&D wages, supplies and fixed capital spending can be justified as an efficient social investment.* Assuming the investing firm immediately writes off the expenses of the project, this would approximately double the anticipated *private* return, thereby equating it to the full *national* return. An example is useful (Table 10).

Reworking the illustration to include alternative tax rates, or to allow only depreciation rather than expensing of the fixed capital component of an R&D project, would naturally modify the estimated private returns, but the same qualitative conclusion would remain. A tax credit of a substantial magnitude is called for to lead the private entrepreneur to make the optimal decision from a national perspective.

This argument can be amplified by recognizing that society can effectively pool the risks of diverse R&D activities to reduce average risk exposure. The individual firm or investor can only do this to a limited extent; therefore, he will require a notably higher anticipated return on R&D projects than on typical fixed capital projects. (This differential is borne out by the rate of return data cited earlier.) Because the risk is reduced for the nation as a whole, a subsidy is indicated again to provide the proper private incentive.

Beyond this specific suggestion, a more *general prescription is to change substantially the national monetary-fiscal policy mix.* Simulations with the DRI model of the US economy indicate that *fiscal restraint offset by monetary ease* would produce a final demand mix significantly slanted toward investment. Table 11 compares a base forecast with an alternative in which government spending has been cut by $10 billion (at 1972 prices) and Federal Reserve policy has been eased in an offsetting manner. The forecast horizon in each case is 1980–1990.

The results are entirely in line with expectations: fixed capital formation is the beneficiary of lower government spending and more generous Federal Reserve interest rate policies. In this exercise, the Fed has pursued a middle course, in that the unemployment rate is slightly high, but real GNP is also higher. If the Fed had been presumed to target precisely on the base-case real output path, employment would be even weaker by definition because of the greater labor productivity in this alternative policy scenario. Conversely, a presumed Fed targeting on the base-case unemployment rate would have raised demand pressures to cut the inflation benefit.

The Critical Nature of the Policy Mix

The Reagan team has certainly proposed spending cuts, but these are paired with even greater tax cuts. The Fed should not be predicted to be willing to accommodate this stimulus, and precisely the wrong policy mixture thus could prevail: strong fiscal/tight credit.

The scenario builders on the budget team dispute this claim, asserting that inflation will plummet as a result of supply expansion produced by the tax cuts. This is an heroic claim which they admit contradicts history. They are not con-

Roger E. Brinner

TABLE 10. The Impact of a 25% R&D Tax Credit on the Private Rate of Return*

Cash Flow	Cash Flow Pattern				% Private Rate of Return
	Year 1	Year 2	Year 3	Year 4	
Gross Flows	−100	15	15	15	15
− Associated Taxes	−50	7.5	7.5	7.5	
= Net Without Credit	−50	7.5	7.5	7.5	15
+ 25% R&D Tax Credit	25	0	0	0	
= Net With Credit	−25	7.5	7.5	7.5	30

*Assume for simplicity: Gross project cost: $100 in year 1, nothing thereafter; Gross project return: $15 per year, year 2 and beyond; Incremental profit tax rate: 50%.

TABLE 11. Changing the Monetary-Fiscal Policy Mix: The Macroeconomic Impacts of Substituting Monetary Policy Ease for Fiscal Stimulus

	Annual Averages 1980–1990		
	$Billions (1972 Prices)	Percentage Change	Percentage Points
GNP	+14.9	+0.8	
Business Fixed Investment	+11.7	+6.2	
Fixed Capital Stock	+41.7	+2.9	
Personal Consumption	+6.6	+0.6	
Federal Purchases	−10.0	−8.4	
Unemployment Rate			+0.2
Inflation Rate			−0.4
Labor Productivity Growth			+0.2
Corporate Bond Rate			−1.1
Treasury Bill Rate			−1.5

cerned about the historical contradiction since they argue that the new regime will produce a structural shift to purely forward-looking expectations, pricing patterns, and wage claims and spending. If they are wrong, the Federal deficit will be massive.

To quantify the budget significance of this dispute over the underlying economic environment, Table 12 indicates the difference between the current Data Resources (DRI) forecast, assuming compromises between Congress and President Reagan, and a "Reaganesque" scenario. Note that these numbers are the *budget differences produced by the different projected economies, not the economy differences produced by alternative fiscal strategies.*

The arbitrary, heroic, Reagan-team assumption of stronger real growth reduces the budget deficit by raising taxes and cutting unemployment and welfare pro-

TABLE 12. Two Different Economies Produce Dramatic Budget Differences

	Average Values for 1982–1983		
	DRI Economy	Approximate Reagan Scenario	1983 Budget Effect ($billion)
Real GNP Growth (%)	3.1	5	30
Inflation (%)	10.4	8	4
Unemployment Rate (%)	7.0	6	9
Treasury Bill Rate (%)	13.4	11	18
Difference in Deficit			61

grams. Lower inflation has a limited deficit impact, except on debt financing costs, since it simultaneously reduces tax revenues and the cost of government programs.

Both the DRI forecast and the scenario involve tighter credit than would be desirable for accelerated capital spending: the Treasury bill rates are both 3% after adjustment for inflation. This must be the case since both projections involve nominal income growth of 13–14% (the sum of real GNP growth and the inflation rate). The Federal Reserve target of approximately 6% nominal money growth cannot be achieved in such an environment without high and probably rising interest rates, because the normal difference between income growth and money demand growth is close to 4%. Thus, the Fed is willing to support 10% nominal income growth, not 13%. The clash between the demand and supply of funds will keep real interest costs high unless the economy is cooled down by tight fiscal policy further than either of these projections indicates.

Tax dollars are too scarce to sacrifice today on major personal tax cuts. Table 13 gives a clear measure of the greater "bang-for-the-buck" obtained by business, rather than personal, tax cuts. The logic of this advantage is straightforward: business tax cuts have a stronger capacity-creation impact and, due to the high rate of return to private investment, reduce total costs.

Therefore, the mix of policy is critical if the medium-term needs for strong capital spending today in the face of recession are not to be sacrificed in the effort to cut inflation through the use of conservative monetary policy. There is room for a range of expanded traditional investment incentives — fixed investment, tax credits, accelerated depreciation, corporate rate cuts — plus a strong R&D tax initiative.

These proposals to stimulate investment are the most effective route to expanding productivity and living standards. They would achieve the long-term goal of controlling inflation without subjecting the economy to recurrent recessions. Stringent monetary policy alone, the pure monetarist alternative, might make a small dent in the current inflation, but it would extract a heavy toll in foregone investment as businesses cut back in response to vanishing final demand and high

TABLE 13. Relative Efficiency of Tax Cuts[a]

	Effect on Potential GNP[b]	Effect on Core Inflation[c]
Personal Tax Cut	0.16	−0.003
Cut in Corporate Tax Rate	0.38	−0.020
Increase in Investment Tax Credit	1.60	−0.061
Depreciation Reform	1.16	−0.71

[a]Assumes government purchase offset.

[b]Defined as increase in level of potential GNP or decrease in core inflation rate both per dollar loss of total revenue, for the year 1985.

[c]Change in core inflation rate per billion of tax cut for the year 1985.

financing costs. An equally misguided approach would be to attempt a *sudden* balancing of the Federal budget. Final demand would be so depressed that capital spending again would decline sharply, rather than rising to absorb the presumed increment to national saving. The best mixture combines selected investment tax incentives, tight Federal spending constraints and more liberal monetary policy.

Notes

1. In Figures 1 through 4 and the accompanying supplementary tables, the growth rates for the subintervals may not appear to be consistent with the full interval in selected cases. In fact, they are fully consistent. The subinterval for 1950–59 presents the rate of increase from the 1950 level to the 1959 level and the subinterval for 1960–69 from the 1960 level to the 1969 level. Thus, the 1959–60 and 1969–70 individual years are not captured in the subintervals, but are included in the 1950–1978 interval.

2. This average is high, relative to the bulk of industries surveyed in Table 1, because the transportation vehicle and equipment industry (SIC Code 37) is included in all manufacturing, but not shown in Table 1 since it includes both motor vehicles and airplane/aerospace industries.

3. Useful references are: (1) Terleckyj, Nestor E., *Effects of R&D on the Productivity Growth of Industries: An Exploratory Study* (Washington, DC: National Planning Association, 1974); (2) Griliches, Zvi, "Research Expenditures and Growth Accounting," Howard Institute of Economic Research Discussion Paper no. 196, 1971; (3) Freeman, Richard B., "Effects of R&D : Social and Private Rates of Return, Investment Opportunities" in J. Herbert Hollomon, Principal Investigator, *Supporting Studies for Alternative Federal Policies Affecting the Use of Technology,* Planning and Policy Analysis Office, Massachusetts Institute of Technology (unpublished); (4) Brinner, Roger E., *Technology, Labor and Economic Potential,* Data Resources, Inc., Special Studies Series, no. 29, 1978. This current essay draws heavily from *Technology, Labor and Economic Potential* and a derivative study, "The Anti-Inflation Leverage of Investment" in C. C. Walton, ed., "Inflation and National Survival," *Proceedings of the Academy of Political Science,* Vol. 33, no. 3 (New York: Academy of Political Science, 1979).

4. Brinner, *Technology, op. cit.,* pp. 97–98.

5. The results are technically drawn from an earlier study of the 1977–1990 time span and would be virtually identical if the 1982–1995 time span were to be evaluated anew.

6. *1985 R&D Funding Projections,* National Science Foundation, NSF 75-314, p. vi.

7. The fixed capital return is drawn from M. Feldstein and L. Summers, "The Rate of Profit: Falling or Cyclical?" (unpublished Discussion Paper).

Technology In Society, Vol. 3, pp. 63–85 (1981)
Printed in the USA. All rights reserved.

0160-791X/81/010063-23$02.00/0
Copyright © 1981 Pergamon Press Ltd

Tax Policy Toward Research and Development

George N. Carlson

Goverment policy makers are understandably concerned over the decline of the US economic growth rate. Suppressed growth aggravates inflationary pressures, retards increases in the standard of living, and makes the United States less competitive in world markets. While real product per unit of labor increased at an average annual rate of 3.5% between 1948 and 1966, it increased by only 2.1% annually between 1966 and 1973, and fell further to 1.1% per year between 1973 and 1978, an overall drop of nearly 2.5 percentage points.[1] Concurrently, research and development (R&D) spending peaked at nearly 3% of gross national product (GNP) in 1964 and then declined gradually until the late 1970s. Quite naturally, questions have arisen regarding the role which reduced levels of R&D spending has played in this growth slowdown and a variety of tax incentives have been suggested to encourage technological innovation in general and R&D in particular.[2] This paper assesses the need for such incentives.[3]

The second section reviews recent trends in R&D spending, both in the United States and in other industrialized nations. Although US R&D spending relative to GNP has fallen since the mid-1960s, it still compares favorably with other countries. More significantly, industry-supported R&D has actually risen since the mid-1960s.

The third section discusses the recent growth slowdown, both in the United States and other countries. It also reviews the available evidence on the impact of R&D on the US economic growth rate. Although the US growth rate fell sharply after 1966, reduced R&D spending is responsible for only about 15% of the overall decline. Weak capital formation is a more important source of the productivity decline. The United States is not alone in the productivity slowdown; it is a problem widely shared by other countries. In fact, some countries have experienced larger declines in their growth rates than has the United States.

The fourth section discusses the impact of R&D on international com-

George N. Carlson is an International Economist in the Office of International Tax Affairs, US Treasury Department. He received a B.A. from the University of Washington and a Ph.D. from the University of Illinois. The opinions expressed are those of the author and not necessarily the views of the Treasury Department.

petitiveness. R&D spending appears to be positively related to export performance in the United States. Since 1960, the United States, for example, has had a trade surplus in R&D-intensive manufactured products and a trade deficit in non-R&D-intensive products. The surplus, however, increased sharply between 1964 and 1975, the period in which R&D spending relative to GNP declined. Although some of the R&D-intensive industries also export their technology, this does not appear to have adversely affected the competitive position of those industries.

Many countries provide preferential taxation of R&D expenditures. The fifth section describes the R&D incentive provisions in the United States and four foreign countries, Belgium, Canada, France and West Germany. The sixth section concludes the paper with a discussion of the issues that should be addressed in considering any additional R&D tax incentives for the United States.

Trends in R&D Spending

Total US R&D spending—from both public and private sources—will reach $60 billion in 1980.[4] As shown in Table 1, private R&D spending has increased relative to Federal government expenditures in the last 15 years, with each now providing about one-half of total R&D funds. Although universities, colleges, and other nonprofit organizations perform significant amounts of R&D activity, they are only minimal sources of R&D funding.[5]

On a historical basis, total US R&D expenditures have increased steadily over the past 25 years, but much of this reflects the impact of inflation. Table 1 also shows that real or price-adjusted R&D expenditures remained roughly constant from the mid-1960s to the mid-1970s, but have recently resumed their climb and will reach a new high of about $35 billion in 1980 (in 1972 dollars).

The United States spends more on R&D than any other country in the world, and more than France, West Germany, Japan and the United Kingdom combined.[6] This is not surprising because the United States also has the world's largest output of goods and services.[7] To adjust for the absolute size of a country's economy, Tables 2 and 3 relate R&D expenditures to GNP for the United States and some of its major trading partners. This method of comparison is popular, although E. F. Denison questions its rationale.

Just because the size of the economy is, say, twice as big, does it take twice as much R&D to obtain the same annual productivity gain? Doubtless it would take twice as much R&D if an economy doubled its size by producing twice as many products, each with a unique technology, and no more of any one product. But why should more R&D be needed if growth occurs by expanding the average output of products rather than their number? An invention that cuts one percent from the production cost of 5 million automobiles should do as much for 10 million.[8]

According to Table 2, R&D spending in the United States reached a peak of nearly 3% of GNP in 1964, declined steadily until the late 1970s when it reached a low of 2.26%, and has recently recovered. Table 2 also shows that the post-1964 decline in R&D spending is attributable solely to reduced Federal spending for defense- and space-related R&D. During this period, industry R&D funding increased relative to GNP and Federal nondefense R&D spending remained constant. The preliminary results of a current study by E. Mansfield, however, indicate that the cost of R&D inputs in research-intensive industries increased faster than the GNP deflator over the last 10 years. Thus, these percentage figures may overestimate real privately-funded R&D performance.[9]

Although US spending for R&D relative to GNP has declined since the mid-1960s, it still compares favorably with other industrialized countries. As shown in Table 3, total R&D expenditures relative to GNP are about equal in the United States and West Germany. Expenditures are lower in the United Kingdom, Japan, France and Canada. Between the mid-1960s and mid-1970s, R&D expenditures increased in West Germany and Japan and decreased in France and the United Kingdom, as well as the United States. But since the mid-1970s, R&D expenditures in each of these countries has been a relatively constant fraction of GNP. The increases in West Germany and Japan have leveled off and the declines in France, the United Kingdom, and the United States have abated.

The relative position of the United States with respect to civilian R&D expenditures, defined as total R&D expenditures less government funds for defense and space R&D, is less favorable. According to Table 3, civilian R&D expenditures in the United States relative to GNP are equal to those in the United Kingdom, higher than in France, but lower than those in West Germany and Japan.

One explanation is that West Germany and Japan have modest defense budgets; most of the R&D expenditures in these countries are for civilian purposes. A recent National Science Foundation publication observes that "the concentration of R&D in civilian areas may have assisted the Japanese and the West Germans to increase productivity rates and be more competitive in world trade."[10] Still, defense- and space-related R&D may have spinoff effects that improve productivity and the quality of output in the civilian economy. Moreover, recent international developments stress the need for the United States to make more — rather than less — defense-related R&D.

Impact of R&D on Economic Growth

Since the mid-1960s, the United States has suffered from a depressed growth rate. The average annual increase in real product per unit of labor, for example, declined from 3.5% in the 1948–1966 period, to 2.1% between 1966 and 1973, and 1.1% between 1973 and 1978.[11] Since R&D spending as a proportion of GNP reached its peak in 1964, attention has understandably focused on the possible role of reduced R&D spending in the growth slowdown. R&D, of course, is only one of many ingredients of economic growth.

Output may be increased by using more resources, such as capital or labor, or by increasing the efficiency or productivity of existing resources. Growth or productivity analysis frequently concentrates on labor productivity or output per unit of labor. But these measures do not necessarily reflect changes in the efficiency of labor. Labor productivity may increase for a variety of reasons: an increase in the amount of capital per worker, an improvement in the quality or education of labor, or a more efficient combination of labor with capital and other resources.

George N. Carlson

TABLE 1. United States Research and Development

		Current Dollars in Millions			
Year	Total	Federal Government	Industry	Universities and Colleges	Other Nonprofit Institutions
1953	5,124	2,753	2,245	72	54
1954	5,644	3,132	2,373	80	59
1955	6,172	3,502	2,520	88	62
1956	8,363	4,852	3,343	96	72
1957	9,775	6,110	3,467	109	89
1958	10,711	6,779	3,707	121	104
1959	12,358	8,046	4,064	134	114
1960	13,523	8,738	4,516	149	120
1961	14,316	9,250	4,757	165	144
1962	15,394	9,911	5,123	185	175
1963	17,059	11,204	5,456	207	192
1964	18,854	12,536	5,888	235	195
1965	20,044	13,012	6,548	267	217
1966	21,846	13,969	7,328	303	246
1967	23,146	14,395	8,142	345	264
1968	24,604	14,926	9,005	391	282
1969	25,631	14,895	10,010	420	306
1970	25,905	14,668	10,439	461	337
1971	26,595	14,892	10,813	529	361
1972	28,413	15,755	11,698	575	385
1973	30,615	16,309	13,278	615	413
1974	32,734	16,754	14,854	677	449
1975	35,200	18,152	15,787	750	511
1976	38,816	19,628	17,804	821	563
1977	43,013	21,751	19,696	893	673
1978	48,286	24,058	22,433	1,029	766
1979	54,296	26,762	25,520	1,150	864
1980*	60,375	29,400	28,710	1,300	965

Office of the Sectretary of the Treasury
Office of Tax Analysis

*Estimated expenditures.

Source: National Science Foundation, *National Patterns of R&D Resources,*
    1953–1977 and *1953*–1978–79, Science Indicators 1978, and *Science Highlights,* May 23, 1980.

Expenditures, by Source of Funds, 1953–1980

| | | | | Other |
| | Federal | | Universities | Nonprofit |
Total	Government	Industry	and Colleges	Institutions
8,702	4,675	3,813	122	92
9,456	5,247	3,976	134	99
10,121	5,743	4,132	144	102
13,296	7,714	5,315	153	114
15,034	9,397	5,332	168	137
16,214	10,262	5,612	183	157
18,303	11,917	6,019	198	169
19,693	12,725	6,576	217	175
20,664	13,351	6,866	238	209
21,820	14,048	7,262	262	248
23,829	15,651	7,621	289	268
25,930	17,241	8,098	323	268
26,970	17,508	8,811	359	292
28,460	18,198	9,547	395	320
29,291	18,217	10,303	437	334
29,798	18,077	10,906	474	341
29,556	17,176	11,543	484	353
28,355	16,055	11,426	505	369
27,697	15,509	11,261	551	376
28,413	15,755	11,698	575	385
28,937	15,415	12,550	581	391
28,214	14,440	12,803	584	387
27,684	14,276	12,416	590	402
29,019	14,674	13,310	614	421
30,374	15,327	13,975	633	439
31,787	16,006	14,638	672	471
33,412	16,641	15,564	718	489
n.a.	n.a.	n.a.	n.a.	n.a.

January 6, 1981

TABLE 2. United States Research and Development Expenditures by Source of Funds as a Percent of GNP, 1953–1980

		Federal				Universities and other
Year	Total	Total	Defense*	Nondefense	Industry	nonprofits
1953	1.40	0.75	0.68	0.07	0.61	0.04
1954	1.54	0.86	0.77	0.09	0.64	0.04
1955	1.55	0.88	0.76	0.12	0.63	0.03
1956	1.99	1.15	0.99	0.16	0.79	0.05
1957	2.20	1.38	1.20	0.18	0.78	0.04
1958	2.39	1.51	1.29	0.22	0.83	0.05
1959	2.54	1.65	1.45	0.20	0.84	0.05
1960	2.67	1.73	1.46	0.27	0.89	0.05
1961	2.74	1.77	1.52	0.25	0.91	0.06
1962	2.73	1.76	1.51	0.25	0.91	0.06
1963	2.87	1.88	1.57	0.31	0.92	0.07
1964	2.97	1.97	1.67	0.30	0.93	0.07
1965	2.91	1.89	1.57	0.32	0.95	0.07
1966	2.90	1.86	1.48	0.38	0.97	0.07
1967	2.91	1.81	1.43	0.38	1.02	0.07
1968	2.83	1.72	1.33	0.39	1.04	0.07
1969	2.74	1.59	1.23	0.36	1.07	0.08
1970	2.64	1.49	1.12	0.37	1.06	0.09
1971	2.50	1.40	1.02	0.38	1.02	0.08
1972	2.43	1.35	0.99	0.36	1.00	0.08
1973	2.34	1.25	0.90	0.35	1.02	0.07
1974	2.32	1.19	0.82	0.37	1.05	0.08
1975	2.30	1.19	0.80	0.39	1.03	0.08
1976	2.28	1.15	0.77	0.38	1.05	0.08
1977	2.26	1.15	0.76	0.39	1.04	0.07
1978	2.27	1.13	0.75	0.38	1.05	0.09
1979	2.29	1.13	0.75	0.38	1.08	0.08
1980	2.34	1.14	n.a.	n.a.	1.11	0.09

Office of the Secretary of the Treasury   January 6, 1981
Office of Tax Analysis

*Includes spending for defense and space purposes.

Source: National Science Foundation, *National Patterns of R&D Resources, 1953–1977* and *1953–1978–79, Science Indicators 1978,* and "Science Highlights," May 23, 1980.

Thus, "increases in output per hour may best be viewed as reflecting the saving of labor per unit of output as the result of the joint effect of all inputs and the way they are combined."[12]

E. F. Denison's landmark studies on the sources of productivity growth illuminate the reasons for the productivity decline and the possible role of R&D.

Denison finds that the growth rate in national income per person employed in the nonresidential business sector declined from 2.7% per year in the 1948 to 1969 period, to 2.1% annually between 1969 and 1973, and to –0.6% per year between 1973 and 1976.[13] Thus, between the 1948–1969 and 1973–1976 periods, productivity growth actually fell by 3.3% per year. Denison has divided this productivity decline into two periods, 1969–1973 and 1973–1976.

In the earlier period, the sources of the productivity decline are about evenly divided between factors affecting input quantity or quality, such as hours worked, education, and capital per worker and factors affecting output per unit of input, such as improved allocation of resources, economies of scale, and a residual described as "advances in knowledge and not elsewhere classified." In contrast, in the 1973–1976 period, all of the productivity decline of 2.7% per year is attributable to factors affecting output per unit of input. The "advance in knowledge and not elsewhere classified" factor accounts for 2.3 percentage points of the 2.7% decline in measure output.[14]

Denison's "advances in knowledge and not elsewhere classified" category has two components.

The contribution of advances in knowledge is, conceptually, a comprehensive measure of the gains in measured output that result from the incorporation into production of new knowledge of any type — managerial and organizational as well as technological — regardless of the source of that knowledge, the way it is transmitted to those who can make use of it, or the way it is incorporated into production.[15]

The "elsewhere classified" component refers to a number of miscellaneous determinants which are not separately specified, but whose effects are "believed small."[16]

Although the contribution of advances in knowledge to the growth in output declined dramatically between the 1969–1973 and 1973–1976 periods, Denison doubts that reduced R&D spending was much of a factor. Based on an earlier estimate, he concludes that only one-sixth of the total contribution of advances in knowledge is related to R&D spending.[17] If correct, this estimate would assign less than 0.40 percentage points of the 2.7% per year decline in output growth to R&D, *i.e.*, about 15% of the total decline. Denison also refers to Z. Griliches' estimate that the maximum contribution of R&D to the growth rate as of 1966 was 0.3 percentage points. Noting the approximately one-fourth drop in total R&D expenditures as a percent of GNP between 1964 and 1976, Denison observes that "if the 0.3 percentage point contribution of R&D to the growth rate of output were reduced proportionately, it would decline by less than 0.1 percentage points."[18] But, he cautions, since industry-supported R&D did not decline at all, "there is no assurance that R&D spending contributed anything to the decline in productivity growth."[19]

In contrast to Denison and Griliches, J. W. Kendrick — using a modified version of Denison's growth accounting framework — estimates a much higher contribution of R&D to productivity growth. But because the decline in the R&D-related source of growth is less drastic than in Denison's analysis, his estimate of the role of R&D in the productivity slowdown is similar to Denison's. According

TABLE 3. Total and Civilian* Research and Development

	Total R&D Percent					
Year	United States	Canada	France	West Germany	Japan	United Kingdom
1961	2.74	n.a.	1.38	n.a.	1.39	2.39
1962	2.73	n.a.	1.46	1.25	1.47	n.a.
1963	2.87	0.9	1.55	1.41	1.44	n.a.
1964	2.97	1.0	1.81	1.57	1.48	2.30
1965	2.91	n.a.	2.01	1.73	1.54	n.a.
1966	2.90	n.a.	2.03	1.81	1.48	2.32
1967	2.91	1.3	2.13	1.97	1.53	2.33
1968	2.83	n.a.	2.08	1.97	1.61	2.29
1969	2.74	1.3	1.94	2.05	1.65	2.23
1970	2.64	1.3	1.91	2.18	1.79	n.a.
1971	2.50	1.3	1.90	2.38	1.84	n.a.
1972	2.43	1.2	1.86	2.33	1.85	2.06
1973	2.34	1.1	1.77	2.32	1.89	n.a.
1974	2.32	1.1	1.81	2.26	1.95	n.a.
1975	2.30	1.5	1.82	2.39	1.94	2.05
1976	2.28	1.0	1.78	2.28	1.94	n.a.
1977	2.26	n.a.	1.79	2.26	n.a.	n.a.
1978	2.27	n.a.	n.a.	2.28	n.a.	n.a.

Office of the Sectretary of the Treasury
Office of Tax Analysis

*Civilian expenditures equal total R&D expenditures less government funds for defense and space R&D

Source: National Science Foundation, *Science Indicators 1978.*

to Kendrick, R&D contributed 0.9 percentage points annually to the growth rate between 1948 and 1966, 0.7 percentage points between 1966 and 1973, and 0.6 percentage points between 1973 and 1978.[20] Thus, R&D was responsible for 0.3 percentage points of the 2.4% annual decline in the growth rate or real product per unit of labor estimated by Kendrick between 1948–1966 and 1973–1978. This is 12.5% of the total decline and similar to Denison's estimate of 15%.

Other investigators have stressed the importance of reduced investment spending in explaining the growth slowdown since the mid-1960s. Citing the decline in the growth rate of the capital stock and the increase in the growth rate in labor hours, M. D. McCarthy concludes that "the slowdown in productivity growth, in the 1970s in particular, can be traced to a very slow growth in the capital/labor ratio in the years 1970–1975."[21] Along with reduced R&D spending, S. P. Zell believes that the decline in the capital/labor ratio is an important cause of the "apparent slowdown" in the rate of technological progress in the United States.[22] Likewise, J. A. Tatom concludes that "the relatively slow pace of capital formation, including research and development capital, has quietly played an important role in productivity's decline."[23]

Expenditures as a Percent of GNP, 1961–1978, Selected Countries

| | Civilian R&D Percent | | | |
United States	France	West Germany	Japan	United Kingdom
1.22	0.97	n.a.	1.37	1.48
1.22	1.03	1.14	1.46	n.a.
1.30	1.10	1.26	1.43	n.a.
1.30	1.34	1.38	1.47	1.46
1.34	1.37	1.53	1.53	n.a.
1.42	1.40	1.62	1.47	1.58
1.48	1.50	1.70	1.51	1.68
1.50	1.54	1.72	1.60	1.70
1.51	1.49	1.81	1.64	1.69
1.52	1.47	1.96	n.a.	n.a.
1.48	1.37	2.16	n.a.	n.a.
1.44	1.39	2.13	n.a.	1.49
1.44	1.30	2.01	n.a.	n.a.
1.50	1.34	2.27	1.91	n.a.
1.50	1.41	2.20	1.91	n.a.
1.51	1.42	2.09	n.a.	1.50
n.a.	n.a.	n.a.	n.a.	n.a.
n.a.	n.a.	n.a.	n.a.	n.a.

January 6, 1981

Like others, J. R. Norsworthy, M. J. Harper, and K. Kunze have divided the productivity slowdown into two periods: 1965–1973 and 1973–1978, with 1948–1965 as the base period. Their method of analysis measures the effect of changes in capital, labor, and a residual described as "other factors." They find that the "other factors" category is important in explainng the earlier slowdown, but that reduced capital formation explains most of the more recent slowdown.

One conclusion is immediate — two slowdowns occurred with two different patterns of contributing causes: the 1965–1973 slowdown is largely unexplained by factors quantified in this analysis, the 1973–1978 slowdown is largely accounted for by the relative weakness in capital formation.[24]

One of the reasons advanced for the weakness of capital formation in the 1973–1978 period is that, compared to the earlier period, the price of capital services increased by nearly four times whereas the price of labor increased by only one-third.[25]

Since the effect of R&D is one of the elements in the "other factors" category, the authors concede it may have been partially responsible for the productivity slowdown in the earlier period. "Although R&D expenditures slowed during this period and may well have contributed to the productivity slowdown, we devised no satisfactory means to take this factor into account."[26]

Even Kendrick, who reports relatively high estimates of the impact of R&D on productivity growth, also stresses the importance of capital formation.

Policies to promote tangible investment . . . would obviously accelerate the growth of real product per unit of labor input. . . . In addition, the acceleration in tangible capital formation would have a positive effect on R&D spending and other tangible investments that are part and parcel of the inventive-innovative process.[27]

The productivity slowdown is not confined to the United States. Although the United States has a relatively high level of productivity, it has a relatively low level of productivity change, but compares favorably with other industrialized countries in the degree to which productivity has decelerated. Tables 4 and 5 highlight the elements of the international productivity comparison.

Table 4 compares the productivity level, or real gross domestic product per employed civilian, for the United States and five other major industrialized nations. As of 1977, the United States had the highest productivity level for the countries under comparison, although each of the five countries had improved its position relative to the United States since 1960. Japan, for example, has a very high productivity growth rate, but its productivity level is less than two-thirds that of the United States.

The deterioration in the relative position of the United States is shown in Table 5 which compares annual growth rates in real gross domestic product per employed civilian for the same countries, plus Italy. For the period 1960–1973, the United States has the smallest growth rate and, for the 1973–1977 period, only Italy has a smaller growth rate. But the United States compares reasonably well with respect to how much productivity has fallen between the two periods. According to the third column of Table 5, only West Germany experienced a significantly smaller productivity slowdown. Thus, although other countries continue to gain on the United States in the productivity race, they are gaining somewhat less quickly.

R&D and Trade

Considerable evidence exists that US R&D spending improves the country's competitive position in world markets. For the United States, D. B. Keesing, for example, compared the percent of an industry's work force involved in R&D activity with that industry's exports as a share of world exports. Keesing finds a linear correlation coefficient of .88 for the 18 manufacturing industries studied; that is, 88% of the variation in export shares is "explained by" variations in R&D activity.[28] Keesing also allows for the influence of other factors on US trade performance, but concludes that

there turns out to be a powerful correlation between the intensity of R&D activity in American industries and their export performance. The association is probably heightened

TABLE 4. Real Gross Domestic Product Per Employed Civilian, for Selected Countries Compared with the United States: 1960–77 *

(Index, United States = 100)

Year	United States	Canada	France	West Germany	Japan	United Kingdom
1960	100	86.6	55.4	52.4	24.7	51.1
1961	100	85.8	57.0	53.1	27.2	49.8
1962	100	85.6	58.0	53.1	27.6	47.9
1963	100	86.2	59.0	53.2	29.6	48.5
1964	100	86.0	60.0	55.2	32.1	49.1
1965	100	85.6	60.8	56.2	32.2	48.2
1966	100	83.5	61.2	58.1	33.4	47.4
1967	100	83.4	63.4	57.3	36.8	49.0
1968	100	84.6	64.2	59.5	40.0	49.7
1969	100	86.2	67.6	63.2	43.9	50.4
1970	100	88.6	71.4	67.0	48.7	52.6
1971	100	90.6	72.9	67.5	50.8	53.9
1972	100	90.7	74.8	68.5	53.9	53.6
1973	100	90.8	76.4	70.2	56.5	54.8
1974	100	93.0	80.0	74.3	58.0	56.0
1975	100	91.9	81.2	74.7	59.5	55.4
1976	100	92.2	83.1	77.7	60.8	55.6
1977†	100	91.6	84.7	79.1	62.2	55.1

Office of the Secretary of the Treasury   January 6, 1981
Office of Tax Analysis

*Output based on international price weights to enable comparable cross-country comparisons.
†Preliminary.

Source: National Science Foundation, *Science Indicators 1978*, p. 157.

TABLE 5. Annual Growth Rates in Real Gross Domestic Product Per Employed Civilian, for Selected Countries, 1960–1973 and 1973–1977

Country	Growth Rates (Percent)		
	1960–73	1973–77	Change (2–1)
United States	2.1	0.3	−1.8
Canada	2.4	0.5	−1.9
France	4.6	2.9	−1.7
West Germany	4.4	3.3	−1.1
Italy	5.8	−0.2	−6.0
Japan	8.8	2.7	−6.1
United Kingdom	2.6	0.4	−2.2

Office of the Secretary of the Treasury   January 6, 1981
Office of Tax Analysis

Source: Edward F. Denison, "Explanations of Declining Productivity Growth," *Survey of Current Business,* August 1979, Part 2, p. 20.

by a tendency for industries that conduct intensive R&D activity to exhibit at the same time economies of scale and high requirements for skills in production. Capital requirements, however, are inversely associated with R&D.[29]

Similarly, W. Gruber, D. Mehta, and R. Vernon's cross-industry study of research effort and export performance finds "a strong export position for industries without large research inputs."[30]

A review of the trade balance performance of R&D-intensive and non-R&D-intensive product groups also indicates the importance of R&D to international competitiveness. Although the US merchandise trade balance has a large deficit ($30 billion in 1979), R&D-intensive manufactured goods have a substantial trade surplus. According to Table 6, the United States has had a trade surplus in R&D-intensive manufactured products since 1960 and a trade deficit in non-R&D-intensive products. R&D-intensive industries are defined as: (1) having at least 2.5% of their work force employed as scientists or engineers engaged in R&D and (2) making R&D expenditures equal to at least 3.5% of net sales.[31] On this basis, only five groups of manufactured products qualify as R&D-intensive: aircraft and parts, chemicals, electrical machinery, nonelectrical machinery, and professional and scientific instruments.[32] All other manufactured products are classified as non-R&D-intensive.

While US R&D spending relative to GNP peaked in the mid-1960s, the US trade surplus in R&D-intensive products increased sharply between 1964 and 1975, nearly tripling between 1972 and 1975. The surplus has fallen slightly since 1975, coinciding with a substantial increase in the trade deficit in non-R&D-intensive goods. The total trade surplus in manufactured products, both R&D-intensive and non-R&D-intensive, fell from a peak of nearly $20 billion in 1975 to about $3 billion in 1977.

In recent years, nearly 90% of the trade surplus in R&D-intensive products has been generated by three product groups: nonelectrical machinery (including computers), chemicals and aircraft.[33] There is some evidence that these industries also are active in the export of technology. US direct investment abroad, for example, will reach nearly $200 billion in 1980.[34] The largest portion of this investment is in manufacturing, with machinery (electrical and nonelectrical) and chemicals being the most important industries.[35] Net receipts (receipts minus payments) of US companies of royalties and fees from foreign affiliates will approach $3 billion in 1980.[36] Again, manufacturing activity generates the largest portion of these receipts, with machinery and chemicals being the most important individual industries.[37] Machinery and transportation equipment, along with chemicals, also are the leading industries in the volume of R&D performed abroad by foreign affiliates of US firms.[38]

Although the machinery and chemical industries are important exporters of technology, S. Okubo doubts that the trade competitiveness of these industries has been adversely affected. Foreign direct investment, she notes, may have encouraged exports. "In general, American exports tend to be enhanced by foreign direct investment, but possibly up to some threshold level after which exports are no longer complementary and the relation between exports and foreign investment appears to be haphazard."[39]

TABLE 6. US Trade Balance[a] in R&D-Intensive and Non-R&D-Intensive Manufactured Product Groups: 1960–77
(Dollars in Millions)

Year	R&D-Intensive			Non-R&D-Intensive			Overall Balance
	Balance	Exports	Imports	Balance	Exports	Imports	
1960	$ 5,891	$ 7,597	$ 1,706	$ −179	$ 4,962	$ 5,141	$ 5,712
1961	6,237	8,018	1,781	−12	4,730	4,742	6,225
1962	6,720	8,715	1,995	−691	4,940	5,631	6,029
1963	6,958	8,975	2,017	−765	5,284	6,049	6,193
1964	7,970	10,267	2,297	−678	6,121	6,799	7,292
1965	8,148	11,078	2,930	−2,027	6,281	8,308	6,121
1966	7,996	12,174	4,178	−3,325	6,913	10,238	4,671
1967	8,817	13,407	4,590	−3,729	7,437	11,166	5,088
1968	9,775	15,312	5,537	−6,581	8,506	15,087	3,194
1969	10,471	16,955	6,484	− 6,698	9,830	16,528	3,773
1970	11,722	19,274	7,552	−8,285	10,069	18,354	3,437
1971	11,727	20,228	8,501	−11,698	10,215	21,913	29
1972	11,012	22,003	10,991	−15,039	11,737	26,776	−4,027
1973	15,101	29,088	13,987	−15,370	15,643	31,013	−269
1974	23,873	41,111	17,238	−15,573	22,412	37,985	8,300
1975	29,344	46,439	17,095	−9,474	24,511	33,985	19,870
1976	28,964	50,830	21,866	−16,499	26,411	42,910	12,465
1977	27,627	53,169	25,542	−24,378	27,284	51,662	3,249

Office of the Secretary of the Treasury
Office of Tax Analysis

January 6, 1981

[a]Exports less imports.
[b]R&D-intensive balance less non-R&D-intensive balance.

Source: National Science Foundation, *Science Indicators 1978*, p. 161.

Taxation of R&D

Business firms undertake R&D activity in order to enhance their future profits. Successful R&D projects produce "properties" that frequently generate income over a number of years. In this respect, R&D is like other types of business investment: the expense is associated with a future stream of income. The intangible properties produced by R&D may be cost-saving processes, innovative marketing techniques, product variations, previously unexploited scientific principles or patents. Aside from the form of the income-earning property that is acquired, R&D expenditures are conceptually like other kinds of business investment. Net income from the use of either an idea or a machine is measured by the annual difference between the additional gross income stream that results and the depreciation of the property due to deterioration and obsolescence.

An income tax system that favored neither R&D nor tangible investment would require the capitalization of all expenses. In the case of R&D, this would require that wages, materials, and depreciation of equipment and structures allocable to R&D would be charged to capital account and depreciated over the earning lifetime of the R&D "property." Whether or not this treatment would be administratively practical, it is the proper standard for neutrality among R&D and tangible investments under an income tax.

Whether dictated by administrative or incentive considerations, many countries provide for preferential taxation of R&D. These provisions are outlined below for the United States and four other countries.

United States

1. Section 174(a) of the Internal Revenue Code permits business taxpayers to deduct research or experimental expenses in the year they are incurred. Alternatively, a taxpayer may elect under section 174(b) to capitalize deductible R&D expenses and amortize them over at least 60 months. This election may be appealing to new or small firms with insufficient income to absorb a current year R&D deduction.

Section 174 does not apply to expenditures for the acquisition or improvement of land or depreciable property used for research or experimental activity. Depreciation allowances themselves, however, are covered by the provision "to the extent that the property to which the allowances relate is used in connection with research or experimentation."[40] R&D expenditures for labor and materials are therefore deducted under section 174 and expenditures for buildings and equipment are depreciated as if employed in current production. A patent acquired from another, rather than resulting from one's own R&D activity, and having a determinable useful life, is depreciated, not expensed. [41]

Congress enacted section 174 into the Code in 1954 "to eliminate uncertainty and to encourage taxpayers to carry on research and experimentation."[42] Prior to 1954, no special statutory provision existed for the treatment of R&D. In some cases, the capital nature of research expense and the difficulty of specifying a useful life combined to deny the deductibility of R&D expenses.

Where they could not be clearly classified as current operating expenses, the courts required their capitalization for tax purposes. Because of the indefinite nature of their useful life, amortization was generally not allowed. Difficulties of proving abandonment of a research project or termination of its utility usually precluded a loss deduction. The end result was disallowance of any deduction for these purposes.[43]

Pre-1954 administrative practice, however, was more liberal than judicial interpretations and sought to allow current expensing of R&D expenditures. A 1924 Treasury Department regulation allowed current expensing, but this option was withdrawn in 1926 in response to a Board of Tax Appeals decision that it contravened the statute.[44] Nonetheless, the Bureau of Internal Revenue continued to permit the current deduction of R&D expenses "where this practice had been consistently followed by a taxpayer."[45] Commissioner Dunlap explained the administrative rationale for this policy in a 1952 appearance before the Joint Committee on Internal Revenue Taxation.

On account of the difficulty of determining the specific costs applicable to various projects and processes, as well as determining in advance, or any time prior to patenting or successful operations, the actual cost of a successful research and development project, the Bureau has allowed all such costs to be deducted annually, except costs of obtaining patents. Many projects take as much as 10 years or more to develop; many are unsuccessful; some unpatentable. . . . The problem of allocating such expenditures to individual projects . . . is most difficult and would require elaborate accounting techniques.[46]

Section 174 thus codified existing practices for taxpayers with a history of deducting R&D expenditures. For new or small businesses, with no established pattern or R&D activity, it meant that such expenditures were clearly deductible. The Treasury Department, in endorsing the 1954 legislation, described its purpose: "Encourage research and experimental activity. Help small, pioneering businesses."[47]

Section 174 contains an additional incentive feature in that expenses need only be paid or incurred "in connection with" a trade or business.[48] In Snow vs. Commissioner, the Supreme Court opined that the "in connection with" language of section 174 is intended "to dilute some of the conception of 'ordinary and necessary' business expenses under ç162(a)."[49] Observing that section 174 was legislated "to encourage expenditure for research and experimentation,"[50] the Court reversed a Court of Appeals decision denying a limited partner his share of a partnership's research and experimental expenses for 1966, even though the partnership made no sales before 1967.

2. To encourage scientific pursuits, individuals and corporations may deduct contributions to educational and scientific organizations operated in the public interest.[51] Individual deductions are limited to 50% of adjusted gross income, corporate deductions to 5% of taxable income.[52]

3. The income of scientific and educational organizations operated in the public interest is exempt from Federal income tax.[53] An organization conducting scientific research will qualify for the exemption if the research "is directed toward benefiting the public."[54] This condition is fulfilled if the research "is published in

a treatise, thesis, trade publication, or in any other form that is available to the interested public."[55] To meet this test, the service has ruled that publication must be "timely."[56] Provided it meets these tests, and even if performed under "a contract or agreement under which the sponsor or sponsors of the research have the right to obtain ownership or control of any patents, copyrights, processes, or formulae resulting from such research,"[57] research may still be regarded as performed in the public interest.

Tax exempt organizations, however, are taxable on income derived from "unrelated" business activities.[58] This is income from a business enterprise which is "not substantially related" to the organization's exempt purpose.[59] A business activity is not "substantially related" to an organization's exempt function if it does not "contribute importantly" to the accomplishment of the organization's exempt purpose.[60]

Thus, the service has held that commercially sponsored research which is published in timely fashion is scientific research carried on in the public interest and related to the organization's exempt purpose. Accordingly, income from that research will not be tainted as unrelated business income.[61] But research — the publication of which is withheld or delayed significantly beyond the time reasonably necessary to establish ownership rights — is not in the public interest and constitutes the conduct of an unrelated trade or business under the statute.[62]

There are other exceptions to the tax on unrelated business income. The following types of research-related income are specifically excluded from the scope of unrelated business income: (1) research income of a college, university, or hospital,[63] and (2) income from any research performed for the United States, a state, or political subdivision.[64] Finally, dividends, interest, and royalties are not unrelated business income, unless received from debt-finance property.[65] This exclusion provides scientific and educational organizations an opportunity to earn passive income without running afoul of the unrelated business income provisions of the Code.

4. Individual inventors who transfer "all substantial rights" to their patents are permitted to treat such revenue as capital gains.[66] In determining whether "all substantial rights" have been transferred, the law distinguishes between the sale of patent rights or the granting of an exclusive license and the nonexclusive licensing of a patent. If a patent is sold, or exclusively licensed, the income is characterized as a capital gain, even though the payment is partly conditioned on future production or profits. If, however, the patent is licensed on a nonexclusive basis, the income is characterized and taxed as ordinary income. The capital gains treatment is an incentive provision since one might consider the sale of patents as ordinary income of an inventor, and it would be so treated without the special exemption provided in the law. Corporations that sell patents or license inventions do not automatically qualify for capital gains treatment, but such transactions may qualify for capital gains treatment as a sale of a capital asset.[67]

Belgium

1. Current research costs are deductible in the year incurred, provided they are related to the business activity of the taxpayer.[68]

2. Capital expenditures — including buildings — by a Belgian enterprise are generally depreciated under either the straight-line or declining-balance method. Scientific research equipment, however, is eligible for accelerated, three-year depreciation.[69]

3. Belgian law provides incentives for investments for specified purposes in economically distressed areas of the country. R&D is one of the purposes entitled to preferential treatment. Accordingly, investment in a development area for a new research laboratory is entitled to exemption from the immovable prepayment tax. The exemption applies to the building, as well as the land and equipment related to it.[70]

4. The sale of patent rights is taxed as ordinary income, provided the patent is used in the normal operation of the taxpayer's business or is the result of a continuous — rather than incidental — inventing program. Alternatively, incidental inventions of a private inventor are taxed at a reduced rate.[71]

5. Contributions to non-commercial, non-profit organizations operated for the promotion of scientific research are tax deductible.[72]

Canada

1. Taxpayers are allowed to deduct both current and capital expenditures (including buildings, but not land) for scientific research in the year incurred, provided that the research is related to the taxpayer's business. To be deductible, current scientific expenditures may be incurred either inside or outside Canada, but capital expenditures must be incurred in Canada. No deduction is allowed for expenditures made to acquire another's patents or other rights arising out of scientific research. The allowable R&D deduction is reduced by any amounts received by the taxpayer pursuant to an Appropriations Act and used for scientific research aimed at improving the technological capability of Canadian manufacturing industry. Repayments of such grants are treated as deductible expenses. The deduction of eligible current scientific expenditure also can be deferred at the taxpayer's option and claimed in future years.[73]

2. Payments to an approved Canadian educational or research institute are deductible, provided they are used for scientific research related to the taxpayer's line of business activity. Payments to a Canadian non-profit organization to be used for scientific research also are deductible.[74]

3. Canadian law provides a general investment tax credit for qualifying capital expenditures. The credit is equal to 7% of eligible expenditures and is limited to the first $15,000 of Federal tax liability plus 50% of any tax liability in excess of $15,000. Unused credits can be carried forward five years.[75] This credit may also be applied to current and capital scientific research expenditures. The deduction for expenditures for scientific research is reduced by the amount of the credit claimed for current scientific expenditures.[76] The effect of this is to make the credit taxable.

4. Business enterprises are allowed an additional deduction equal to 50% of qualifying scientific expenditures in excess of a three-year base period amount. The expenditures must be incurred in Canada for scientific activities related to the taxpayer's line of business. Both current and capital expenditures are eligible for

the special allowance and the investment tax credit may also be claimed with respect to such expenditures.[77]

France

1. Current research costs must be deducted in the year they are incurred. No option exists to capitalize and amortize these expenses.[78]

2. Capital equipment and buildings used for scientific purposes must be depreciated. While straight-line depreciation is usually mandatory in France for depreciable assets, declining-balance depreciation may be taken on certain types of assets, including scientific and technical research equipment, provided the assets are new when purchased and have a useful life of at least three years.[79]

3. Buildings generally may not be depreciated on the declining-balance basis. A special first-year allowance permits companies to write off 50% of the cost of acquiring or constructing buildings dedicated to scientific research. The remaining 50% of the cost is depreciated on a straight-line basis over the life of the structure.[80]

4. Enterprises may deduct 50% of their investment in the shares of approved research companies. When sold, such shares are taxed as a capital gain.[81]

5. Contributions to organizations operating in the public interest and carrying on scientific research are deductible. Corporate contributions are limited to 0.3% of gross sales, individual contributions to 1.5% of net income.[82]

6. Profits resulting from the sale or licensing of patent rights are taxed at the long-term capital gains rate. Transactions involving a sale, exclusive license, or nonexclusive license of patent rights are all eligible for the capital gains rate. To qualify for this preferential taxation, the patent must have been held by the transferor for at least two years, unless it was self-developed.[83]

West Germany

1. Current R&D expenditures are deductible in the year incurred. Capital expenditures, such as for laboratories, buildings and equipment, are depreciated as if employed in current production.[84]

2. The cost of acquiring another party's research results — such as a patent — must be depreciated over the useful life of the asset acquired.[85]

3. Taxpayers may claim an investment tax credit equal to 7.5% of the acquisition or construction costs of capital assets used for R&D purposes. The assets must be used for at least three years in the taxpayer's trade or business. To qualify for the credit, movable fixed assets must be used exclusively for R&D and at least two-thirds of a building must be devoted to R&D. The credit does not reduce the depreciable basis of the asset on which it is claimed.[86]

4. Inventors, both independent and employed, are eligible for preferential tax treatment. An independent inventor is taxed at one-half the normal rate on income earned on the development of a patentable invention provided it is not exploited in the taxpayer's own trade or business. Similarly, a 50% reduction in the

wage tax imposed on payments made by an employer to an employee is available for qualifying inventions.[87]

5. Organizations engaged in R&D activity for the public or common good are entitled to exemption from the income and net wealth taxes. Within limits, contributions to these institutions are tax deductible.[88]

Consideration of Additional R&D Tax Incentives

In considering any additional R&D tax incentives for the United States, the following issues should be addressed.

1. Are additional incentives necessary? Although total R&D spending relative to GNP has fallen along with the growth rate since the mid-1960s, industry-supported R&D has increased steadily. The continued strong performance of private R&D is significant because this is the sector that would be most affected by additional tax incentives. Industry spokesmen have noted that the capacity of business to properly absorb the results of successful R&D is limited.

Greater funding for R&D is not responsive to the problem. . . . The balance between creating new technology and applying it seems out of whack. The coming decade is a time when we as a nation must see that our R&D results and our accumulated knowledge and technique are applied to tangible engineering projects aimed at specific goals.[89]

Twenty years earlier, when private R&D spending was much lower, another executive echoed similar sentiments.

There is . . . the question of the rate at which a company or industry can effectively absorb and commercialize the good results coming from its research and development program. Generally the scaling up of new processes costs a great deal more in money and manpower than laboratory research and development and leads to even larger requirements for new production and distribution facilities.[90]

2. Are additional R&D tax incentives the best way to improve productivity or the trade balance? Available studies indicate that reduced R&D spending may have been associated with about 15% of the post-1960s productivity decline. The United States already has a large trade surplus in R&D-intensive goods. Although not dismissing the importance of R&D incentives, recent studies stress capital formation incentives as the preferred way of improving economic performance. The Committee for Economic Development concluded that "a more rapid capital recovery allowance is the first-priority action among *all* the alternative tax measures."[91] Similarly, the Advisory Subcommittee on Economic and Trade Policy, a group of business community representatives, stated that "the removal of disincentives to savings and investment should be the primary purpose of tax policy designed to encourage innovation."[92]

3. Do international comparisons suggest a need for more R&D incentives? The United States spends more on R&D than France, Germany, Japan and the United Kingdom combined. Relative to GNP, its total R&D expenditures compare favorably with other countries, but its civilian R&D expenditures lag somewhat.

Most industrial nations — not just the United States — have experienced a post-1960 growth slowdown. Other countries tend to have more generous R&D tax incentives than the United States, but this may simply reflect a different form of support for R&D. Although the percentage has declined in recent years, over 50% of total US R&D funding is from government sources. Industry provides a larger share of the R&D budget in West Germany and Japan.[93] Whether the United States should tilt its support of R&D away from direct expenditure and toward tax incentives is a separate question.

4. Are additional tax incentives preferable to direct expenditures? Additional R&D tax incentives would require new definitions and guidelines to identify the eligible expenditures. It may be difficult, for example, to determine how much of the salaries paid to workers in "white coats" is for product research or development compared to quality control or market analysis. This generally is not necessary under current law since R&D may be expensed whether it generates current or future income. Accordingly, R&D is not even reported separately on the tax return, but is included as part of wages and salaries and other expense items. The Financial Accounting Standards Board set forth broad guidelines identifying R&D activities in its statement requiring the expensing of R&D, but decided against more precise definitions.

Differences among enterprises and among industries are so great that a detailed prescription of the activities and related costs includable in research and development, either for all companies or on an industry-by-industry basis, is not a realistic undertaking for the FASB.[94]

It may not be a "realistic undertaking" either for the Internal Revenue Service, but a "detailed prescription of . . . activities and . . . costs" would be necessary if significant new tax benefits depended on the definition.

In addition to the definitional problem, tax incentives raise other issues. Like expenditures, they absorb government funds. But unlike expenditures, they are a form of Federal financing outside the scrutiny and rigor of the normal budget appropriation process. A tax incentive aimed at a particular segment of the R&D community, such as "technology-based" firms or universities, may redistribute rather than increase total R&D activity. No matter how precisely the intended beneficiary of the incentive is defined, it is difficult to avoid rewarding expenditures that would have been made without the incentive. Making an incentive incremental compounds the administrative problems.

5. If a new R&D tax incentive is necessary, the most sensible would be a R&D tax credit for privately funded R&D expenditures on wages and equipment. Since the government would be sharing the cost of R&D, the taxpayers' R&D deduction should be reduced by the amount of the credit. The credit should also be non-refundable. Such a credit would be relatively neutral among R&D projects. It would reduce the cost of all R&D spending, except for structures, by the same proportion regardless of the economic life of the projects, the mix of current and capital expenditures, or the tax circumstances of most taxpayers. Unlike an incentive aimed at particular R&D expenditures, there would be no incentive for a tax-

payer to redistribute — but not increase — its R&D expenditures to qualify for the credit. The credit would work within the market mechanism as firms would be free to pursue the most profitable innovations and technologies. Government officials would not have to make difficult, subjective judgments concerning the relative merits of various innovations and technologies. Still, the problem of determining the particular outlays eligible for the credit, as discussed in point four above, would remain.

Notes and References

1. John W. Kendrick, "Productivity and Economic Growth," *The AEI Economist,* November 1980, p. 3.
2. For example, see Aerospace Industries Association of America, *Research and Development, A Foundation for Innovation and Economic Growth* (1980); Committee for Economic Development, *Stimulating Technological Progress* (1980); and John W. Kendrick, "Productivity Trends and the Recent Slowdown: Historical Perspective, Causal Factors, and Policy Options," *Contemporary Economic Problems* (American Enterprise Institute, 1979), pp. 17–69.
3. The author wishes to thank Carole Garland, Barbara Hall and Elsa Vargas for their assistance in the preparation of this manuscript. This article appeard in substantially the same form in *OTA* (Office of Tax Analysis) *Papers,* no. 45, United States Treasury Department, January 1981. The opinions expressed are those of the author and not necessarily the views of the Treasury Department.
4. National Science Foundation, *Highlights,* May 23, 1980, p. 2.
5. According to the National Science Foundation, universities and other non-profits performed 17% of total R&D activity in 1980, but provided only 4% of total funding.
6. National Science Foundation, *Science Indicators 1978,* p. 6.
7. US Department of Commerce, Bureau of the Census, *Statistical Abstract of the United States 1979,* Washington, p. 895.
8. Edward F. Denison, "Explanations of Declining Productivity Growth," *Survey of Current Business,* August 1979, p. 6.
9. Edwin Mansfield, "Research and Development, Productivity and Inflation," *Science,* September 5, 1980, pp. 1082–93.
10. National Science Foundation, *Science Indicators 1978,* p. 9.
11. Kendrick, "Productivity and Economic Growth," *op. cit.,* p. 3.
12. Steven P. Zell, "Productivity in the U.S. Economy: Trends and Implications," *Economic Review,* Federal Reserve Bank of Kansas City, November 1979, p. 13.
13. *Ibid.,* p. 19.
14. *Ibid.*
15. Denison, *op. cit.,* pp. 3–4.
16. *Ibid.,* p. 4.
17. Edward F. Denison, *The Sources of Economic Growth in the United States* (Committee for Economic Development, 1962), p. 245.
18. Denison, "Explanation of Declining Productivity Growth," *op. cit.,* p. 33.
19. *Ibid.*
20. Kendrick, "Productivity Trends and the Recent Slowdown," *op. cit.,* p. 33.
21. Michael D. McCarthy, "The U.S. Productivity Growth Recession: History and Prospects for the Future," *The Journal of Finance,* June 1978, p. 977.
22. Zell, *op. cit.,* p. 20.
23. John A. Tatom, "The Productivity Problem," *Review,* Federal Reserve Bank of St. Louis, September 1979, p. 15.
24. J.R. Norsworthy, Michael J. Harper and Kent Kunze, "The Slowdown in Productivity Growth: Analysis of Some Contributing Factors," *Brookings Papers on Economic Activity* 2:1979, p. 415.
25. *Ibid.,* p. 420.
26. *Ibid.,* p. 421.
27. Kendrick, "Productivity Trends and the Recent Slowdown," *op. cit.,* p. 51.
28. Donald B. Keesing, "The Impact of Research and Development on United States Trade," *Journal of Political Economy,* February 1967, p. 39.

29. *Ibid.*, p. 45.
30. William Gruber, Dileep Mehta and Raymond Vernon, "The R&D Factor in International Trade and International Investment of United States Industries," *Journal of Political Economy*, February 1967, p. 23.
31. National Science Foundation, *Science Indicators 1978*, p. 30.
32. *Ibid.*
33. *Ibid.*, p. 162.
34. Obie G. Whicard, "U.S. Direct Investment Abroad in 1979," *Survey of Current Business*, August 1980, pp. 16–36, and author's estimate for 1980.
35. *Ibid.*, p. 27.
36. *Ibid.*, p. 23, and author's estimate for 1980.
37. *Ibid.*, pp. 23, 33–36.
38. Sumiye Okubo, "The Impact of Technology Transfer on the Competitiveness of U.S. Producers," paper presented to Trade Policy Staff Committee, July 18, 1980, p. 15.
39. *Ibid.*, p. 39.
40. Internal Revenue Code, Paragraph 1.174-2(b)(1).
41. *Ibid.*, Paragraph 1.167(a)-3.
42. House Report 1337, 83rd Congress, 2nd Session (1954), p. 28.
43. William M. Horne, Jr., "Research and Development Expenditures," *Tax Revision Compendium*, Vol. 2, House Committee on Ways and Means, November 16, 1959, p. 1116.
44. Charles R. Orem, Jr., "Research and Development Costs," *Tax Revision Compendium, op. cit.*, p. 1111.
45. *Ibid.*, p. 1112.
46. *Ibid.*
47. Hearings on HR 8300, Senate Finance Committee, 83rd Congress, 2nd Session (April 1954), p. 105.
48. Internal Revenue Code Section 174(a)(1).
49. Snow vs. Commissioner, 416 US 502.
50. 416 U.S. 504.
51. Internal Revenue Code, Section 170(a).
52. *Ibid.*, Section 170(b)(1); Section 170(b)(2).
53. *Ibid.*, Section 501(a) and 501(c)(3).
54. *Ibid.*, Paragraph 1.501(c)(3)-1(d)(5)(iii)(c).
55. *Ibid.*, Paragraph 1.501(c)(3)-1(d)(5)(iii)(c)(2).
56. Rev. Rul. 76-296; 1976-2 C.B. 141.
57. Internal Revenue Code, Paragraph 1.501(c)(3)-1(d) (5)(iii)(c)(4).
58. *Ibid.*, Section 511(a)(1).
59. *Ibid.*, Section 513(a).
60. *Ibid.*, Paragraph 1.513-1(d)(2).
61. Rev. Rul. 76-296; 1976-2 C.B. 141.
62. *Ibid.*
63. Internal Revenue Code, Section 512(b)(8).
64. *Ibid.*, Section 512(b)(7).
65. *Ibid.*, Section 512(b)(1,2).
66. *Ibid.*, Section 1235.
67. *Ibid.*, Section 1231.
68. C. Sibille, "Belgium: Tax Measures and Direct Incentives Applicable to Research and Development," *European Taxation*, 1977, p. 256.
69. *Ibid.*, p. 258.
70. *Ibid.*, p. 259.
71. *Ibid.*, p. 262.
72. *Ibid.*
73. Commerce Clearing House, *Canadian Master Tax Guide*, 1980, Paragraph 2810.
74. *Ibid.*
75. *Ibid.*, Paragraph 9077.
76. *Ibid.*, Paragraph 2810.
77. *Ibid.*, Paragraph 2852.
78. C. Sibille, "France: Tax Treatment of Research and Development and the Result of Research," *European Taxation*, 1978, p. 78.
79. *Ibid.*
80. *Ibid.*, pp. 78–79.

81. *Ibid.*, p. 80.
82. *Ibid.*, p. 82.
83. *Ibid.*, pp. 84–85.
84. E. Jehle, "German Federal Republic: The Tax Treatment of Research and Development," *European Taxation*, p. 345.
85. *Ibid.*, p. 348.
86. *Ibid.*, p. 349.
87. *Ibid.*, p. 351.
88. *Ibid.*, p. 355.
89. E.E. David, Jr., President, Exxon Research and Engineering Company, "Engineering and Its Impact on the 1980's," Speech before the Conference of the American Association of Engineering Societies, Houston, Texas, October 16, 1980.
90. Robert W. Cairns, "Income Tax Provisions Regarding Research and Development Expenditures," *Tax Revision Compendium, op. cit.*, p. 1106.
91. Committee for Economic Development, *op. cit.*, p. 31.
92. Advisory Subcommittee on Economic and Trade Policy, "Final Report on Economic and Trade Policy," Advisory Committee on Industrial Innovation, February 1979, p. 13.
93. National Science Foundation, *Science Indicators 1978*, p. 7.
94. Financial Accounting Standards Board, "Accounting for Research and Development Costs," October 1974, Paragraph 24.

Technology In Society

New York / Oxford / Toronto / PERGAMON PRESS / Paris / Frankfurt / Sydney

Technology In Society, Vol. 3, pp. 87–98 (1981)
Printed in the USA. All rights reserved.

Tax Policies for Encouraging Innovation: A Survey

Joseph J. Cordes

The US economy has recently been plagued by sluggish economic growth and unacceptably high rates of inflation. Declining productivity growth has been identified as a significant cause of such poor economic performance. Because the level and quality of industrial innovation is an important determinant of productivity growth, public policies toward innovation have received substantial attention.

This article summarizes and compares the main tax policy options which have been proposed for encouraging innovation. The next section briefly discusses the principal conclusions of four recent reports which examine the relationship between government policy and innovative activity. The various tax policies identified in each of the reports are then examined and compared in more detail. The concluding section discusses areas of apparent consensus as well as disagreement among four studies.

Overview of Reports and Recommendations

Several government and private groups have attempted to identify public policies that appear to discourage innovation, as well as policies that might stimulate innovation. The results of these efforts are presented in four studies: (1) the draft report of the Industry Advisory Subcommittee on Economic and Trade Policy convened by the Secretary of Commerce as part of the Domestic Policy Review (DPR Industry Report); (2) a report, "Recommendation for Creating Jobs Through the Success of Small, Innovative Business," prepared for the Commerce Technical Advisory Board (CTAB Report); (3) a monograph, "The Impact of Tax and Financial

Joseph J. Cordes has a Ph.D. in economics from the University of Wisconsin/Madison, and is currently an Associate Professor of Economics at The George Washington University. Journals in which his work has been published include The Journal of Public Economics, Public Finance, Land Economics *and* The Journal of Economics and Business. *Dr. Cordes is also co-author of a monograph,* The Impact of Tax and Financial Policies on Innovation, *published by the National Academy of Engineering.*

Regulatory Policies on Industrial Innovation," prepared under the auspices of the Committee on Technology and International and Trade Issues, National Academy of Engineering (NAE monograph); and (4) an analysis, "Stimulating Technological Progress," prepared by the Committee for Economic Development (CED Report). With the exception of the NAE monograph, the reports discuss a wide range of policy issues.[1] The focus of this review, however, is the specific theme of tax policy.

DPR *Industry Report*

This document presents recommendations made by the Industry Advisory Sub-committee on Economic and Trade Policy as part of the Domestic Policy Review conducted during 1978 and 1979. Twelve tax policy recommendations are presented addressing the issues of general tax incentives for saving and invest-ment; calculating the revenue impact of tax proposals; tax treatment of research and development; taxation of multinational firms; taxation of small, innovative firms; and tax treatment of patents. In addition, four recommendations are made pertaining to government regulation of financial markets. Of the various recom-mendations, improved general tax incentives for savings by individuals and invest-ment by established corporations are viewed as having the greatest potential significance for innovation.

CTAB *Report*

The CTAB report emphasizes government policies toward small business. Five tax policy recommendations are offered dealing with taxation of capital gains; cor-porate taxation of small firms; taxation of stock option plans; and tax treatment of costs incurred by small firms in complying with government regulations. Recom-mendations are also made concerning changes in government spending policies, and in government regulation of capital markets. The report assigns highest priority to tax and financial regulatory policies that increase the availability of capital and management expertise in small businesses.

The CED *Report*

This report, prepared under private auspices, argues that accelerating the pace of US technological innovation requires improvements in four areas of public policy: tax policy, government regulation, government patent policies, and government support for R&D. Of these, changes in tax policy are viewed as the most impor-tant, in particular, changes that would improve existing incentives for capital spending by industry.

The NAE *Monograph*

This study sponsored by the Committee on Technology and International

Economic and Trade Issues of the Assembly of Engineering, National Academy of Engineering, focuses exclusively on the relation between innovation and tax financial regulatory policies. Numerous changes in tax and financial regulatory policies which would favor increased innovation are identified. These changes are quite similar to those discussed in the DPR industry, CTAB and CED reports. A basic theme of the NAE report is that stimulating industrial innovation cannot be separated from the objective of stimulating capital formation. Consequently, the NAE report assigns the highest priority to general macroeconomic policies that make the investment environment more stable, and to policies that improve existing general tax incentives for investment by corporations.

Tax Policy and Industrial Innovation

Each report summarized above discusses a variety of tax policies affecting the level and mix of innovation. This section examines in greater detail the specific conclusions of the four analyses which pertain to corporate and individual income tax policies.

Corporate Income Tax Policy

The corporate income tax affects business investment decisions through its impact on after-tax returns and liquidity. Since innovation is a form of investment, corporate tax policy can influence the amount and/or type of industrial innovation. Aspects of corporate tax policy examined in the four studies are: (1) tax incentives for capital spending; (2) tax treatment of research and development (R&D) expenditures; (3) tax treatment of US multinationals, and (4) tax treatment of small firms.

Tax Incentives for Capital Spending

Tax incentives for capital spending affect innovation in several ways. Jacob Schmookler (1966) has shown that increases (or decreases) in capital goods innovations were typically preceded by increases (or decreases) in capital spending; consequently, government policies that either encourage or discourage capital spending are likely to encourage or discourage innovations in capital goods industries. Moreover, studies by Mueller (1976) and Grabowski (1968) have found that R&D expenditures are affected by corporate liquidity, which is partly determined by tax incentives available to the firm. Finally, since much innovation is embodied in new capital equipment, measures that stimulate new investment speed the rate at which the benefits of innovation spread throughout the economy.

During the 1960s and early 1970s, tax incentives for capital spending were provided through reductions in the corporate tax rate, accelerated depreciation, and investment tax credits. Empirical studies of investment tax incentives have generally found that such measures stimulate corporate investment spendings. However, estimates differ as to the size of the stimulus. Some studies have concluded that tax incentives provide only modest stimulus to corporate investment spending, while others have found the investment stimulus provided by such measures to be quite substantial.[2]

The value of these tax incentives has been reduced by inflation. This is particularly so in the case of depreciation allowances which are based on historical, rather than replacement, costs. Computing depreciation on the basis of historical rather than replacement costs understates true capital costs during periods of inflation. Recent calculations by Gramlich (1976) suggest that current procedures have substantially reduced the real value of depreciation deductions.[3]

Changes in corporate tax policy enacted in the Revenue Act of 1978 provide some stimulus in the statutory corporate income tax rate from 48% to 46%, permanent enactment of the existing 10% investment tax credit, a broadening of the tax credit to permit corporations to use the credit to offset 90% of their corporate tax liability instead of 50%, and allowing corporations a full write-off for expenditures on pollution control equipment. However, these changes do not adequately deal with distortions introduced into the income tax base by inflation.[4]

In view of these considerations, it is not surprising that the DPR report, NAE monograph, and CED report all conclude that improved tax incentives for capital spending are the most promising way of stimulating innovation. The CTAB report does not specifically endorse broad tax incentives for capital spending. This is largely attributable to that report's emphasis on the role of small unestablished businesses in innovation. However, the CTAB report does endorse measures which would reduce the effective corporate tax on small firms, and which would ensure that new firms in their early years are able to make full use of investment tax incentives provided to established corporations.

There are several alternative ways of stimulating capital spending through changes in corporate tax policy. These include: (a) reducing corporate income tax rates, (b) permitting depreciation allowances to be indexed for rising replacement costs, (c) permitting faster write-offs for depreciation, and (d) increasing the current tax credit for new investment.

The NAE monograph, Industry DPR report and the CED report assign a relatively low priority to further reductions in the corporate income tax rate. This position is consistent with the view that general rate reductions are the least effective means, per dollar of foregone tax revenue, of stimulating capital spending. This is so because the tax savings provided by rate reductions do not depend on the investment activities of the firm.

Both the Industry DPR and the CED reports explicitly favor more rapid capital recovery through depreciation. The CED report recommends that this be done by shortening the useful lives over which investments may be depreciated. The basis for this recommendation is that such a change would be easily understood and implemented by firms.

Neither the NAE monograph nor the CED report specifically endorses increasing the existing tax credit for new investment. The Industry DPR report mentions enhancing the investment tax credit, but assigns this lower priority than improving capital recovery through depreciation. This is significant since the investment tax credit has traditionally been viewed by many tax scholars as an extremely effective way of encouraging new investment.[5]

There are, however, several reasons why further increases in the investment tax credit (ITC) should not be assigned high priority as a means of encouraging innovation. First, since the ITC encourages the use of shorter-lived assets in production, further expansion of this tax incentive may conflict with the objective of encouraging a greater commitment of resources to long-term investments in innovation. Second, unlike depreciation allowances, the real value of the ITC has not been eroded by inflation.[6] This is so because the value of the tax credit increases automatically with the cost of new investment purchases.

Tax Incentives for Research and Development

Research and development (R&D) is an integral part of the innovation process. Therefore, policies that lower the net cost of R&D are likely to encourage innovation. Currently, Section 174 of the US Internal Revenue Code permits firms to fully deduct some R&D expenditures in the year they are incurred, even though R&D may produce an intangible asset with a useful life of more than one year.

Expenditures that qualify for immediate expensing include all costs incurred in connection with the taxpayer's trade or business which represent R&D in the experimental or laboratory sense. There are, however, some relevant costs of R&D that may not be expensed. While the costs of obtaining one's own patent, or developing one's own model or process can be expensed, the costs of acquiring someone else's patent, model, or process may not. Instead, these items are treated like other capital expenditures, to be amortized over their useful lives. In addition, structures and equipment used in R&D activities may not be immediately expensed. The costs of such R&D depreciable assets are recovered through general depreciation allowances for investments.

Because Section 174 is equivalent to granting instantaneous depreciation to some portion of R&D, it is viewed as a tax incentive for investments in R&D. A potential way of encouraging innovation would be to expand this tax incentive. One way of achieving this objective would be to broaden the coverage of Section 174 to include expenses for plant and equipment used in R&D as well as expenses incurred to purchase patents on processes. Another approach would be to enact new specific tax credits for R&D.

The DPR Industry report, the NAE monograph, and the CED report all recommend that consideration be given to increasing tax incentives for R&D. However, the reports differ somewhat in the strength of their support for such measures.

The NAE monograph is the least enthusiastic of the three analyses about tax incentives for R&D as a means of stimulating industrial innovation. The reason given for this view is that innovation is a complex process in which R&D is but one part. Not only must a technically viable concept for a new or improved product be developed; it must also be rendered commercially viable. The NAE monograph acknowledges that tax incentives for R&D may have a substantial impact in industries where research and development costs are a significant portion of the total costs of innovation. However, in many industries, R&D expenditures are a modest share of the costs of innovation—perhaps 10% to 20%. In such cases, tax incentives for R&D would have a modest impact on innovation. In addition, the monograph also notes that if lagging innovation is due to pessimistic expectations about profits, the prospect of receiving tax savings through tax incentives for R&D may not offer much encouragement to innovation.

Consistent with these views, providing additional tax incentives for R&D is assigned a lower priority in the NAE monograph than other measures such as changes in personal income taxation and in government regulation of financial markets. Moreover, no specific tax incentive is endorsed in the NAE analysis.

The CED report qualifies its support of R&D tax incentives by noting that such selective incentives are most likely to encourage innovation if they are introduced along with, rather than separately from, general tax incentives for capital spending. However, the CED report regards R&D tax incentives as sufficiently promising to devote considerable discussion to such measures. Specifically, the CED report recommends that: (a) Section 174 be broadened to permit immediate expensing of plant and equipment used in R&D; (b) plant and equipment used in R&D be given a double tax credit; (c) the useful life governing depreciation of patents be shortened to a maximum of 10 years; and (d) corporations be given a tax credit for contributions to university research.

Of the 12 tax policy recommendations presented in the DPR, four pertain to R&D tax incentives. The specific measures proposed are basically quite similar to those discussed in the CED report, though there are some differences. Like the CED report, the DPR Industry report recommends extending Section 174 to plant and equipment, providing a larger tax credit for plant and equipment used in R&D, permitting patents to be depreciated more rapidly and providing tax credits for contributions to university research. Unlike the CED report, the DPR Industry report does not stipulate the amount by which tax credits should increase for R&D-related investments. Furthermore, the DPR Industry report recommends that tax credits be provided for those R&D-related expenditures that are not currently eligible for the investment tax credit. This is a measure not mentioned in the CED report.

If additional tax credits are extended to R&D, further attention must be given to: the size of the tax credit; defining eligibility for the tax credit; and whether tax credits should be limited to R&D expenditures that exceed some "base-line" effort by the firm. The latter two issues are particularly relevant to the objective of not subsidizing activities that either: (a) are innovative, but which would have been funded in the absence of tax incentives; or (b) are more or less conventional investment activities that have simply been redefined on paper as "innovative" in order to qualify for tax incentives.[7]

Taxation of US Multinationals

A recent Treasury regulation, 1.861-8, requires multinationals to allocate some of their domestic R&D expenditures against foreign source income. This reduces foreign source income for US tax purposes. However, unless foreign governments allow tax deductions for R&D expenditures incurred in the US, this procedure would not reduce taxable income for foreign tax purposes. Since the foreign tax credit is based on the Treasury's definition of foreign source income, this guideline reduces the credit that multinationals may take against US taxes without reducing their actual foreign tax liability. Because of this, it is argued that multinationals have a tax incentive to move their R&D activities overseas.

Regulation 861 is discussed in the NAE monograph and in both the DPR and CED reports. The NAE monograph recommends that further research be devoted to assess the amount of tax revenue raised by this provision, and to determine whether Regulation 861 has seriously discouraged innovation. If such research determines that small additional revenues are obtained at the expense of significant reductions in innovation by US multinationals, the NAE monograph recommends the repeal of Regulation 861. In contrast to the NAE report, both the DPR Industry and CED reports advocate either repeal or revision of Regulation 861. Repeal of this provision is recommended in the DPR Industry report, while the CED report recommends the regulation be limited to the portion of US multinationals' R&D expenses directly related and traceable to foreign earnings. However, revision of Regulation 861 is ranked behind general tax incentives for capital spending, and specific tax incentives for R&D, in all three analyses.

Corporate Tax Treatment of Small Firms

Certain small enterprises seem to play an important role in the innovation process.[8] Some observers claim that small firms have contributed a disproportionate share of inventions in industries such as instrumentation and electronics. Others have been more cautious in assigning *sole* credit for inventions to small firms, pointing to the involvement of larger firms either at the beginning or the end of the invention process. However, under both views, small technology-based firms are considered to play a vital role *at some point* in the development of innovations.

All four reports consider policies for encouraging the formation and profitability of small, innovative firms. Indeed, the CTAB report is primarily concerned with public policy toward small firms. All four reports agree on two broad issues. First, the analyses emphasize the role of the individual income tax and government regulations of financial markets as opposed to the corporation tax. Second, in discussing corporate tax policy, none of the analyses advocate new corporate tax incentives for small businesses. Instead, the analyses focus either on expanding existing tax preferences for small firms, or on ensuring that small, unestablished firms are able to take full advantage of tax incentives available to all firms.

With one exception, recommendations concerning corporate tax policy deal with deductibility of losses incurred by small firms. Ensuring adequate tax deductibility of losses is one way of encouraging investor participation in new, innovative firms which are likely to be unprofitable in their early years. Subchapter

S treatment of corporations with 15 or fewer shareholders as partnerships for tax purposes, as well as various provisions allowing individual investors to deduct losses from investments in small business from ordinary income are current efforts to provide adequate loss offsets. Both the DPR Industry and CED reports recommend the expansion of the first provision. The DPR Industry report recommends that the qualifications for Subchapter S treatment be liberalized for small firms which spend more than a certain percentage of revenues in research and development. The CED report recommends that the Subchapter limit on shareholders be increased from 15 to 100 investors. In contrast to the DPR Industry proposal, no mention is made in the CED report of limiting this change to R&D intensive small firms.

Some features of the corporate income tax may unintentionally discriminate against small firms, in particular new firms. Loss offsets, depreciation deductions, and investment tax credits are not of immediate value to new, initially unprofitable firms because they face no corporate tax liability. The NAE monograph notes that this will discriminate against such firms if carry-forward provisions for unused operating losses are inadequate. The CED and CTAB reports maintain that current provisions — which allow losses to be carried forward for five years — are not adequate, and should be extended. The CTAB report specifically recommends increasing the carry-forward period from five to 10 years. The CTAB report also recommends further reductions in the taxation of firms with net earnings of less than $200,000 per year in order to place such firms on a more equal footing with large, established corporations.

If specific corporate tax incentives are to be used to encourage innovation by small firms, one must decide whether to extend such tax preferences to small business in general, or to limit them to small innovative firms. While research has shown that some small firms have made significant and disproportionate contributions to innovation, these findings do not apply to small businesses generally. Limiting the scope of tax preferences requires, however, that one distinguish between "innovative" and other firms. Such distinctions are difficult to make in practice. For example, the DPR report, which favors limiting the scope of small business tax incentives, merely recommends extending such tax incentives to "small businesses, properly defined, which spend more than a given percentage of revenues on research and development."

Personal Income Tax Policy

The personal income tax affects both how much households save and how they allocate their savings among different investments. Since household savings are an important source of investment capital, the personal income tax — albeit indirectly — affects both the amount and the composition of private investment.

The feature of the individual income tax given the most attention in the four studies is taxation of capital gains. There are two major reasons for this emphasis. First, the returns to corporate stock ownership and other equity investments are directly affected by capital gains taxation. Certain innovative activities, particularly those undertaken by small firms, depend on equity as a major source of finance. In addition, the willingness of investors to assume risk is sensitive to capital gains taxation, and investments in innovation are relatively riskier than other investments.

Long-term capital gains have traditionally received preferential tax treatment. Until recently, the tax advantage conferred on capital gains had been eroding due to both tax law changes and inflation. Prior to 1969, the maximum effective tax on capital gains was 25%. However, the Tax Reform Acts of 1969 and 1976 increased the maximum rate to 49%. In addition, inflation had distorted the computation of capital gains, increasing the effective tax on real capital gains. The trend toward increased taxation of capital gain was reversed by changes enacted in the Revenue Act of 1978. The changes lower the maximum capital gains tax from 49.1% to 28%, and lower capital gains taxes for investors in all income brackets.

The changes enacted in the Revenue Act of 1978 are either implicitly or explicitly endorsed by the NAE monograph, and the DPR Industry, CED, and CTAB reports. Moreover, three of these studies, the DPR Industry, CED, and CTAB reports, propose additional liberalization of capital gains taxes.

One proposal, made in the DPR Industry and CTAB reports, would extend the coverage of existing tax preferences by liberalizing provisions for employee stock option plans. Specifically, the DPR Industry report recommends increasing the qualified options time from five to 10 years and postponing taxation of non-qualified options until the shares have been sold, rather than taxing such options when they are exercised. The CTAB report recommends a similar change. However, the DPR Industry report proposes that this change be applied only to small businesses that are R&D intensive. The CTAB report recommends that the change apply to small business, generally.

Other proposals involve increasing general tax preferences for capital gains. These can be grouped into three broad categories: (a) reductions in capital gains tax rates; (b) liberalized deductibility of capital losses; and (c) changes to minimize the lock-in effect.

Those favoring preferential treatment of capital gains maintain that risk-taking would be discouraged if capital gains were taxed as other income.[9] Theoretical analyses of the relationship between capital gains taxation and risk-taking have highlighted the relation between risk-taking, taxation, and adequate deductibility of capital losses. Taxation of capital gains permits the government to share in the returns of an investment if it is successful. Full deductibility of capital losses requires the government to share in the losses from an unsuccessful investment. In evaluating a risky investment, one should consider both the after-tax return earned if it is successful and the after-tax loss suffered if it is not. Decreases in capital gains taxes increase potential after-tax returns, while liberalizing deductibility of capital losses reduces potential after-tax losses. Thus, both actions favor investment in risky investments.

The DPR Industry, CED, and CTAB reports all recommend further reductions in capital gains tax rates. The CTAB study recommends lowering the maximum tax rate on capital gains to the pre-1969 rate of 25% when those gains are realized on sales of stock held for more than three years in businesses with 500 or fewer employees. The report also recommends reducing the maximum rate to 10% for firms with 100 or fewer employees. The CED report indirectly favors reducing the maximum rate on capital gains from 28% to 20%. The DPR report in its first recommendation supports the general principle of reducing the burden of the capital gains tax. However, it does not propose any specific rates. Finally, reducing capital gains tax rates is mentioned in the NAE monograph as one of several policies for encouraging investors to purchase the equity offerings of small technological firms. However, it is not specifically endorsed.

Improved Capital Loss Deductibility

Both the NAE monograph and the CED report also suggest that deductibility of capital losses be improved, though neither study recommends specific measures along these lines. Currently, investors with net capital losses may deduct such losses against up to only $3000 of ordinary income each year and must exclude 50% of long-term capital losses when doing so. The inadequacy of these loss-offset provisions is demonstrated by recent US Treasury calculations which show the presence of significant undeducted capital losses in each income class.[10] There are several ways in which loss offsets could be made more complete. The most substantial change would permit full deductibility of capital losses against ordinary income. Less drastic changes would involve increasing the dollar income limit and/or increasing the fraction of long-term capital losses deductible within the limit.

Finally, three of the four studies discuss changes that would permit investors to defer paying capital gains taxes on sales of stock in small firms, provided that such sales are "rolled over" to purchase securities of other small firms. These measures are all intended to reduce the lock-in effect of the capital gains tax. Capital gains are only taxed when realized into income and in many cases may be passed on to heirs virtually tax free. Consequently, investors have an incentive to postpone sales of assets. Bailey (1969) and Feldstein and Yitzhaki (1978) present evidence that the lock-in incentive may be quite strong. Hence, investors may be discouraged from efficiently allocating capital in response to new investment opportunities.

The three studies differ somewhat in the coverage of the rollover positions that are discussed. Both the NAE monograph and the DPR Industry report support tax-free rollover of equity investments in small technological firms. The CTAB report supports tax-free rollover for equity investments in all small firms.

Several issues arise in using tax preferences for capital gains to encourage innovation. A major issue is whether general reductions in capital gains taxes are the most effective stimulus to innovation. The CED report appears to favor reducing capital gains tax rates and increasing capital loss offsets for all taxpayers. This view is consistent with the first recommendation of the DPR report. However, subsequent DPR Industry recommendations seem to favor restricting further capital gains tax concessions to small technological firms. Finally, the CTAB report favors restricting the coverage of capital gains tax concessions to equity investments in small firms (less than 500 employees at the time of purchase), and further recommends denying eligibility for such concessions to capital gains realized from real estate.

Another issue is whether rate reductions and increases in loss offsets should be viewed as competing options. This is particularly important if recommendations pertain to general tax concessions. Though reducing capital gains tax encourages investment in risky activities, it also encourages investments that are neither particularly risky nor innovative, but which legally qualify as capital gains. This is less likely to occur if capital gains tax relief is provided by liberalizing deductibility of capital losses because more tax relief, per dollar of revenue loss, is extended to those making risky investments.

Policy Implications and Conclusions

The various tax incentives identified in the four studies offer a variety of options to the policymaker. However, several issues must be resolved if any or all of these tax incentives are to be implemented. A major issue is whether the specific measures mentioned should be viewed as competing alternatives or as elements of an overall package of specific tax incentives. Both the CED and DPR Industry reports suggest that as many of such measures as are feasible should be implemented. However, constraints imposed by the political process may preclude adopting more than one or two of these tax incentives.

One must also consider how additional tax incentives for capital spending are to be financed. Tax policies that stimulate innovation entail, at least initially, some revenue loss to the US Treasury. However as emphasized in the CED and DPR Industry reports, there is considerable disagreement about how to estimate the "true" revenue losses from tax cuts once the response of firms and individuals to such tax cuts have been taken into account.

If the various tax incentives discussed above are viewed as competing alternatives, one must determine which option is the most desirable. The reports surveyed above disagree about the ranking of specific policy measures. These differences reflect divergent views about: the importance of R&D in the innovation process; the contribution to innovation made by small firms; and the relative merits of general as opposed to "innovation-specific" tax incentives. However, there does appear to be considerable agreement about the general focus of tax policies toward innovation. That is, such policies should encourage: general capital spending, research and development, and the formation of small innovation-oriented firms.

Notes

1. For example, the CED report devotes considerable attention to the relation between government regulation and innovation. The DPR report also devotes attention to government regulation, as well as to foreign trade issues.
2. A number of empirical studies of the impact of investment tax incentives on corporate investment behavior may be found in Fromm (1971). Among these studies, that of Hall and Jorgenson is the most optimistic in

its assessment of the impact of investment tax incentives, while Coen, and Klein and Taubman find a considerably more modest impact of tax policy than Hall and Jorgenson.

3. Specifically, Gramlich's estimates suggest a decline, due to inflation, in the present value of depreciation deductions of roughly 23–41%.

4. For example, Gramlich (1976) estimates that the corporate tax rate would have to be cut from 48% to 40% to offset the impact of inflation on historic cost depreciation.

5. See Break (1974), pp. 217–219.

6. Furthermore, since relatively short-lived assets are favored by tax credits, further increasing the tax credit would favor short-lived rather than long-lived investment projects.

7. This concern is raised by Mansfield in National Science Foundation (1977).

8. See Jewkes, *et al.* (1969).

10. See Wetzler (1976).

References

Break, G. "The Incidence and Economic Effects of Taxation," in *The Economics of Public Finance* (Washington, D.C.: Brookings Institution, 1974).

Feldstein, M., "Personal Taxation and Portfolio Compositino: An Econometric Analysis," *Econometrics,* July 1976.

Feldstein, M. and Yitzhaki, S., "The Effect of the Capital Gains Tax on the Selling and Switching of Common Stock," *Journal of Public Economics,* 1978.

Fromm, G., *Tax Incentives and Capital Spending* (Washington, DC: Brookings Institution, 1971).

Grabowski, H., "The Determinants of Industrial Research and Development: A Study of the Chemical, Drug, and Petroleum Industries," *Journal of Political Economy,* March–April 1968.

Gramlich, E., "The Economic and Budgetary Effects of Indexing the Tax System," in H. Aaron, ed., *Inflation and the Income Tax* (Washington, D.C.: Brookings Institution, 1976).

Harberger, A., and Bailey, M.J., *The Taxation of Income from Capital* (Washington, D.C.: Brookings Institution, 1969).

Kaplan, R.S., *Tax Policies for R&D and Technological Innovation, Chapter 1; Tax Policies of U.S. and Foreign Nations in Support of R&D and Innovation* (Pittsburgh: Carnegie-Mellon University, 1976).

Mueller, D.C., "The Firm Decision Process: An Econometric Investigation" *Quarterly Journal of Economics,* February 1967.

National Science Foundation, *Preliminary Papers for a Colloquium on the Relationships Between R&D and Economic Growth/Productivity* (Washington, D.C.: National Science Foundation, 1977).

Schmookler, Jacob, *Invention and Economic Growth* (Cambridge, Massachusetts: Harvard University Press, 1966).

Wetzler, J. "Capital Gains and Losses," in J. Pechman, ed., *Comprehensive Income Taxation* (Washington, D.C.: Brookings Institution, 1977).

Technology In Society, Vol. 3, pp. 99–105 (1981)
Printed in the USA. All rights reserved.

Critical Mass and Innovation

Robert F. Dee

As one considers the history of the world, it is apparent that truly new events occur in a pattern that is hard to explain. Not only is the progress of physical evolution in the human marked by enormous gaps during which very little change has occurred, but human use of apparently simple processes—grazing of herds, agriculture, the making of pottery, the discovery of iron—has erupted only after thousands of years during which all traces of them seem to have been absent.

Innovation, then, appears to be an erratic event. Indeed, if the innovative accomplishments of humanity were arranged on a one-year calendar, humankind's greatest burst of creative activity would be seen to occur in the last few minutes before New Year's Eve. In the face of these puzzling facts about the nature of technological advance, it is difficult to predict what conditions are necessary to encourage innovation in our time.

The author's own view is that innovation is the result of a great number of complex factors all working together over a space of time until a critical mass and a subsequent insight produce the creative event. A profitable way to think about the innovative process would be to consider what some of these factors are and whether or not any of them can be deliberately encouraged.

The staff of the Joint Economic Committee of the Congress has recently published a useful analysis of research and innovation in the United States. They have stressed the fact that capital investment is the key to new innovation and that government fiscal, regulatory and science policy have hindered such investment for many years. Such a view is consistent with the thesis of critical mass. It is a well known principle of capitalism that a certain level of capital accrual is essential before any new endeavor can be successfully undertaken, and government policies that discourage capital formation have a negative impact on research and development.

The attitude of a government toward its national research potential is obviously

Robert F. Dee is Chairman of the Board and Chief Executive Officer of SmithKline Corporation which he joined in 1948. After holding positions in pharmaceutical research and development, sales and personnel, he was elected Vice President in 1967 and Group Vice President and member of the Board of Directors in 1969. Prior to his election as Chairman in 1976, Mr. Dee had served as President and Chief Executive Officer since 1972. A spokesman for democratic capitalism and a member of the Business Council, The Conference Board, the National Association of Manufacturers, and the Policy Committee of the Business Roundtable, he has been influential in shaping policies and perspectives in the American business community.

one of the most vital factors in stimulating innovation in the modern world. The governments of most major democracies have grasped this point, and have initiated positive incentives for the private sector and for academic research organizations. Japan, Germany and France are notable examples of how these incentives can produce concrete results.

The Joint Committee report on research and innovation makes clear that such efforts can, and have, also worked in the United States. The history of computer, agriculture and space technologies shows how industry, government and universities can work toward positive technological goals. Exchanges of ideas, information and personnel enhance the process. Technologies can often interrelate, so that elements from one technology help another to develop. Computer technology has interrelated with space technology and to some degree with agriculture. Without the computer there could have been no first landing on the moon for the United States in 1969.

A Rare Phenomenon

Yet this cooperative relationship between government and American technology has been a rare phenomenon during the past two decades. In fact, for the most part the US government has demonstrated, through its bureaucracies, a positive antagonism toward the private sector and an increasingly indifferent attitude towards the academy.

The result has been a loss of leadership for American technology and decreasing gains in US productivity. Output per hour growth for all goods and services produced in this country for the 1970s was 1.4% per year, compared to 3% during the 1960s and 2.6% during the 1950s.

The decline in American technology as a result of government indifference and bureaucratic hostility has often been cited. Research spending in the United States hit a peak in 1968. Since then, it has flattened out at a level far below what the US must have for national economic growth. In a talk the author gave at The Franklin Institute in 1979, he made the categorical charge that the present technology lag has been largely engineered by government.

There are three aspects of government policy that are especially harmful to innovation.

The first is a Federal policy that discourages savings. The United States has the highest per capita income in the world and the lowest rate of savings of any industrial country. Yet two-thirds of the financial capital needed for investment in economic growth in this country comes from personal savings. Nearly every US law affecting saving is negative and actually discourages thrift.

It is perfectly clear from statistics like these that one of the chief elements needed for a critical mass in American capital is sadly missing.

The second negative policy of US government in recent years consists of regulations that impose enormous financial burdens on the private sector while at the same time creating a psychological climate inimical to inventiveness. Government regulation costs business and consumers upward of $130 billion a year. There are 55 regulatory agencies employing about 80,000 people on a budget more than double what it was in 1974. The burden of regulation, much of it misguided, has made it impossible for many small innovative businesses to launch creative new ideas. At the same time, it has brought hardship to many large companies. Despite differing opinions on the true cause of Chrysler Company's difficulties, the author has no doubt that onerous regulation of the automobile industry played a significant role.

So regulation, too, like US savings policy, militates against the formation of the critical mass so necessary to the birth of invention.

The Disadvantageous Tax Code

The third disadvantage to innovation sponsored by the government is taxation. The US tax code favors consumption, discourages investment, and prevents capital formation. There are no real incentives for ventures involving high spending on research and development. Inventors do invent, but they cannot find investors to bring their inventions to the market place. Taxation on income, capital gains, personal savings, dividends—on every crucial aspect of American fiscal life—is the third most grievous affront to the formation of the critical mass needed to beget new inventions.

America is not unaware of this problem. Several members of Congress have addressed the matter, notably and most recently Congressman Don Fuqua, Chairman of the House Committee on Science and Technology. Congressman Fuqua went to the heart of the matter when he said, "Innovation by its very nature involves risk for it deals with what is new and untried. Thus, it can only be encouraged in an environment which is inspirational to risk-taking. . . . At the moment, I think we generally lack the sense of urgency to risk, to innovate, to test the waters in the face of all odds."

For years Representative Thomas Curtis of Missouri introduced legislation to provide a tax credit for basic research. He believed that a credit system was far preferable to a program under which the government underwrites the costs of research. Congressman Curtis's efforts did not succeed. But in 1971, President Nixon rekindled the flame of hope on this issue; in a major economic speech, he directed his Secretary of the Treasury to recommend to Congress "new tax proposals for stimulating research and development of new industries and new technologies to help provide 20 million new jobs."

The Commerce Department then began to press for Federal subsidy of research and development in the form of tax relief, loans and repeal of antitrust legislation; but the Treasury Department resisted these pressures, maintaining that it did not want to use the tax system for anything but revenue raising.

The late Congressman Jerry L. Pettis introduced a bill in 1971 that would have provided a 7% investment tax credit to "qualified" research and experimental expenditures. He argued, very cogently, that the existing investment tax credit for capital investment had the least beneficial effect in the very sector of industry most sorely in need of encouragement—the R&D-oriented, high-technology sector that is not normally capital-intensive. But the Pettis legislative proposal too was unsuccessful.

Federal Policy and Innovation

Perhaps the next largest effort—apart from other unsuccessful attempts by members of Congress to alter the prevailing pattern of tax discrimination against research-intensive companies—was President Carter's appointment of a task force to examine how Federal policy discourages or encourages innovation. This task force included hundreds of experts from government, industry and consumer groups. It submitted recommendations for basic changes in Federal policy to stimulate innovation by industry.

Unfortunately, President Carter only saw fit to recommend action on a few of the 41 recommendations of the task force. He put off tax, capital investment, and depreciation incentives for business until decisions could be made about the 1981 fiscal budget—which remains at this writing (March 1981) still in a state of considerable indecision. The recommendations President Carter did endorse were fundamentally nonfiscal, but the real critical mass of American research is one of capital-building, against which the entire set of the US government for nearly 50 years has been visibly in opposition.

It is to be hoped that the new Administration will recognize the "unwisdom" of opposing the country's capital-building obligations, that it will clearly perceive the wisdom of stimulating innovation as a stimulant of productivity. The author feels confident that such a view will ultimately prevail. But it will not do so without the concerted effort of all who understand the situation as it now stands.

The basic tax rule in the United States now is that research and experimental expenditures may be deducted as current expenses in the year they are paid or incurred. At the taxpayer's election, however, such expenditures may be treated as deferred expenses deductible ratably over a period of not less than five years (starting when the taxpayer first realizes profit from the expenditure), so long as they are not attributable to property subject to regular tax depreciation or amortization over its useful life.

No investment credit is allowed, such as would be allowed if the expenditures were made to acquire tangible capital assets for use in producing income. Industry has argued that it is unfair to view research and development expenditures of long duration and questionable outcome as current expenses. It has argued that they should be viewed as capital expenditures.

But to truly appreciate the shortsightedness of US tax policy affecting research and development, one must understand the impact of a relatively new regulation under Section 861 of the Internal Revenue Code. This regulation has a profoundly adverse effect on research conducted in the United States. What the research tax provisions described earlier in this article allow, this newest Treasury interpretation can effectively take away.

It is important to describe Section 861 in some detail to give a clear impression of the anti-research bias of the present Federal bureaucracy.

Section 861(b) of the Internal Revenue Code requires that income from US sources be reduced by "the expenses, losses, and other deductions properly apportioned or allocated thereto." The US Treasury, exercising its authority to interpret this language, has issued a regulation allocating certain US-incurred expenses (primarily those in R&D) against foreign-source income by use of complex formulas. The effect is to inflate US taxable income, while reducing foreign-source net income for US tax purposes.

The result is to reduce the amount of foreign tax credits that can be used to offset the US tax on the same foreign income. Consequently, foreign tax credits representing taxes actually paid to foreign countries cannot be availed of—and will expire *unused* unless special and sometimes artificial tax-planning devices are employed.

But how does this regulation affect research and development expenditures specifically? That is the important point for the scientist and the concerned layman to understand.

Companies with overseas operations allocate a portion of their US-incurred R&D expenses against foreign-source income. They do so by using a ratio of foreign versus domestic gross income. And they do so even though the research and development was performed by the US parent company. The fact that R&D is also performed abroad by the company's subsidiaries is ignored.

A Strong Disincentive

It follows, therefore, that the 861 expense allocation tends to inflate the parent company's US source income and to reduce foreign-source income. Consequently, there is a strong disincentive for the parent company to perform research and development in the United States. And there is a corresponding incentive to move its research operations to a foreign subsidiary.

In practice, tax advisors typically react to this inequitable situation by advising their managements *not* to expand research operations at home, but to move them to overseas locations. In addition to discouraging the expansion of R&D facilities and expenditures in the United States, the failure to grant the same tax benefits to US research and development as that given to any other type of American business expense gives a further edge to research-intensive foreign firms, such as Japanese or German companies. These companies, by the way, already enjoy more favorable treatment in their own countries than even US basic tax laws provide.

Nearly every country in Western Europe, as well as in Canada and Japan, offers incentives to encourage technological development. Among the principal methods other countries use to encourage research and development are tax benefits, government-sponsored associations and institutes, grants, loans, loan guarantees, interest and employment subsidies, favorable patent coverage and technical assistance. Of these, tax benefits are the most frequently used. These include deductions, exemptions, accelerated depreciation allowances and tax credits.

Canada, for example, allows a 100% write-off of current and capital research and development expenditures (except for land) in the year they are made. This is supplemented by an investment tax credit on current and capital R&D outlays, which vary by region from 5% to 10%. Canada also offers special tax credits for costs of approved research programs, or cash grants for capital investment in R&D projects—at the taxpayer's election.

West Germany has offered up to a 50% write-off for R&D investments and a 10% subsidy for capital investment in R&D. Cash premiums and investment grants for research and development are now offered.

Japan has granted up to three-year tax holidays for profits on "new and important" products. Japan also offers a corporation tax credit for R&D expenses above those of a certain base period.

Norway allows an immediate deduction not only for current costs for research, but also for capital expenditures related to research. Belgium grants non-interest-bearing loans of up to 80% of the expenditure to finance R&D of new products and new production techniques. The loans are repayable when the research and development objective has been met and manufacturing or commercial use has begun.

Industry in the United States has, almost uniformly, not sought or received direct grants or subsidies from government to aid in performing its mission. In the case of US agriculture, of course, subsidies have become a common form of financing. US industry, on the other hand, has typically asked government for protection against unfair competition, domestic or foreign. And industry has consistently asked government not to burden it with excessive administrative and tax restraints on its ability to develop and market products and to earn adequate profits.

Fear of Government Help

Americans have traditionally feared the hand of government—even if extended in help—lest it might at some future date take advantage of its beneficence. The hand that bears the gift can wield the hatchet.

The author believes this is a sound tradition, based on solid principles. He thinks government handouts to the private sector should be rejected, except for the support of academic research, with the understanding that a close relationship will be engendered between industry and the academy. The additional government bureacracy required to operate handout programs is a burden one can well live without.

But, as an alternative, American industry—hand in hand with American academic science—must demand, must find a method to remove, the constraints on free enterprise and free intellectual inquiry that have been binding them for years.

It is delightful that the staff of The Joint Economic Committee of Congress, which was referred to earlier, has made recommendations that American business can endorse. The author hopes to see those recommendations acted upon by the new Administration and Congress, and what, it is hoped, will be a greatly remodelled government apparatus.

Recommendations

The author's recommendations are:

1. Expansion of the investment tax credit to cover R&D business expenditures

and to allow additional credit for investment in R&D structure and equipment. More favorable treatment should be given to firms who *increase* their levels of R&D spending.

2. Enactment of tax incentives for contributions made by individuals and corporations to research-oriented programs.

3. Provision of a tax exemption on capital gains from the sale of venture capital stock if the capital gains are reinvested in new R&D oriented businesses within a specified time period.

4. Increase in the amount of losses that can be deducted from ordinary income by an individual who invests in a new, high-technology company.

5. Continuing Federal support for academic research. Funding increases in real terms for a number of years will be necessary to compensate for substantial declines in this funding between 1968 and 1976 and for the soaring costs facing universities.

6. Federal assistance to universities to modernize their facilities for basic scientific research. A protracted period of low investment for research plant and equipment for universities has caused many installations to become obsolete and inadequate for current research projects.

7. Provisions that encourage personal savings. Such provisions could exclude a greater amount of interest income from taxation and decrease the tax rate on capital gains.

8. A change in the Section 861 regulation to relieve domestic R&D operations from the onerous burden that this Treasury Department regulation imposes upon them. There are several alternative ways by which such a change can be made, but made it must be.

9. A complete, methodical and swift evaluation of those regulatory agencies and those regulations that impede America's ability to innovate and compete with its innovations in foreign markets, followed promptly by the elimination of such regulations and/or agencies.

In conclusion, what is needed now in the United States, and the author has great confidence that it will come, is a new understanding of the importance of innovation in the lives of all Americans, and its *central* importance to the continuation—indeed, the survival—of the US free economy.

Technology In Society

New York / Oxford / Toronto / PERGAMON PRESS / Paris / Frankfurt / Sydney

Technology In Society, Vol. 3, pp. 107–111 (1981)
Printed in the USA. All rights reserved.

Venture Capital, Technology and Taxes

Reid W. Dennis

Throughout history men and women with adventurous spirits have been willing to accept the exposure to inordinate risks in return for the promise of extraordinary rewards. The discovery of America in 1492 was essentially "a venture capital" project, although Christopher Columbus may have lacked some of the attributes of today's skilled professional managers and Queen Isabella of Spain probably did not consider herself a venture capitalist when she used the royal jewels to finance the voyage. In the United States, the venture capital "industry" began to emerge during World War II and its development accelerated in the immediate postwar period as the electronic age burst forth upon the nation.

The earliest participants in venture capital investments were primarily wealthy individuals who operated either individually or through pooled family funds, with the Rockefeller, Phipps and Whitney families setting the example. The institutionalization of the industry began in 1946 with the organization of the American Research and Development Corporation of Boston, financed in part by the John Hancock Mutual Life Insurance Company and the Rosenwald family. However, it was not until 12 years later with the passage of the Small Business Investment Act of 1958 that the banks and insurance companies began to participate in the industry in a meaningful way. From 1960 through 1962 approximately 585 Small Business Investment Company (SBIC) licenses were approved and more than $200 million in private capital was raised to finance their operation.

The SBICs were off to a fast start, but disappointment set in almost immediately. Investor expectations were unreasonable, and managements lacked experience as well as an appreciation of the discipline required in the venture investment process. There was too much emphasis on short-term results, particularly by the publicly held SBICs, and the industry was burdened by cumbersome and excessive government regulation. Unfavorable economic conditions and a weak stock

Reid W. Dennis is Managing Partner of Institutional Venture Partners, Menlo Park, California, and a Director and Past President of the National Venture Capital Association. From 1952 until 1973 he was active in the investment operations of Firemen's Fund Insurance Company, San Francisco, and the American Express Company. He resigned as President of the American Express Investment Management Company in 1974 in order to form Institutional Venture Associates; Institutional Venture Partners was formed in 1980. Active in the venture capital investment field for 30 years, Mr. Dennis is director of a number of corporations.

market also contributed to poor financial performance and investors rapidly grew disenchanted. Indeed, the infant industry almost died in the process of being born.

Partly in response to the difficulties facing the SBICs, in the mid-1960s and early 1970s a number of new private venture capital firms were formed. These new firms — which did not require governmental approval and, therefore, avoided the attendant regulations — were almost all formed as limited partnerships, although a few of the largest firms were structured as corporations. Their professional managers were often technically trained, possessed master's degrees in business administration, and had usually gained considerable investment experience working for other financial organizations. Their investors included insurance companies, pension funds, major corporations, foundations, endowments, wealthy individuals and families. It is these independent, private venture capital firms that today represent the core of the venture capital industry, and it is these firms that over the past decade have been the most active in the financing of emerging, innovative, high-technology enterprises.

The relative importance of the private firms in the industry is shown in Table 1.

Although the data for the early years are sketchy, it is believed that the total capital committed to the industry remained relatively static during the period from 1969 through 1977 and ranged from approximately $2.5 billion to $3 billion. Thus, the $4.5 billion as of December 31, 1980, represents a gain of 50% or more in the total capital committed during the past three years. However, during this same period, the capital committed to the independent private firms has increased at least 150%.

Resurgence of the Private Sector

There are several reasons for the dramatic resurgence of the independent private sector of the industry. Certainly the outstanding investment record of some of the major firms has become more visible, at least in part, as some of their more successful portfolio companies have completed their initial public offerings. Over the past seven or eight years, a number of leading venture capital partnerships have achieved an internal rate of return on their investor's funds of 24–40%, and a few have even exceeded that range. Such results compare very favorably to the rates of return that have generally been achieved in marketable securities and, of course, far outstrip the results obtained by investing in high-grade medium and long-term bonds.

A venture capital investment typically involves a commitment for four to eight years with little or no liquidity along the way and with the probability that additional funds will be required from time to time before success can be assured. Because of the very long-term nature of the investment, the venture investor often will be actively involved in providing advice and counsel to the management of the enterprise, either informally or through participation on the company's board of directors. To quote one West Coast venture capitalist: "Venture capital investors are different from other types of investors in that they get to blow on the dice!"

The venture capital investor's principal objective can be simply stated: to

**TABLE 1. Total Capital Committed to the Organized Venture Capital Industry
(Estimate at December 31, 1980)**

Independent Private Venture Capital Firms	$1.8 billion
Small Business Investment Companies	1.4 billion
Corporate Subsidiaries (Financial and Non-Financial)	1.3 billion
Total	$4.5 billion

Source: Venture Capital Journal

achieve — over an extended period of time — a significantly above-average rate of return on invested assets through both realized and unrealized long-term capital gains. As a result, the most meaningful incentive for investors, investment managers and entrepreneurs alike has been the existence of substantial *differential* between the maximum tax rate on realized long-term capital gains and the maximum rate on ordinary income. Table 2 shows that this differential has varied widely over the past 18 years.

The differential between the two key tax rates declined substantially from 3.6 times in 1963 to 1.4 times in 1977. This decline had a demoralizing effect on the attitude of investors toward investments promising long-term capital gains. The effect was further amplified as investors realized that much of the gain was the result of inflation. Thus, not only did investors have to cope with inflation, but, in addition, they had to pay a heavy tax on inflation. Under these conditions, investors shifted their emphasis toward the generation of current income. Indeed, the entire nation shifted its emphasis toward consumption rather than production.

Would-be entrepreneurs in senior and middle management positions in established companies were also discouraged from venturing forth into new enterprises. The changing rates on capital gains and the 50% limitation on personal service income evolved to the point that the maximum tax rate on these two very different forms of remuneration were essentially the same. In 1977 and 1978 there was little incentive to give up a well-paying position and risk a successful career in order to join a young struggling company — no matter how promising its future might be!

A Major Reversal

The Tax Reform Act of 1978, which emerged from the debate generated by the "Steiger Amendment," marked a major reversal in the long-term trend of tax policy. As a result, the differential in rates shown in Table 2 actually increased significantly from 1.4 times to 2.5 times, and several bills currently before the 97th Congress hold the promise that the differential may be widened still further to approximately 3.0 times. The change in rates enacted in 1978, more than any other single factor, has had a dramatic impact on the venture capital industry. Table 3 shows that, during the past three years, the private sector of the industry has had new capital committed to it at an unprecedented rate. This table shows that the total new private capital committed during the past three years ($1,789

TABLE 2. Maximum Incremental Federal Tax Rate for Individuals

Taxable Year	(A) % Long-Term Capital Gains	(B) % Personal Service Income	(C) % Ordinary[a] or Unearned Income[b]	Differential (C) ÷ (A)
1963	25	N.A.[c]	91	3.6 x
1965	25	N.A.[c]	70	2.8 x
1970	35	50	70	2.0 x
1977	49	50	70	1.4 x
1979	28	50	70	2.5 x

[a]1969 and prior years
[b]1970 and subsequent years
[c]Not applicable

TABLE 3. Estimated Fundings and Disbursements
(Millions of Dollars)

Year	New Private Capital Committed to Venture Capital Firms	Disbursements to Portfolio Companies	Initial Public Offerings of Companies with Net Worth of $5 Million or Less	
			Number	Amount
1969	$171	$ 450	698	$1,367
1970	97	350	198	375
1971	95	410	248	551
1972	62	425	409	896
1973	56	450	69	160
1974	57	350	9	16
1975	10	250	4	16
1976	50	300	29	145
1977	39	400	13	43
1978	570	550	21	89
1979	319	1,000	46	183
1980	900	1,000	135	820

Source: Venture Capital Journal

million) was almost four times the total committed during the previous eight years ($466 million). This veritable flood of new capital has resulted in a record rate of disbursements into portfolio companies. At no time in its history has the organized venture capital industry ever been more active than it has been during the past 12 months. If past experience is a reliable guide, this recent high level of investment activity will result in the creation of many of the nation's most rapidly growing enterprises during the decade of the 1980s and beyond.

Table 3 also shows that the climate for initial public offerings of securities of small companies has improved during the past three years. This is also vital to the venture capital process, for ultimate liquidity is an important objective of both investors and entrepreneurs. To the extent that the public market is available, small companies have the opportunity to raise the additional capital they require and still remain independent. When the public market is not available, a merger with a larger and financially stronger firm may be the only course of action open to the small company in order to satisfy the requirements, both for liquidity for its shareholders and additional capital for its growth.

The good health of the public securities market can be very fragile and is particularly affected by the moods and emotions of investors. Euphoria sometimes follows a change in national administration; depression often accompanies an unexpected crisis; the forces of greed and fear are constantly pitted against one another. It is futile to try to protect public investors against themselves, but both corporate managers and securities underwriters need to act responsibly in order to treat public investors fairly. The wild price gyrations of some recent public securities offerings raise large caution flags. Certain of these new issues are going to have a difficult — if not impossible — task in living up to investor expectations indicated by their extremely high prices. There is little or no room for error or unforeseen delays, and one may wonder if some companies are not "going public" before they are ready to assume the heavy responsibility that accompanies such a course of action.

Clearly, the recent changes in capital gains tax rates have improved the risk/reward ratio for both investors and entrepreneurs. The proposed changes now being considered, if enacted, will further lower the barriers to capital transactions and will result in the still more efficient reallocation of capital to its most productive use. Additional progress has also been made in the liberalization of S.E.C. Rule 144 pertaining to the sale of securities acquired in private transactions, and the Department of Labor has revised its proposed Plan Asset Regulation, permitting pension funds to once again invest more freely in venture capital firms.

Disincentives Still Remain

The venture capital process is beginning to work extremely well, but enormous disincentives to investment and personal risk-taking still remain. The 70% tax rate on investment income, the double taxation of dividends, the partial exclusion of the deductibility of capital losses and investment interest expense, and the punitive tax treatment of stock options are all candidates for revisions and all would have a beneficial effect on the nation's economy.

The tax rates on long-term capital gains should be reduced and the "differential" referred to in Table 2 increased still further. In both Germany and Japan capital gains tax rates are essentially zero, and the personal savings rate is three to five times that enjoyed by this country. In an era when the United States lags the leading industrial nations of the world in the rate of capital formation and productivity increase, in an era when it desperately needs to put more people to work, it would appear to be very poor national policy to retain a capital gains tax rate that is significantly higher than that of its principal competitors in world markets. As a nation, there is still so very much to be done!

Technology In Society

New York / Oxford / Toronto / PERGAMON PRESS / Paris / Frankfurt / Sydney

Technology In Society, Vol. 3, pp. 113–121 (1981)
Printed in the USA. All rights reserved.

0160-791X/81/010113-09$02.00/0

Removing the False Assumptions from Economic Policymaking

J. Peter Grace

For far too long, Congressional policymakers have approached tax cuts as static phenomena resulting in revenue losses. The widespread underlying assumption connected with this approach is that *tax revenues* move proportionately and in the same direction as tax *rates*. Raise rates, it is assumed, and revenues go up. Lower rates, and revenues go down.

Raising the question of tax cuts leads almost inevitably to arguments about how to divide a remaining smaller pie; how to allocate fewer *revenue* dollars brought about by cuts in tax *rates*. In all of this, too little is being said about the stimulative effects tax cuts have on investment—and, therefore, on technology and jobs.

The author's worry is that the United States is losing valuable time needed to recoup the loss which has already occurred in its national technological posture vis-à-vis other industrial countries.

Two Significant Quotes

The United States has the highest percentage of obsolete plants, the lowest percentage of capital investment, and the lowest growth in productivity and savings of any major industrial country. (Federal Trade Commission)

An astonishing total of 130,000 cases of alleged fraud and related illegal acts have been found in 21 major departments and agencies over a two-and-a-half-year period. The fact that most of this information comes from field offices, with little awareness of these problems in Washington, indicates weakness in policy level oversight. (US General Accounting Office)

As Table 1 shows, the number of scientists and engineers measured as a portion of the US labor force (number per 10,000 persons) has sunk to 57.4 in 1977 from

J. Peter Grace is Chairman and Chief Executive Officer of W.R. Grace & Co. with whom he has been associated since 1936. He is a Director of Citicorp and Citibank, N.A., Kennecott Copper Corporation, Ingersoll-Rand Company, Stone and Webster, Inc., Branscan Limited, and Milliken & Company. Mr. Grace is also a Trustee of the Atlantic Mutual Insurance Company and Chairman and Director of Chemed Corporation, and serves as a member of the Development Committee of the National Bureau of Economic Research, Inc., and a Director of the International Center for Economic Policy Studies.

TABLE 1. The Research and Development Effort

	Scientists and Engineers per 10,000 Persons in the Labor Force			R&D Spending as % of GNP		
	1965	1977	% Incr./(Decr.) 1965–1977	1964	1977	% Incr./(Decr.) 1964–1977
(1) Germany	22.6	40.5	79.2	1.6	2.3	43.8
(2) Japan	24.6	49.9	102.8	1.5	1.9	26.7
(3) France	21.0	29.9	42.4	1.8	1.8	—
(4) U.K.	21.4	32.8	53.3	2.3	2.0	(13.0)
(5) U.S.	64.1	57.4	(10.5)	3.0	2.3	(23.3)

64.1 in 1965. Germany, Japan, France and the UK show significant increases for the same period.

The data also reveal a similar pattern in research and development spending, measured as a percentage of the gross national product. For the 1965–1977 period, the US percentage has declined 23.3%.

Not surprisingly, the US balance of patents with (other) major countries has suffered a deterioration in this environment (see Table 2).

The concern is that national policymakers are failing to grasp the stimulative potential of targeted tax cuts designed to get investment in new technology going again.

The most notable gap is the failure to address the role of capital formation and its necessary relationship to the impact of tax rates on investment.

The US economy will continue to underproduce until this troublesome assumption is rejected.

Taxing the Vitality Out of the National Technological Posture

The present tax structure is a failure because the US has not, first, attended to the overblown role and size of government, and it is destructive of the capital formation and investment process.

To quote one responsible politician, Congressman Jack F. Kemp:

If you tax something, you get less of it. If you subsidize something, you get more of it. The problem with the United States today is that we tax work, savings, thrift, production, capital, and we subsidize non-work, welfare and consumption.

As shown by Figure 1, US taxes on capital are contrary to practices of most developed nations and, predictably, performance of its economy has been relatively poor.

The maximum tax in 1978 on capital gains in the United States was 49.1%. In Japan, France, the Netherlands, Australia, Belgium, Italy and Germany, there is no such tax.

TABLE 2. The U.S. Balance of Patents With Major Countries

	Patents Granted By Foreign Countries to U.S. Inventors	Patents Granted By the U.S. to Foreign Inventors	Patents Granted to U.S. Inventors vs. Patents Granted to Foreign Inventors	
			Number	Ratio
(1) 1966	58,905	13,706	45,199•	4.3X
(2) 1971	61,822	22,192	39,630	2.8
(3) 1976	40,967	25,516	15,451	1.6
(4) %Change 1966–1976	**(30.5)%**	**86.2%**	**(65.8)%**	

The result? For four critical measures of economic growth over the long term—average investment as a percentage of GNP; government spending (excluding transfer payments) as a percentage of GNP; productivity growth, and real economic growth overall—the US ranks worst.

In the US, average investment as a percentage of GNP is 17.5%. Government spending (excluding transfer payments) as a percentage of GNP is 21.4%. The annual productivity growth rate is 2.7%. Real economic growth *per annum* is 3.5%.

In Japan, average investment as a percentage of GNP is 32.0%. Government spending (excluding transfer payments) as a percentage of GNP is 8.8%. The annual productivity growth rate is 8.2%. Real economic growth *per annum* is 8.3%.

In Germany, average investment as a percentage of GNP is 24.6%. Government spending (excluding transfer payments) as a percentage of GNP is 16.9%. The annual productivity growth rate is 5.4%. Real economic growth *per annum* is 3.7%.

The correlation is obvious. Taxes on capital formation in the US have led to slow economic growth. Bigger, costlier government—the natural outcome of the private sector's inability to perform adequately under such circumstances—has compounded the problem.

The OPEC Myth

One hears a lot about how OPEC threw the US into the current recession, but the countries described above depend far more heavily on imported oil than does the US (see Table 3).

Germany and Japan, for example, depend two and three times, respectively, on foreign oil compared with the US.

Japan's foreign-oil dependence is especially noteworthy because as Figure 1 demonstrates, Japan nevertheless significantly exceeds the US in rates of investment, productivity and GNP growth—and manages to hold government expenditures in line.

		(1)	(2)	(3)	(4)	(5)
		Average Investment As % of GNP	Government Spending(a) As % of GNP	Productivity	Real GNP	1978 Maximum Capital Gains Tax
		1962–1978				
				(Avg. Ann. % Increase)		
(1)	Japan	32.0 %	8.8 %	8.2 %	8.3 %	0 %
(2)	France	22.8	13.2	5.5	4.7	0
(3)	Netherlands	23.6	16.0	6.8	4.4	0
(4)	Australia	25.4	13.2	3.3	4.4	0
(5)	Belgium	21.7	14.1	7.0	4.2	0
(6)	Italy	20.7	13.7	5.2	3.9	0
(7)	Germany	24.6	16.9	5.4	3.7	0
(8)	United States	17.5	21.4	2.7	3.5	49.1 %

(a) Federal, state and local current spending excluding transfer payments and capital spending.

FIGURE 1. The Disincentivization of America.

Japan Versus U.S.

83% Higher Investment Rate
59% Lower Gov't Expenditures
3X Productivity Growth
137% Higher GNP Growth

As the data above show, Japan's investment rate is 83% higher than the US's. Government expenditures are 59% lower in terms of their portion of the economy. Productivity growth exceeds the US's by three times. The Japanese economy is growing 137% times faster than ours. It's time the US faced the real problem.

TABLE 3. Oil Import Dependence (Second Half 1979)

	Value of Oil Imports as % of Value of Energy Consumption	Value of Oil Imports as % of Value of Total Exports	
		Amount	Rank
(1) Japan	74.0	32.6	2
(2) Italy	67.0	18.5	3
(3) France	59.0	16.0	4
(4) Germany	53.0	11.0	5
(5) U.S.	21.0	32.9	1

The No-Growth Social Theory

Proposals to cut capital gains taxes in order to unlock investment and get the economy going again are often described as "windfalls for millionaires and two bits for the average taxpayer" (see Table 4).

While it is widely assumed that the "millionaires" are walking away with all the capital gains, the fact is that 65% of the capital gains in this country are made by persons with adjusted gross incomes of $25,000 or less. Thirty-five percent of the capital gains are made by persons with adjusted gross incomes of more than $25,000.

Policymakers are indulging in too much rhetoric and too little substance, spending too much time allocating the fruits of the past instead of permitting private enterprise to find the best way to produce the fruits of the future.

"Smart Money"

The basic problem comes out clearly in Table 5, showing what happens to the after-tax value of an investment over the average holding period of 7.2 years, under varying inflation rates and varying pre-tax profits.

Suppose such an investor has a $5,000 profit on a $10,000 investment for the 7.2-year period in question. That would be a 50% nominal gain. Enter inflation and the 28% maximum tax rate in effect today on long-term capital gains. What seems like a handsome nominal profit is in fact an after-tax loss in real dollars. The only variable is the inflation rate—or how much one loses.

At 5% inflation, the real-dollar loss is $609. At 13%—a rate hardly unfamiliar—the loss is greater than the investment itself, $10,508.

At 13% inflation, a *100% gain* on $10,000—$10,000—translates to a real-dollar loss of $6,908 for the average holding period at current tax rates.

Even if one is a genius and miraculously turns $10,000 into $25,000 — a $15,000, 150% profit — one still loses $3,308.

These effects are bad enough on individual investors, but, as shown in Table 6, look what has happened to capital formation by small companies.

TABLE 4. Percent Distribution of Capital Gains Taxpayers for Two Income Groups*

	Percentage of Individuals With Adjusted Gross Incomes Under $25,000	Percentage of Individuals With Adjusted Gross Incomes Over $25,000
(1) 1966	87.9	12.1
(2) 1967	85.8	14.2
(3) 1968	87.6	12.4
(4) 1969	88.0	12.0
(5) 1970	87.4	12.6
(6) 1971	84.8	15.2
(7) 1972	82.2	17.8
(8) 1973	79.2	20.8
(9) 1974	77.8	22.2
(10) 1975	75.1	24.9
(11) 1976	70.6	29.4
(12) 1977	66.7	33.3
(13) 1978	65.0	35.0

*This, despite President Carter's statement that the Capital Gains Tax cut was a windfall for millionaires and two-bits for the average taxpayer.

TABLE 5. Real Investment Results Over 7.2 Years* With a 28% Nominal Capital Gains Tax Rate

Percentage of Annual Inflation Rate	Results from a $10,000 Investment		
	Nominal Pretax Gain		
(1)	$ 5,000 50% Profit	$ 10,000 100% Profit	$ 15,000 150% Profit
	Real After-Tax Profit/(Loss)		
(2) 5	$ (609)	$ 2,991	$ 6,591
(3) 6	(1,613)	1,987	5,587
(4) 7	(2,677)	923	4,523
(5) 8	(3,804)	(204)	3,396
(6) 9	(4,998)	(1,398)	2,202
(7) 10	(6,262)	(2,662)	938
(8) 11	(7,600)	(4,000)	(400)
(9) 12	(9,014)	(5,414)	(1,814)
(10) 13	**(10,508)**	**(6,908)**	**(3,308)**
(11) 15	(13,754)	(10,154)	(6,554)
(12) 20	(23,563)	(19,963)	(16,363)

This is after getting the Federal Capital Gains Tax reduced to 28% from the previous 49.1% and the 50.5% President Carter wanted, and does not include state and local taxes.
*According to the U.S. Treasury Department, 7.2 years it the average holding period for securities.

A decade ago, when inflation was a fourth of what it is today, the then-approximately equivalent tax rate on capital gains allowed the smaller, technology-intensive companies to grow.

In 1969, 698 new issues, by companies with a net worth under $5 million, raised $2.9 billion in constant 1980 dollars. That was the peak year.

The following year, a doubled capital gains tax rate went into effect. Immediately, the amount of new capital raised by these companies fell to $375 million and reached a low of $42.6 million in 1977.

The passage of The Revenue Act of 1978 lowered the maximum capital gains tax to 28%, in spite of President Carter's recommendation to increase it to 50.5%. Even with an exacerbated inflation problem, the results have been extremely stimulative.

According to the latest data, the number of new issues for the first 11 months of 1980 is up 414.3% from the corresponding 1978 level.

While it is acknowledged that small companies are an important source of new technology and also heavily dependent upon healthy conditions for investor risk-taking, what's often overlooked is their role in the economy. Simply put, small companies employ the bulk of America's workers (see Table 7).

As a percentage of total new jobs, 66% come from firms with 20 or fewer

TABLE 6. Equity Capital (millions of $) Raised by Companies Having a Net Worth of Under $5 Million

Year	No. of Offerings	Funds Raised	
		Current $	Constant 1980 $
(1) 1968	358	$ 745.3	$1,643.3
(2) 1969	698	1,366.9	2,869.5
(3) 1970	198	375.0	747.3
(4) 1971	248	550.9	1,044.5
(5) 1972	409	896.0	1,631.2
(6) 1973	69	159.7	274.8
(7) 1974	9	16.1	25.3
(8) 1975	4	16.2	23.2
(9) 1976	29	144.8	197.0
(10) 1977	13	42.6	54.8
(11) 1978	21[a]	89.3[b]	106.9
(12) 1979	46	182.9	201.1
(13) 1980 (11 Months)	108[a]	631.9[b]	631.9

[a]Up by 414.3%
[b]Up by 607.6%

J. Peter Grace

TABLE 7. Net New Jobs Created By Size of Firm, 1969–1976

Number of Employees In Each Firm	Northeast	Midwest	West	South	Total United States
(1) 20 or Fewer	727,771	1,125,154	1,070,803	1,536,087	4,459,815
(2) 21–50	26,555	201,421	208,717	322,816	759,509
(3) 51–100	(71,588)	87,876	113,909	158,800	288,997
(4) 101–500	(136,629)	51,781	167,214	270,835	353,201
(5) 501 +	(135,219)	208,050	239,469	585,081	897,381
(6) Total	410,890	1,674,282	1,800,112	2,873,619	6,758,903
			As % Of Total New Jobs		
(7) 20 or Fewer	177.1	67.2	59.5	53.5	**66.0***
(8) 21–50	6.5	12.0	11.6	11.2	**11.2***
(9) 51–100	(17.4)	5.2	6.3	5.5	**4.3***
(10) 101–500	(33.3)	3.1	9.3	9.4	5.2
(11) 501 +	(32.9)	12.4	13.3	20.4	13.3

*81.5% in firms of 100 employees or fewer.

employees. Slightly more than 11% come from firms with 21–50 employees. Another 4.3% come from firms with 51–100 employees.

Net net, 81.5% of the new jobs created in America are with firms employing 100 persons or less.

We can talk all we like about investors who are being decapitalized by high tax rates and inflation, but what about America's workers? The egalitarianists are enforcing their no-growth moral code with America's jobs.

In net, there is no basis for any capital gains tax. By definition such taxes reduce the capital formation process which is so essential to attaining adequate productivity and economic growth. Thus, on grounds of inflationary conditions that exist and persist, as well as the dictates of philosophically sound economic policy, the capital gains tax should be eliminated completely.

Can the advocates of increased or unlowered capital gains taxes justify the price of this incorrectly premised morality? The price is jobs.

Technology In Society

New York / Oxford / Toronto / PERGAMON PRESS / Paris / Frankfurt / Sydney

Technology In Society, Vol. 3, pp. 123–139 (1981)
Printed in the USA. All rights reserved.

0160-791X/81/010123-17$02.00/0

Toward a US Tax Policy for Innovative Labor

Alvin Jay Harman

A labor component has been overlooked in the portfolio of policies for stimulating industrial innovation in the United States. This is not to say that labor interests have been ignored. Rather, much of the attention has been devoted to defensive strategies (*e.g.,* worker health and safety) and to the fostering of a "healthy" macroeconomic climate for encouraging both innovation and full employment.

Such policies are important, as is encouraging new capital format, if the US is to have a dynamic economy in which, over the course of decades, useful new products and services are created. But especially during the early formation of industries, *individuals* with special talents, vision, and zeal are needed. Most often during the past half century or so, their talent and vision have been exercised in the context of the organized application of science and technology for economic, social, or other societal benefit.

This paper will explore a tax policy for the direct encouragement of such individuals engaged in innovative processes and for the indirect support of their enterprises. Its advantages and drawbacks are discussed with the intention of encouraging more thorough consideration of the best way to formulate and implement such a policy.

Innovation and Infant Industries

In past decades and centuries, temporary tariff barriers for infant industries made sense to protect the firms' growth within domestic markets. An "infant industry" is one in which "a line of production is subject to increasing returns or decreasing costs based on external economies, imperfect knowledge, or learning by doing."[1]

The views expressed in this paper should not be interpreted as those of Rand, of IIASA, nor of either institution's research sponsors.

Alvin Jay Harman is a research scholar at the International Institute for Applied Systems Analysis, Laxenburg, Austria, on leave from the Rand Corporation where he was Program Director for R&D and Acquisition Studies from 1972 to 1975. At Rand he led and conducted research on domestic and national security topics related to technological innovation spanning several economic sectors: aerospace, computers, machine tools, medical technology, and the diverse "lower tiers" of the defense industrial base. At IIASA he is contributing to the development of an international collaborative network for the analysis of the process of technological innovation and of governmental policies that affect it.

A tariff would allow producers to attain more efficient production levels; if the policy were used appropriately, eventually the tariff would be removed — when the country's firms were no longer in their "infancy" stage.

In a dynamic world, it is essential to distinguish between two types of infant industries: the industry just being developed in a particular country but already existing elsewhere, and the *new* industry — developing for the first time. The former includes both the diffusion of technologies among the developed countries and technology and industrial transfers to the less developed world. The latter occurs less frequently. Historical examples include the textile and iron and steel industries in the United Kingdom in the 18th and 19th centuries, and the automobile and computer industries in the United States in the 20th century. Public policy for "infant industries" of the "new" type is the subject of this paper. For the occasional and temporary encouragement of such industries today, the mobility of labor and capital across national boundaries and the development of a more integrated world economy make the tariff barrier policy undesirable and ineffective.

Economists have frequently pointed out that a *subsidy* to the firms in the infant industry would also achieve the desired result. But direct transfer payments from government to firms is a textbook solution, not a practical policy alternative. The electronics industry in the 1940s and 1950s — during its "infancy" — received substantial US government backing in the form of Defense Department funds for product development and — even more importantly — procurement of the final products.[2] But future new industries — such as for solar energy or biotechnologies — may not produce products of use to the Defense Department.

To formulate an effective public policy for encouragement of new industries, one must first identify what it is that needs encouragement. In particular, should individual product developments receive support — *e.g.*, through government procurements, patent policy, etc. — or is another form of backing more appropriate? In an extensive analysis of the computer industry, the author has shown that, from a theoretical standpoint, the firm rather than the individual product deserves primary attention.[3] Recently, much has been said and written about both the complexities of the industrial innovation process within the firm, and of the many governmental policies that affect it. This paper concentrates on the special aspects of the personnel needed by the firm in a new industry, and on a public policy designed to encourage such labor and to indirectly subsidize such firms. Several features of the work environment of the firm deserve consideration before the specific policy proposal can be discussed.

Creative Teamwork

The importance of a broad and coordinated spectrum of talents for the success of industrial inovation has been widely discussed in the literature. Of course, this includes the R&D teams such as those organized around rare talents — for example, Gene Amdahl (IBM) or Seymour Cray (CDC) in the computer industry, each of whom ultimately formed his own company. R&D teams are instrumental both to the development of new ideas and to a firm's ability to adapt innovations developed elsewhere. The latter process has major significance for the economies of nations; for example, it has been important to Japan's competitive entry into the world market for computers.

But the teamwork in innovative firms transcends the R&D team. IBM achieved its dominance in the computer industry in the late 1950s—a decade after the founding of the first "computer" companies and well after larger firms like GE had become active. IBM's success rested on shrewd marketing and support policies and capabilities. Decades of research on innovation have confirmed the generality of this experience—R&D may be necessary to participation in "high-technology" industries, but the marketplace also plays a critical role in successful innovation.[4] To anticipate the needs of the ultimate users, marketing efforts and the product planning and development processes must be highly interactive. To encourage innovation, it would be insufficient by itself to simply subsidize R&D.

Appropriability

Research on industrial innovation has been rightly concerned with whether, and for how long, *firms* can capture the returns of their innovative investments. Less attention has been given to whether the personnel within a firm can capture the full returns of their efforts. Based on his research in connection with US versus IBM, Fisher has observed that R&D teams specifically, and managerial skills generally, may not receive the full returns for their added efficiency—especially in large firms dealing with complicated and delicate technologies.[5]

In the past, good teams could "spin off" from larger firms, as did the Control Data Corporation from Sperry Rand's UNIVAC Division (surviving a law suit in the process). The semi-conductor industry is replete with such examples. But the tax climate has turned less favorable to new business formations in the last decade (*e.g.*, changes in capital gains taxation; removal of the qualified stock option). Such formations may be particularly difficult for new, high-technology firms, which are particularly dependent on the availability of venture capital.[6] Thus, past public policy has changed the climate for *new entry* into technology-based industries. Even in the case of the Amdahl Corporation, an individual with a commanding international reputation suffered extreme difficulties and frustrations forming a successful company during the 1970s—not over technical but over financial uncertainties.[7]

One expects uncertainties for such ventures, of course. But the government-induced reductions in the opportunity for high-technology teams to strike out in new businesses has also constrained the ability of such teams to capture the full returns of their efforts.

Risk and Return

Unlike the above problem of insufficient "entry" into an industry, there are also personal costs of inadvertent "exit"—high failure rates of high-technology firms, especially small ones. this is partly a consequence of the life-cycle of industries. Many small firms in the semi-conductor industry are being squeezed out as larger capital investments are required, whereas new firms are still prominent in solar energy[8] as well as the newly developing "bioindustries."

Of course, the high risks of these businesses are compensated for, at least in theory (with many specific success stories to support it), by high financial returns. Such careful empirical work as has been done *suggests* that the returns to society at the margin (of encouraging more innovation) are higher than the returns to the firm itself.[9] If this result were conclusive, a public subsidy would be warranted. But the results to date are merely suggestive, based on small, selective samples and individual cases.

Leaving aside the question of adequate reward to the firms for innovative risks, firms do fail—especially small ones. For capitalists, the tax code provides some compensation for losses. But when firms fail, people lose jobs. Not all high job mobility in the semi-conductor industry results from a desire for change. Unemployment insurance provides a temporary relief for many individuals, and others find attractive opportunities quickly. Still, it is important to ask whether the risks taken by individuals in innovative *new* industries provide the society at large with benefits that may deserve additional public encouragement.

To address this question, another brief excursion into economic theory will be useful. Most of the time economic activity involves what Joseph Schumpeter described as "the circular flows of economic life"—agricultural processes and businesses operating in well-known ways to satisfy well-known needs by methods handed down from past generations.[10] Neoclassical economic theory provides a parsimonious and often powerful explanation of economic behavior of this sort. But at infrequent intervals new directions of economic affairs become opportune. Who would have included the computer as an important element of economic life in a 30-year technological forecast from the late 1930s?

Today the importance of information technologies is appreciated, but what innovations may occur in five or 10 years that will provide for further opportunities (and challenges) to man's capacity for improving the well-being of society and its members? Burton Klein has effectively argued that an economic system needs a capacity both for "dynamic efficiency"—in which new opportunities and directions of economic affairs are surfaced—as well as the more traditional kinds of efficiency within the "circular flow." Dynamic efficiency is best achieved by encouraging a diversity of activities at the micro-economic level. For this type of "dynamic competition" to occur, *risk takers* are required.[11]

Thus, technological innovation can yield new industries which provide society with useful products and capabilities. They also provide the economy with new opportunities for employment and with an improved competitive position in world markets. When individuals—including technical specialists and those in production, sales, and management—must function in a world fraught with risk and uncertainty to develop such infant industries, they must be allowed generous current compensation for their activities.

Proposal to Encourage Innovative Labor

Many ingredients and actions are needed to launch an innovative enterprise successfully in a new industry. In particular, the conceptual legitimacy for temporary public subsidy during the "infant industry" state, and the need for risk-taking, creative individuals who receive the full returns for their efforts were discussed above. Thus, to encourage innovative labor for such enterprises, consider the following proposal:

> *Grant a temporary personal income tax credit on wages and salaries earned by individuals employed by highly R&D-intensive, for-profit firms.*

This proposal would make selective use of the personal income tax system to provide a direct subsidy to "innovative labor," identified as personnel—whether in laboratories, in production, in sales, or even in management—of firms intensively undertaking research and development (R&D).

Discussion of several clarifying details may be useful. There are existing practices of the Internal Revenue Service (IRS) for defining expenditures on R&D. Of course, the problems of drawing the line between R&D and various kinds of market development and promotion activities are non-trivial; these problems already exist for current favorable tax treatment of R&D. Following existing IRS practices on the measurement for R&D adds no new problems, and it simplifies the implementation of this aspect of the proposal.

"R&D intensity" can be measured as the proportion of a firm's R&D to its sales over some recent period—say two years for existing firms and at least two quarters for new firms. Some might prefer R&D per employee as a measure of intensity, but to encourage newly created small firms with very low initial sales, the former definition would be particularly desirable.

High R&D intensity could be handled by several levels of R&D intensity—*i.e.*, the greater the intensity, the larger the tax credit. The choice of levels of R&D intensity—perhaps 7%, 13%, and even 18%—and the size of the personal income tax credit—perhaps 10%, 20%, and 25% respectively—would deserve careful analytical attention to assess the likely reduction of tax revenues from the proposal and distribution of the initial impacts by sector of the economy and size of firm. Although *very* high R&D intensities are included, large, established firms would find it undesirable to commit such resources to R&D.[12]

Successful technological innovation requires a broad spectrum of activities to be performed; R&D is an important and highly leveraged investment, ordinarily consuming only a small percentage of the total resources involved. Very high R&D intensities would only make sense for newly established, technology-intensive ventures that have not yet achieved significant sales (assuming cheating on classifying expenditures can be controlled—a subject to which the author will return). The formation rate of such new firms has slumped significantly in the last decade.[13]

Finally, the proposal is for a *temporary* tax credit, to encourage the development of new industries through their "infancy" period. Since important benefits from this proposal would come through indirect effects, as discussed below, this temporary period should be at least a decade and perhaps as long as the life of a patent.

The immediate effect of this proposal would be to increase the take-home pay of all individuals employed by highly R&D intensive firms: a "reward" to *all* those within the firm whose efforts are necessary to successfully innovate. Not all activities will be successful, of course. And not all individuals will keep the reward, as will be discussed below.

The first argument favoring tax policy as the vehicle for this "reward" relates to costs of policy implementation. If one wants the initial benefits to accrue to all those regularly employed by innovative firms—those earning wages and salaries but excluding bonuses, commissions, and consulting fees—it would be enormously complex to provide this "reward" by any instrument other than the personal income tax system. The desirability of such direct benefits to the individuals can be justified partly on psychological grounds. What better way for the government to provide a tangible "reward" to thousands of individuals, in this virtually cashless society, than by a visible credit on the tax form that Americans take particularly seriously? The discussion below will clarify some other, more important, reasons for granting individuals some control over their "reward."

This "reward"is warranted for the "risk" and "appropriability" reasons discussed above. This proposal affords individuals increased take-home pay as a compensation for higher uncertainties that they personally face compared to those whose economic life is part of the customary "circular flow." It helps counter the "appropriability" problem by directly rewarding these individuals. Also, an employee may take the tax credit with him if he should decide to leave his firm to help found another (and the rate of tax credit may be even higher than he would qualify for in his original firm).

In this way, the proposed tax credit would provide encouragement similar to that which capital gains tax benefits provided to university-based scientists and engineers in the past, to stimulate the creation of new businesses.[14] The proposal also avoids the perverse distributional implications of many current capital gains tax proposals, which tend to provide tax relief mainly in high income tax brackets.[15]

Over time, some firms would undoubtedly *capture* benefits, for they could hire some services (*e.g.,* from unskilled workers) below previously prevailing (real) wage rates in various geographic areas. That is, many types of clerical and production line personnel may be willing to work for the same take-home pay as before; the tax credit would provide an indirect subsidy to firms. Is this undesirable? Certainly not! If such firms are expected to be as competitive as possible in regional, national and world markets, they must be encouraged to be cost-conscious in labor markets. And the (temporary) subsidy to the firm is itself justified by the "infant industry" argument.

Further Benefits of the Proposal

The principal features of this proposal—encouraging innovative labor for new industries and indirectly subsidizing the firms—have several additional aspects that deserve brief discussion.

Flexibility

The use of the personal income tax system as the mechanism for providing a reward/subsidy for innovative activity in new industries would produce very flexible incentives at the individual, firm, and national levels. For some individuals, the tax credit would provide a modest encouragement to strike out in a new enterprise; this would be especially effective if the size of the credit increases with R&D intensity, if an individual's current firm is not sufficiently R&D-intensive to qualify for the credit, or if the firm has captured the credit as an indirect subsidy. Thus, on one hand the credit would encourage the formation of new enterprises.

On the other hand, the policy would provide firms that capture some of the credit with additional working capital without requiring new investment. The proceeds of such subsidies could be used by the firm to hire more labor or to invest further in R&D, in capital equipment, or elsewhere as the firm sees fit — subject to existing regulatory and other governmental "guidance" to the firms, and to the future discipline of the marketplace.[16]

But most importantly, if the *right kind* of firms are selected — those venturing into *new industries* — on the basis of high R&D intensity (or by some other means as discussed below), they would essentially be using the subsidy to explore *new solutions* to the nation's economic challenges. And from a national perspective, it is not necessary to specify the most promising economic sectors.

Today it appears that the tax credit would encourage ventures in solar energy and the biotechnologies, but new discoveries will spark innovative activities that are not now foreseeable. Because the credit is restricted to a specified period of time (a decade or so) rather than to a particular size of firm, it would not discriminate against small firms that — through success — grow and provide larger economic benefits inherent in scale economies; this is the core of the infant-industry argument for such a subsidy. A well-tailored range of R&D intensities and tax credits may help small firms to rely on internal growth, rather than on the more secure sources of working capital from larger firms that might wish to acquire them.

National Security

Another aspect of the "flexibility" of the proposal does not involve the infant-industry motivation. Government-supported R&D has been deliberately included in the proposed calculation of R&D intensity, so a number of firms in the aerospace, electronics, and nuclear industries may qualify on the basis of this source of funding. This approach is desirable because the Department of Defense may face some serious impediments to industrial readiness in the event that an international crisis requires a large and sustained surge in defense-related industrial product. Research results several years ago indicated that a scarcity of *skilled labor* would be the most serious problem defense producers would face in meeting such a surge in military demands for high-technology products.[17] This potential deficiency has been missed by the DOD's Industrial Preparedness Planning Program with its emphasis on plant and equipment and on "planning" for thousands of individual final products. The proposed tax credit would help to attract more skilled labor into defense-related industries. And to the extent that an indirect subsidy to firms occurs, it may help the producers not currently involved in defense-related work to overcome the entry barriers arising out of military specifications and other specialized buying practices.

Training

An OECD assessment of long-term world economic development identified rigidities of labor markets in most of the developed countries as a central problem; the *Interfutures* report attributes some of the causes to current tax regulations.[18] To the extent that the proposed credit is captured as an indirect subsidy, real wages paid by firms would be lowered and new hiring would be encouraged. Such hiring would encourage new careers in highly innovative fields. Moreover, the firms may find it desirable to provide on-the-job training for their new recruits. This is not likely to involve formal programs in small, R&D-intensive firms, but the employees would find themselves in an environment particularly open to new ideas.

Also, such a tax credit would provide young people — in colleges and universities or just entering the job market — with "guideposts" to the sectors of industry and specialties that may have particularly promising, although riskier, futures. Recruiters for firms and student counselors could probably use information about the tax credit, including perhaps IRS-published indicators of fields with the greatest number of employees receiving the credit. Such "guideposts" would provide encouragement for those pursuing scientific and technical education to consider a broad range of possible careers.[19]

Palatability

For a proposed policy intervention to be effective, it must first be enacted. Thus *political palatability* must be considered. It seems clear from Congressional hearings and debates and parts of the President's 1978 Domestic Policy Review on Innovation that direct subsidy (or tax benefits) to business face some real political obstacles. For this reason, the indirect subsidy through labor looks attractive. Of course, since price "distortion" is involved, it is important to determine whether prices are *more* distorted before or after the change in tax policy. For the reasons already discussed, this tax credit proposal should help to lessen the distortion (and alleviate other elements of "non-market failure") that seems to be present. Moreover, the credit is certainly more intellectually palatable than many international protectionist policies to save declining industries. And it may be beneficial to delegate to the marketplace (for labor services) the ultimate distribution of the benefits of the proposal between labor and business. This vagueness regarding ultimate beneficiaries may be helpful to the process of forming coalitions necessary for political action.

Possible Deficiencies of Policy Implementation

Even the best-intentioned government interventions have costs, and opportunities for failure of government actions abound. Tax dollars are only one of many dimensions of the costs. Mistakes in implementation and unanticipated, perverse side effects can also have severe economic consequences. Seven perspectives on the limitations of the proposal are given below. Most do not question the conceptual arguments for encouraging "innovative labor" for new industries. But government cannot implement concepts — only explicitly articulated policies.

Policing/Enforcement

However carefully R&D expenditures and sales are defined, some firms will try to redefine their expenditures to give the appearance of higher R&D-intensity. Control of *cheating* is a difficult problem for many economic and social policies. The current tax code already has such difficulties with current expensing of R&D.

Attempts at universal review of firms claiming the tax credit for their employees could involve administrative costs greater than the potential benefits. Thorough review of large firms for major *changes* in R&D intensity from past reports could be undertaken, and smaller firms could be reviewed on a statistical sampling basis. Sizeable penalties for cheating should be specified — perhaps three times the value of the tax revenues involved (regardless of whether the firm captures the credit as a subsidy).

Existing Non-Pecuniary Incentives

Good teams of scientists enjoy working together and the challenges of their work, often with little expectation of large pecuniary benefits. Why give them a special tax break? Successful innovation requires an "innovation team" with a much broader range of talents. These include not just technologists but production engineering, marketing capabilities, and overall planning and management. Quality control "circles," the Japanese approach to quality control in manufacturing, is an example of teamwork in the production domain.[20]

Some individuals will already be satisfied with their pecuniary returns, and the tax credit will become an indirect subsidy to the firm. It has already been argued here that this is a desirable secondary effect of the tax proposal. However, some individuals — especially, for example, in sales — will respond when an *increase* in take-home pay can be achieved by working for a highly R&D-intensive firm. Since "demand pull" has been verified to be an important element in successful innovation, and since marketing and sales personnel provide an important link between the firm and the market needs, it is desirable that highly qualified and talented personnel be attracted to regular employment in firms in new industries.

Subsidizing Costs

Would it not be better to reward firms that successfully achieve certain outputs, rather than to reward/subsidize inputs? Reimbursement of "legitimate" costs in the defense sector often leads to an inclination to justify costs rather than to reduce them; similar incentives exist for the reimbursement of health care costs. A tax benefit related to high R&D costs might encourage firms to justify larger expenditures than would be socially desirable.

This danger provides one of the best reasons for implementing the tax credit with an explicit termination after a decade or some other long, but finite, period (a termination phase-out should be given careful consideration). The "infancy" period for new industries must not be allowed to become permanent.

If temporary, subsidizing of costs *is* preferable to rewarding successful outputs, for the former strategy supplements badly needed working capital for pursuing innovative activities. This occurs in part by the subsidy itself and in part by increasing the attractiveness of these firms for venture capital investments. To wait until successful output has been obtained is to ignore the critical role of uncertainty. Many sensibly planned and executed activities will undoubtedly fail. Society's benefit comes from the higher probability that successful new paths will be found through a diversity of attempts, and from the social returns from innovative activity.

Subsidizing Existing Employment

Initially, the tax credit would benefit those already employed in highly R&D-intensive firms, with little impact likely on their behavior. The principal reason for a rather long lifetime of the credit is that there are several important secondary effects that will take time to be realized.

First, one source of new entry is "existing" employment—by existing firms that decide to enter new industries or markets, or by individuals or teams employed by existing firms (or universities) that "spin off."[21] The latter may occur if the individuals either do not qualify for the tax credit or do not retain their "appropriate" share. Over the time period of the credit, the "training guideposts" discussed above would also yield *new* talent for industrial innovation. Moreover, reductions in wages for some skills and firms would result in new labor hired into these firms.

Finally, thousands of individual taxpayers would be reminded yearly on their income tax forms that they belong to teams that their society values. Even those whose take-home pay does not increase as a result of the tax credit can take pride in the visible dollars and cents of subsidy they are contributing to the success of their firm. This may sound like a trivial point, but the importance of developing a "team spirit" in complex, high-technology projects should not be underestimated; for example, observers have argued that team spirit is key to the industrial success of the Japanese.

Substitution Effects

Through the indirect subsidy, would this proposal cause firms to use more labor than desirable? Some of the price changes resulting from the proposal would *correct* previous market and non-market distortions (*e.g.*, on "appropriability" and "risk" grounds). But some wage-rate distortion would undoubtedly occur in this less than perfectly competitive world. Of course, policies such as accelerated depreciation lower the after-tax cost of capital—with similar possibilities for undesirable substitution effects favoring capital formation. A further danger worthy of attention is that the proposed credit would provide a subsidy to firms that could simply substitute public for private venture capital funds.

Here, short-run efficiency and macro-economic policies may be at odds with policies favoring long-run dynamic efficiency and international competitiveness. Further analysis will be needed to reveal the dimensions on which societal judgment may have to be made.

Subsidize Only "Usefully Innovative" Firms

High R&D intensity is really neither a necessary nor a sufficient condition for a firm to be an innovative contributor to a new industry. Why not limit the proposal to highly innovative firms that make socially useful accomplishments? By promoting socially useful innovations, this proposal would be undertaken in the context of a vast array of governmental regulations and actions tailored to promote certain social objectives and to limit certain social costs. Encouragement of innovation through this proposal would be guided and shaped by these other policy actions.

Even leaving aside the "useful" concern, some small firms in new industries, as in the solar energy field, are at an exploratory stage of product design and find it necessary to let their first users do some of the product testing.[22] And sometimes *users* of processes, rather than equipment manufacturers, are important innovators.[23]

Perhaps the proposal should seek to provide a tax credit only to employees of "highly innovative" enterprises, whether supplier or user. Two difficulties would immediately arise.

First, there is the intrinsic uncertainty of innovative activities. The Department of Defense has had the most extensive experience with attempting to back such enterprises, and has had the additional advantage of being the final user of the high-technology products it supports through the development process. Still, choices cannot be narrowed too early because of the intrinsic uncertainties.

The Defense Department has repeatedly confirmed the utility of parallel developments—to develop several initial concepts into testable hardware before making a final selection among sources. This approach was used widely in the 1950s, but largely abandoned in the 1960s on the grounds that better planning could help to avoid the "duplicate" expenses.[24] By the end of that decade, however, a Commission on Government Procurement had recommended the reintroduction of "prototyping"; it has since become formally supported by the Office of Federal Procurement Policy. In several cases in the 1970s, prototype development has led to a choice of a *different* contractor for the full-scale development and production effort than would have been chosen based on the initial proposals.[25] Thus, in selecting "good" firms, actions that in retrospect could be described as "wasteful failures" would need to be encouraged.

Second, a governmental selection process—necessarily bureaucratic—would have to exhibit intelligence and savvy in its machinations. Planned economies have been grappling with the issue of encouraging "good behavior" by enterprises for many years. Apparently simple and "objective" standards that can be applied to the fostering of innovations—*e.g.,* reward for new products—have often yielded more "new" products that are "pseudo-new" product differentiations or uneconomic (less productive per unit of cost than what they replace). It can be argued that in the planned economies the *buyers* of the innovations may screen new products much less effectively than their counterparts in the US domestic economy; that is, the buyers of intermediate and capital goods in the Soviet Union may not have the strong incentives for assuring that the "innovative" products acquired are really worth the price.

The foregoing discussion suggests that the choice of "good" firms for private-sector innovation in the US is both intrinsically fraught with uncertainty, and hard to design and implement into a bureaucratic decision-making process. Is there any alternative, then, to "high-R&D intensity" as a useful indicator?

A conceptually attractive, but politically impractical, alternative would be to create an industrial-innovation "patent office." This would mean giving a government office or agency the temporary authority (for 10 years or so) to certify that an enterprise has the range of staff talent to make a "credible effort" at innovating in the new industrial field(s) of its specification. Certainly this would not require that the office verify the likelihood of success of innnovative activities; the intrinsic uncertainties and government's remoteness from "the marketplace" would doom any such task to failure. And if this tax proposal is to be any benefit to small and newly formed firms, the requirements for qualification must not require the services of a sophisticated legal team.

The mode of operation of the Office of Naval Research after World War II may provide a useful analogy.[26] But the objective of this proposal would remain to reward/subsidize the *full range* of labor services necessary for successful innovation, and not simply project funding of R&D. Perhaps such a temporary office could best be organized and empowered within the technologically sophisticated parts of the Department of Commerce. The success of such an alternative would be critically dependent on the personnel recruited to carry out the function, and would suffer all the dangers of appeals for "fairness" when limits were drawn. By contrast, the more impersonal approach of "accurately" measuring R&D intensity and granting benefits through only a small (but important) subset of innovative firms may be a more pragmatic approach.

A Subsidy for Foreign-Owned Firms?

Since some foreign-owned firms are highly R&D intensive and since some tax benefits for a firm's employees may become indirect subsidies to the firm, it is clear that implementation of this proposal would benefit foreign-owned firms, unless they were specifically excluded. In this connection, it may be useful to look more closely at the role of the foreign capitalist in the development of US technology.

Using the Amdahl Corporation as an example once again, it was built, in part, with the help of venture capital investment from Nixdorf of West Germany and Fujitsu of Japan.[27] The arrangements for these investments included commitments for Amdahl to provide technical assistance to the Japanese firm. One may ask whether or not these transactions constituted a technology transfer from the US to Japan, with potentially adverse effects on US domestic and international competitiveness, as Dr. Gene Amdahl was asked two years ago.[28] Amdahl's reply emphasized the distinction between the *conception* of a new technology and its *realization*. The "technology" existed nowhere in the world at the time of the foreign capitalists' investments. And without those investments it would not have been brought into existence. In that sense, Amdahl argues, the investments constituted a technology transfer from abroad to the United States!

In short, economic activities based on new (and changing) technologies cannot be viewed in static terms. One should not confuse what is feasible with what is commercialized. US society is rather open to the flow of ideas; this has led serious observers to question the utility of the generation of new knowledge by American institutions when Americans have difficulty capturing the returns. Such returns for the firms depend in part on the opportunities for patenting or maintaining trade secrets, and in part on the lead time advantage over other firms.[29]

For the individual, the returns take the form of current earnings, learning-by-doing experience in using the new technology, and access to better and cheaper products and services. Except in extreme cases—like the monopoly or strong control by foreign ownership of a sector vital to the nation's defense—the US gains from foreign capital backing for high-technology firms both as consumers, and as the people in whom experience with the technology is embodied. Provided that *new* infant industries are encouraged and *new entry* into high technology sectors of the economy is preserved (and these are the principal objectives of this tax credit proposal), the US can continue to benefit from playing the role of technological entrepreneur as the world moves toward a global economy.

If So, Why Now?

Any public sector intervention into economic and business affairs is bound to have a multitude of direct and indirect effects. Further careful analysis and quantitative assessments are needed to determine the costs and some of the benefits of specific formulations of this policy proposal. Any judgments are required regarding qualitative aspects of the proposal and its likely influence on the behavior of diverse individuals.

Without further presumption regarding its desirability, consider briefly the timing for such a policy for the US. There is now a convergence of current events and longer historical trends that makes the encouragement of new industries through innovative efforts particularly attractive.

The widespread view that American business is less innovative than in earlier decades has received some support from careful research.[30] This is partly a result of declining resources devoted to R&D, and partly due to changes in the composition of R&D, with shifts away from long-term projects in some sectors. America's place in the international community is also determined in part by the activities and successes in other nations. As the history of the computer industry illustrates, an international advantage based on technology is intrinsically temporary, it resides in a nation's firms more than in individual products, and it may well last for a long time.[31]

Compounding the uncertainties of technological advancement has been a concatenation of price changes, particularly significant in materials and energy sources, but also of prices in general. Under such circumstances, economic flexibility has become much more important than in earlier decades. As Klein has effectively argued, a society's chances for macroeconomic stability and development under such circumstances are enhanced by a diversity of activities and exploration of options at the microeconomic level.[32] What looks like "wasteful duplication and failure" in retrospect, may have originally been option exploration and preservation in the face of diverse uncertainties. But few government officials will repeatedly subject themselves to public chastisement for "wasteful duplication." Present-day circumstances make public encouragement of a diversity of innovative activities timely, and perhaps this may be best accomplished on a decentralized, tax policy basis.

A less widely appreciated line of historical reasoning also supports prompt public encouragement of new industries. Kuznets has traced "long waves" in economic growth—with successive decades of prosperity, then recession, then depression, and then recovery occurring repeatedly—back to the late 18th century.[33] Van Duijn has extended this type of analysis to the mid-1970s (with the last "recession" period ending in 1975).[34] Mensch has extensively supplemented this historical data with information on two centuries of "basic" innovations.[35] He concludes that innovations are the driving force in economic recovery.

Marchetti has related information on innovations to long-term trends in use of and substitutions among energy sources.[36] In contrast to Mensch, Marchetti argues that the trends of innovative activity are so regular that no public intervention is needed (nor would any be effective in the long run). He expects the next wave of innovative activity to begin in this decade.[37] Most recently Graham and Senge have related "long waves" in economic growth to waves of capital formation.[38] They suggest that the "conventional wisdom"—that policies to stimulate investment are necessary and constructive—may only be true for some periods within "long waves."

This is not the place to evaluate the merits of competing interpretations of economic history. Suffice it to say that no one theory has gained universal acceptance, no more so than any one theory of industrial innovation reigns supreme. Perhaps the greatest strength of these arguments is that they reveal the long historical roots of current trends in economic development, and focus attention on the possible role of innovation in these trends.

However, the interpretation of innovation as a major source of economic recovery and change, as put forward by some analysts, does not reveal where, geographically, the next round of major innovations will occur. The unique environment and capacity for fostering the formation of new technology-based businesses and the growth of small ones make the United States an ideal spawning ground for the next wave of such innovations.[39] A policy such as the one proposed here, that encourages some existing innovative firms and new entry may be a desirable component of the portfolio of policies for stimulating industrial innovation in the US.

The proposal presented in this paper is for *temporary* public support for pathbreaking industrial innovation engaged in by some individuals, *timed* to open up new technological options for society that empirical evidence suggests are available and are already being encouraged by global economic trends. But technological innovation offers complex challenges for culture as well as genuine opportunities.[40] Should the personal income tax system be used to temporarily favor individuals and firms engaged in industrial innovation? The issue of equity of this proposal — deliberately and temporarily suspending "neutrality" in the impact of the tax code on individuals — requires a societal judgment that no amount of analytical rigor will fully resolve.

Acknowledgments

Early support for the research leading to this proposal was provided by The Rand Corporation, as part of its program of public service. Further encouragement to develop and refine the concept was received from G. Shubert and C. Wolf, Jr., of Rand, from A. Lee and R. Levien of IIASA, and from Senator H. Cannon, then chairman of the Committee on Commerce, Science and Transportation, US Senate. Helpful assistance, comments, and suggestions (not always in the context of this tax policy proposal) have also been received from Y. Dror, F. M. Fisher, L. Hervey, J. Hirschhorn, S. Merrill, N. Nimitz, A. Palmer, R. Solow, R. Starnes, and R. Vernon, as well as from W. Goldberg and N. Terleckyj in connection with the oral presentation of a preliminary version of this paper at the "International Conference on Technology Transfer," sponsored by the International Institute of Management, Berlin (West), December 1980. These sources of support, encouragement, and constructive criticism are gratefully acknowledged, but the proposal and views expressed here are those of the author, and are not necessarily shared by these individuals.

Notes and References

1. C.P. Kindleberger, *International Economics* (5th ed.) (Homewood, Illinois: Richard D. Irwin, Inc., 1973), p. 113.
2. J. Utterback and A. Murray, "The Influence of Defense Procurement and Sponsorship of Research and Development on the Development of the Civilian Electronics Industry," Center for Policy Alternatives, CPA-77-5, Massachusetts Institute of Technology, 1977.
3. A.J. Harman, *The International Computer Industry: Innovative and Comparative Advantage* (Cambridge, Massachusetts: Harvard University Press, 1977); see especially the discussion culminating on page 44. Furthermore, Pavitt and Wald found that opportunities for small firms tend to be greatest in the earliest stages of the "product cycle," when successful new entry to an industry is largely dependent on scientific and technological capability in a highly uncertain environment. See, K. Pavitt, and S. Wald, *The Conditions for Success in Technological Innovation* (Paris, France: Organization for Economic Cooperation and Development, 1971).
4. D. Mowery and N. Rosenberg, "The Influence of Market Demand Upon Innovation: A Critical Review of Some Recent Empirical Studies," *Research Policy,* Vol. 8 (1979), pp. 102–153.

5. F.M. Fisher, "Diagnosing Monopoly," *The Quarterly Review of Economics and Business,* Vol. 19, no. 2 (Summer 1979).

6. Charles River Associates, *An Analysis of Venture Capital Market Imperfections.* Prepared for the Experimental Technology Incentives Program, US Department of Commerce, February 1976.

7. US Senate, Committee on Commerce, Science and Transportation, *Industrial Technology,* Serial No. 95-138 (Washington, DC: US Government Printing Office, 1978), pp. 37–41, 49–51.

8. E.M. Rogers, "Technological Innovation in High Technology Industries," presented at the International Conference on Technology Transfer sponsored by the International Institute of Management, Berlin (West), December 1980; proceedings forthcoming.

9. See E. Mansfield, J. Rapoport, A. Romeo, S. Wagner, and G. Beardsley, "Social and Private Rates of Return from Industrial Innovations," *The Quarterly Journal of Economics,* Vol. XCI, No. 2 (1977), pp. 221–240.

10. J.A. Schumpeter, *The Theory of Economic Development* (New York: Oxford University Press, 1934).

11. B.H. Klein, *Dynamic Economics* (Cambridge, Massachusetts: Harvard University Press, 1977).

12. Clearly, this proposal would need considerable refinement before such a tax policy could be enacted. The description of a brief but explicit proposal in this section is offered to discuss the merits of the concept of encouraging "innovative labor" for new industries. At this point, however, please note that further consideration should be given to whether or not R&D consulting firms or design-only enterprises should be deliberately excluded, since the proposal as stated might encourage some firms to divest their R&D divisions to reap tax benefits. Since such design-only enterprises have worked very effectively in other contexts (see, for example, A.J. Alexander, *R&D in Soviet Aviation,* R-589-PR, The Rand Corporation, 1970), the resolution of this refinement is by no means obvious. Note also that not-for-profit firms have been excluded since they already have a special tax status. In fields like medical technology, where firms respond to a very complex mixture of market and regulatory forces, such enterprises could become important innovators.

13. The National Research Council (prepared by J.J. Cordes). *The Impact of Tax and Financial Regulatory Policies on Industrial Innovation* (Washington, DC: National Academy of Sciences, 1980).

14. D.H. Holland, "The Effect of Taxation on Effort: Some Results for Business Executives," in S.J. Bowers, ed., *Proceedings of the Sixty-Second Annual Conference on Taxation* (Columbus, Ohio: National Tax Association, 1970), especially pp. 482–501.

15. R.A. Musgrave, "The Hansen-Steiger Amendment and Other Capital Gains Tax Proposals," *Taxation With Representation Fund,* 1978.

16. In an earlier paper in which I first suggested this proposal, I devoted a technical appendix to an exploration of the uses to which such a subsidy might be put. Based on the model used, if the firm's production function has an elasticity of substitution greater than unity, it would invest in improving labor productivity. See A.J. Harman, "Industrial Innovation and Governmental Policy: A Review and Proposal Based on Observations of the US Electronics Sector," *Technological Forecasting and Social Change,* Vol. 18 (October 1980), Appendix. Unfortunately, economic research to measure the elasticity of substitution by sector and size of firm does not exist.

17. G.G. Baubusch, P.D. Fleischauer, A.J. Harman, and M.D. Miller, *Defense Industrial Planning for a Surge in Military Demand,* R-2360-AF (Santa Monica, California: The Rand Corporation, September, 1978); G.G. Baumbusch and A.J. Harman, *Peacetime Adequacy of the Lower Tiers of the Defense Industrial Base,* R-2184/1-AF (Santa Monica, California: The Rand Corporation, November 1977), especially Section V.

18. Interfutures, *Facing the Future: Mastering the Probable and Managing the Unpredictable* (Paris, France: Organization for Economic Cooperation and Development, 1979).

19. L.S. Kubie, "Some Unsolved Problems of the Scientific Career," Parts I and II, *American Scientist,* Vol. 41 (1953), pp. 596–613; Vol. 42 (1954), pp. 104–112.

20. See, for example, C. Holden, "Innovation: Japan Races Ahead as U.S. Falters, *Science,* Vol. 210, No. 14 (November 1980), pp. 751–754.

21. See R. Rothwell and W. Zegveld, "Small and Medium Sized Manufacturing Firms: Their Role and Problems in Innovation: Government Policy in Europe, the U.S.A., Canada, Japan, and Israel," Volumes I and II, Six Countries Programme Secretariat, TNO, Postbox 215, Delft, the Netherlands, November 1977.

22. See Note 8.

23. E. von Hippel, "Appropriability of Innovation Benefit as a Predictor of the Functional Locus of Innovation," presented at the International Conference on Technology Transfer (see Note 8).

24. See R.L. Perry, G.K. Smith, A.J. Harman, and S. Henrichsen, *Systems Acquisition Strategies,* R-733-PR/ARPA (Santa Monica, CA.: The Rand Corporation, 1971).

25. See G.K. Smith, "An Overview of Acquisition Policy Effectiveness in the 1970s," in *Department of Defense Contract Profit Policy,* Hearing before the Senate Committee on Banking, Housing and Urban Affairs held jointly with the Subcommittee on Priorities and Economy in Government of the Joint Economic Commit-

tee, March 21, 1979; see also E. Dews, *et al., Acquisition Policy Effectiveness: Department of Defense Experience in the 1970s,* R-2516-DR&E, The Rand Corporation, October 1979.

26. J.G. Wirt, A.J. Lieberman, and R.E. Levien, *R&D Management* (Lexington, Mass.: Lexington Books, 1975), pp. 39–45.

27. For futher details on corporate structure and product development at Amdahl, see A.J. Harman, A.J. Alexander, M. Davis and A.D. Lee, *Technological Innovation by Firms: Enhancement of Product Quality,* R-2237-NSF, the Rand Corporation, 1977, section III.

28. See Note 7.

29. See Note 23.

30. For example, E. Mansfield, "Technology Transfer, Innovation, and Public Policy," presented at the International Conference on Technology Transfer (see note 8).

31. See Note 3.

32. See Note 11.

33. S. Kuznets, *Economic Change* (New York: Norton, 1953).

34. J.J. van Duijn, "The Long Wave in Economic Life," *de Economist,* Vol. 125 (1977), pp. 544–576.

35. G. Mensch, *Stalemate in Technology: Innovations Overcome the Depression* (Cambridge, Massachusetts: Ballinger Publishing Co., 1979), translated from the 1975 German original.

36. See, for example, C. Marchetti, "The Evolution of the Energy Systems and the Aircraft Industry," *Chemical Economy and Engineering Review,* Vol. 12, No. 5 (May 1980), pp. 7–13.

37. C. Marchetti, presentation during "IIASA Dialogue with Industry," November 22, 1980, Laxenberg, Austria.

38. A.K. Graham and P.M. Senge, "A Long-Wave Hypothesis of Innovation," *Technological Forecasting and Social Change,* Vol. 17 (198]), pp. 283–311.

39. See Note 21.

40. J. Ladriere, *The Challenge Presented to Cultures by Science and Technology* (Paris, France: United Nations Educational, Scientific and Cultural Organization, 1977).

Technology In Society

New York / Oxford / Toronto / PERGAMON PRESS / Paris / Frankfurt / Sydney

Technology In Society, Vol. 3, pp. 141–149 (1981)
Printed in the USA. All rights reserved.

0160-791X/81/010141-09$02.00/0

Applying Tax Policy to Generate and Implement Technology

Gary Clyde Hufbauer

The US rate of productivity growth has badly slumped in recent years. Productivity growth depends on a number of factors—worker skills and attitudes, abundance of natural resources, capital stock and technology. The particular concern of this paper is how tax policy can be deployed to foster the more rapid generation and implementation of technology.

The Technology Pressure Points

In principle, tax policy can influence the generation and implementation of technology at three pressure points: first, the *level of expenditures* on research and development; second, the *success rate* of those expenditures; and third, the *speed* at which successful innovations make their appearance in new machinery and new products.

This discussion of the application of tax policy to these pressure points will follow a "tax sequence" rather than a "technology sequence." Thus, first to be discussed is the implementation of new technology; second, R&D expenditures; and last, the R&D success rate. This sequence is designed to facilitate consideration of tax policy first in larger terms and then in smaller terms.

Tax policy encompasses three separate but related realms. First, there is the realm of fiscal policy — namely, the extent to which government spending is matched by tax revenues. Second, there is the realm of broad tax structure — namely, the distribution of the tax burden between types of taxes (income taxes, excise taxes, etc.) and between classes of taxpayers (individuals, corporations,

Gary Clyde Hufbauer is Deputy Director of the International Law Institute at Georgetown University Law School and Counsel to Chapman, Duff and Paul. He is a former Deputy Assistant Secretary for Trade and Investment Policy and Director of the International Tax Staff of the US Treasury Department. Dr. Hufbauer has been a Professor of Economics at the University of New Mexico, and holds degrees from Harvard College; King's College, Cambridge; and Georgetown Law School.

etc.). Actions within the fiscal policy realm and the broad tax structure realm principally affect the speed of implementing new technology.

The third realm is the realm of detailed tax structure. Much popular and legislative attention is focused on tax details, namely, how within the broad structural framework the tax burden will be distributed as between kinds of transactions and categories of income. Actions within this realm have the greatest impact on the generation of new technology.

Implementation of New Technology

The most expensive step in translating new ideas into greater productivity is to embody them in new processes in the factory and new products in the marketplace. If new ideas are generated at a given rate, and if the average number of years between the generation of a new idea and its widespread commercial adoption remains constant, then implementation speed can be characterized as a neutral factor in the overall technology sequence. But if the average number of years is lengthening, implementation speed must be characterized as an adverse factor.

It is often said that implementation speeds are becoming slower in the United States. Three reasons are assigned for the consequent lengthening of gestation periods: regulatory delays, obstructive labor practices, and sluggish investment in plant and equipment. Not only do longer gestation periods cause a slowing of productivity growth, they can also make the return on R&D expenditure itself less attractive. A project which might be attractive if commercialized in five years may well be unattractive if delayed for 10 years.

Tax policies are not really suitable for reducing regulatory lag and overcoming restrictive labor practices. But fiscal policy and broad tax structure policy can make plant and equipment investment more attractive relative both to consumption and to inflation-proof (but also productivity-proof) investments in bricks and mortar. By making plant and equipment investment more attractive, tax policy can contribute to faster implementation speeds.

Fiscal Policy

The connection between plant and equipment investment and fiscal policy is fairly straightforward. The basic "crowding out" thesis, popularized by the *Wall Street Journal,* is familiar. To the extent public expenditures are not matched by tax revenues, the government must issue more bonds. In the eyes of savers, government bonds are just as satisfactory an asset as plant and equipment or other productive investments. Therefore, an increase in the outstanding issue of government bonds, necessitated by a government deficit, must crowd out productive investment. And with less productive investment, the pace at which the economy can implement new technology will be slowed.

A key proposition in the "crowding out" logic is that the level of private saving is set by exogenous behavior. The author has never put much faith in this proposition. Individual and corporate savings behavior are, he believes, highly responsive to after-tax real rates of return.

If this is correct, then *in principle*, there is no reason why government deficits cannot be accompanied by higher after-tax rates of return. If this happened, private savings would swell and only those investments that could not pay the higher real rates of return would be deferred. Since investments that are designed to implement new technologies typically yield high real rates of return, they should be among the last crowded out.

In practice, the problem is more difficult. Government deficits are usually accompanied by pro-inflationary policies. The combination of inflation and taxation takes a heavy toll on income from productive capital. And inflation often spawns policies that insulate certain low-productivity investments from the need to pay higher real rates of return.

In the pro-inflationary category are the Federal Reserve practice (largely abandoned since Paul Volcker became chairman) of "accommodating" the budget deficit by purchasing government securities, and the US Treasury's habit (still very much alive), of issuing huge amounts of short-term bills that have many characteristics of money. The rapid growth of money and near-money that accompanies Federal deficits fuels inflation. The interaction between higher inflation and a corporate tax based on *nominal* income means that the prospective yield on investments must increase very significantly in order to make investment projects worthwhile during times of accelerating inflation.

This point is illustrated in Table 1. Suppose the inflation rate is zero in Period One and rises to 15% in Period Two. Suppose that the corporate tax rate on nominal income is 40%, and that the after-tax real rate of return demanded for an investment is 10%. Under these circumstances, the before-tax nominal return must increase from 16.6% to 41.7% when inflation increases from 0% to 15%.

If Period Two describes a steady-state equilibrium when all adjustments have taken place, both in actual prices and in expected prices, a 41.7% before-tax nominal rate of return may not be regarded as a high threshold test. But during a transition period of accelerating inflation, this test could scare off a great deal of productive investment in plant and equipment.

In the insulation category are policies designed to ensure a regular flow of credit at low-tax or tax-free yields to favored sectors, particularly housing and state and

TABLE 1. Taxable Investment

	Period One %	Period Two %
Before-tax nominal return on investment	16.6	41.7
Corporate tax rate	40.0	25.0
After-tax nominal return on investment	10.0	25.0
Inflation rate	0.0	15.0
After-tax real return on investment	10.0	10.0

local public works. These insulation policies shift the crowding-out burden to other types of investment, especially plant and equipment investment. In turn, this means that the anticipated before-tax nominal rates of return on disfavored forms of investment must rise more than 1% for each 1% increase in the inflation rate. By contrast, the anticipated before-tax nominal rates of return on favored forms of investment need only rise by the amount of inflation. This point is illustrated by contrasting Table 1 with Table 2.

In order to preserve the same after-tax real return, the *ratio* of before-tax nominal returns as between the taxable and tax-free investments must remain constant at 1.667 (*i.e.*, $1/(1 - t)$), where t is the tax rate of 40%. This means that an increase in inflation substantially enlarges the required *arithmetic* difference in before-tax rates of return between the taxable and the tax-free investment.

Moreover, when inflation is accelerating, it is often more comforting to invest in bricks and mortar. The capital value of bricks and mortar is usually projected to increase, on a tax-free basis, *pari passu* with inflation. By contrast, equipment must generate a rapidly growing taxable cash flow to justify its existence.

Taking into account these practical features, it is evident that appropriate fiscal policy can contribute to the faster implementation of technology by slowing inflation. A lower rate of inflation reduces the required before-tax nominal return on productive equipment and reduces the arithmetic margin of preference for alternative assets.

Broad Tax Structures

Tax policy can increase the amount of savings out of a given income by taxing more lightly those types of income which are more likely to be saved. More savings enables more total investment, and more total investment means, *inter alia*, more productive investment. More savings also means less inflation. Thus, to enhance productivity, the tax structure should favor savings and disfavor consumption. In broad terms, the types of taxes which should be favored are sales, excise and value-added taxes (with appropriate exemptions for capital goods). The types of taxes which should be disfavored are high marginal tax rates on personal income whether "earned" or "unearned," taxes on corporate profits and capital gains and wealth taxes.

Conventional wisdom says that it is politically difficult to impart a pro-savings tilt to the tax structure. Business firms and high-income individuals are responsible for most savings, and a $5 billion decrease in "soak-the-rich" taxes will never

TABLE 2. Tax-Free Investment

	Period One %	Period Two %
Before-tax nominal return on investment	10.0	25.0
Inflation rate	0.0	15.0
After-tax real return on investment	10.0	10.0

win as many votes as a $5 billion decrease in "middle-America" taxes. But the post-1950 history of the US tax structure is really a history of pro-savings features: lower marginal rates, higher depreciation allowances, the Keogh plan, the ESOP plan, the maximum tax on "earned" income, lower corporate rates and so forth. At a time when the nation is concerned about productivity, there is no reason why further chapters in this history cannot be written.

R&D Expenditures

US research and development expenditures are widely believed to be inadequate. Underlying this view are two observations and a model. One observation is that Japan and West Germany have increased their R&D expenditures relative to their own GNP levels and relative to the United States. The second observation is that Japan, West Germany and many other European countries have experienced better rates of productivity growth than the United States.

The basic model is that larger R&D expenditures translate into more innovation, which in turn paves the way for new products and new machines, which mean higher productivity. Since R&D expenditures are a small percentage of GNP, the model promises a sort of magic multiplier: an additional one percent of GNP devoted to R&D would soon repay itself in higher GNP growth.

The basic model does not explain why American firms underspend on research and development. After all, if the potential gains are large, why don't firms simply increase their R&D budgets?

An explanation that often appears in more sophisticated models is that R&D expenditures are a hyperfunction of profits, and that industry-wide profit performance has been mediocre, largely due to poor productivity growth. A vicious (or virtuous) circle is at work. When profits decline, R&D is disproportionately cut; when profits rise, R&D disproportionately rises. Why? Because R&D is expensed annually on the profit and loss statement even though it has the economic character of a long-term investment. An accounting convention thus leads firms to irrationally shorten their investment horizons in bad times as a device for smoothing earnings per share. Whether or not there is truth to this explanation, it seems doubtful that government tax policy should be mobilized to offset private accounting conventions.

There is another explanation for inadequate private R&D expenditure that deserves more government attention. Private returns to successful R&D projects are much less than social returns.[1] This is so for two reasons. First, the legal mechanisms that protect the fruits of successful R&D from imitation by other producers are not entirely effective. Second, new technology often leads to lower prices, and consumers of inframarginal units are thereby treated to a larger "consumers' surplus."[2]

Thus, a successful R&D project might yield social benefits of $10 million, but only pay its private creator $3 million. The other $7 million would be shared by business imitators and by the public at large. There is an argument for returning part of this $7 million back to the entrepreneur through tax incentives.

US law already contains certain incentives for R&D expenditures *per se:*

• Under Internal Revenue Code Section 174(a), a business taxpayer may deduct R&D outlays currently, or, if it chooses, capitalize and amortize them over a period of 60 months or more. The immediate write-off is limited to current R&D expense and does not extend to plant and equipment dedicated to R&D use.

• A taxpayer may deduct contributions to an educational or scientific organization which carries on research in the public interest. Provided the research results are published in a timely manner, the deduction is available, even if patents are assigned to the sponsor.

Additional means have been suggested for rewarding R&D expenditure *per se*, for example:

• Allow a deduction for more than the amount of current R&D outlays. Canada, for example, allows both a regular deduction for R&D expense and an additional deduction of 50% of the excess of R&D outlays over a three-year base.

• Allow capital expenditures on R&D plant and equipment to be expensed at an accelerated rate. For example, France allows 50% of the cost of a building to be expensed in the first year.

• Allow a deduction for investment in the shares of an approved research company. Again, France has a provision of this sort.

The present US approach embodied in Section 174(d) extends the same tax treatment to R&D as the tax treatment of "ordinary and necessary" business expenses which are not easily distinguished from R&D — for example, routine quality inspection, market testing, the effort of patent attorneys, and so forth. Thus, the present tax law has the virtue of furthering easy tax administration. A more extensive incentive for R&D expenditure would require either a more precise, and difficult to draft, definition of R&D activity or a case-by-case certification procedure. To be sure, the United States has used the certification approach for tax incentives for the renovation of historic buildings. It could be extended to R&D by assigning certification responsibility, for example, to the National Science Foundation.

However, in the author's view a better policy would reward not expense, but success. The discussion now turns to the middle element in the sequence between R&D expenditure and commercial implementation, namely, the R&D success rate.

R&D Success Rate

R&D expenditure is not an end in itself. The goal is successful product and process innovations. Yet expenditure is often used as a surrogate for the target, on the argument that plain luck separates R&D failures from R&D successes. In this view, more R&D "shots" will increase the probability of a "hit," but nothing much can be done to shape the underlying probability distribution.

Frankly, the author is not entirely persuaded of this view. Some scientists consistently perform better than others. And some companies consistently get superior results from their R&D efforts. Moreover, the differences between companies transcend the careers of particular individuals. This suggests that the art of research management can be successfully practiced and that there is more to the art than simply hiring the best and brightest in a particular field at a particular time. Tax policy can play a role not only in encouraging firms to increase their R&D expenditures, but also in targeting those expenditures in a manner calculated to achieve results.

The difference between tax policy that encourages *greater expenditure* on R&D and tax policy that provides greater rewards for *successful* innovations is very similar to the difference between the tax provision for the expensing of intangible drilling costs and the provision of a percentage depletion allowance (really a tax-free income stream) for petroleum production.

Percentage depletion encourages the drilling and pumping of *successful* wells. The expensing of intangible drilling costs encourages drilling *per se*. Both incentives can be justified on the grounds that either a gusher or a dry hole conveys valuable knowledge to adjacent landowners. Two additional arguments have been marshalled to support the intangible drilling cost provision:

•The driller lacks the cash resources to await successful results; he needs tax assistance today, not tomorrow.

•Success is largely a matter of luck. Therefore, in the aggregate what counts is more effort, not larger rewards for the lucky few.

The strong argument against the intangible drilling cost provision is that it encourages ill-considered outlays at the taxpayer's expense. By contrast, the percentage depletion allowance only rewards success.

Obviously, drilling contains a random factor. And, obviously, R&D contains a random factor. But at least so far as R&D is concerned, the author believes that effective management—highly attuned to the commercial potential—can make an enormous difference in R&D results.

In addition, tax policies ought to be designed to promote the development of a better functioning R&D market. The way to do this is to reward success, not expense.

In the United States, the market for technology is inhibited by a number of factors.

First, if one company licenses another company, and places strict field of use, pricing of final product, geographic or similar limits on the exploitation of that technology, it may offend the antitrust laws. An offense to the antitrust laws not only brings a risk of Justice Department prosecution, but also raises the spectre of private treble damage actions. However, the company can price and sell almost at will, and earn the income of a discriminating monopolist if it exploits the technology through its own corporate structure. Thus, many companies shy away from licensing their technology to outside firms.

Secondly, there is a real danger that a patent licensee—once he understands the technology—will attack the patent.

Third, if know-how which is not protected by a patent is sold or licensed, the danger of inadvertent disclosure to third parties, and exploitation by them, is increased.

Modified Laws and Tax Policy

In principle, these market imperfections could be addressed directly. But, direct solutions would require modification of fundamental antitrust and patent laws at the Federal level and trade secret laws at the state level. This would take decades to achieve. Another way to offset the imperfections would be through tax policy—specifically taxing patent and know-how income at reduced rates.

Under present law, income derived by individual inventors from patents sold, or licensed on an exclusive basis, is taxed at capital gains rates. However, this concession does not apply to non-exclusive licenses. A corporation that sells or exclusively licenses a patent will qualify for capital gains treatment only if the patent is a capital asset, that is to say, not part of the ordinary stock in trade of the corporation. Moreover, no tax concession is extended to the sale of know-how.

To be sure, firms may cross-license their patents on a tax-free basis. But cross-licensing arrangements are generally confined to firms with approximately equivalent patent values in their portfolios.

The author's suggestion is that *all* receipts from any *publicly registered* licensing or sale of patents or know-how to *unrelated* parties should be tax-free. In other words, royalty payments should be tax-free to the seller, but remain deductible to the buyer. This provision would reward R&D success, not merely expenditure. And it would greatly broaden the market for technology.

The *unrelated* party requirement is designed both to speed the diffusion of technology to outside firms, and to avoid disputes between the Internal Revenue Service and the taxpayer as to transfer pricing practices within the corporate family.

The *public registration* requirement is designed to provide a ready source of information on the commercial terms at which the market for technology is operating so that new entrants will have a better idea of prevailing commercial conditions and rates.

President Reagan's Tax Program

President Reagan has announced his fiscal and tax policies in broad terms:

- Sharply reduce the growth of non-defense spending in fiscal year 1982 and beyond;
- Reduce individual tax rates by 10% per year for each of the next three years;
- Make investment more attractive through "10-5-3" depreciation or a similar plan.

This program deserves two cheers from the productivity buffs. It should reduce inflation and the consequent inflationary bias against productive investment. And it should directly stimulate private savings, private investment and thus the implementation of technology.

But the program is missing a targeted incentive for the generation of successful new technology. The author's own third cheer is reserved for a tax-free royalty provision.

Note and Reference

1. *Relationship Between R&D and Returns from Technology,* National Science Foundation Colloquium, May 21, 1977.
2. Consumer surplus is the difference between what the purchaser would pay if the alternative was not to buy the product at all, and the market price. The marginal consumer is just willing to pay the market price.

Technology In Society

New York / Oxford / Toronto / PERGAMON PRESS / Paris / Frankfurt / Sydney

Technology In Society, Vol. 3, pp. 151–171 (1981)
Printed in the USA. All rights reserved.

Taxation and Technical Change

Dale W. Jorgenson

The growth of the US economy in the postwar period has been very rapid by historical standards. The rate of economic growth reached its maximum during the period 1960 to 1966. Growth rates have slowed substantially since 1966 and declined further since 1973. A major source of uncertainty in projections of the future of the US economy is whether patterns of growth will better conform to the rapid growth of the early 1960s, the more moderate growth of the late 1960s and early 1970s or the disappointing growth since 1973.

The purpose of this paper is to consider the prospects for restoring moderate economic growth through tax policy. For this purpose the growth of output during the postwar period is decomposed into contributions of capital input, labor input and the rate of technical change. For the period 1948 to 1976 it is found that all three sources of economic growth are significant and must be considered in analyzing future growth potential. For the postwar period, capital input has made the most important contribution to the growth of output, technical change has been next most important, and labor input has been least important.

Focusing on the period 1973 to 1976, one finds that the fall in the rate of economic growth has been due to a dramatic decline in the rate of technical change. Declines in the contributions of capital and labor input are much less significant in explaining the slowdown. The conclusion is that the future development of technology should be the primary focus of efforts to stimulate future US economic growth.

Given the importance of technical change in future economic growth, an attempt is made to analyze the slowdown in the rate of technical change for the US economy as a whole in greater detail. For this purpose technical change during the

This article was first prepared as the Bernard I. Fain Lecture at Brown University on October 22, 1980. Thanks are due to Alan Auerbach and Barbara Fraumeni for joint research that contributed to the results presented in this paper. Any remaining errors are the sole responsibility of the author.

Dale W. Jorgenson is Frederick Eaton Abbe Professor of Economics at Harvard University where he has taught economics since 1969. He is a member of the National Academy of Sciences and was awarded the prestigious John Bates Clark Medal of the American Economic Association in 1971.

postwar period is decomposed into components that can be identified with
technical change at the sectoral level and with reallocations of output, capital input and labor input among sectors. For the period 1948 to 1976, these reallocations are found to be insignificant relative to sectoral technical change. The combined effect of all three reallocations is slightly negative, but sufficiently small in
magnitude to be negligible as a source of aggregate technical change.

Again focusing on the period 1973 to 1976, it is possible that the economic
dislocations that accompanied the severe economic contraction of 1974 and 1975
could have resulted in shifts of output and inputs among sectors that contributed
to the slowdown of the aggregate rate of technical change. If this were true, then
economic policy should be focused on reallocation of output among sectors. This
appears to be the objective of industrial revitalization programs, such as the program proposed by the Carter Administration. Alternatively, sources of the
slowdown in the aggregate rate of technical change might be found in falling rates
of technical change at the level of individual industrial sectors. In this case, the
objective of economic policy should be to stimulate the development of new
technology for all industrial sectors.

Reallocations of output and inputs among sectors are found to have made
positive, rather than negative, contributions to economic growth during the
period 1973–1976. Economic policies oriented toward revitalization of the
economy by reallocating economic activity among industries appear to be
misguided. The conclusion is that declines in rates of technical change for the individual industrial sectors of the US economy must bear the full burden of explaining the slowdown in the rate of technical change for the economy as a whole.
The major focus for economic policy should be to stimulate the development of
new technology for all industries.

An Econometric Analysis

To identify policies that can stimulate the development of new technology, the
results of an econometric analysis of the determinants of productivity growth at
the sectoral level are presented. The econometric model determines the growth of
sectoral productivity as a function of relative prices of sectoral inputs. For each sector inputs are divided among capital, labor, energy and material inputs.
Allowance is made for the fact that the value of sectoral output includes the value
of intermediate inputs — energy and materials — as well as the value of primary factors production — capital and labor. Differences in relative prices for inputs are
associated with differences in the rate of technical change for each sector.

After fitting this econometric model of productivity growth to data for individual industrial sectors, it was found that the rate of technical change decreases
with an increase in the price of capital input for a very large proportion of US industries. Similarly, the rate of technical change falls with higher prices of labor input for a large proportion of industries. The impact of higher energy prices is also
to slow the rate of technical change for a large proportion of industries. By contrast an increase in the price of materials input is found to be associated with increases in rates of technical change for almost all industries.

Tax policies over the postwar period have resulted in wide variations in effective rates of taxation on income from corporate capital. Effective tax rates at the beginning of the postwar period were greater than or equal to the statutory rate of 52%. Beginning in 1954, a series of tax reforms resulted in a steady decline in effective tax rates through 1965. For some assets the effective tax rate on corporate capital was reduced by more than half. Effective tax rates rose sharply from 1965 to 1969 and fell over the period from 1969 to 1973. Since 1973 effective tax rates have remained relatively stable.

Examining the postwar development of technology for the economy as a whole, technical change was found to attain its maximum during the period 1960–1966, when effective rates of taxation on income from corporate capital were falling. During the period 1966–1969, when effective rates were increasing dramatically, the rate of technical change declined to the lowest level in the postwar period up to 1969. The rate of technical change recovered to levels close to the postwar average during the period of 1969–1973, when effective tax rates were falling.

Since 1973 the relative prices of capital, labor, energy, and materials inputs have been altered radically as a consequence of the increase in the price of energy relative to other productive inputs. Higher world petroleum prices following the Arab oil embargo of late 1973 and 1974 have resulted in sharp increases in prices for all forms of energy in the US economy—oil, natural gas, coal, and electricity generated from fossil fuels and other sources. Although the US economy has been partly shielded from the impact of higher world petroleum prices through a system of price controls, all industrial sectors have experienced large increases in the price of energy relative to other inputs.

The econometric model reveals that slower productivity growth at the sectoral level is associated with higher prices of capital and energy relative to other inputs. The first conclusion is that the pattern of increases and decreases in the aggregate rate of technical change over the postwar period is inversely correlated with changes in the price-effective rate of taxation on capital. High effective rates of taxation are associated with low rates of technical change, while low effective tax rates are associated with high rates of technical change.

The second conclusion is that the slowdown in sectoral rates of technical change since 1973 is at least partly due to the sharp increase in the price of energy relative to other productive inputs. This increase began with the run-up of world petroleum prices in late 1973 and early 1974. The fall in sectoral rates of technical change after 1973 is responsible in turn for the decline in the rate of technical change for the US economy as a whole. Slower technical change is the primary source of the slowdown in the US economic growth since 1973.

During 1979 and early 1980 world petroleum prices have jumped 130% to 140%, following the Iranian revolution of late 1978. Since the outbreak of the Iran-Iraq War in 1980, spot petroleum prices have begun to increase relative to the higher levels established in 1979 and early 1980. Based on the performance of the US economy since 1973, a further slowdown in the rate of economic growth can be anticipated along with a decline in the rate of technical change for the economy as a whole and declines in sectoral rates of technical change for a wide range of industries.

To offset the drag on the development of new technology for the US economy as a whole due to higher energy prices, it is important to take immediate steps to reduce the effective rate of taxation on capital. Reduction in effective tax rates on capital has been thoroughly tested as a policy instrument for stimulating technical change. For this purpose a new approach to capital recovery under tax laws is proposed to counteract the effects of higher energy prices.

The Growth Slowdown

This section begins an analysis of the slowdown in US economic growth by decomposing the growth of output for the economy as a whole into the contributions of capital input, labor input, and technical change.[1] The results are given in Table 1 for the postwar period 1948–1976 and for the following seven subperiods — 1948–1953, 1953–1957, 1957–1960, 1960–1966, 1966–1969, 1969–1973, and 1973–1976.[2] Except for the period from 1973 to 1976, each of the subperiods covers economic activity from one cyclical peak to the next. The last period covers economic activity from the cyclical peak in 1973 to 1976, a year of recovery from the sharp downturn in economic activity in 1974 and 1975.

Rates of growth for output, capital input, labor input, and the rate of technical change for the US economy are presented first. For the postwar period as a whole output grew at 3.5% per year, capital input grew at 4.01% and labor grew at 1.28%. The rate of technical change averaged 1.14% per year. The rate of economic growth reached its maximum at 4.83% during the period 1960–1966 and grew at only 0.89% during the recession and partial recovery of 1973–1976. The growth of capital input was more even, exceeding 5% in 1948–1953 and 1966–1969, and falling to 3.12% in 1973–1976. The growth of labor input reached its maximum in the period 1960–1966 at 1.99% and fell to 0.58% in 1973–1976, which was above the minimum of 0.23% in the period 1953–1957.

The rate of growth of output for the US economy as a whole can be expressed as the sum of a weighted average of the rates of growth of capital and labor inputs and the rate of technical change. The weights associated with capital and labor inputs are average shares of these inputs in the value of output. The contribution of each input is the product of the average shares of this input and corresponding input growth rate. Contributions of capital and labor inputs to US economic growth for the period 1948–1976 and for seven subperiods are presented in Table 1. Considering technical change, it is found that the maximum rate occurred from 1960 to 1966 at 2.11% per year. During the period 1966–1969 the rate of technical change was almost negligible at 0.04%. The rate of technical change recovered to 0.95% during the period 1969–1973 and fell to a negative 0.70% during 1973–1976.

Since the value shares of capital and labor inputs are stable over the period 1948–1976, the movements of the contributions of these inputs to the growth of output largely parallel those of the growth rates of the inputs themselves. For the postwar period as a whole the contribution of capital input of 1.61% is the most important source of output growth. Technical change is next most important at 1.14%, while the contribution of labor input is the third most important at 0.75%. All three sources of growth are significant and must be considered in an analysis of the slowdown of economic growth during the period 1973–1976.

TABLE 1. Growth of Output and Inputs for the US Economy, 1948–1976

	1948–1976	1948–1953	1953–1957	1957–1960	1960–1966	1966–1969	1969–1973	1973–1976
Growth Rates:								
Output	0.0350	0.0457	0.0313	0.0279	0.0483	0.0324	0.0324	0.0089
Capital input	0.0401	0.0507	0.0393	0.0274	0.0376	0.0506	0.0396	0.0312
Labor input	0.0128	0.0160	0.0023	0.0099	0.0199	0.0185	0.0116	0.0058
Rate of technical change	0.0114	0.0166	0.0146	0.0113	0.0211	0.0004	0.0095	−0.0070
Contributions:								
Capital input	0.0161	0.0194	0.0154	0.0109	0.0156	0.0211	0.0161	0.0126
Labor input	0.0075	0.0097	0.0013	0.0057	0.0116	0.0108	0.0068	0.0033

However, capital input is clearly the most important contributor to the rapid growth of the US economy during the postwar period.[3]

Focusing on the period 1973 to 1976, the contribution of capital input is found to have fallen to 1.26% for a drop of 0.35% from the postwar average, the contribution of labor input fell to 0.33% for a drop of 0.42%, and that the rate of technical change at a negative 0.70% dropped 1.84%. The conclusion is that the fall in the rate of US economic growth during the period 1973–1976 was largely due to the fall in the rate of technical change. Declines in the contributions of capital and labor inputs are much less significant in explaining the slowdown. A detailed explanation of the fall in the rate of technical change is needed to account for the slowdown in US economic growth.

To analyze the sharp decline in the rate of technical change for the US economy as a whole during the period 1973 to 1976 in greater detail data are employed on rates of technical change for individual industrial sectors. For this purpose it is important to distinguish between technical change at the aggregate level and technical change at the sectoral level. At the aggregate level the appropriate concept of output is value added, defined as the sum of the values of capital and labor inputs for all sectors of the economy. At the sectoral level the appropriate concept of output includes the value of primary factors of production at the sectoral level — capital and labor inputs — and the value of intermediate inputs — energy and material inputs. In aggregating over sectors to obtain output for the US economy as a whole the production and consumption of intermediate goods cancel out, so that values of energy and materials inputs do not appear at the aggregate level.

The Sum of Four Components

The rate of technical change for the US economy as a whole can be expressed as the sum of four components. The first component is a weighted sum of rates of technical change for individual industrial sectors. The weights are ratios of the value of output in each sector to value added in that sector. The sum of these weights over all sectors exceeds unity, since technical change in each sector contributes to the growth of output in that sector and to the growth of output in other sectors through deliveries of intermediate inputs to those sectors. The remaining components of aggregate technical change represent the contributions of reallocations of value added, capital input and labor input among sectors to technical change for the economy as a whole.[4]

The role of reallocations of output, capital input and labor input among sectors is easily understood. For example, if capital input moves from a sector with a relatively low rate of return to a sector with a high rate of return, the quantity of capital input for the economy as a whole is unchanged, but the level of output is increased, so that productivity has improved. Similarly, if labor input moves from a sector with low wages to a sector with high wages, labor input is unchanged, but productivity has improved.

Technical change for the economy as a whole is a combination of improvements in technology at the sectoral level and reallocations of output, capital input, and labor input among sectors. Data on reallocations of output, capital input and labor input for the postwar period 1948 to 1976 and for seven subperiods are given in Table 2.[5]

For the postwar period as a whole, technical change at the aggregate level is dominated by the contribution of sectoral technical change of 1.24% per year. The contributions of reallocations of output, capital input and labor input are a negative 0.16%, a positive 0.08%, and a negative 0.02%. Adding these contributions together one finds that the combined effect of the three reallocations is a negative 0.10%, which is negligible by comparison with the effect of technical change at the sectoral level. The rate of technical change at the aggregate level provides an accurate picture of average rates of technical change for individual countries; this picture is not distorted in an important way by the effect of reallocation of output and inputs among sectors.

Again focusing on the period 1973–1976, it is found that the contribution of sectoral technical change to technical change for the economy as a whole fell to a negative 1.13% for a drop of 2.37% from the postwar average. By contrast the contribution of reallocations of output rose to 0.46% for a gain of 0.62% from the postwar average. The contribution of the reallocation of capital input was unchanged at 0.08%, while the contribution of labor input fell to a negative 0.11% for a drop of 0.09% from the postwar average.

The combined contribution of all three allocations rose 0.53%, partially offsetting the precipitous decline in rates of technical change at the sectoral level. The conclusion is that declines in rates of technical change for the individual industrial sectors of the US economy are more than sufficient to explain the decline in the rate of technical change for the economy as a whole.

To summarize the findings on the slowdown of US economic growth during the period 1973–1976, the drop in the growth of output of 2.61% per year from the postwar average was found to be the sum of a decline in the contribution of labor input of 0.42% per year, a sharp dip in sectoral rates of technical change of 2.37%, a rise in the role of reallocations of output among sectors of 0.62% per year, no change in the reallocations of capital input, and a decline in the contribution of reallocations of labor input of 0.09% per year. Whatever the causes of the slowdown, they are to be found in the collapse of technical change at the sectoral level rather than a slowdown in the growth of capital and labor inputs at the aggregate level or the reallocations of output, capital input or labor input among sectors.

The decomposition of economic growth into the contributions of capital input, labor input and the rate of technical change is helpful in pinpointing the causes of the slowdown. The further decomposition of technical change for the economy as a whole into contributions of sectoral rates of technical change and reallocations of output, capital input and labor input is useful in providing additional detail. However, the measure of the sectoral rate of technical change is simply the unexplained residual between growth of sectoral output and the contributions of sectoral capital, labor, energy and materials inputs. The problem remains of providing an explanation for the fall in rates of technical change at the sectoral level.

TABLE 2. The Rate of Technical Change for the US Economy 1948–1976

	1948–1976	1948–1953	1953–1957	1957–1960	1960–1966	1966–1969	1969–1973	1973–1976
Sectoral rates of technical change:	0.0124	0.0219	0.0177	0.0145	0.0217	0.0025	0.0048	−0.0113
Reallocation of value added:	−0.0016	−0.0075	−0.0030	−0.0010	−0.0016	−0.0025	0.0030	0.0046
Reallocation of capital input:	0.0008	0.0022	0.0008	−0.0001	0.0002	0.0001	0.0010	0.0008
Reallocation of labor input:	−0.0002	−0.000	−0.0008	−0.0021	0.0008	0.0004	0.0006	−0.0011

Sectoral Rates of Technical Change

The decline in the rate of technical growth at the level of individual industrial sectors within the US economy has now been identified as the main culprit in the slowdown of US economic growth that took place after 1966. To provide an explanation for the slowdown one must go behind the measurements to identify the determinants of technical change at the sectoral level. For this purpose an econometric model of sectoral technical change is required. This section contains a summary of the results of applying such an econometric model to detailed data on sectoral output and capital, labor, energy and materials inputs for 35 individual industries in the United States.

The complete econometric model is based on sectoral price functions for each of the 35 industries included in the study.[6] Each price function gives the price of the output of the corresponding industrial sector as a function of the prices of capital, labor, energy and materials inputs and time, where time represents the level of technology in the sector.[7]

Obviously, an increase in the price of one of the inputs—holding the prices of the other inputs and the level of technology constant—will necessitate an increase in the price of output. Similarly, if the level of technology in a sector improves and the prices of all inputs into the sector remain the same, the price of output must fall. Price functions summarize these and other relationships among the prices of output, capital, labor, energy, and materials inputs and the level of technology.

Although the sectoral price functions provide a complete model of production patterns for each sector, it is useful to express this model in an alternative and equivalent form. The shares of each of the four inputs—capital, labor, energy, and materials—can be expressed in the value of output as functions of the prices of these inputs and time, again representing the level of technology.[8] One can add to these four equations for the value shares an equation that expresses the rate of technical change as a function of the prices of the four inputs and time.[9] In fact, the negative of the rate of technical change is a function of the four input prices and time. This equation is the econometric model of sectoral technical change.[10]

Like any econometric model, the relationship determining the value shares of capital, labor, energy and materials inputs and the negative of the rate of technical change involve unknown parameters that must be estimated from data for the individual industries. Included among these unknown parameters are biases of technical change that indicate the effect of changes in the level of technology on the value shares of each of the four inputs.[11] For example, the bias of technical change for capital input gives the change in the share of capital input in the value of output in response to changes in the level of technology represented by time. Similarly, biases of technical change for labor, energy, and materials inputs give changes in the shares of labor, energy, and materials inputs in the value of output that results from changes in the level of technology.

Capital Using / Capital Saving

It is said that technical change is capital using if the bias of technical change for
capital input is positive — that is, if changes in the level of technology result in an
increase in the share of capital input in the value of output, holding all input
prices constant. The quantity of capital input increases as technology changes, so
that it is said that the change in technology is capital using. Similarly, it is said
that technical change is capital saving if the bias of technical change for capital input is negative. As technology changes, the production process uses less capital input, so that the change in technology is capital saving.

Similarly, it can be said that technical change is labor using or labor saving if
the bias of technical change for labor input is positive or negative. As technology
changes, the production process uses more or less labor input, depending on
whether the change in technology is labor-using or labor-saving. Energy-using or
energy-saving technical change can be associated with positive or negative biases
of technical change for energy input. Finally, materials-using or materials-saving
technical change can be associated with positive or negative biases of technical
change for materials input. Since the shares of all four inputs — capital, labor,
energy, and materials — sum to unity, technical change that "uses" or "saves" all
four inputs is impossible. In fact, the sum of the biases for all four must be
precisely zero, since the changes in all four shares with any change in technology
must sum to zero.

It has beeen pointed out that this econometric model for each industrial sector
of the US economy includes an equation giving the negative of the sectoral rate of
technical change as a function of the prices of the four inputs and time. The
biases of technical change with respect to each of the four inputs appear as the
coefficients of time — representing the level of technology — in the four equations
for the value shares of all four inputs. The biases also appear as coefficients of the
prices in the equation for the negative of the sectoral rate of technical change.
This feature of this econometric model makes it possible to use information about
changes in the value shares with time and changes in the rate of sectoral technical
change with prices in determining estimates of the biases of technical change.

The biases of technical change express the dependence of value shares of the
four inputs on the level of technology and also express the dependence of the
negative of the rate of technical change on the input prices. One can say that
capital-using technical change, associated with a positive bias of technical change
for capital input, implies that an increase in the price of capital input decreases
the rate of technical change (or increases the negative of the rate of technical
change). Similarly, capital-saving technical change, associated with a negative bias
for capital input, implies that an increase in the price of capital input increases
the rate of technical change. Analogous relationships hold between biases of
labor, energy, and materials inputs and the direction of the impact of changes in
the prices of each of these inputs on the rate of technical change.[12]

Jorgenson and Fraumeni (1980) have fitted biases of technical change for 35 industrial sectors that make up the whole of the producing sector of the US
economy. They have also fitted the other parameters of the econometric model

that has been described above. Since the primary concern in this section is to analyze the determinants of rates of technical change at the sectoral level, the focus is on the patterns of technical change revealed in Table 3. Listed are the industries characterized by each of the possible combinations of biases of technical change, consisting of one or more positive biases and one or more negative biases.[13]

The pattern of technical change that occurs most frequently in Table 3 is capital-using, labor-using, energy-using and materials-saving technical change. This pattern occurs for 19 of the 35 industries analyzed by Jorgenson and Fraumeni. For this pattern of technical change the biases of technical change for capital input, labor input and energy input are positive, and the bias of technical change for materials input is negative. This pattern implies that increases in the prices of capital input, labor input and energy input decrease the rate of technical change, while increases in the price of materials input increase the rate of technical change.

Considering all patterns of technical change included in Table 3, technical change is found to be capital-using for 25 of the 35 industries included in the study. Technical change is capital-saving for the remaining 10 industries. Similarly, technical change is labor-using for 31 of the 35 industries and labor-saving for the remaining four industries; technical change is energy-using for 29 of the 35 industries included in Table 3 and is energy-saving for the remaining six. Finally, technical change is materials-using for only two of the 35 industries and is materials-saving for the remaining 33. The conclusion is that, for a very large proportion of industries, the rate of technical change decreases with increases in the prices of capital, labor, and energy inputs, and increases with the price of materials inputs.

Tax Policy

To identify the sources of variations in rates of technical change for industrial sectors of the US economy, next to be considered is the evolution of tax policy over the postwar period. Under current law, taxpayers are permitted to deduct depreciation as an expense in arriving at income for tax purposes. Taxpayers are also allowed to reduce their tax liability by means of an investment tax credit based on purchases of equipment.[14] As tax rates at corporate and personal levels have increased, provisions for capital recovery under the tax code have become increasingly significant for economic policy. These provisions have an important impact on stimulating or retarding changes in the level of technology.

An ideal system for capital recovery would enable taxpayers to recover economic depreciation on each asset they hold. Economic depreciation is the decline in the value of an asset with age. Depreciation can be measured by simply looking at the profile of asset prices corresponding to assets of different ages at a given point in time. An ideal system of capital recovery would permit taxpayers to deduct the decline in the value of all their assets with age in arriving at taxable income.[15]

Although it is a very straightforward matter to describe an ideal system for capital recovery, such a system is difficult to implement. Normally, business ex-

TABLE 3. Classification of Industries by Biases of Technical Change

Pattern of Biases	Industries
Capital using Labor using Energy using Material saving	Agriculture, metal mining, crude petroleum and natural gas, non-metallic mining, textiles, apparel, lumber, furniture, printing, leather, fabricated metals, electrical machinery, motor vehicles, instruments, miscellaneous manufacturing, transportation, trade, finance, insurance and real estate, services.
Capital using Labor using Energy saving Material saving	Coal mining, tobacco manufactures, communications, government enterprises.
Capital using Labor saving Energy using Materials saving	Petroleum refining
Capital using Labor saving Energy saving Material using	Construction
Capital saving Labor saving Energy using Material saving	Electric utilities
Capital saving Labor using Energy saving Material saving	Primary metals
Capital saving Labor using Energy using Material saving	Paper, chemicals, rubber, stone, clay and glass, machinery except electrical, transportation equipment and ordnance, gas utilities
Capital saving Labor saving Energy using Material using	Food

penses under the tax code are linked to actual puchases of goods and services. The approach to capital recovery embodied in US tax law is based on the historical cost of an asset. This cost is allocated over the useful life of the asset in accord with accounting formulas.

In the absence of inflation, an approach to capital recovery based on historical cost has many advantages. Perhaps the most important advantage is that capital-consumption allowances, like other business expenses, can be linked to actual transactions. However, a capital recovery system based on historical cost fails to provide the necessary link between capital consumption allowances and economic depreciation when there is inflation in the prices of assets.

With inflation the profile of prices corresponding to assets of different ages rises over time due to increases in the prices of newly produced assets. Even capital-consumption allowances that accurately reflect the profile of asset prices when the asset is originally acquired rapidly fall behind economic depreciation as inflation takes place. As a consequence, effective rates of taxation have increased substantially and sectoral rates of technical change have been retarded.

The system for capital recovery embodied in current tax law is the result of extended efforts to deal with the problem of inflation in the value of assets. In 1954 a system of capital-consumption allowances was adopted that permitted taxpayers to use accelerated formulas for allocating capital recovery over the useful lifetime of an asset. Accelerated depreciation was adopted in response to the rapid inflation in prices of assets during the Second World War and the Korean War.

Between 1954 and 1962 the lifetimes used in calculating capital consumption allowances were gradually reduced. In 1962 a new set of guideline lifetimes was adopted for tax purposes. These guideline lifetimes represented a further acceleration in capital recovery. In addition, an investment tax credit for purchases of equipment was adopted in 1962. The combination of the guideline lifetimes and the investment tax credit resulted in a dramatic stimulus to capital formation. Business fixed investment rose by 40% over the four years from 1962 to 1966.

In the original legislation providing for the investment tax credit, the credit was linked to capital recovery by reducing the basis for calculating capital consumption allowances by the amount of the credit. This feature of the investment tax credit—the so-called Long Amendment—was repealed in 1964. As inflation rates began to rise in the late 1960s pressure began to build to adjust lifetimes for tax purposes to levels below the guidelines of 1962. In 1971 the Asset Depreciation Range System was adopted, permitting taxpayers to reduce lifetimes by as much as 20%.

These developments can be summarized by saying that the current system has developed through successive liberalization of depreciation formulas and lifetimes for tax purposes and through the introduction of the investment tax credit. These changes in the capital recovery provisions of the tax code have been motivated by the need to bring capital-consumption allowances into line with economic depreciation. However, double-digit inflation in the early 1970s has undercut the effectiveness of the earlier reforms.

Inflation and Effective Tax Rates

To analyze the impact of inflation on capital recovery under the existing law, effective tax rates were measured on five representative classes of assets. The asset classes are described in detail in Table 4. For each asset is given the tax lifetime embodied in current law, and the economic depreciation rate as calculated in a comprehensive study for the Department of the Treasury by Hulten and Wykoff (1979). Also given is the proportion of nonresidential fixed investment in 1974 for each asset class. Together these five assets accounted for about a third of investment in that year.

TABLE 4. Assets and Their Characteristics

Asset Class	Type	Tax Lifetime[a]	Economic Depreciation Rate[b]	Percentage of 1974 Investment
Construction machinery (CM)	Equipment	5.5 (7.0*)	.172	2.8
General industrial equipment (GIE)	Equipment	8.6	.122	4.4
Trucks, buses and trailers (TBT)	Equipment	5.5 (7.0*)	.254	9.0
Industrial buildings (IB)	Structures	23.8	.036	5.2
Commercial buildings (CB)	Structures	31.8	.025	11.0

[a]Tax Lifetimes equal guideline lives for structures and eighty percent of guideline lives for equipment, as permitted under current law (*except where a lengthening of tax lifetime is preferred to obtain a full investment tax credit).
[b]Economic Depreciation Rates are annual rates of decline in asset value with age, as estimated by Wykoff and Hulten (1979).

To analyze the impact of changes in capital recovery provisions of the tax law over the postwar period, the effective tax rate for each class of asset in Table 4 was calculated. Effective tax rates represent that fraction of each project's gross income which goes toward corporate taxes. Since such rates may vary from year to year, this figure represents the average tax rate faced by a new asset over its lifetime. To calculate an effective tax rate, first the gross rate of return that a particular investment would have — if the corporate tax rate were zero and there were no investment tax credit — is calculated. Then the net rate of return is calculated taking account of corporate taxes and adjusting for depreciation deductions and the investment tax credit. The net rate of return is subtracted from the gross rate of return and this difference divided by the gross rate to find the proportion of the gross return paid in taxes.

To assess the impact of the tax law prevailing in each year from 1952 to 1979 on capital recovery, effective tax rates for all five classes of assets for each year are presented in Table 5. For purposes of comparison, also given is the statutory rate on corporate income in each year. Under an ideal system for capital recovery the effective tax rates would be equal to the statutory rates for all assets.[16] The first conclusion to be drawn from Table 5 is that effective tax rates have varied widely among assets and over time, depending on the provisions of the tax code and the rate of inflation.

Before 1954 effective tax rates for structures were in line with the statutory rate on corporate income of 52%. However, effective tax rates for equipment far exceeded the statutory rates. While effective tax rates for both structures and equipment were reduced by the adoption of accelerated depreciation in 1954, effective tax rates for equipment remained above statutory rates until the adoption of the guideline lifetimes and the investment tax credit in 1962. With the repeal of the Long Amendment in 1964 there was a further reduction in the effective tax rates on equipment to levels well below the statutory rate.

As the pace of inflation quickened during the late 1960s the effective tax rates on equipment rose gradually; repeal of the investment tax credit in 1969 raised effective tax rates to levels comparable to those that had prevailed before 1962. Similarly, inflation and restriction of accelerated depreciation on structures to the 150% declining method after 1966 resulted in increases in the effective tax rates for structures to levels that exceeded those that prevailed before 1954. For equipment reinstitution of the investment tax credit in 1970, adoption of the Asset Depreciation Range system in 1971, and the increase in the rate of the credit from seven to 10% resulted in effective tax rates well below the statutory rate, even in the face of double-digit inflation in 1973 and again in 1979.

The Inverse Correlation

The overall conclusion is that effective tax rates on corporate income are inversely correlated with rates of technical change for the US economy as a whole. Effective tax rates declined sharply between 1960 and 1965; the rate of technical change attained its postwar peak of 2.11% per year during this period. The weighted sum of sectoral rates of technical change was 2.17% from 1960 to 1966. Effective tax

TABLE 5. Effective Tax Rates Since 1952

Year	Statutory Tax Rate	CM	GIE	TBT	IB	CB
1952	.52	.57	.59	.65	.51	.51
1953	.52	.57	.59	.65	.51	.51
1954	.52	,58	.60	.66	.52	.52
1955	.52	.58	.60	.66	.52	.52
1956	.52	.54	.57	.62	.49	.49
1957	.52	.54	.57	.62	.49	.49
1958	.52	.54	.57	.62	.50	.50
1959	.52	.55	.58	.63	.50	.50
1960	.52	.56	.58	.63	.51	.50
1961	.52	.54	.57	.62	.50	.50
1962	.52	.41	.43	.49	.49	.49
1963	.52	.40	.43	.49	.49	.49
1964	.52	.31	.34	.38	.48	.48
1965	.48	.26	.29	.34	.45	.45
1966	.48	.35	.38	.43	.46	.46
1967	.48	.37	.40	.45	.47	.47
1968	.48	.35	.38	.43	.48	.48
1969	.48	.53	.56	.61	.52	.51
1970	.48	.43	.44	.51	.53	.52
1971	.48	.35	.37	.42	.53	.52
1972	.48	.35	.37	.43	.53	.52
1973	.48	.39	.40	.47	.54	.53
1974	.48	.43	.44	.51	.55	.54
1975	.48	.33	.36	.40	.56	.54
1976	.48	.34	.37	.42	.56	.54
1977	.48	.37	.39	.45	.56	.55
1978	.48	.36	.39	.44	.56	.55
1979	.46	.32	.35	.39	.54	.53

Note: Assumes real discount rate to be four percent and relevant inflation rate to be unweighted five-year moving average of past inflation rates. Discount rates appropriate for calculating effective tax rates are discussed by Fraumeni and Jorgenson (1980)

rates rose dramatically from 1965 to 1969; the rate of technical change declined to 0.05% per year during the period 1966–1969, a drop of 2.07%; the weighted sum of sectoral rates of technical change declined to 0.25% per year, a drop of 1.92%.

Effective tax rates declined from 1969 to 1972 and have remained relatively constant since then, increasing slightly for some assets and declining slightly for others. The rate of technical change climbed from 0.4% per year for the period 1966–1969 to 0.95% per year for the period 1969–1973, an increase of 0.91% or slightly less than half of the drop from 1960–1966 to 1966–1969. The rise in the weighted sum of sectoral rates of technical change from 0.25% per year for the period 1966–1969 to 0.48% per year for the period 1969–1973 was less dramatic, but still substantial.

The most striking change in the relative prices of capital, labor, energy, and materials inputs that has taken place since 1973 is the staggering increase in the price of energy. The rise in energy prices began in 1972 before the Arab oil embargo, as the US economy moved toward the double digit inflation that characterized 1973. In late 1973 and early 1974 the price of petroleum on world markets increased by a factor of four, precipitating a rise in domestic prices of petroleum products, natural gas, coal, and uranium. All industrial sectors of the US economy experienced sharp increases in the price of energy relative to other inputs.

Slower growth in productivity at the sectoral level is associated with higher energy prices for 29 of the 35 industries that make up the producing sector of the US economy. The dramatic increases in energy prices contributed to the slowdown in productivity growth at the sectoral level. The preceding section showed that the fall in sectoral productivity growth after 1973 is the primary explanation for the decline in productivity for the US economy as a whole. Finally, it has been shown that the slowdown in productivity growth during the period 1973–1976 is the main source of the fall in the rate of US economic growth since 1973.

Recommendations

The objective in this concluding section of the paper is to provide recommendations for changes in tax policy to stimulate future US economic growth. For this purpose it is not possible to rely on the extrapolation of past trends in technical change. From 1960 to 1965 tax policy stimulated sectoral rates of technical change; from 1965 to 1969 tax policy retarded technical change; from 1969 to 1973 tax policy again acted as a stimulant. Comparing the period after 1973 with the rest of the post-war period, part of the decline in the rate of technical change can be associated with the dramatic increase in energy prices that followed the Arab oil embargo in late 1973 and early 1974.

During 1979 there was a further sharp increase in world petroleum prices, following the interruption of Iranian petroleum exports that accompanied the revolution that took place in that country in late 1978. Although prices of petroleum sold by different petroleum exporting countries differ widely, the average price of petroleum imported into the United States has risen by 130% to 140% since December 1978. In January 1981 President Reagan announced that prices of petroleum products would be decontrolled immediately. As a consequence domestic natural gas prices will also be subject to gradual decontrol, moving to world levels as early as 1985 or, at the latest, 1987.

Given the sharp increase in the price of energy relative to the prices of other productive inputs, the prospects for productivity growth at the sectoral level are dismal. In the absence of any reduction in prices of capital and labor inputs during the 1980s, a decline in productivity growth can be expected for a wide range of US industries, a decline in the growth of productivity for the US economy as a whole, and a further slowdown in the rate of US economic growth. To avoid a repetition of the unsatisfactory economic performance of the 1970s, it is essential to undertake measures to reduce the price of capital input and labor inputs. The price of capital input can be reduced by cutting taxes on income from capital.[18]

In considering economic policies to stimulate US economic growth, top priority should be given to the design of a new system for capital recovery that results in a substantial tax cut. Auerbach and Jorgenson have proposed that taxpayers should be allowed to deduct the present value of economic depreciation as an expense in arriving at income for tax purposes. The deduction would be allowed in the year an asset is acquired. Accordingly, they refer to the proposed system for capital recovery as the First Year Capital Recovery System.

Like the present system for capital recovery, the First Year Capital Recovery System is based on actual purchases of depreciable plant and equipment. However, to avoid the deterioration in the value of capital consumption allowances with inflation, the present value of economic depreciation is allowed as a deduction in the same year that the asset is acquired. As a consequence, the capital consumption allowances are unaffected by inflation or by variations in the rate at which inflation takes place.

It is important to recognize that economic depreciation actually occurs in the years after the asset is originally acquired. Future economic depreciation must be discounted back to the present to arrive at a present value of economic depreciation. For example, the present value of one dollar's worth of investment in a long-lived asset such as a manufacturing plant might be 50 cents, while the present value of one dollar's worth of investment in a short-lived asset such as a pickup truck might be 75 cents.

Under the First Year Capital Recovery System capital consumption allowances would be described by a schedule of present values of economic depreciation for one dollar's worth of investment in each class of assets. It would be possible to use 30 classes of assets — perhaps 10 types of structures and 20 types of equipment. The whole capital recovery system could then be described in terms of 30 numbers, giving the first year capital recovery allowances for all classes of assets.

The First Year Capital Recovery System would represent a vast simplification of current tax law. Rather than choosing among a range of asset lifetimes and a number of alternative depreciation formulas for tax purposes, taxpayers would simply apply the first year capital recovery allowance to their purchases of depreciable plant and equipment. No records of past purchases would be required to substantiate capital consumption allowances taken in a given year.

The First Year Capital Recovery System is a direct attack on the problem confronting tax policy makers — namely, to design a system of capital recovery that can cope with high, moderate, and low rates of inflation without the distortions resulting from the current system. While the First Year System would provide a substantial stimulus to capital formation, it would also contribute to improving the allocation of capital. The system would enhance rather than dissipate the impact of a higher rate of capital formation on productivity and economic growth.

The First Year Capital Recovery System would result in increases in effective tax rates on some assets and decreases in effective tax rates on others. To provide a stimulus to sectoral rates of technical change it is essential to combine adoption of the First Year System with a sizeable reduction in tax rates. This could be achieved by reducing the statutory tax rate of 46%. Alternatively, the effective tax rate could be reduced on new investment through an investment tax credit on all assets. The rates for such an investment tax credit must reflect differences on economic depreciation rates, so that effective tax rates remain the same for all assets.

Notes

1. The methodology that underlies our decomposition of the growth of output is presented in detail in Jorgenson (1980).
2. The results presented in Table 1 are those of Fraumeni and Jorgenson (1980), who also provide annual data for output and inputs.
3. This conclusion contrasts sharply with that of Denison (1979). For a comparison of our methodology with that of Denison, see Jorgenson and Griliches (1972).
4. The methodology that underlies our decomposition of productivity growth is presented in detail in Jorgenson (1980).
5. The results presented in Table 2 are those of Fraumeni and Jorgenson (1980), who also provide annual data for productivity growth.
6. Econometric models for each of the 35 industries are given by Jorgenson and Fraumeni (1981).
7. The price function was introduced by Samuelson (1953). A complete characterization of the sectoral price functions employed in this study is provided by Jorgenson and Fraumeni (1981).
8. Our sectoral price functions are based on the translog price function introduced by Christensen, Jorgenson, and Lau (1971, 1973). The translog price function was first applied at the sectoral level by Berndt and Jorgenson (1973) and Berndt and Wood (1975). References to sectoral production studies incorporating energy and materials inputs are given by Berndt and Wood (1979).
9. Productivity growth is represented by the translog index introduced by Christensen and Jorgenson (1970). The translog index of technical change was first derived from the translog price function by Diewert (1980) and by Jorgenson and Lau (1981).
10. This model of sectoral technical change is based on that of Jorgenson and Lau (1981).
11. The bias of technical change was introduced by Hicks (1932). An alternative definition of the bias of technical change was introduced by Binswanger (1974a, 1974b). The definition of the bias of technical change employed in our econometric model is due to Jorgenson and Lau (1981.
12. A complete characterization of biases of technical change is given by Jorgenson and Fraumeni (1981).
13. The results presented in Table 3 are those of Jorgenson and Fraumeni (1981). Of the 14 logically possible combinations of biases of technical change, only the eight patterns presented in Table 3 occur empirically.
14. A history of capital recovery provisions under US tax law, an analysis of current tax provisions, and detailed references to the literature are provided by Gravelle (1979).
15. The concept of economic depreciation is discussed in greater detail by Jorgenson (1973).
16. The criterion that effective tax rates should be the same for all assets is discussed in more detail by Auerbach (1980).
17. The bias toward equipment is not due to the impact of inflation under current capital recovery provisions; biases under current tax law are discussed in more detail by Auerbach (1979).
18. An analysis of alternative proposals for cutting taxes on income from capital is presented by Auerbach and Jorgenson (1980). A later and amplified version was published by Jorgenson and Sullivan in March 1981 through the Harvard Institute of Economic Research.

References

Auerbach, Alan J., "Inflation and the Choice of Asset Life," *Journal of Political Economy*, Vol. 87, no. 3 (June 1979), pp. 621–638.

Auerbach, Alan J., "Tax Neutrality and the Social Discount Rate: A Suggested Framework," Discussion Paper no. 742, Harvard Institute of Economic Research, January 1980.

Auerbach, Alan J., and Dale W. Jorgenson, "Inflation-Proof Depreciation of Assets," *Harvard Business Review*, Vol. 58, no. 5 (September-October 1980), pp. 113–118.

Berndt, Ernst R., and Dale W. Jorgenson, "Productive Structure," chapter 3 in Dale W. Jorgenson and Hendrik S. Houthakker, eds., *U.S. Energy Resources and Economic Growth* (Washington: Energy Policy Project, 1973).

Berndt, Ernst R., and David O. Wood, "Technology, Prices, and the Derived Demand for Energy," *Review of Economics and Statistics,* Vol. 56, no. 3 (August 1975), pp. 259–268.

Berndt, Ernst R., and David O. Wood, "Engineering and Econometric Interpretations of Energy-Capital Complementarity," *American Economic Review,* Vol. 69, no. 3 (September 1979), pp. 342–354.

Binswanger, Hans P., "The Measurement of Technical Change Biases With Many Factors of Production," *American Economic Review,* Vol. 64, no. 5 (December 1974), pp. 964–976.

Binswanger, Hans P., "A Microeconomic Approach to Induced Innovation," *Economic Journal,* Vol. 84, no. 336 (December 1974), pp. 940–958.

Christensen, Laurits R., and Dale W. Jorgenson, "U.S. Real Product and Real Factor Input, 1929–1967," *Review of Income and Wealth,* Series 16, no. 1 (March 1970), pp. 19–50.

Christensen, Laurits R., Dale W. Jorgenson and Lawrence J. Lau, "Conjugate Duality and the Transcendental Logarithmic Production Function," *Econometrica,* Vol. 39, no. 4 (July 1971), pp. 255–256.

Christensen, Laurits R., Dale W. Jorgenson and Lawrence J. Lau, "Transcendental Logarithmic Production Frontiers," *Review of Economics and Statistics,* Vol. 55, 1 (February 1973), pp. 28–45.

Denison, Edward F., *Accounting for Slower Economic Growth* (Washington: The Brookings Institution, 1979).

Diewert, W. Erwin, "Aggregation Problems in the Measurement of Capital" in Dan Usher, ed., *The Measurement of Capital* (Chicago: University of Chicago Press, 1980), pp. 433–538.

Fraumeni, Barbara M. and Dale W. Jorgenson, "The Role of Capital in U.S. Economic Growth, 1948–1976" in George M. von Furstenberg, ed., *Capital, Efficiency and Growth* (Cambridge: Ballinger, 1980), pp. 9–250.

Gravelle, Jane G., "The Capital Cost Recovery System and the Corporate Income Tax," Report No. 79-230E, Congressional Research Service, November 1979.

Hicks, John R., *The Theory of Wages* (London: Macmillan, 1932; 2nd edition, 1963).

Jorgenson, Dale W., "The Economic Theory of Replacement and Depreciation," in Willy Sellekaerts, ed., *Econometrics and Economic Theory* (New York: Macmillan, 1973), pp. 189–221.

Jorgenson, Dale W., "Accounting for Capital," in George M. von Furstenberg, ed., *Capital Efficiency and Growth* (Cambridge: Ballinger, 1980), pp. 251–319.

Jorgenson, Dale W., and Barbara M. Fraumeni (1981), "Substitution and Technical Change in Production," in Ernst R. Berndt and Barry Field, eds., *The Economics of Substitution in Production* (Cambridge, M.I.T. Press, forthcoming).

Jorgenson, Dale W. and Zvi Griliches (1972), "Issues in Growth Accounting: A Reply to Edward F. Denison," *Survey of Current Business,* Vol. 52, No. 5, Part II, pp. 65–94.

Jorgenson, Dale W. and Lawrence J. Lau (1981), *Transcendental Logarithmic Production Functions* (Amsterdam, North-Holland, forthcoming).

Samuelson, Paul A. (1953), "Prices of Factors and Goods in General Equilibrium," *Review of Economic Studies,* Vol. 21, No. 1, October, pp. 1–20.

Investment Bibliography

Jorgenson, Dale W., "Capital Theory and Investment Behavior," *American Economic Review,* Vol. 53, no. 2 (May 1963), pp. 247–259; reprinted in R.A. Gordon and L.R. Klein, eds., *Readings in Business Cycles* (Homewood: Irwin, 1965, pp. 366–378; reprinted in *Bobbs-Merrill Reprint Series in Economics,* Econ-167.

Jorgenson, Dale W., "Anticipations and Investment Behavior," in U.S.

Duesenberry, G. Fromm, L.R. Klein, and E. Kuh, eds., *The Brookings Quarterly Econometric Model of the United States* (Chicago: Rand McNally, 1965), pp. 35–92.

Jorgenson, Dale W., and J.A. Stephenson, "The Time Structure of Investment Behavior in United States Manufacturing, 1947–60," *Review of Economics and Statistics,* Vol. 49, No. 1, February 1967, pp. 16–27.

Jorgenson, Dale W., and J.A. Stephenson, "Investment Behavior in U.S. Manufacturing, 1947–60," *Econometrica,* Vol. 35, no. 2, April 1967, pp. 169–220.

Hall, Robert E., and Dale W. Jorgenson, "Tax Policy and Investment Behavior," *American Economic Review,* Vol. 57, no. 3 (June 1967), pp. 391–414; reprinted in *Bobbs-Merrill Reprint Series in Economics,* Econ.-130.

Jorgenson, Dale W., "The Theory of Investment Behavior," in R. Ferber, ed., *The Determinants of Investment Behavior,* Conference of the Universities—National Bureau Committee for Economic Research (New York: Columbia University Press, 1967), pp. 129–156; reprinted in Harold R. Williams and John D. Huffnagle (eds.), Macroeconomic Theory: *Selected Readings* (New York: Appleton-Century-Crofts, 1969), pp. 207–230; reprinted in S. Mittra, ed., *Dimensions of Macroeconomics* (New York: Random House, 1971), pp. 161–178.

Jorgenson, Dale W., and C.D. Siebert, "A Comparison of Alternative Theories of Corporate Investment Behavior," *American Economic Review,* Vol. 58, no. 4 (September 1968), pp. 681–712.

Jorgenson, Dale W., and C.D. Siebert, "Optimal Capital Accumulation and Corporate Investment Behavior," *Journal of Political Economy,* Vol. 76, no. 6 (November/December 1968), pp. 1123–1151.

Jorgenson, Dale W., and J.A. Stephenson, "Anticipations and Investment Behavior in U.S. Manufacturing, 1947–60," *Journal of the American Statistical Association*, Vol. 64, no. 325 (March 1969), pp. 67–89.

Hall, Robert E., and Dale W. Jorgenson, "Tax Policy and Investment Behavior: Reply and Further Results," *American Economic Review*, Vol. 59, no. 3 (June 1969), pp. 388–401.

Jorgenson, Dale W., J. Hunter and M.I. Nadiri, "A Comparison of Alternative Econometric Models of Quarterly Investment Behavior," *Econometrica*, Vol. 38, no. 2 (March 1970), pp. 187–212.

Jorgenson, Dale W., J. Hunter and M.I. Nadiri, "The Predictive Performance of Econometric Models of Quarterly Investment Behavior," *Econometrica*, Vol. 38, no. 2 (March 1970), pp. 213–224.

Jorgenson, Dale W., and S.S. Handel, "Investment Behavior in U.S. Regulated Industries," *Bell Journal of Economics and Management Science*, Vol. 2, no. 1 (Spring 1971), pp. 213–264.

Jorgenson, Dale W., "Econometric Studies of Investment Behavior: A Review," *Journal of Economic Literature*, Vol. 9, no. 4 (December 1971), pp. 111–1147.

Hall, Robert E., and Dale W. Jorgenson, "Application of the Theory of Optimum Capital Accumulation," in G. Fromm, (ed.), *Tax Incentives and Capital Spending* (Amsterdam: North Holland, 1971), pp. 9–60.

Jorgenson, Dale W., "The Economic Impact of Investment Incentives," in Joint Economic Committee, *Long-Term Implications of Current Tax and Spending Proposals*, Washington, Ninety-Second Congress, First Session (1971), pp. 176–192; reprinted in W.E. Mitchell, J.H. Hand, and I. Walter, *Readings in Macroeconomics* (New York: McGraw-Hill, 1974), pp. 174–183.

Jorgenson, Dale W., "Investment Behavior and the Production Function," *Bell Journal of Economics and Management Science*, Vol. 3, no. 1 (Spring 1972), pp. 220–251.

Jorgenson, Dale W., and C.D. Siebert, "An Empirical Evaluation of Alternative Theories of Corporate Investment," in K. Brunner, ed., *Problems and Issues in Current Econometric Practice* (Columbus: Ohio State University, 1972), pp. 155–218.

Jorgenson, Dale W., "Technology and Decision Rules in the Theory of Investment Behavior," *Quarterly Journal of Economics*, Vol. 97, no. 4 (November 1973), pp. 523–543.

Jorgenson, Dale W., "The Economic Theory of Replacement and Depreciation," in W. Sellekaerts, ed. *Econometrics and Economic Theory* (New York: MacMillan, 1973), pp. 189–221.

Jorgenson, Dale W., "Investment and Production: A Review" in M. Intriligator and D. Kendrick, eds., *Frontiers of Quantitative Economics*, Vol. II (Amsterdam: North-Holland, 1974), pp. 341–366.

Gordon, R., and Dale W. Jorgenson, "The Investment Tax Credit and Counter-Cyclical Policy," in O. Eckstein, ed., *Parameters and Policies in the U.S. Economy* (Amsterdam: North-Holland, 1976), pp ½ 275–314.

Jorgenson, Dale W., "Investitions Theorie," in M. Beckmann, G. Menges and R. Selten, eds., *Hand Wörterbuch der Mathematischen Wirtschaftswissenschaften*, Band 1 (Wiesbaden: Verlag Dr. Th. Gabler KC, 1980), pp. 113–118.

Auerbach, Alan J., and Dale W. Jorgenson, "The First Year Capital Recovery System," *Harvard Business Review*, forthcoming; reprinted in Committee on Ways and Means, United States House of Representatives, *Tax Restructuring Act of 1979*, Washington, Ninety-Sixth Congress, First Session (1980), pp. 66–76; and in Committee on Finance, United States Senate, *Miscellaneous Tax Bills III*, Washington, Ninety-Sixth Congress, First Session (1980), pp. 349–378.

Note: Requests for reprints of articles should be addressed to Professor Jorgenson, Harvard University, 122 Littauer Ctr., Cambridge, MA 02138 (617-495-4661).

Technology In Society

New York / Oxford / Toronto / PERGAMON PRESS / Paris / Frankfurt / Sydney

Technology In Society, Vol. 3, pp. 173–203 (1981)
Printed in the USA. All rights reserved.

0160-791X/81/010173-31 $02.00/0

A Tax to Internalize Risks

Burton H. Klein

Over the past 15 years the United States economy has been characterized by declining productivity gains, a worsening ability to compete in international markets, and the reemergence of a business cycle in which declines in the rate of productivity growth anticipate downturns. Why? These changes, it will be argued, reflect a worsening of the dynamic performance of the US economy, brought about by a preoccupation with both short-term profits and short-term stability.

What should be done? The purpose of this paper is to stimulate thinking with respect to a tax proposal that would (a) encourage more rapid productivity gains by providing substantial tax benefits for risk-taking, (b) dampen inflationary pressures by tying rewards to better price performance, and (c) reduce the amplitude of the business cycle by substituting continuous for intermittent pressure when bringing about productivity gains. To stimulate such thinking a fairly specific proposal will be made. However, it should be emphasized at the outset that the proposal does contain some serious problems. Indeed, inasmuch as no such proposal has ever been made, it would be surprising if an initial attempt were free of difficulties. The questions which need to be debated are, first, whether it might be possible to devise a better way for rewarding on the basis of performance; and, second, if fully satisfactory alternatives cannot be found, would a highly-imperfect method of rewarding on the basis of performance be perhaps better than none?

In the past, improvements in productivity have come about mainly as a result of pressure on firms by their rivals to improve their ability to compete in terms of price. Indeed, such pressure has not only provided a major stimulus to productivity gains, but it has provided a major deterrent to wage increases. Where wage escalation has been most rapid is not in the high, but in the low productivity in-

The author wishes to thank Bruce Cain, Ed Green, Carl Lydick, Gordon McRae, Stephen Selinger and Evsey Domar for helpful suggestions. He is mainly indebted to David Feinstein.

Burton H. Klein received his Ph.D. from Harvard University in 1952 and is a member of the Council of Economic Advisers. He was employed by the Rand Corporation from 1954–1967 where, he says, he "tried to understand why making money in the military market was an entirely different proposition from making money in the civilian market." In 1967 he went to the California Institute of Technology "because I wanted to make economics into a more worldly subject (i.e., a more dynamic subject matter) and because I hoped to obtain some useful clues from physicists, chemists and geologists. As it turned out, I profited most from the chemists."

dustries — where there is a smaller degree of constraint upon both price and wage increases.

Therefore, assume that one wants a tax that both stimulates productivity advances and constrains wage increases. A tax based upon this logic would reward firms on the basis of improvement of their own price performance relative to the industry's average performance during the preceding year. Suppose that, for the purpose of judging the industry's performance during the previous year, the firm utilizes price data published by the government. If the firm increases its prices at the same or greater rate than the industry as a whole, it will pay taxes at a rate equivalent to the previous year. But, assume that to the extent it improves its price performance, then it will be able to reduce its tax burden considerably.

The logic of such a tax, it should be apparent, is to encourage firms to take risks to escape from paying higher taxes. To better appreciate how such a tax might operate, consider an industry with, say, six firms. Suppose that initially only one firm, "A," elects to take risks to escape the tax, while the others simply continue to make pricing decisions as usual. To simplify the discussion, assume that firm "B" is representative of the latter group.

As Table 1 indicates, in the first period A's prices were about the same as its competitors. But, even though prices industrywide had been increasing about 10% per year, A makes a strategic decision to hold its increase to only half of that of the preceding year for the next several years while the others continue a policy resulting in prices increasing at a more or less 10% rate.

Now, A's gain from reducing prices will be reflected in a tax savings as well as in increased sales of its product at the lower price. So, let us assume that A predicates its strategic decision on increasing output by say, 5% — and that this increase in output is realized at the expense of the other five firms in the industry. As the lower portion of the table indicates, such price performance clearly benefits the consumers of A's product. While customers of the other firms in the industry must pay almost 10% more for the products they buy (measured in terms of first-year prices and second-year output), A's buyers save 25,000 dollars in total as a result of his pricing decision. Moreover, should A continue such a policy, it will almost certainly induce the other firms in the market to reduce their costs and, ultimately, their prices too. Once such an effort gains momentum, the entire industry can increase its output at the expense of other domestic and foreign industries.

What would A have to do to make such strategy possible? By taking greater risks in R&D, it might be possible to generate alternatives at no sacrifice in quality that would cost the firm 5% less. Judged in terms of historical perspective, this would be a relatively modest accomplishment. Or lower prices might be made possible by a combination of risk-taking in R&D and a greater degree of wage constraint than that which is generally practiced.

Why a Special Tax Inducement?

If A can so increase his profits, why is a special tax inducement needed? The essential reason is that, inasmuch as the benefits derived from following such

TABLE 1. Illustration of Performance Tax Impact

	Firm A			Firm B		
Commodity	Average Price	Quantity Sold	Dollars Sales	Average Price	Quantity Sold	Dollar Sales
Period One						
1	$132.00	1050	$138.60	$134.00	1040	$139.40
2	152.00	1030	156.60	151.00	1050	158.60
3	165.00	900	148.50	166.00	890	147.70
			$443.70			$445.70
Period Two						
1	139.00	1100	152.90	147.00	1030	151.40
2	160.00	1080	172.80	147.00	1030	151.40
3	173.00	945	163.50	182.00	881	160.30
			$489.20			$484.30

Computation of Average Price Increase:
Second Year's Output Measured in Terms of First Year's Prices

1	$132 × 1100 = $145.20	$134 × 1030 = $138.00
2	152 × 1080 = 164.20	151 × 1040 = 157.00
3	165 × 945 = 155.90	166 × 881 = 146.20
	$465.30	$441.20

Average percentage price increase $\dfrac{489.2}{465.3} = 105.1\%$ Average percentage price increase $\dfrac{484.3}{441.2} = 109.7\%$

strategy are highly uncertain, the requisite animal spirits are likely to be found only in newly established firms. Consequently, special measures are required to rekindle vigor in mature firms.

Given the unwillingness of firms to take risks when precise calculations cannot be made, the kind of tax benefit needed to promote behavior such as A undertakes is as follows: assume that A's cost people compute the difference between the sums that consumers would pay for the firm's products at the average prices charged during the year, and the amount they would pay had prices increased as much as they did during the previous year. If the former were not smaller than the latter, the firm would obtain no tax advantage. But every percentage point of "cost savings" could reduce the tax it otherwise would have to pay by, say, 10%. In the above example, firm A would be able to reduce its computed corporation tax by 50%. Or assume that for every percentage point reduction the tax savings were 20%. If profits after taxes averaged 5% of sales, the tax loss would be more or less the same as the customers of A's products gained. And, if one takes into account the impacts of A's pricing decisions on other firm's pricing behavior, the total consumer gain would be greater than the tax loss. However, there is a danger in going this far: firms could engage in price wars at no cost to themselves.

To be sure, firms willing to take risks to lower their taxes might incur losses for a year or two. But, if they could carry not only losses forward (as they can for a ten-year period under current laws), but also average their price computations over a period of, say, five years, the risk of early losses would not be weighed so greatly — and firms would be motivated to think in terms of a longer time horizon.

The principal advantage of such a tax scheme over one that would advocate more liberal allowances for R&D spending or more liberal treatment of capital gains is that it rewards on the basis of *performance*. By contrast, the benefits of rewarding on the basis of inputs are very uncertain. For example, it is questionable what impact, if any, a 10% increase in R&D spending would have on the rate of productivity gain. What is important is not so much the total amount spent but the amount spent on high-risk projects. Indeed, as the propensity to engage in risk-taking has declined, so has the "productivity" of R&D dollars, as measured in terms of the associated rate of productivity gains.

The proposed tax scheme would also have an obvious advantage over schemes aimed at restraining inflation by providing tax advantages to firms that exercised a greater degree of wage constraint; by recognizing that higher wages alone do not create inflation, it would not single out higher labor costs for special tax treatment.

On the other hand, as will be pointed out in the concluding section, the proposed tax does have some serious problems; particularly, there is the danger that it would provide an incentive for reducing quality.

Figure 1 indicates why it is important to have steady, rather than intermittent, pressure to bring about productivity gains. The vertical axis measures year-to-year changes in production and productivity indices; the horizontal axis, time. As the chart shows, in US manufacturing industries productivity gains lagged during the booms and were pushed up most rapidly during recoveries from recessions. The common explanation for the cyclical swings in productivity is that during the booms various bottlenecks emerge, and during the downswings firms are loath to lay off workers as rapidly as output declines. However, while such factors can explain something like 5% plus or minus variations around a *zero* rate of productivity growth, they cannot explain the big swings in *productivity rates* shown in Figure 1. Consider, for example, the Great Depression when, according to the conventional wisdom, productivity gains might be expected to have fallen to zero. Yet, whether productivity gains are measured in terms of output per man-hour or per unit of capital and labor inputs, between 1929 and 1937, according to both indices, productivity rose by about 17%. Paradoxical as it may seem, industries, such as the automobile industry, were involved in more risk-taking during the Great Depression than they are today!

Also clearly indicated by Figure 1 are the economic reasons for applying steady pressures on firms to keep the average rate of productivity gains in manufacturing above 5% per year. The period 1948 to 1965, it can be agreed, was somewhat of a Golden Age. True, during that period productivity gains were somewhat below

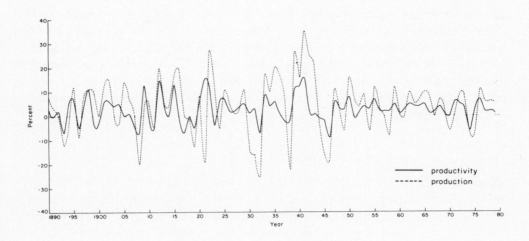

FIGURE 1. Changes in Manufacturing Productivity and Production Indices.

an annual 5%. But, nevertheless, though during that period the amplitude of the cycles was declining, they remained remarkably steady. On the other hand, a glance at the left side of the chart will reveal that only if the annual rate of productivity gain rose above 5% during a boom would a depression be followed by a quick recovery. Conversely, when productivity rates did not rise much above 5% and the trend was generally downward, this was followed by the panic of 1907, in one case, and the Great Depression, in the other.

The Future Outlook

What is the outlook for the future? The 1970 and 1974–1975 downturns were not only relatively large but resulted in the reemergence of a pattern in which a decline in the rate of productivity advance anticipated downturns (with an average lag of about four months). However, it should not be assumed that we are entering a period of short and sharp cycles such as occurred in the 1900s. It would be overly optimistic to assume that, like the 1915 economy, the 1980 US economy is sufficiently robust to attain productivity gains well above 5% during a boom, suffer twice the decline in output as occurred during the 1974–1975 downturn and reach another peak in a year or two. But neither can we be confident that the economy will return to the performance it exhibited during the period 1948 to 1965, when the United States was still benefiting in several ways from World War II.

There are good reasons for assuming that downturns anticipated by declining productivity rates are to be expected in the future. In particular, while in every period of history there are industries engaged in rivalry to reduce costs or improve quality — the steel industry in the 1890s, the computer and semiconductor industries at present — the so-called mature industries slacken their efforts to bring about productivity gains during boom times, and behave like rivalrous industries only when recessions bring their backsides to the fire. To be sure, continuous pressure to bring about productivity gains will not eliminate the business cycle. But, by insuring that firms will more or less continuously deal with new circumstances, the probability of a series of recessions as deep or deeper than the last will be minimized.

Wishful Thinking

No doubt, there are many politicians and business economists who choose to believe that, except for being regulated, the current American economy possesses all the vitality it ever had. However, to deny there is serious risk that the dynamic stability of the economy — its ability to make smooth adjustments to new circumstances — will not be further impaired is to engage in wishful thinking. The time has come to make a US goal of the adoption of measures aimed at gradually pushing up the average rate of productivity gains in manufacturing to 5% a year — and keeping them there.

The following discussion is divided into four parts. The first discusses the logic of a tax designed to spur gains in productivity. It will be seen that the proposed tax has precisely the same impact on progress as does economic rivalry (as distinct from static economists' concept of competition). It also will be seen that a tax designed to achieve the same effect was proposed as long ago as 1825 by Sadi Carnot (who is mainly known for having discovered the key ideas contained in the second law of thermodynamics).

Part II will discuss two important analytic points: the requirements for steady progress, and the impact on economic stability when risk-taking declines below some crucial level. The substance of this discussion is based on a book, *The Hidden Foot,* that David I. Feinstein (an applied mathematician) and this author are writing on a dynamic model designed to predict accelerations and decelerations in the rate of progress as well as cyclical movements in productivity. However, this paper will not be concerned with the model per se, but, rather, with only a few of its key results.

Part III will show why, to develop an effective tax proposal, it is imperative to understand the relationship between productivity gains and inflation. Contrary to common wisdom, rising wage rates during periods of prosperity do not fuel inflation, but sagging productivity rates do!

Part IV will discuss some of the practical issues encountered when designing a tax that will permit business firms to serve their country by better serving their own longer-run interests.

The Concept of the Hidden Foot

Rivalry is here defined, in common sense terms, as competition to generate better or cheaper alternatives. The degree of rivalry depends on the size of advances firms in an industry seek. Assume that in a progressive industry, such as semiconductors or computers, firms undertake to bring about significant advances, and, by doing so, pressure their rivals to undertake risks. Now, no firm in such an industry will be told it must bring about significant advances. The leaders of the firm will be entirely free to choose whether to engage in bringing about insignificant or significant advances — to aim for survival in the short run or the long run. But, if the former strategy is chosen, they risk going out of business in a few years. And an industry, in which firms preferring to stay in business take risks that are likely to bear fruit only in several years hence, can be described as having a highly effective hidden foot; or alternatively, as an industry in which the "tax" rate for failure to take risks is far greater than that proposed above.

However, the proposed tax will have an impact not only on those firms that choose to take risks to lower their tax burdens, but also on those who, by not so choosing, find that they have jeopardized their ability to compete.

Is the enunciation of such a concept tantamount to the renunciation of Adam Smith? By no means. The fact of the matter is that, while Adam Smith's concept of competition was the man in the streets — to his way of thinking, competition was rivalry between both buyers and sellers — as of the time he wrote *The Wealth of Nations* (1776), the rivalry between firms that enormously increased Britain's wealth in the 19th century was only beginning. For example, to observe the impact of rivalry on the rate of progress in the iron and steel industries he would have had to have written *The Wealth of Nations* something like 100 years later. Moreover, while equilibrium economists claim him as one of their own, his words attest otherwise: "The progressive state is the hearty state, the stationary state dull, the declining state melancholy."[1] So, how can one do Adam Smith more honor than by returning to the task he left undone?

There are three principal differences between a dynamic-rivalry concept of competition and the concept of competition adopted by those static economists who defected from Adam Smith to the theory later developed by the mathematician Cournot.

1. *Whereas the theory of pure competition is a mechanistic theory, rivalry is a behavioral theory of competition.*

The static theory of competition assumes that the "goodness" of competition is determined by the number of sellers in a market: when the number is great, each can have but an insignificant effect on price, and a condition of "perfect" competition is said to exist. On the other hand, the effectiveness of dynamic competition depends upon motivating entrepreneurs to ask burning questions which will lead to searches for the feedback required to overcome limits, and, hopefully, escape the "tax." As for the stimulating effect of genuine challenges, Samuel Johnson made the general point very well when he said, "Depend upon it, sir, when a man knows he is to be hanged in a fortnight, it concentrates his mind wonderfully."

2. *Dynamic competition results in a positive-sum game.*

The conventional theory of competition implies a zero-sum game in which the size of the pie is strictly fixed. Consequently, more competition can result in greater allocative efficiency — a once-and-for-all gain equivalent to a few percent of the GNP — but it cannot result in exponential progress. On the other hand, dynamic competition is a positive-sum game from the point of view of both participants and consumers which, as will be shown, can generate progress at compound interest rates (*e.g.*, doubling bits/cent every two or three years).

Now it is true, if individual moves in the game were considered, dynamic competition might seem to be a zero-sum game. When one firm brings about a startling advance in the field of semiconductors it gains, and the other firms lose. When one surgical team discovers a way to reduce fatalities associated with heart operations, the immediate effect is to gain patients at the expense of other surgical teams. When one baseball team wins the World Series, the other loses.

The Elasticity of Demand

However, if we look more deeply, what may seem to be a zero-sum game at first glance really is not. It is no accident that rivalry mainly occurs in fields in which the potential elasticity of demand with respect to quite large quality or price changes happens to be very high. To be sure, firms have no way of calculating the elasticity of demand beforehand; for example, Henry Ford had no way of knowing that the demand for a rugged, $600 car would turn out to be highly elastic.

But, when the demand becomes elastic for large price or quality changes, what may have seemed to be a zero-sum game will actually be a positive-sum cooperative game. For example, by engaging in keen competition with other teams to draw large crowds to see their games, baseball players may be thought of as engaging in a form of cooperation to make their salaries much higher. Teams of heart surgeons voluntarily agree to engage in much the same kind of rivalry because, by so doing, they can increase the total number of heart operations; and when the semiconductor people engage in rivalry, they too make total sales greater than they otherwise would be.

This is not to say, however, that the demand for everything is highly elastic. In fact, this is one reason for proposing a tax that would not involve penalties for failure to bring about productivity gains. What is needed is a tax that would have a minimum impact on distorting the workings of the marketplace.

3. *Whereas perfect competition occurs under conditions of perfect information, rivalry changes the probability distributions of the world.*

With perfect competition, firms must take their environments as given, and cannot change them. If they cannot change their information, then obviously they cannot change their environments.

However, with rivalry, firms do not take their information as given. The name of the game is to understand the strong and weak points of the rivals' products so well that in the next round of the game one can best him. And, when one does, it will have changed the probability distributions of the world. Thus, after the invention of the DC-3, both aircraft companies and airlines calculated the odds of certain events differently. Beforehand, however, entrepreneurs have no way of calculating the odds of being successful. It is only to avoid the certainty of paying higher "taxes" to a rival that they are motivated to take relatively small-scale incalculable risks. In short, only in a world of calculable risks would no hidden-foot be needed.

The proposed tax to spur larger increases in productivity and smaller increases in prices is also designed to change the probability distribution of the world. Entrepreneurs will find that the probability of selling creative ideas to top management will increase. Top management will find that by becoming more decentralized and better listeners they will be able to increase the probability of competing more satisfactorily with German and Japanese firms. When consumers shop at the market, they will discover that the probability of finding bargains has increased. And not only that. If firms go as far as possible to avoid paying higher taxes, everyone can be less nervous about the probability of a serious downturn!

Sadi Carnot's Tax Proposal (1824)

As of the time, the competing theory of farming — a static theory commonly regarded as the very essence of scientific farming — was that put forth by Lavoisier. On his model farm near Blois, managed according to the principle that knowledge neither could be created nor destroyed, Lavoisier kept precise information on inputs, outputs, prices, and costs. And he made decisions in a way to maximize profits, or in other words, to maximize static efficiency.

Now, Carnot clearly recognized that by assailing static efficiency he was also attacking the economists of his generation:

Taxes are regarded by economists as an evil, but as a necessary evil, since they provide public expenses. Consequently, economists think that if the government possessed sufficient revenues, in domains, for example, the suppression of all taxes would be a desirable matter.[2]

He further argued that, static economists notwithstanding, "Taxes are a means of influencing production and commerce to give them a direction they would not have taken."[3] In his view, apparently, taxes were regarded as an appropriate means for driving a system away from an equilibrium. How did he propose to do this?

A tax on the rent of a farm would be much better than a tax on the land itself. Proprietors then could only avoid taxes by themselves improving their property. As it is, they merely collect the rents, and usually employ their surplus in unproductive expenditure, while the proprietary farmers voluntarily devote theirs to the improvement of the land.[4]

One effect of such a tax, Carnot believed, would be to cause a decentralization of farm operations:

Proprietors, becoming cultivators to escape the taxes, would settle in the country, where their presence would disseminate intelligence and comfort; their revenues, before spent unprofitably, would then pay expenses and improvements on their property.[5]

In short, Sadi Carnot proposed a differential tax to increase dynamic efficiency by providing an incentive for decentralization. It must be emphasized, however, that had there been a way to bring pressure on the landlords to prevent them from increasing prices by as much as costs, decentralization could have been accomplished without having them move to the countryside. Once such pressure was brought to bear, landlords would have been provided with an incentive to reward operators in terms of their contributions toward improving the productivity of the land.

It can be seen, therefore, that the logic of Sadi Carnot's tax proposal is precisely the same as the logic involved in dynamic competition: both involve a "differential tax," from which escape requires decentralization of risk-taking. And, in both cases, the effect is to increase the rate of progress.

Moreover, it also must be observed that the incentives guiding the pursuit of self-interest by French landlords are not different from those that guide the pursuit of self-interest of many large corporations. Most are owned by thousands of absentee landlords who, it may be assumed, are mainly interested in short-term gains. According to a recent article in *Scientific American,* in Japan the story is entirely different.[6] There, stockholders are principally interested in longer-term capital gains. And, if true, this single fact could very well explain much of the difference between performance of Japanese and American industrial firms.

Is it fair to say that Sadi Carnot not only overthrew Lavoisier's caloric law, but also his farming law? The price France had to pay for protecting an overcentralized system of management was that agriculture became the most protected sector of the French economy — the most protected because French landlords were maximizing profits subject to obsolete information with respect to the possibilities for improving productivity.

On the other hand, it is known that in the form of rivalry, at least since the end of the Civil War, American farmers have had a self-imposed "tax" for improving the productivity of farms. Although the demand for farm products is very inelastic, this tax took the form of rivalry between entire communities of farmers. The institutions associated with rivalry were the state and county fairs that began in New England in 1810 which were promoted mainly by the more successful farmers and a variety of periodicals subscribed to by farmers dealing with ideas that seemed to work best in farming. This included advice with respect to fertilizing land, making tastier cider, breeding animals, seed selection — and even the choice of a good farm wife! So, if science is defined as "what works," it can be said that from a very early date there was scientific farming in America. The father of scientific farming, it may be noted, was Thomas Jefferson, who, when Ambassador to France, frequently visited the French countryside to gather seeds to experiment with on his American farm.

Table 2 provides a rough idea of how scientific farming evolved in America. It can be agreed that, in comparison with the six-fold reduction in the cost of automobiles between 1910 and 1925 or the 40% annual increase in performance of semiconductors during the past 20 years, the decade-to-decade improvements in agricultural productivity were minuscule. Yet, what is surprising about this table is the steadiness of the gains and the acceleration in the rate of progress in wheat and corn that began about 1900. Ironically, Jefferson's approach to farming succeeded in the North long before it did in the South.

It must be acknowledged that the agricultural experimental stations had some

TABLE 2. Changes in Farm Productivity*

Year	Wheat		Corn for grain		Cotton	
	Yield per acre (bu.)	Manhours per 100 bushels	Yield per acre (bu.)	Manhours per 100 bushels	Yield per acre (bu.)	Manhours per 100 bushels
1800	15.0	373	25.0	344	147	601
1840	15.0	233	25.0	276	147	438
1880	13.2	152	25.6	180	188	303
1900	13.9	108	25.9	147	189	284
1910–1914	14.4	106	26.0	135	201	276
1915–1919	13.9	98	25.9	132	168	299
1920–1924	13.8	90	26.8	122	155	296
1925–1929	14.1	74	26.3	115	171	268
1930–1934	13.5	70	23.0	123	184	252
1935–1939	13.2	67	26.1	108	226	209
1940–1944	17.1	44	32.2	79	260	182
1945–1949	16.9	34	36.1	53	273	146
1950–1954	17.3	27	39.4	34	296	107
1955–1959	22.3	17	48.7	20	428	74
1960–1964	25.2	12	62.2	11	475	47
1965–1969	27.5	11	77.4	7	485	.30
1970	31.0	9	71.6	7	438	26

*Figures for 5-year periods are annual averages.
Source: *Historical Statistics of the United States*. U.S. Department of Commerce.

influence with the acceleration in the rate of progress. This example is often quoted as evidence in support of Federal aid to R&D; but the problem in using it as basis for making sweeping generalizations is that it does not take the farmers into active consideration. Had there not been a keen demand on the part of farmers for new ideas, the agricultural experimental stations would have come to naught.

The Agriculture Advantage

In any event, there are apparently cases in which the tortoise — a tortoise that is stimulated to gradually quicken its pace — can catch up with the hare and gradually overtake him. The United States' advantage is greatest, relative to the rest of the world, in the field of agriculture. There can be no question, therefore, that Carnot not only overthrew Lavoisier's caloric theory — but also his static theory of farming designed to insure a dull stationary economy.

What Should the Future Look Like?

To return to a question raised earlier: if one takes farming as an example of an activity in which there are more or less continuous pressures to bring about productivity gains, what should the cycles look like? One can expect to observe business cycles because, even if not generated in the activities in question, they will be affected by cycles arising in the less progressive sector of the economy. But one can also expect to observe cycles in which there is no slackening of productivity gains during periods of prosperity. And as Figure 2 shows, while farmers have suffered from serious downturns, they certainly have not contributed to economic declines (note the absence of lags between productivity and output declines).

As for the high correlation between declines in production and productivity, this is easy to explain: farming is an activity in which employment remains relatively steady over the business cycle. So, output declines will automatically be reflected in a decline in productivity. This is not to say, of course, that if Jefferson's agrarian society had been able to completely isolate itself from the Hamiltonian sector of the economy it would have suffered no downturns; there certainly would have been years of bad harvests, invasions by various insects, and so forth. But, while farmers have had to respond to cycles, their role in propagating them has been relatively minor.

In the case of farming there are enough data available to obtain insights on the impact of the tax as was proposed above. To appreciate the relevance of the data, it is important to keep in mind that the rate of progress depends not only on the "tax rate," so to speak, but also on farmers' incomes. If the rates were the same in two periods, but in the second their real incomes were greater, then one obviously would expect a more rapid rate of progress. Conversely, if the rates increased while real incomes remained more or less the same, then one would expect a more rapid rate of progress.

The first row of Table 3 shows the decade-to-decade changes in the "tax rate"; the second, farmers' average incomes (including government subsidies) divided by an index of what they actually paid for living expenses and farm production inputs. It will be noted that, because the data for particular farm commodities increased more throughout the period than did changes in output per unit of input. And productivity measured on a man-hour basis rose much faster than did productivity measured in terms of total inputs, because during the first half of the period farm machinery was substituted for farm labor, and during the second, chemicals.

Now, there were two periods in which productivity did not behave as might be expected: 1932 to 1942 and 1942 to 1952. The second is relatively easy to explain. Due to the draft, during World War II, the exodus from farming was almost twice the rate of the previous decade. Moreover, the period 1942–1952 was relatively free of economic downturns. And these two facts alone can easily account for the rapid rise in productivity during World War II. However, the author is unable to explain why, during the Great Depression, when farm price supports resulted in an annual 6% increase in prices over costs, the rate of productivity advance substantially increased over the rate of the 1920s. Was there enough economic adversity in the country at large to supply all the motivation needed?

In any event, it is easy to explain the poor performance during the period 1900 to 1920 on the basis of relatively low real incomes, and performance since World War II on the basis of changes in the "tax rate": when it was positive, productivity gains accelerated; when it was negative, they decelerated.

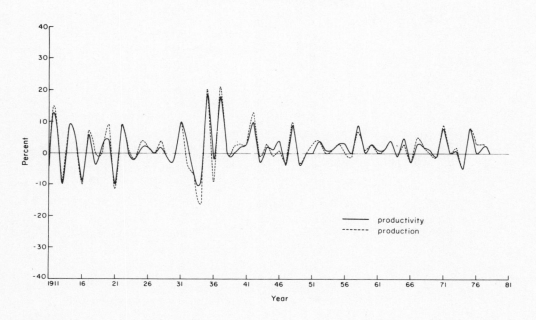

FIGURE 2. Changes in Farm Productivity and Production Indices.

These computations should serve to chasten those economists who believe now, as did economists in Sadi Carnot's day, that all US ills would be solved by simply reducing taxes. Quite clearly, if increasing income will do the trick, then in the period 1972–1978 there should have been a spectacular increase in the rate of productivity gain.

Dynamic Efficiency

Dynamic efficiency is the efficiency associated with obtaining either a given output with fewer inputs or a higher quality output with fewer inputs. The term "efficiency" is used because it is assumed that resources are fixed, and that the name of the game is to use them in a manner so as to buy as much progress as possible. The term "dynamic" is used because, whereas all static processes occur under given conditions, the essence of dynamic processes consists of changing initial conditions.

Gains in dynamic efficiency can occur as a result of employing more efficient machines or changing the slope of learning curves. For example, in a recent article, James A. Cunningham, an executive of the National Semiconductor Corporation, points out in some detail how greater pressure to reduce costs resulted in discoveries that reduced a 75% learning curve to 65% and an 80% curve to 75%.

Where did the people in the semiconductor industry get the idea to use the learning curve as a management tool? According to Cunningham, the author of the concept was none other than Henry Ford.

TABLE 3. Farmers' Revealed Response to Hiden-Foot and Hidden-Hand Feedback

	1912–22	1922–32	1932–42	1942–52	1952–62	1962–72	1972–78
Percentage change in prices recovered/ Percentage change in prices paid	– .3	.4	6.2	2.1	– 1.9	– 1.4	4.2
Real income per farm	2170	1850	1820	3610	3235	3990	7000
Decade to decade percentage changes in output per unit of input	– .9	– 5.5	.9	2.3	1.8	2.1	1.6
Average percentage changes in man-hours per unit of output							
Wheat (100 bushels)	.9	1.3	1.6	1.6	2.2	2.5	0
Corn (100 bushels)	1.0	0	1.6	2.3	3.0	5.5	5.0
Cotton (bale)	– 1.0	1.7	1.4	1.7	2.3	6.2	5.6
Hay (ton)	0	.7	1.2	1.8	1.6	3.2	2.5
Potatoes (ton)	.8	.9	2.3	2.1	1.6	2.0	5.0
Tobacco (100 lbs)	– .5	– .3	.9	1.2	1.4	4.7	1.2
Milk cows (CWT)	.5	.6	.3	1.4	1.8	6.2	18.0
Cattle (CWT)	.2	.4	.7	1.1	1.4	1.6	6.7
Chickens (CWT)	.2	0	1.1	1.2	1.8	NA*	NA
Turkeys (CWT)	.4	1.1	1.4	2.9	5.2	NA	NA

*NA = Not available.
Source: U.S. Department of Agriculture.

Almost 50 years ago, after manufacturing more than 15 million Model T autos, Henry Ford noted that "we have the firm policy of steady price reduction" and explained why "we have never considered any costs as fixed."

"One of the ways of discovering what a cost ought to be," he wrote, "is to name a price so low to force everyone in the place to the highest point of efficiency. The low price makes everyone dig for profits. We make more discoveries concerning manufacturing and selling by this forced method than by any method of leisurely investigation."[7]

The most important gains in dynamic efficiency result either from developing new products or new processes. And, when in a given round of the game, one firm wins the gamble by introducing an alternative embodying a significant advance before its rivals, it also wins handsomely in terms of profits. What makes winning very lucrative is not simply that it displaces a rival from a profitable market; more basically, the real gain occurs when, as a consequence of overcoming market and technical limits not overcome before, the actual elasticity of demand turns out to be very high, and its sales will expand rapidly: Indeed, the very essence of dynamic behavior consists of bringing about discontinuous and unpredictable advances — advances resulting in the discovery of "loopholes" in the static law of supply and demand.

A representation of the process of overcoming limits is shown in Figure 3. On the vertical axis product performance of a new product or process is measured; on the horizontal axis, time.

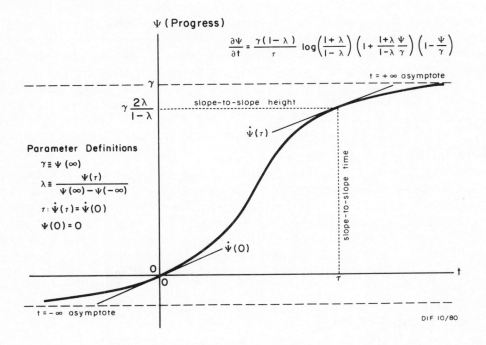

$$\frac{\partial \Psi}{\partial t} = \frac{\gamma(1-\lambda)}{\tau} \log\left(\frac{1+\lambda}{1-\lambda}\right)\left(1+\frac{1+\lambda}{1-\lambda}\frac{\Psi}{\gamma}\right)\left(1-\frac{\Psi}{\gamma}\right)$$

Parameter Definitions

$\gamma \equiv \Psi(\infty)$

$\lambda \equiv \dfrac{\Psi(\tau)}{\Psi(\infty) - \Psi(-\infty)}$

$\tau : \dot\Psi(\tau) = \dot\Psi(0)$

$\Psi(0) = 0$

FIGURE 3. Overcoming Limits.

It is assumed that the developer begins with some ideas on how to overcome significant limits with respect to improving performance. Gamma represents the maximum performance that might be achieved were the developer to spend an infinite effort on polishing these ideas. Tau is the point at which the rate of progress is as it was at the inception of the effort. And lambda is the total fraction of asymptote to asymptote height explored in lambda.

Departure from a previous "s"-shaped curve begins with fresh ideas whose mutual interaction supplies exponential growth. They have been variously described as "an appreciation of the significance of traveling wave tubes for developing a lower-cost microwave system" or "the realization that automobile emissions can be decreased by an order of magnitude, and gasoline consumption can be reduced by half when thinking of the combustion process of an engine in an entirely different way." Such descriptions, however, do not explain the manner in which the discoveries were made.

The process of discovery can be better described as the freeing of habits of thinking which occur when one tries to understand the potential role of either new ideas or new rules. In turn, key insights generated before development is underway lead to the discovery of subsidiary ideas to increase performance, and the more or less continuous redefinition of the system in the light of what was learned. Finally, as Figure 3 shows, rapidly diminishing returns set in. This stage is described as "involution" rather than "evolution" because, whereas evolution is an outward-looking process, involution is an inward-looking process.

It is true that diminishing returns in a temporal sense need not imply diminishing economic returns. Logically speaking, slowdowns in the rate of progress could be accompanied by reductions in the cost. Nevertheless, there are good empirical reasons for assuming that diminishing returns in an economic sense occur more rapidly. Fresh ideas result in rapid progress, which usually turns out to be relatively inexpensive. But, when the curve finally flattens, progress becomes very expensive, because it involves dealing with dozens of tiny optimizations. Indeed, for this reason entrepreneurs pressed by their rivals typically take as their motto, "better early than best."

In brief, there are two distinctive forms of cognitive discovery: "elaboration," which is mapping and surveying with the span of ideas already discovered, and "violation," the unplanned intuitive leap that illuminates new realms. Elaboration yields progress which, when charted opposite time, resembles a skewed letter "s." This is the standard "growth-against-limits" curve known to biologists. Driven stochastically by violations, progress over longer times becomes an irregular staircase of "s" curves, each coupled continuously and smoothly with its predecessor.

In addition to being circumscribed by the initial conditions of their birth points, "s" curves (resulting from first order quadratic differential equations) require two additional parameters to be unique. As was indicated above, tau (τ) measures the time taken for the slope of an "s" curve to reattain the value it had at the birthpoint. Thus, tau (τ) is the "slope-to-slope" time. Lambda (λ) governs the sharpness of an "s" curve. It is defined as the ratio of the slope-to-slope height to the "asymptote-to-asymptote" height of the curve. Equivalently, it is half the ratio of the slope-to-slope height to the "tau/2-to-infinity" height. (Equivalent, because the "s" curves are symmetric about their tau/2 point.) Lambda is a measure of learning and adaptivity. In general, the more important the limits overcome and the more the system is adapted to take advantage of new knowledge, the greater the value of lambda.

Bringing about violations to keep one jump in front of the "tax collector" requires two kinds of feedback: opportunity and violation. Opportunity feedback is obtained by studying the strong and weak points of a rival's products; and its role is to stimulate questions to determine how best to overtake the opposition. On the other hand, violation feedback is that needed to answer the questions provoked by opportunity feedback, as, for example, when Henry Ford realized that a French racing car was constructed with a type of steel that he needed for building a rugged car.

Why Tau?

Why was tau selected rather than some earlier or later benchmark? Tau was selected because it is assumed that the firm wants to make as much money as possible *subject to taking the actions of its rivals into account*. In particular, the developer might wait beyond tau on the premise that, even though the product will cost a good deal to develop, the consumer will be willing to pay more for a product better specialized to meet his particular needs.

But, if the developer should wait, he would risk having another firm capture the prize. Moreover, by having a second team work on specializing the product for particular applications, while a first team initiates the development of a new product, the developer can have his cake and eat it too! Providing, of course, that ideas are forthcoming to initiate a new s-shaped curve with the same curvature as the present one — why waste the first team on a less profitable activity when it can be used on a more profitable one? Why not release products before, say, tau? The essential reason is that releasing products very early in the game typically involves reliability problems. So, by releasing too early the developer risks acquiring the reputation of producing clever but unreliable products.

What, then, determines lambda? In part, lambda is determined by the cost of experimentation: the smaller the cost, the more progress that can be bought per dollar of expenditure.

But the height also depends on the capacity of the developers' team to engage in rapid learning, both before and after the initiation of development. At one extreme are the developers who have such a small capacity for learning that they can only imitate. In this case, the value of lambda would be zero. However, as will be seen in the next section, while a strategy of pure imitation can be more profitable in the short run than operating at relatively small values of lambda, in the long run such a policy is very unpromising, indeed.

If entrepreneurs are young enough in spirit to learn, on what does their learning depend? To maximize the curvature and, hence, the longer-run height attained by a series of "s" curves, the following conditions need to be met:

First, to maximize the flow of opportunity and violation feedback, engineers and workmen as well need to be rewarded on the basis of their ability to generate creative ideas — and no one should be promoted who has never made a mistake.

The greater the degree of risk the firm must take — either to escape from a tax imposed by its rivals or to escape from paying higher corporation taxes — the more it must do to create an internal environment that is highly conducive to risk-taking. A reward system that motivates people to widen their search for ideas creates a highly interactive organization: interactive within, with its customers — present and potential — and with universities.

Suppose that a firm is willing to take significant risks to reduce its tax burden, how can it measure its internal response to such a strategic decision? Data would have to be collected on telephone calls or trips before and after its internal incentives were changed; and it will be found that, measured in terms of the randomness of the internal communications, it has become a more fluid organization.

Second, while ideas are indispensable for overcoming limits, only experimentation can reveal whether they are promising. Generally speaking, the ratio of the doubters to the nondoubters increases exponentially with the size of the advance. Therefore, to insure rapid learning during research, and experimentation preceding development, firms must budget separately for relatively high-risk projects. If they insist upon making comparisons between high- and low-risk projects, the inevitable result will be to drive out the high-risk projects. Now, the proportion of R&D a firm devotes to high-risk projects will obviously depend on how anxious it is to escape from paying higher "taxes." The greater the desire, the more that will be set aside in the form of risk capital. In turn, the greater the proportion, the more that the risk-taking function is decentralized.

Third, the principle of decentralization requires that development be decoupled from production, and particular individuals be made responsible for development. When R&D and production decisions are coupled, the inevitable consequence is an organization in which everyone is responsible for everything, and no one is in charge of anything — an organization in which lambda is made artificially small. Every firm should be completely free to decide whether or not to observe this rule. Nevertheless, if they chose not to follow it, firms would, so to speak, expose themselves to double taxation. On the one hand, under the proposed tax system they would be paying higher taxes than necessary. On the other hand, they would continue to pay the exorbitantly high "taxes" Japanese and German firms are levying on them.

The Relationship Between Microbehavior and Macroperformance

While space does not permit a detailed development of the mathematical argument, the logic is relatively simple. It assumes a division of labor between man and God, in which God throws dice to determine the timing of violations to initiate new s-shaped curves, and man determines the curvature of the "s" curves. To develop a predictive theory, the question is: which set of rules comes closest to capturing earthly reality?

David Feinstein and the author decided that the best set of rules they could find was one that described the *waiting time* between violations in terms of a negative exponential distribution. Employing such a distribution is tantamount to assuming that the probability that one company will make a discovery is independent from the probability that another will also. It should be noted, however, that this assumption does not apply to what goes on *inside* a dynamic organization. Highly interactive organizations can greatly augment the role of luck which increases the rate of violations and, consequently, their rate of (exponential) growth. However, unless the advances are trivial, what they cannot do is to schedule the time when limits will be overcome.

In order to present the conclusion of the analysis, let us rephrase our question thusly: how many discoveries are required before tau so the "s" curves can grow upon themselves and provide us with exponential progress? On the vertical axis of Figure 4 is shown the percentage change in performance per unit of time (τ); and on the horizontal axis, the mean number of violations in tau.

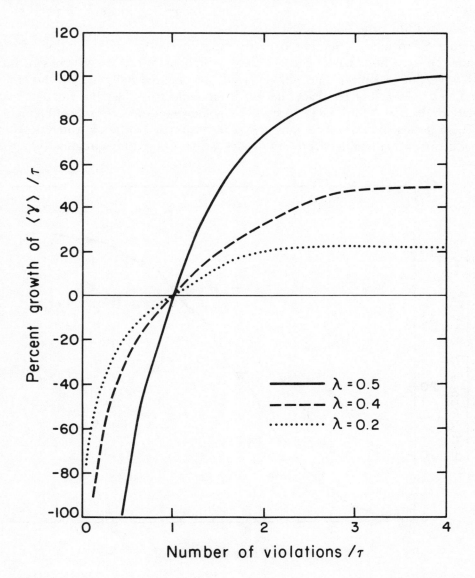

FIGURE 4. Sketch of Percent Growth Rate of Performance Versus Violation Rate.

As Figure 4 indicates, the requirements for exponential progress — for progress occurring at compound rates of interest — are, on the one hand, relatively modest, and, on the other, razor sharp. They are relatively modest because, even if the vaue of lambda is high, only three independent experiments are required, on the average per tau, to provide a .93 probability of making the "s" curves couple before tau which insures continual exponential progress. And, after that point, further experiments increase the probability at a rapidly diminishing rate. It may be noted, when significant advances are involved, the laws of probability insure that the "s" curves of various firms will not be synchronized — which puts them in almost as good a position to learn from each other as if their activities had been planned in that way. On the other hand, let the number of experiments drop to one in tau and we obtain only linear progress; with fewer experiments, progress will die out completely.

Figure 5 provides, in somewhat overly simplified form, an illustration of the results. To show how the "s" curves couple, a high lambda value was chosen. But with any value of lambda one will get steady exponential progress. On the other hand, let hidden-foot feedback die out of an industry — let the frequency of violations decline — and the picture will be as shown on the right side of Figure 5.

These results should not be interpreted to mean that with only three firms in an industry a reasonable degree of rivalry will insure steady progress. On the

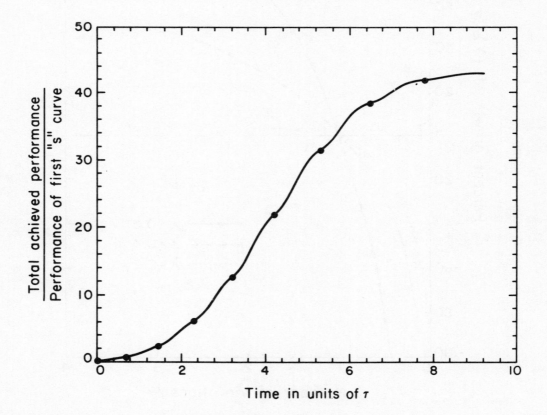

FIGURE 5. Envelope of "s" Curves.

assumption that success will likely be followed by relaxation, that a few failures will be followed by retrenchment, and that a fair degree of internal risk-taking will produce at least one dud, about twice as many firms are required to provide an adequate amount of redundancy. It is true that individual firms can undertake a sufficient number of experiments to make smooth progress. But there is not need to debate that issue, because in the near future there should be good enough estimates of lambda to measure their dynamic performance.

If the requirement for steady exponential progress is relatively modest, why does progress die out of an industry? The basic reason is related to the fact that, when organizations become highly structured, people stop asking questions, which, in turn, has the effect of defining the technology more and more narrowly. Consequently, if the definition is later broadened, almost always it will be a newcomer to the industry or a firm from another industry that makes the revitalizing discovery.

A declining violation rate is commonly associated with a declining entry of new firms. A number of studies have shown, when evolution is the order of the day, new firms make more than their share of important discoveries, and, by doing so, bring a good deal of pressure against established firms.[8] A case in point: the much greater dynamic performance of Bell Telephone Laboratories after World War II surely had a good deal to do with the fact that it faced far more serious challenges from new entrants.

However, due to the fact that entry costs increase by two or three orders of magnitude, there is an almost inevitable decline in entry as a technology matures.

The proposed tax would not encourage the entry of new firms to develop entirely new products. But new firms and firms from other industries would be provided with a motivation to enter industries if they thought they could reduce the rate of inflation.

The Concept of Bifurcation

The phenomenon to be discussed is imitation that results in short-term benefits at the expense of long-term paralysis. It should be emphasized at the outset, however, that not all imitation is self-defeating. In about 1860, when the United States began producing Bessemer steel, a number of firms engaged in imitation of British firms — to the point of hiring British foremen.[9] But rivalry between firms led to ways to lower costs, with the consequence that — by 1900 — Scottish shipbuilding firms were importing steel from the United States. And in Japan, too, what began as lavish imitation often was followed by creativity — by gradually pushing up the values of lamdba.

Then there are the chemical firms that engage in both the development of new chemicals and the granting of licenses to other companies to produce new chemicals. It can be assumed that they are engaged in a type of trade that is mutually beneficial. Why is it so? If one chemical firm can license the production of a chemical developed by another firm, it can concentrate its first-class talent on generating higher values of lambda than otherwise would be possible. When all chemical firms engage in this type of trade, total chemical sales are increased. In short, this is a type of trade that produces better results than could be achieved in a zero-sum game.

There are other types of imitation and near imitation which can have a favorable impact on shorter-run profits, but will jeopardize longer-term gains. These types of imitation — generally described by economists as "product differentiation" — are the result of a lack of rivalry, on the one hand, and a high degree of centralization, on the other.[10] The bifurcation illustrated by Figure 6 is a short-run phenomenon. The vertical axis of Figure 6 shows the performance of a product measured in dimensionless terms. The depth axis measures lambda. (Recall high lambda correlates with relatively unstructured and highly decentralized organizations.) This results from the belief that the next model to be developed (*e.g.,* the K car, the Model T Ford or the 1955 color television set) will be the last word on the subject, and an associated desire to maximize short-run profits. As a consequence the developer is encouraged to evolve either towards high lambda values or very low lambda values, depending crucially on his starting position.

In particular, it can be predicted that a highly centralized firm that operates on the basis of issuing commands will be pulled towards the region of lambda values approaching zero. The horizontal axis measures time, again normalized. When t/τ is greater than one, development is being carried to the stage of rapidly diminishing returns. It should be noted, however, that diminishing returns in an economic sense is sharper than in a temporal sense. Suppose that one were to plot cumulative development expenditures until the time bifurcation first appears. In a typical case it would be found at that point that cumulative development expenditures were something like four or five times what they were at tau.

The mathematics used to generate these curves is the same as that employed to generate the "s" curves described earlier. The only difference is in the interpretation of the "s" curves. In the previous description it was assumed that an "s" curve applied to a single product; however, here it applies not only to the original product, but also to subsequent modifications. Thus, when Hewlett-Packard began providing an entirely new family of scientific computers, that marked the beginning of an "s" curve with a relatively high lambda value. On the other hand, when American automobile companies began to develop compact cars with features found in foreign automobiles five to eight years earlier, that marked the beginning of a lambda curve with relatively slight learning: in the limiting case — pure copying without any learning — the curvature would be zero. It must not be assumed, however, that from the point of view of an insider the value of lambda is as it appears from the perspective of an outsider. Quite obviously, bringing about a greater degree of curvature requires dealing with a higher degree of uncertainty. So, as an insider accustomed to operating at a point where lambda is close to zero, engaging in a bit more imaginative copying might be quite as challenging as developing an entirely new breed of computers.

In the following discussion, the picture of economic reality implicit in the saddle point will be described; and then it will be shown why myopic profit maximization can involve relatively large longer-run costs.

It will be observed that, while all of the "s" curves start at the same slope, when t/τ is in the neighborhood of 1.5 to 2.0 the "saddle point" begins to emerge

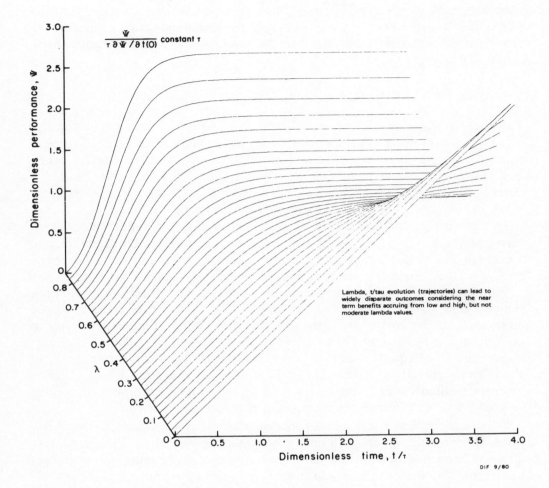

FIGURE 6. Projected Performance When Technological Innovation Stops.

(technically $\partial Y/\partial \lambda \ (\lambda = 0) = 0$ at $t/\tau = 1.47$). Then as t/τ attains greater and greater values, the "saddle" widens.

How is this to be explained? By observing the extreme right portion of the diagram, it can be assumed that innovations are being considered that, on the one hand, produce relatively small advances and, on the other, are fairly easy to copy. For example, an automobile designed to capture the image of the P-38 airplane by providing it with long tail fins results in an insignificant advance that is relatively easy to copy. On the other hand, when considering the extreme left portion of the curve, it can be assumed that the high lambda curves are not easily dislodged. So, if progress is about to stop, a firm can establish a "monopoly" in the traditional sense of the term. After the initial pioneering discoveries, a firm may develop a series of new products or — as in the case of the Model T Ford or the DC-3 airplane — it may not improve its products beyond tau. In either case, the firm in question quickly develops such a reputation for excellence as to pro-

vide the product with a high growth potential as far as sales are concerned. Between these extreme examples one finds on both sides of the ravine a variety of intermediate cases that result in a saddle point when lambda reaches some
minimum value.

The Wrong Side of the Ravine

The essential reason the developer gets pulled to the right is, on the one hand, his
quest for short-term profits and, on the other, a belief that, as far as future
technical progress is concerned, the clock is about to stop. Nevertheless, when
new challenges emerge, firms that are highly centralized and operate by the issuance of commands are completely unable to jump across the ravine to gradually
push up the value of lambda, because that would involve dealing with a higher
degree of uncertainty than their attenuated uncertainty thresholds would allow.
Living on the wrong side of the ravine means living in a world of microstability —
a world in which organizations are so insistent upon short-run predictability in the
small that they can only cope with well-defined types of uncertainty.

But, inasmuch as they must deal with hidden-foot feedback by overcoming
limits if they want to survive, macrostability or long-term predictability in the
large must be the goal of the left-bank operators. While it is relatively easy to
cross the ravine by becoming obsessed with the desire for microstability, it is by no
means easy to reacquire a taste for adventure once it has been surrendered. In
short, firms operating on the right side of the ravine are much like Carnot's
absentee landlords who — because they could only copy each other's procedures
— could not learn from experience what the game was all about.

What are the longer-run costs of imitation that involve minor product variation? The previous graph indicated what would happen should progress cease
after the last innovation; and in that case the advantages of imitation were striking. Figure 7 indicates what would happen if progress continued over 12 generations of products. As is indicated, from a longer-run perspective the advantage of
operating at higher, rather than lower, values of lambda is completely unam-
biguous. The ticks in the diagram demarcate each new generation of products
(violations). Assume that the time required for generation is three years. Then, in
15 years a developer operating at .4 lambda would have a 33% advantage over a
straight imitator, and one that operated at .2, a 16% advantage. The conclusion:
when firms in an industry act as imitators, they become easy prey to the process of
creative destruction.

Implications

Over the past 15 years the United States has experienced both a decline in the rate
of productivity advance and a weakening in its ability to engage in foreign competition (Table 4). How are these related? Assume that productivity advances can
be measured in either terms of reductions in costs or improvements in quality.
Then, when one country improves its productivity by generating either better or

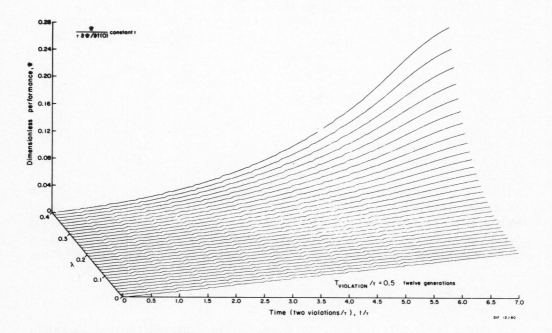

FIGURE 7. Long-Term Dimensionless Performance as a Function of λ and Time.

cheaper alternatives, it can expect to be an exporter of the commodity in question — and an importer, when its rate of productivity advance declines relative to that of other countries. Thus, it is no accident that for many years the British economy has exhibited both lower productivity and poor trade performances.

In turn, myopic profit maximization leads to both poor trade and lower productivity performance. When the synthetic fibers industry challenges the cotton textile industry, an opportunity is created for US textile machinery developers. But, if the US cotton textile machinery developers continue to think in myopic terms while the Germans and Japanese bring about significant advances, the US will end up importing half of its cotton textile machinery.

Conversely, during the 1930s, when US aircraft firms were reducing drag to lower the cost of airliners while European countries were engaged in reducing drag to obtain better gliders and racing planes, US firms were thinking in less mypoic terms. Consequently, US firms brought about a 50% reduction in per-seat-mile costs while European manufacturers continued to imitate the Ford trimotor airplane. It should be emphasized that imitation can take many forms. But all produce unfortunate longer-run results without any conscious recognition on the part of the developer that he is in fact imitating.

Suppose, for example, that firms in an industry decide to make R&D decisions more or less in the same highly calculable way they make investment decisions. When they do, this will inevitably lead to a decline in opportunity feedback and in the number of violations. Therefore, the result will be the same as if they openly conspired to imitate each other.

TABLE 4. Sales by United States Firms as a Percentage of Total U.S. Sales

Industry	1960 %	1970 %	1979 %
Autos	95.9	32.8	70.0
Steel	95.0	85.7	86.0
Apparel	98.2	94.8	90.0
Electrical components	99.5	94.4	79.9
Farm machinery	92.8	92.2	84.7
Industrial inorganic chemicals	98.0	91.5	81.0
Consumer electronics	94.4	68.4	49.4
Footwear	97.7	85.4	82.7
Metal-cutting machine tools	96.7	89.4	73.6
Food processing machinery	97.0	91.9	81.3
Metal-forming machine tools	96.8	93.2	75.4
Textile machinery	93.4	67.1	54.5
Calculating and adding machines	95.0	63.8	56.9

Source: Department of Commerce. *Business Week*, June 30, 1980, p. 60.

So, there is left the conclusion that decline of the wealth of a nation is brought about by a worsening ability to deal with the new challenges which, in turn, is brought about by the absence of hidden-foot feedback. Moreover, to close the circle, when in the absence of continuous hidden-foot feedback firms slack off in bringing about productivity advances during good times, this inevitably results in business cycles with a greater amplitude than would otherwise occur. Thus, from several points of view, operation on the left bank leads to a "hearty" economy, and, on the right bank, to a "melancholy" economy.

What should be done? There are, of course, the monetarists who say that if the US could only keep the money supply stable, the economy would remain stable. People who seriously believe this are daydreaming. Those who believe that a static equilibrium is inherently stable are thinking of heaven and not of earth. In heaven, firms may ignore the feedback generated by their rivals, and maximize their profits subject to fixed and unchanging inputs and production functions. But, if one can find a firm doing that on earth, one should rush to the stockbroker and tell him to sell its stock short. Therefore, the monetarists' prescription applies to heaven and not earth; a fact of life that many industrialists in the United Kingdom are more aware of today than they were several years ago.

The conclusion? Reindustrializing America will not simply involve remedying the capital shortage of the stagnating industries (as the US once sought to remedy the problems of underdeveloped countries by supplying them with capital). More fundamentally, reindustrializing America will require appropriate incentives to pull firms down the right bank so they can reacquire the degree of heartiness associated with operations on the left bank.

The primary reason for not recommending a tax that would impose penalties for failure to bring about productivity gains is that every firm should have the option to decide for itself whether or not to make the crossing, and at what speed.

Suppose that in some particular industry firms are highly centralized. And suppose that in those industries 50% to 60% of managerial compensation takes the form of bonuses awarded during prosperous times, which cannot be withdrawn until the manager in question retires. Now, such an incentive scheme is ideal for operations on the right bank: yes-men are promoted, and young imaginative engineers are discouraged from entering the industry.

If such a firm refuses to take risks to lower its tax burden, because it wants to preserve a way of life, it will sooner or later fail to remain in business. However, it should be guaranteed the right to be a failure. In fact, there is a need for a constitutional amendment that would make it illegal for public officials to prevent any firm — large or small — from going out of business.

On the other hand, assuming that firms will be persuaded to take risks to lower their tax burdens, they should have the opportunity to proceed at their own speed when transforming their internal incentives and associated organizational characteristics. For example, it will not be easy for firms that now make development and production decisions as if they were one to separate R&D from production — even though combining these activities makes the value of lambda artificially small. If firms do not make this separation, they will inevitably find that foreign competition will be taking a greater and greater toll: recall the difference between progress at linear rates and exponential rates.

Nor will it be easy for firms that have not been rewarding in terms of creative accomplishments to begin to do so. When the present bureaucracy has been rewarding on the basis of seniority and administrative position, it can be counted upon to stoutly resent such a move. But, again, unless firms devise a reward scheme that induces people to think in terms of working for the firm as a whole rather than individual departments, US firms will be no match for Japanese firms.

Finally, it must be recognized that productivity gains are also hindered by union work rules. For example, a machine breaks down and, although they know the cause, the workers are forbidden to do anything but have a cup of coffee while a repair team comes in to fix the problem. But, again, when workers begin to appreciate that higher wages and greater productivity go hand in hand, because they are given on-the-spot promotions when they think of the operation as a whole, everybody will be made better off.

In brief, the basic purpose of the proposed tax is to drive the economy to a point at which it can achieve better results than in a zero-sum game.

The Inflation Problem

Figure 8 shows average annual percentage changes in manufacturing for output, productivity, unit wage costs, and prices. Changes in unit wage costs are merely the reciprocal of changes in productivity. They are included in the chart merely to make the relationships more clear between productivity and price changes.
As the figure indicates, productivity performance began to worsen during the 1960s — and, had it not been for the war in Vietnam, it seems likely that a serious downturn would have occurred in the 1960s. As for the earlier period, World War II undoubtedly affected the impressive degree of stability. Not only

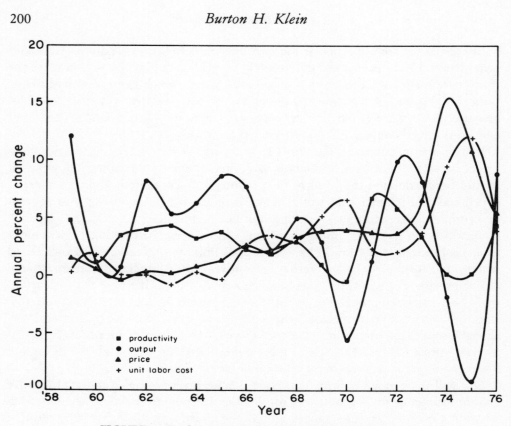

FIGURE 8. Performance of Manufacturing Industries.

did wartime technology find postwar applications, it also trained an entire generation of entrepreneurs to work in areas of high lambda numbers. Moreover, after
World War II, funds for starting high technology firms were more plentiful than
are available today. But most important, perhaps, were the returning GIs who,
having learned to innovate on the battlefield, brought to American business a
spirit that had been lacking during the Great Depression.

However, such windfalls could not be expected to last very long. So it is not
surprising that in the 1970s the economy began to reacquire the same
characteristics it had demonstrated before World War II. As far as inflation is concerned, the facts are these. First, while there is not necessarily a short-run correlation between unit labor costs and prices, during each successive downturn since
World War II prices moved less flexibly than in the last. Consequently, the correlation coefficient between changes in unit wage costs and prices almost doubled
in the second half of the period. Second, conventional wisdom notwithstanding,
rising wage rates during prosperous times play a relatively minor role in initiating
inflation. Inflation gains momentum, not during recovery periods, but when the
country is heading into a recession.

If wages rose as rapidly as prices, there would be nothing to break the development of a cost-plus economy. But they do not. And when consumers' real incomes
fall quite significantly, it is change in their buying habits that does what the
monetary authorities cannot do.

The proposed tax will provide an incentive for firms to increase prices less than they otherwise would during periods of economic decline — and, to the extent that firms respond, the public deficit will be made larger. However, unlike deficits incurred to provide consumers with more spending power, the deficit resulting from the proposed tax is noninflationary. Hence, it would ease the task of the monetary authorities during periods such as the present. Moreover, to the extent that such deficits mitigated the seriousness of downturns they would result in less deficit financing in the longer run.

Several Serious Problems

Is it practical?

As was indicated in the introduction, there are several serious problems inherent in the proposed tax scheme. Very briefly, they are as follows:

Classification of Products

The price data published by the government are not for individual products with well-defined technical characteristics. The proposed tax would not hinder a firm from developing new commodities which would come under a different price classification from those it is now producing. Often, opportunities for reducing prices and costs are better perceived by newly established firms or firms from another industry. And, if such firms infuse a sagging industry with vitality, they ought to be rewarded.

The problem, however, is that existing firms in an industry might be motivated to take advantage of such a tax by switching to those price categories which would make their own performances seem more favorable without actually decreasing production or customer costs. In short, there are more ways than one to stay ahead of the "tax collector." That the danger is a real one, there can be no question. Consequently, further research is necessary to determine if there are ways to minimize this danger, ways that would not involve an enormous policing effort.

Measurable Improvements in Quality

There are products whose improvements in quality are quite as measurable as reductions in costs. For example, improvements in the efficiency of machines can be quite accurately measured. And there are generally agreed upon measures of the performance of computer chips.

It should be apparent that, when measurable improvements in quality occur, price indices should be adjusted to reflect such improvements. How might this be accomplished? One relatively simple way would be for firms in the industry concerned to jointly work out mutually acceptable measures, which, in turn, could be used to adjust prices. In short, this would involve a good deal of work, but it does not seem to be an insurmountable problem. It would provide better incentives for many industries — including the machinery industry, where improvements are sorely needed.

Unmeasurable Improvements in Productivity

Dealing with this problem undoubtedly represents the main difficulty for the proposed tax, particularly with respect to consumer products industries in which the buyers are relatively poor judges of quality. Indeed, quality deterioration of many consumer products is a serious problem today, and there is no doubt that on this account alone the rate of inflation in the United States is understated. Moreover, it cannot be denied that the proposed tax would provide an incentive for firms to overlook its impact on quality.

On the other hand, it also cannot be denied that for some industries there already is in existence as good a means of checking quality deterioration as can be devised: competition from Japanese firms. But this still leaves open the question about the responsiveness of American firms to quality as well as price competition. Do they respond by merely improving quality? Or do they respond by more clever advertising? And, if greater expenditure on advertising can serve as a substitute for bona fide quality improvements, is there an effective way to deal with this problem (*e.g.,* by limiting advertising expenditures that can qualify as tax deductions).

There are, indeed, thorny questions that will require further study. But the main point to keep in mind is that, lacking an effective way to change the incentives of firms there is a real danger that the American economy will deteriorate to the point where the trend toward a more static and more unstable economy will become irreversible.

The question of whether some kind of reasonably effective method for rewarding on the basis of performance is, therefore, a terribly important question — terribly important because all of the other ways for dealing with the present economic predicament might be far worse.

References

1. Adam Smith, *The Wealth of Nations*, p. 72.
2. N.L.S. Carnot in R.H. Thurston, Ed., *Reflections on the Motive Power of Heat* (John Wiley and Sons, 1890), p. 212.
3. *Ibid*, p. 212.
4. *Ibid*, p. 212.
5. *Ibid*, p. 213.
6. James C. Abegglen and Akio Etori, "Japanese Technology Today," *Scientific American*, October 1980.
7. James A. Cunningham, "Using the Learning Curve as a Management Tool, *IEEE Spectrum*, June 1980.

8. See, for example, F.M. Scherer, *Industrial Market Structure and Economic Performance* (Rand McNally Economic Series, 1970), pp. 376:377.

9. For an excellent account, see Elting E. Morison, *Men, Machines, and Modern Times* (MIT Press), pp. 125–175).

10. Harold Hotelling, "Stability in Competition," *The Economic Journal*, March 1929.

Technology In Society

New York / Oxford / Toronto / PERGAMON PRESS / Paris / Frankfurt / Sydney

Technology In Society, Vol. 3, pp. 205–212 (1981)
Printed in the USA. All rights reserved.

0160-791X/81/010205-08$02.00/0

Tax Policies and Economic Expansion in the US

L. R. Klein

The Problem

There is little doubt that all is not well with the US economy, but what to do about it? Before trying to prescribe remedies it is natural and good practice to try to diagnose the present situation. Policy prescription, at least on an indicative basis, will then follow.

Among our many ills, the following are representative:
- Inflation is too high
- Growth has fallen, partly by cyclical recessions (1974–75, 1980) and partly in the longer run.
- Productivity growth has fallen, even to the point of declining. This too is cyclical and secular.
- Energy is expensive and its delivery is unreliable.
- The quality of life has been deteriorating.

The first two items combine to produce the concept of "stagflation"—rising prices, high or rising unemployment, lower growth rates of production. Aspirations, based on memories of better times in the 1950s and 1960s, would suggest that the country would be more comfortable with inflation under 5% annually, preferably as low as 2%; unemployment at about 4%, and GNP growth at about 4%. As the situation stands now, the nation can hope to bring inflation below 10% with a great deal of effort, but it is far from getting to 5% or below.

Real growth which was formerly on a 4% trend for a long stretch of time ap-

Lawrence R. Klein is Benjamin Franklin Professor of Economics and Finance of the University of Pennsylvania. He has contributed to Macroeconomic Analysis in The Keynesian Revolution *(1974) and many research papers, and has built statistical models of the US and other economies, beginning in 1946, the first of which were published in* Economic Fluctuations in the United States, 1921–1941 *(1950). Dr. Klein published* A Textbook of Econometrics *(1952),* An Introduction to Econometrics *(1962), and several research papers in applied and theoretical econometrics. He is a past president of the Econometric Society and American Economic Association. Presently a member of the National Academy of Sciences, the American Academy of the Arts and Sciences, and the American Philosophical Society, he is founder and chairman of the Professional Board of Wharton Econometric Forecasting Associates.*

pears to have fallen to about 3%. This figure averages slower rates during cyclical decline and faster rates during recoveries. When growth used to be at 4%, unemployment was held at 4% of the labor force on a fairly steady basis. This was considered to be "full employment" in the American context. The rise of multiple earner families, the absorption of the youths born in the late 1940s–early 1950s (baby boom generation), generous unemployment benefits, the entrance of more women into the labor force and other socio-demographic trends changed the country's perceptions of full employment. This would lead one to accept 5% unemployment as a desirable figure, but if the surge of women entrants into the labor force is over and if youthful entrants are much reduced in a relative sense, then the nation may aspire to the 4% figure again in the middle of this decade.

The productivity decline may well be at the root of many of the economic ills of these times. Productivity growth makes it possible for all segments of society to participate in economic advancement; it also restrains inflation and makes stable growth possible. If the US is to go any distance at all towards meeting its aspirations at the more favorable ends of possible ranges, it will be necessary to lift the growth rate of productivity. At the first point, it was expanding at more than 3% annually; now it is cyclically depressed at zero-to-negative rates.

A possible reason for the decline in productivity growth is the economic dislocation of shifting from an energy-cheap to an energy-dear economy. The country has become temporarily diverted to finding substitutes, making capital more energy efficient and trying to conserve energy use. While the transition is taking place, the oil import bill soars and the overall economy has to be restricted in order to relieve pressures on the foreign trade accounts and on inflationary bottlenecks. Apart from the all important issue of national security, energy problems account for many of the other problems in the list cited above.

With low productivity, many services, especially social services, are difficult to maintain on former standards. It appears that the social environment is being taken care of on a lower level of quality. In addition, there are pollution, congestion and the scarring of the earth's surface, partly associated with energy problems and partly issues in their own right.

An Analysis of Possible Cures

Since this paper is more concerned with policy proposals for improvement of the economy than with a full discussion of the present troubles, it is worthwhile to abbreviate their diagnosis and proceed with an analysis of possible cures. A complete treatment would extend into many lines of economic policy, but for sharper focus, this paper will be devoted to tax policies. Related to the economic ills of the United States at the present time is a high rate of taxation. This, in itself could be considered as an ill, but more importantly, it may be a major factor in causing such ills as stagflation and the productivity slowdown. Total government receipts (excluding social insurance contributions and Federal transfers to state/local government) reached 24% of GNP in 1980, just below the "rule of thumb" ceiling of 25%, cited by Colin Clark many years ago. If the proposition that people are highly taxed or, possibly, over taxed, is accepted, then candidates for reduction should be considered, keeping in mind the need for contributing to the betterment of the basic economic ills.

Federal taxes are larger than state/local taxes and can be dealt with on a unified basis; therefore, priority should be given to cuts at the national level. Indirect taxes (sales, property, excises) would be admirable candidates for cutting because they figure directly in business costs and account for a significant part of the main price indexes. If they were to be reduced there would be an immediate, but once-and-for-all reduction in the rate of inflation. That would be a welcome fillip to the economy at this time, but would be very difficult to implement. All 50 states and thousands of local governmental units would have to be given grants to make up for lost revenues, and it would be very difficult to do this on an equitable basis. The possibility of reducing indirect taxes offers many attractive results, but it should be given secondary consideration at the present time, although not deleted from the menu of alternatives.

Similarly, social insurance collection should not be considered now, favorable as that might be, because so many people have an uneasy feeling about the need for preserving solvency in the trust funds. Social Security contributions (or taxes) are like indirect taxes, in that a large portion—the employer's portion—is a major component of business costs. If Social Security contributions could be cut back or restrained from statutory escalation, this would provide relief to business costs and make for a once-and-for-all reduction in the rate of inflation. The fund for social insurance benefits would, of course, have to be supplemented, but part of the benefits are not for actuarially insurable risks. Those parts—medicare and unemployment compensation—could be financed from general revenues, while the old-age retirement system could be run on proper insurance principles. Such tax reductions and shifts, like the cutting of indirect taxes, could help the short-run inflation problem, and help economic stimulus at the same time, as would any other tax cut.

Cuts in Direct Taxes

Among the remaining, direct taxes, cuts may be contemplated for
•personal income taxes
•capital gains taxes (business and personal)
•corporate profits taxes
  a. tax credits
  b. depreciation revaluations
  c. overall rates

The arguments for reducing the burden of personal income taxation are two-fold. On the one hand there is justified need for relief from the ravages of inflation or reduction of "bracket-creep." In an inflationary period, tax collections accelerate under a progressive system as people are pushed into ever higher tax brackets. A second rationale for personal tax reduction is that the country has allowed successive rounds of tax legislation over the years to increase progressivity to the point at which marginal rates become very punitive and possibly harmful toward work incentives.

Reduction of personal income tax rates, across the board, by given percentages (10% annually for three years running), according to the Kemp-Roth proposal, is based on the populist assertion that work incentives would be greatly enhanced by lower bracket rates. The stimulation of economic activity, enlarging the taxable base, and the enhancement of work incentives are expected by the populist argument to bring in more revenues, step up productivity growth and hold down inflation — all providing dramatic rejuvenation to the economy.

True enough, the Kennedy-Johnson tax cut of 1964 was enormously successful in stimulating economic growth and in promptly bringing in additional revenues.[1] It was a textbook case but would it work as well in today's environment as it did in 1964? The tax cut of the 1960s had excellent productivity growth already in place. It was implemented in a non-inflationary environment, just prior to the escalation of the war in Vietnam, the point at which the long inflationary push began. The country needs desperately to get productivity moving again along an expansive path before it can enjoy the fruits of progress in the form of large personal tax cuts. If the full Kemp-Roth package were to be implemented now, for three years running, there would be large budget deficits with incremental public borrowing on a scale that would add to existing upward pressures on interest rates, thus setting back those areas of the economy where one looks for progress in contributing to productivity growth.

This is not to say that all personal income tax relief is to be avoided or postponed. There are valid reasons for reducing the balance of "bracket-creep." It is the magnitude of the full Kemp-Roth proposal that imposes a staggering fiscal burden on the economy. The supply-side arguments that productivity and work effort would respond to sharply lower marginal rates has no scientific support. Careful statistical tests fail to indicate a powerful relationship between labor supply and the marginal tax rate, when other relevant factors are also taken into account. In fact, the relationship might even be perverse, according to the time honored economic concept of the "backward bending supply curve of labor."

Capital Gains Taxation

Capital gains taxes were lowered in 1978 by the Steiger amendment. Confident arguments then abounded, reminiscent in their lack of scientific credibility of the present populist supply-side analysis, that the stock market would respond favorably, that the better tone of equity prices would bring forth more capital investment. Nothing like this happened.

This does not mean that the Steiger amendment was wrong or unproductive, but it does mean extravagant claims should be treated very suspiciously. If the Steiger Amendment has, in fact been successful, it is by virtue of its contribution to the raising of venture capital. There are some crude indications that trading on the American Stock Exchange and on the Over-the-Counter Market moved into favorable range and that some new ventures were launched with equity capital that would not have been forthcoming, had the capital gains rates not been lowered. These developments are all to the good but need to be firmly established and quantified in proper context. It appears that further concessions of capital gains taxes are worthy of research investigation and trial programs ought to be implemented. This line of tax policy can be helpful.

Other Business Taxes

Business taxes offer many promising lines for improvement, not so much on an overall basis for general stimulus to the economy, but on a highly structured basis tailored to promote capital formation with higher productivity. It is generally agreed that fixed-capital formation was less than prominent in the recovery from the widespread recession of 1974–75 than were consumer spending, inventory restocking, and residential construction. There are many explanations for the lagging activity in fixed capital formation, but one important component is surely the rate of return on capital. An objective of tax policy is, therefore, a search for proposals that will improve the (after-tax) rate of return.

In this respect it might be surmised that an overall reduction in the corporate rate would encourage capital formation by making more funds available. To a large extent, however, enterprises tend to be indifferent between the use of internal or external funds. What really matters is the rate of return on the investment in relation to the cost of either internal or external funds. A cut in the general corporate rate will do much to affect the distribution of income between profits and other income sources but will probably do less for capital formation than will tax policies that are aimed directly at capital formation itself.

Although there may be many ways of structuring tax policy to encourage investment by improving the (after-tax) rate of return, there are two that are frequently cited and have had some history of success, namely investment tax credits and accelerated depreciation. These two schemes by themselves and in various styles can always be reduced to an equivalence in terms of enhancement of the rate of return. They were used effectively in the Kennedy Administration and have had a checkered career of cut-back/enlargement since then.[2] These investment incentives were used as a component of short-run, cyclical stabilization policy, but they dealt with long-run capital expansion decisions. This was probably a mistake. They should be used now on a long-term basis to see complete capital projects brought into use, with enough experience to realize potential productivity gains. Steady and long term—those should be the main characteristics of new thrusts in this area of tax policy.

There is, indeed, room for improvement of the rate of return even though such tax policies are already in effect. The present investment tax credit does not cover all types of new equipment spending, and it does not cover structures at all. There is clearly room for expansion here. In addition, the credit rate is only 10% and can be raised markedly. It can also be made refundable for enterprises that do not make a profit and have current tax liabilities. Guideline lives for capital depreciation are far from reaching complete contraction. They can be cut back considerably, as under 10-5-3 or 2-4-7-10 proposals. There is thus no lack of leverage with which to work.

Investment may be desirable for its own sake, mainly because it has not properly recovered and also because this is a period when the nation is looking for near-term GNP growth. But the fundamental reason for focusing on capital formation is the idea that it is closely associated with productivity growth. In adapting the capital stock to the new energy situation — particularly in coping with expensive energy costs by becoming more energy efficient — there has been a set-back to productivity growth. The sooner the adaptation is made, the sooner the US will be able to restore productivity. Furthermore, the present stock of capital has become obsolete in some lines such as steel, and new elements of high technology need to be installed in fresh areas of activity. The expansion of capital facilities that modernize and use the latest technical improvements should contribute significantly to productivity growth.

Model Simulations for Alternative Tax Policies

Simulations with the Wharton Long Term Model of the US economy have been examined to see how projections with and without tax-based investment incentives compare with one another (Table 1). The investment incentives introduced in this policy exercise are obtained (hypothetically) through an increase in the investment tax credit — by doubling it from 10% to 20% and extending it to cover plant as well as equipment. These results could just as well have been attained, approximately, by shortening of depreciation guideline lives by amounts that improve the rate of return equivalently.

Broadly speaking, the implementation of tax incentives for investment induce higher real growth for the economy, lower inflation, and increased productivity improvement. All the figures in Table 1 are stated in terms of differentials in percentage growth rates. By mid-decade, the improvement in the growth rate of real output expansion appears to peter out, but the productivity gains and better tone for inflation are more persistent.

This simulated tax concession works out well for the kind of policies being considered in this analysis. Higher investment rates lead to better productivity growth and therefore lower inflation rates. This is fundamental; it is the *real* way to combat inflation, reducing it gradually over time through basic improvements in the economy.

But none of the entries in Table 1 is very large. The entire fight against inflation cannot be carried by more investment activity; it is only one of many anti-inflationary policies to be pursued. A sizable jump in the investment tax credit can add up to one-half point in growth and take off somewhat less than that in inflation; nevertheless, every modest gain in this battle is worth earning. It is simply a matter of counseling policymakers and interested observers not to expect too much from any one approach by itself.

Another look at the effects of tax policy from the point of view of short-run analysis comes from simulations of the Wharton Quarterly Model (Table 2). A tax cut of $20 billion was projected by three different tax packages in comparison with a baseline case:

(i) baseline — no statutory changes
(ii) personal exemption increased to $1250, guideline lives reduced by 20%, investment tax credit (equipment only) increased to 15%.
(iii) roll-back statutory increase in Social Security contributions, guideline lives

TABLE 1. Effects of Investment Tax Credit, Wharton Annual Model
(Differences Between Baseline Case and Case With Higher Credit)

	1981	1982	1983	1984	1985	1986	1987	1988	1989
GNP real growth rate	0.6	0.4	0.2	0.4	0.1	0.0	−0.1	0.1	−0.2
Inflation rate	−0.2	−0.2	−0.2	−0.3	−0.4	−0.3	−0.3	−0.4	−0.4
Productivity growth rate	0.3	0.2	0.2	0.3	0.1	0.1	0.1	0.3	0.0

TABLE 2. Effects of Alternative Tax Policies,
Wharton Quarterly Model — Annual Average
(Differences Between Each Alternative and Baseline Case)

	1981	1982
GNP real growth rate		
(ii)–(i)	0.44	0.73
(iii)–(i)	0.62	1.09
(iv)–(i)	0.34	0.19
Inflation rate		
(ii)–(i)	−0.17	−0.41
(iii)–(i)	−0.39	−0.34
(iv)–(i)	−0.01	0.07
Productivity growth rate		
(ii)–(i)	0.30	0.28
(iii)–(i)	0.43	0.45
(iv)–(i)	0.23	−0.01

reduced by 20%, investment tax credit (equipment only) increased to 15%.

(iv) personal exemption increased to $1250, corporate income tax rates reduced.

The best overall performance goes to the policy (iii) that jointly acts on capital formation and lowers personal taxes by reducing Social Security contributions. That is because the initial impact — for 1981 — is so strong in reducing inflation by virtue of the roll back of statutory increases in Social Security contributions. This is an impact effect that will tend to fade away after the first two years or so. The lower inflation rate, coupled with the stimuli to business and personal spending, make for strong growth performance in both the first and second years of implementation. A conventional reduction in personal income taxes, done here through an increase in the personal exemption because of computer programming simplicity and a reduction in guideline lives (ii), comes between the best and worst cases.

Across-the-board reduction in personal and business income taxes (iv) does the least for the economy among the policies considered because it simply puts more purchasing power in the personal and business hands without channeling these extra funds into capital formation, productivity improvement and lower inflation. It is not necessarily a bad policy in terms of the need to offset bracket creep or higher social insurance contributions, but it is simply a macro policy without specific direction for capital formation.

This brief summary suggests that within the ranges of tax policy alone there are many things to be done to improve economic performance in the United States. Since many options are available, it makes sense to ask for a good set. The author would not claim that all possible combinations or proposals have been considered here or even that an optimal set has been found among those simulated through the Wharton Models. It does appear, however, that some choices are to be made and some are likely to be better than others. It should be possible to choose tax policies that lead to distinct improvements.

As for the whole range of policies that will deal comprehensively with the large number of economic ailments of our times, that would involve many structural or microeconomic policies that go beyond the overall tax proposals of this paper.

References

1. L.R. Klein, "Econometric Analysis of the Tax Cut of 1964," in J. Duesenberry, et al., eds., *The Brookings Model: Some Further Results* (Chicago: Rand McNally, 1969), pp. 458–72.
2. See G. Fromm, ed., *Tax Incentives and Capital Spending* (Amsterdam: North-Holland, 1971).

Technology In Society, Vol. 3, pp. 213–239 (1981)
Printed in the USA. All rights reserved.

0160-791X/81/010213-27$02.00/0
Copyright © 1981 Pergamon Press Ltd

Taxes — Their Impact on Technological Innovation Decision-Making

Ralph Landau

In October 1980 the National Academy of Engineering issued a report of a colloquium (held in December 1979) on innovation, entitled "Industrial Innovation and Public Policy Options." This report summarized and reviewed all the recent inquiries undertaken on the suddenly topical subject of *Innovation*. Literally hundreds, if not thousands, of busy and active citizens from every community: business, government, academia, labor, public-interest groups, non-profit organizations, etc., were deeply involved, and made many useful and important suggestions. However, to date, all those intellectual man-hours have largely been in vain, because no implementation of any important recommendations has occurred. Yet it is widely recognized that innovation, especially technological innovation, is vitally necessary for the continuing and improved health and growth of the American economy.

Many studies have led to this consensus, but the overwhelming factor is the decline in American productivity growth, and, concomitantly, America's competitive position. *The Economist* puts it thus:

"The brave American clout of which [President Reagan] dreams was created by a small lead in productivity growth in the Grant-to-Truman years, and it has been eroding in a big relative productivity lag in the Eisenhower-to-Carter ones. There is likely to be a crash during the Reagan Presidency unless he changes economic policy. . ."

The figures that their article further cites are convincing: from 1870–1950, American productivity increase averaged 1.8% per year versus 1.2% in Britain, 1.1% in Germany and 1% in Japan. This 0.6–0.8% annual lead, compounded, brought the US from a log cabin slave economy to the economic and political leadership of the world. Since 1950, American productivity growth has been 3–5% lower than West Germany's and Japan's because their governments have followed more sensible pro-investment and pro-business policies. Even the minuscule annual average increase in US productivity since 1974 has been achiev-

Ralph Landau is Chairman of The Halcon SD Group. A widely recognized chemical entrepreneur-technologist, he was awarded the Winthrop Sears Medal, the Newcomen Award, Chemical Industry Medal and Perkin Medal. He is a trustee of the University of Pennsylvania and of MIT, a member of the National Academy of Engineering and a director of ALCOA. Dr. Landau is Adjunct Professor of Technology, Management and Society at the University of Pennsylvania.

ed only with an inflation twice that of West Germany and Japan; for the last three consecutive years, non-farm productivity has fallen.[1]

During this period, the personal savings of Americans as a share of disposable personal income declined from about 8.5% to 5%,[2] clearly a directly-related phenomenon as well as one plausible explanation. The article goes on to point out that these policies have resulted in much younger Japanese plants than those in America, based on later technology and more efficient in consequence, with lower inventories and higher productivity. "There really are bigger productivity gaps emerging than will be bridged by . . . proposed faster depreciation allowances."[3] In this connection, it must be remembered that productivity measures express only quantitative increases in output per unit of input, and not changes in the quality of that output. Certainly, many of America's products have also been improving qualitatively (as in the high technology industries generally), but so have those of its international competitors. Although no real measuring sticks exist to evaluate the comparative advantage of the United States in any general sense, the increasing ability of foreign products to compete successfully in the domestic American market on quality grounds likewise gives no basis for complacency.

It should not be concluded that government policies bear all the blame for the poor recent performance. There are also outmoded management thought habits and practices, some of which are responses to the environment in which the managements have had to function; but in this paper, emphasis will be placed on the *reaction* by individuals and business to policies established by governments.

Innovation

Innovation is not the exclusive province of either the individual entrepreneur, the small company, or big business. They all innovate, to a greater or lesser extent, and with great variability, when they are permitted to. The Academy report mentioned emphasizes that it is the *climate* for innovation which most stands in need of improvement.

Many aspects of the increasingly unfavorable climate for innovation are reviewed in the report, but it seems abundantly clear that the central feature needing remedying, especially in this era of high inflation, is the taxation policy of the US. The inverse relation between inflation rates and capital formation, which is linked to tax policy, for a number of European countries,[4] clearly shows how important this issue is. A further indicator of this in the US comes from recognition of the increasing percentage of GNP which goes to total spending (taxation plus borrowing) by governments at all levels — Federal, State and local, now approaching 35%[5]; this results in large budget deficits, and reduces the funds available for private investment required to increase productivity, economic growth and jobs. Another indicator is the more rapid increase in taxation: from 1977 to 1980 the nominal GNP grew by 36% but individual Federal income tax revenues increased by 54%.[6]

The impact of taxation on technological innovation becomes even more apparent when it is divided into its two principal phases:

1. The research and development (R&D), or invention;
2. The entrepreneurial, or the first commercialization.[7]

Many economic studies have shown that phase 2 is the expensive one, requiring up to 90% of the total cost of commercializing an invention. While R&D is a *cost*, the completed innovation is an economic *benefit*. This benefit can be realized however, only through phase 2. Commercialization, whether by an individual or a company, requires capital and a variety of skills such as management, marketing, engineering, finance, legal, etc.

Lag in Risk-Taking Capital

Thus, while R&D expenditures in the US have declined slowly over the past decades in real terms (from about 3% to 2% of GNP),[8] whereas German and Japanese expenditures have been relatively rising — although flat or declining slightly more recently — the closer analysis provided in the Academy Colloquium report shows that it is the risk-taking concomitant capital investment required by phase 2 which has really been lagging.

Why is this important? Because economists have shown that technological change has been the principal driving force in growth of the American economy for a long time.[9] Although Denison's[10] and Kendrick's quantitative analyses and methodology in this area (discussed by Lloyd Bentsen in this issue as well as by Roger Brinner) are disputed to some degree by Dale Jorgenson's very recent and detailed studies (see his article), nevertheless there seems to be agreement among them as well as Z. Griliches of Harvard that recent lags in the American economy are the result in significant measure of inadequate technological investment, with somewhat differing interpretation of how much of this is directly related to R&D expenditures, how much to general advances in knowledge of various kinds, and how much to capital investment in physical facilities embodying new or improved technology or knowledge. These are very difficult numbers to develop with precision from the available data and methodology of macroeconomics. Indeed a striking example of the lag between R&D expenditure and the commercialization phase leading to such physical embodiment can be found in Great Britain.[11] The facts of US declining international competitiveness also bear this out.

Therefore, in completing the innovation studies referred to above, attention must above all be paid to taxation and its effects on technologically important capital investment. Even where economists may differ on ideology it seems to be the consensus that tax cuts which increase productivity are anti-inflationary.[12] The conclusions of the various studies cited in the National Academy of Engineering Colloquium with regard to taxation are contained in Cordes's paper in this volume. The author's own views are presented herein from the standpoint of the decision-makers, whether individuals or companies, who face choices among investments and indeed whether to invest at all, or rather to consume more freely. The author has been fortunate to have been able to participate actively in such decisions over 35 years as (1) a chief executive officer of a technologically intensive R&D-oriented company which he co-founded; (2) a top policy maker in a major entrepreneurial chemical company based on new technology, which he also co-founded, and which grew in 10 years to a billion dollars/year sales volume; (3) a board member of a large Dow–Jones industrial corporation; (4) a scientist-engineer, engaged not only in his company's private activities, but also associated with three prestigious universities; and (5) an individual investor seeking diversification of his own assets.

It is not the purpose here to engage in extensive theoretical discussions, or to consider to any significant degree politics, tax theory, tax equity, or tax neutrality, etc., but, rather, to give as plainly as possible the viewpoint of the decision-maker. Others may act differently in individual cases, and therefore these recommendations are not based solely on the author's own experiences but on those of others with whom he has associated over the years in the various roles described above. But however difficult politically a particular kind of tax cut may be, or however wise economically the balance is that needs to be struck between supply and demand stimulation or between personal and business tax cuts, it remains clear that some revision of the tax structure to reduce the drag on growth and innovation is urgently necessary.[13] This is the direction of the remaining section of the paper.

Furthermore, it is the underlying thesis of this paper that tax cuts cannot be targeted too specifically at exactly the kind of investor or exactly the kind of investment one might wish to see. Thus, for example, a generally healthy stock market would also be beneficial for new equity issues of technological companies. No government agency has the wisdom to direct such strategy; it is far better to allow the pluralistic decision-making processes of the market to select out the paths which will be followed, within broad general macroeconomic policies that make overall sense for the country. In the process, some people or companies may well prosper that may not be technological in character, or real contributors to productivity growth, etc.; and indeed some may misspend the monies they acquire in this way, or simply be failures. But the virtue of the market is that it sooner or later rewards the diligent and successful, and punishes the dilettantes and failures, to the benefit of the overall economy.

Long Range Investment Fund Distribution

Before taking up the various aspects of decision-making by the principal categories of investors in US industrial facilities, it is helpful to take a broad look at the long-range investment picture in the United States. The most comprehensive readily available data known are contained in the volume entitled *1981 Prospects for Financial Markets* by Henry Kaufman and colleagues at Salomon Brothers. Tables 1, 2, and 3 have been extracted from their figures. (The Department of Commerce very shortly before New Year 1981 issued revised investment and savings figures since 1970 for the United States. A check with Salomon Brothers indicated that these changes would have no materially significant effect on the conclusions of their volume, although physical investment by business may have been around 10% greater in 1979 than was previously calculated by the government, and there was somewhat less of a differential in the earlier years revised.)

TABLE 1. Long Term Capital — Sources and Uses — Increases/\<Decreases\> in 1980 ($ Billions)

Providers of Funds/Users of Funds	Private Mortgages	Corp. & Foreign Bonds	Tax Exempts	Governments	Corporate Equity	Total
Banks, Savings Institutions	40.8	0.7	15.0	31.0	—	87.5
Insurance Companies	14.1	11.9	9.4	7.3	3.1	45.8
Pension/Retirement Funds, Foundations	1.1	12.8	\< 1.0\>	10.7	25.0	48.6
Foreign	—	5.0	—	5.1	4.8	14.9
Individuals	16.0	11.2	6.9	52.5	\<21.8\>	64.8
Other	\< 2.9\>	\< 0.1\>	\< 0.3\>	4.7	1.0	2.4
Total	69.1	41.5	30.0	111.3	12.1	264.0

TABLE 2. Long Term Capital — Sources and Uses (Projected) — Increases/\<Decreases\> in 1981 ($ Billions)

Providers of Funds/Users of Funds	Private Mortgages	Corp. & Foreign Bonds	Tax Exempts	Governments	Corporate Equity	Total
Banks, Savings Institutions	72.6	1.0	12.9	28.0	0.3	114.8
Insurance Companies	15.0	14.2	8.5	8.5	4.3	50.5
Pension/Retirement Funds, Foundations	1.6	12.2	\< 0.5\>	9.2	29.0	51.5
Foreign	—	3.5	—	\< 3.0\>	3.5	4.0
Individuals	11.5	7.6	13.6	57.7	\<20.6\>	69.8
Other	\< 0.2\>	0.5	\< 1.5\>	7.5	1.5	7.8
Total	100.5	39.0	33.0	107.9	18.0	298.4

TABLE 3. Long Term Capital — Sources and Uses (Balances — Dec. 31, 1980)
($ Billions)

Providers of Funds/Users of Funds	Private Mortgages	Corp. & Foreign Bonds	Tax Exempts	Governments	Corporate Equity	Total
Banks, Savings Institutions	875.0	27.1	153.3	235.5	4.8	1,295.7
Insurance Companies	132.9	196.7	91.0	39.3	81.5	541.4
Pension/Retirement Funds, Foundations	15.3	165.7	2.9	68.0	287.9	539.8
Foreign	–	15.0	–	138.4	105.5	258.9
Individuals	120.2	119.3	108.1	351.5	996.4	1,695.5
Other	19.7	0.4	4.3	69.7	3.9	98.0
Total	1,163.1	524.2	359.6	902.4	1,480.0	4,429.3

These tables show in principal categories the sources of such long-range funds and the principal users, as calculated for 1980 and estimated for 1981. They also show the total outstanding balances up to the end of 1980 for the same categories.

Without going into too much detail, these figures reveal certain basic underlying facts essential to the understanding of the decision-making process, as described further in the following sections. Some principal points to note are:

1. As far as the individual investor is concerned, his principal direct investments (after provision for personal residence requirements) are to be found in government securities and corporate equities. Tax exempts, corporate bonds and private mortgage investment are nearly equal to each other, and together constitute the third leg of the individual's program.

2. However, corporate equities investments by individuals are diminishing in recent years and have been negative, reflecting the instability of the stock markets. As a result, there is very little *net* new corporate equity investment from the public. Corporations therefore derive their funds from other sources (see Tables 4 and 5).

3. The major financial institutions have different roles in different markets. Thus, banks and savings institutions are most active in private mortgages and government securities. They also constitute an important component of the tax exempt market, because of special tax rulings permitting deduction of interest while still holding tax exempts (a privilege not accorded individuals) but this may be decreasing — perhaps partially as a reflection of recent changes in the applicable IRS policies. Life insurance companies are heavily regulated and are not in the tax exempt market, so that their activity is concentrated in the other forms of mortgages and corporate bonds, with less in government securities. Property casualty insurance companies do invest in tax exempts, but recently this may also be diminishing, due in large part to losses in the insurance business which offset the taxes on their taxable securities. The funds, such as pension, foundations, etc., which are exempt from taxes, basically invest in corporate and government securities for high pre-tax income which of course equals after-tax income.

4. The private mortgage market attracts a large proportion of the total annual increase in long-term capital investment. Government securities are roughly equal, while corporate bonds are much lower. Indeed, the sum of corporate bonds plus equity is less than 20% of the total capital which flows into mortgages and various government securities (in the latter, the tax exempts often include funding for housing as well). Thus, it is again evident how important corporate internal cash flow is for the needs of the industrial sector, which traditionally has obtained about 85% of its equity funding from this source.

Although the tables do not show it, a related publication[14] by one of the authors states that if one adds up all credit market debt (government, business and individual) and compares it with the market value of outstanding equities, it is evident that the ratio of such debt was about 2:1 from the early 1950s to about the mid-1960s. However in the past 15 years this ratio has irregularly worsened to 3:1 during the past five years. Although Table 3 shows about $3 trillion long-term business and government debt, the total credit market debt was over $4.5 trillion.

TABLE 4. Sources of Funds for Non-Financial Corporations ($ Billions)

Source	1980	1981
Internal Cash Flow (Corrected for Inventory Adjustments)	158.0	186.5
Physical Investment	249.0	282.5
Plus Net Trade and Consumer Credit	2.5	7.0
Requirements for Financial Assets	12.8	22.5
External Cash Requirements (By difference)	106.3	125.5

TABLE 5. Sources of External Cash Requirements ($ Billions)

Source	1980	1981
Mortgage Debt	15.1	21.5
Bank Term Loans (5–7 Years)	12.0	20.5
Bank Short-term Loans	16.9	14.5
Finance Company Loans	0.9	8.0
US Government Loans	1.8	1.5
Net Sales of Open-Market Paper	12.4	10.0
Net New Tax-Exempt Bonds	3.1	3.5
Net New Taxable Bonds	33.5	30.0
Net New Stock Issues	10.6	16.0
Total	106.3	125.5

6. This same publication also draws attention to the growing government intervention in the credit markets. During the two previous periods of acute credit stringencies in 1969 and 1974, the Federal government's preemption of market share was 2% and 16%, respectively. In 1980, with unprecedented inflation, high interest rates and economic uncertainty, the Federal government will preempt 25% of all funds raised in the American credit market. As shown under item 2 above, this "crowding out" has resulted in corporations being unable to obtain sufficient long-term credit at fixed rates, and being forced increasingly into the short-term market at higher floating rates, or at best into the medium-term market (5–7 years) — a condition unconducive, to say the least, to long-term risk-taking planning, which particularly impacts technological decision-making.

Individual Decision-Making

The average taxpayer is basically uninvolved in decisions affecting technological investment. He lacks both knowledge and the ability to discriminate among risks. In recent years, in fact, the new additions to the equities investment ranks from among the smaller investors of more modest means have centered increasingly on speculative shorter range investments, in an attempt to hit a "jackpot."[15] And, certainly, consideration of risk-taking and the potential rewards is the key ingredient in longer-range investment decisions of a technological character. Institutional investors — bank trust departments, insurance companies, and pension and mutual funds — have not been buying the new issues.[16] They do invest in the more established technological companies, among others.

But among the 30 million equity investors (restored from a low of 25 million in 1975, probably largely as a consequence of the decreased capital gains taxation), the much smaller number of venture capitalists, and the number who invest in other income-producing securities such as bonds, etc., there are the major investors *who, either as individuals but more often through venture capital groups, are the bulwark of the new technological companies.*[16] They are influenced by a relatively few primary facts which shape their investment strategy. These facts are:

1. The capital gains tax is lower than either the earned income (50%) or the investment income (70%) maximum tax.

This has been true only since the Revenue Act of 1978, which reduced it to 28%. The recent history of the capital gains tax is an interesting example of how so many economists and politicians have grossly misjudged the real world of the individual risk-taker. Ever since 1969, this tax has been steadily increasing, until, in 1976, it rose to 49.1% as a maximum. Although inflation at that point was much lower than today, such a high level successfully stifled venture capital and the new equities issues market. Despite all the conventional wisdom (in fact, the author can remember only one prominent academic economist who spoke out in favor of cutting this top rate, and that was Dr. Martin Feldstein of Harvard), the Congress and the American people proved smarter, and forced on a reluctant Administration the reduction to today's rate. Immediately, among other significant positive effects on the market, the new issues market began to revive, and venture capital increased sharply.[17] Despite the uneasy economic climate in 1980, the number of companies offering stock to the public for the first time was the greatest since 1972.[18] Some 237 companies that initially sold shares raised $1.4 billion, far surpassing 1979's 81 companies which raised $506.5 million.

Lest we welcome the millenium, however, remember that in 1969 there were 1,026 firms which raised $2.6 billion by going public for the first time. And, in 1972, although only 568 companies offered their stock, they raised $2.7 billion.

Another perspective on the size and nature of venture capital is to be found in the activities of the venture capital industry, a widely-used vehicle for individuals interested in risk-taking, longer-range investments. In 1980 about $700 million flowed into venture capital companies from such individuals,[19] a significant proportion of all the new issue equity raised in that year. The cumulative balance in 1980 of the venture capital industry was about $4.5 billion; this should be compared with the various balances shown in Table 3.

While only a tiny fraction of the total equities outstanding by year-end 1980, its importance is much greater. It is from these small high-risk companies that there sometimes emerge the breakthrough technologies of the future, the potential Xeroxes, Texas Instruments, Intels, Digital Equipments, etc. This is the genius of America's innovation at work, and here is where the innovators can find the risk capital they require.

During the national debate in 1978, any comprehension of its ultimate significance was lacking on the part of many tax "experts," and there were dire predictions that the cut in the capital gains rate would cost the Treasury at least two billion dollars a year in lost revenue, based on the usual static econometric predictions practiced by them. In fact in 1979 the evidence of a recent Treasury study shows that the government actually *gained* about $1.1 billion in such revenues.[20] Of course, it is well known that stock market volume has also increased, and thus 1980 may also have shown such gains in revenue when the data become available. In any event, the impact on the Federal budget is small compared to the dynamic and beneficial effects on the economy, some of which have been cited above.

During the period since November 1978, the Standard & Poor's 400 Index (*i.e.,* for industrial corporations) has gone up 43%, while the American Stock Exchange index, which has a bias toward smaller companies, has gained 133%.[21] The relationship to the cut in the tax is also quite marked.

The above evidence is submitted only to confirm what all decision-makers know: that they react to the rules of the game by trying to optimize their own results, and that if enough do so, the macro-results are different from what could have been predicted from a static model of the economy. As an engineer, the author is all too aware of the meaning of feedback, which is what has been described here, but few economists have quantified the relationships which result, causing the US economy to be *dynamic,* not static (one such is Burton Klein, the author of a book entitled "Dynamic Economics," who has contributed a paper to this issue).

Fundamentally, of course, this phenomenon of feedback is what is currently being described under the rubric of supply-side economics, but it has existed for years! As a result of these problems in quantification, there are few econometric models which take feedbacks (or expectations) into account.[22] A splendid example of the most sophisticated look at current models in the context of this issue is contained in Lawrence Klein's paper; as is well-known, he created modern model-making and presides over the Wharton Econometric model. Brinner's paper in this issue gives some results from the well-regarded Data Resources model.

As Alice Rivlin, Director of the Congressional Budget Office, has put it, "Indeed, one of the major benefits of the current controversy over supply side economics . . . is that it serves to focus the attention of model builders and economists generally on the effect of governmental policy change, especially the long-run effects of changes in marginal tax rates and the mechanism through which these policy changes operate."[23]

*2. Investment income, classified as "unearned" by US tax law (*i.e., *dividends, interest, etc.), is taxed at a maximum of 70%.*

While the average taxpayer is unaware of this category, any one who receives and has income above $215,000/year if married, or $108,000/year if single, knows it very well. It is a most unattractive form of income. Take the example of such an investor in New York, who, in addition, would have to pay, after deduction from the Federal return, a net of 4 + % state income tax. For him, this means that the governments (Federal and state) get three dollars for every dollar he keeps as net income!

If, in addition, fixed income securities lose their face value with inflation, it becomes very clear why such securities are shunned by individuals.[24] They recognize full well that they are receiving a negative rate of return on their money. For example, if the inflation rate is 10% and the interest is 13%, their real return at the margin is minus 7% per year after paying Federal and New York taxes!

As a result, individuals who are in the position to take risks in longer-term investments (stocks, bonds, etc.) are discouraged and diverted instead into "tax shelters" of various kinds. Hence, as pointed out above, institutions are increasingly the lenders or investors in fixed income markets, and in the established equities markets. A recent Senate staff study suggests that the ownership of the common stock in America's corporations has become increasingly concentrated with perhaps as few as 15 banks and insurance companies playing the major role,[25] particularly in the leading corporations. But, institutional and foreign investors now own about 35% of *all* of the outstanding market value of US stocks[26]; in 1949, this was 9%; in 1959, 12% and in 1969, 18%. Many of these institutions, such as pension funds or foundation portfolios, are tax exempt, so that the return is much more attractive to them than to the tax-paying individual; some are regulated in various ways as to what they can purchase, others are speculators or count on short-term changes in the bond market and seldom hold securities to maturity. Officers of such institutions are conscious of their fiduciary investment policy, even without the strictures of ERISA, and they tend to avoid the more risk-taking, primarily-new issues, markets for both stocks and bonds. They also tend to follow similar paths because of constant interchange of information. This conservatism is one of the factors behind the lagging innovation process in this country, since managements of firms in turn become cautious and conservative, with a short-term orientation instead of a longer-term risk-taking outlook more characteristic of the Japanese (or of Americans 15 years ago).

3. Tax shelters.

Accordingly, individuals increasingly search out various tax shelters. It is a fallacy among some economists to think that incentives to invest are useless, because tax reductions would simply increase consumption. Only institutions, which tend to avoid risk, and affluent individuals, have significant savings to invest. Such individuals seek the investment that offers them the particularly desired combination of security of principal, of income, and of appreciation. If a specific form of capital investment seems unattractive to them, they go elsewhere, but it is really not a choice between investment or blowing their funds on more fur coats or a fancier wine cellar! Buying gold is quite a different phenomenon.

Furthermore, tax shelters are not the exclusive precinct of the rich. The middle classes indeed have the largest of all in private housing. A recent article[27] attempts to define "middle class," but it certainly covers a large number of American households. For these, primary among tax shelters is the private home.[28] For typical American middle class homeowners in 1976–79 their investment has resulted in appreciation of 63-½% per year on initial equity, which in most cases will be realized tax-free. Another way of looking at this is to say that they have paid a real after-tax interest rate at the margin of something like minus 5%. As a result, in the last few years mortgages equaled 145% of the actual cost of new housing, so that Americans were cashing in on the value of their homes rather than putting in new money. Of course, coupled with such "winners" were also the "losers" — the savers, many of modest means, who lent their money out to the mortgage holders via various savings institutions which paid them low after-tax interest, kept that way by government law!

The spectacular returns went to any homeowner who in 1976 bought, with a 20% downpayment, a typical house which then inflated at the national annual average home price of 12.7% in those years. The negative interest rate, which is the result of the same interplay of the key factors explained above for the case of the *most affluent* taxpayer, comes about simply if one assumes for the *middle class* average a 40% marginal tax rate and a 12% mortgage. *The Economist* points out that not only does this constitute

. . . a good deal for the homeowner, it also crowds out the credit demands of industry. The capital value of private American houses must now be over $2 trillion, so a 12.7% recent annual average house price rise must have meant annual capital gains over $250 billion [untaxed for those over 55 up to $100,000; in addition, of course, property taxes and mortgage interest are deductible against the homeowner's other income]. About four million Americans change their houses each year, and the average new mortgage they take on is about $25,000 above the old one. That produces a demand for $100 billion of additional credit a year. The private market cannot provide $100 billion of additional credit, so something like 30–40% of new mortgage credit is held under some form of government credit guarantee. This additional flood of mainly untaxed purchasing power comes into the hands of people selling their houses at a profit, and the addition to consumer demand from it exceeds that from the Federal budget deficit. The subsidies to mortgages also introduce absurd distortions into the capital market. Today, more American capital flows into mortgages than flows into any other use [*i.e.,* debt instrument, etc.], including into the business investment on which Americans' future real income mainly depends.

The base data for this gloomy revelation come from a recent article by A. Downs in the *Brookings Bulletin*.[29] These results are a direct consequence of government tax policies, within an inflationary environment, and likewise dramatically illustrate the existence of feedback effects in the economy. It should be noted that this recent economic behavior is mostly by middle class Americans, who do indeed see this giant loophole as a way of increasing their income for consumption and overcoming the effects of inflation. It is not too surprising that saving for other investment purposes by the middle classes has been diminishing. Thus, Mr. Downs states that in 1979 the net increase in homeowner's equity came to about $119 billion, while total savings of all other kinds came to $74 billion!

In contrast, therefore, to the high value of individuals' real estate holdings, which the volume by Kaufman *et al.,* cited earlier, points out has tripled from $750 billion in 1970 to $2.5 trillion at year-end 1980, their corporate stock holdings have risen only 45%, to less than $1.1 trillion (including mutual fund shares) even with the relatively strong recent market. This quite confirms *The*

Economist's analysis, and illuminates the problem of declining production-oriented investment in another way.

For the affluent investor, however, governed by a different strategy, the US government provides excellent tax shelters in commercial real estate, via accelerated depreciation, investment credit, full deductibility of interest, etc., but most of all by the non-applicability of "at risk" rules, whereby an investor may put in as little as, say, 10% of the equity in a property, then mortgage the property itself for the remaining 90% without himself being personally liable for the repayment of the loan, while deducting against his income from other sources the depreciation, etc., on 100% of the property!

Recently, a tax bill has been enacted which gives favorable treatment to pension funds if they invest in real estate property, by allowing them to acquire mortgaged real property on a tax-free basis. As a result they will no longer pay taxes on the subsequent income from any acquired mortgaged properties.[30] Once, again, one can see the tax laws being used to favor skewing investments away from industry. Clearly, tax policy has favored real property investment by all classes of investors, and attracted capital away from industry and, above all, technological capital formation, upon which productivity and economic growth heavily depend.

There are other shelters too, although some are limited by the so-called "at risk" rules, such as oil and gas, wood waste pelletizing, equipment leasing, tax-free municipal bonds, etc., some of which draw the individual's capital away from the investment most needed for the industrial growth of the country. There are also many more speculative devices such as straddles, puts and calls, commodity futures, etc.[31] There should therefore be a re-examination of the policy in light of the proven consequences of the past decade — one of high taxation and high inflation. Borrowers must be favored less, and lenders more; consumers less, and savers more. The next section will deal with tax effects that would improve the situation without requiring any major "reforms." There have been too many and too extensive tax reforms in the past 20 years; the ground rules change too frequently, and mostly adversely. It is time for a longer-range, steadier policy, designed to reach a better equilibrium.

Tax Measures for Individuals to Improve Technological Innovation and Capital Formation

The Capital Gains Tax

The basic problem with the present capital gains tax is that the rate is the same whether the property is held for one year or 100 years. In the real world of inflation, it is evident that the longer an asset is held, the more inflation represents the principal part of the appreciation. The average length of time stock in a new technological venture is held in the US is about seven years. When it is sold, then, the tax primarily confiscates capital, not profit. To encourage longer term risk-taking investment this effect must be recognized. A striking calculation of the mathematics involved was recently published as an advertisement in "The National Economic Survey" of *The New York Times,*[32] and is included in the paper by J. Peter Grace in this issue.

One way to accomplish appropriate relief would be to index costs so that gains would be limited to the economic appreciation. Another way would be to reduce the capital gains tax with length of holding (the British call this "tapering"). One additional advantage of such tax treatment would be that the entrepreneur would be less tempted to sell out to a larger company on a tax-free merger, but would find it more advantageous to seek a public market for his shares. (Here, consideration could well be given to revision of estate tax schedules, so that smaller entrepreneurial companies would not have to sell out or go public, for tax reasons, but remain in the family if they chose.)

Another method would simply be to reduce the tax altogether. The present level of 28% is too high to encourage "patient" money. It is noteworthy that only in the United Kingdom are capital gains tax rates at that level (they are 30%). They are lower or non-existent in many other countries. In Germany and Japan, whose economies have certainly been vigorous while that of the US has vacillated, there is no capital gains tax at all! Even in highly-taxed Sweden, it is 23%.[33]

The Tax on Investment Income

All income earned, from whatever source (wages, salaries, dividends, interest, etc.), should be taxed so that various governments (Federal and local) never take more than one dollar for every dollar retained by the investor, *i.e.,* 50% maximum tax. A higher combined tax discourages incremental work or investment for more earnings, since the taxpayer instinctively rebels at working more for the benefit of the government than for himself.

Since many states have an income tax of their own, this proposal needs to be accomplished by setting a maximum Federal tax rate at, say, 45%, and decreeing by law that no state or local income tax can bring the total beyond 50%. In a sense, this constitutes a form of automatic provision for and ceiling on one type of revenue sharing, but clearly relates the revenue raising to spending at the local level, rather than leaving it in the hands of the Federal government. *Of course, lower maximum rates on all types of income would be even more productive of new investment.*

The marginal tax rate average Americans will pay in 1981 will in fact be more than 50% when all taxes — Federal, State, and local — as well as transfer payments which must be given up as earnings rise, are calculated. For the majority of Americans, therefore, it is more profitable to conceal or shelter a dollar of existing income than to earn an additional dollar.[34]

There is an immensely important psychological barrier to any individual if governments transgress beyond this basic principle of an equal balance between maximum rate of taxation and retention. The author is convinced that, if at least this degree of equality were to be recognized, many of the more or less artificial tax shelters mentioned above — some of very dubious national value — would rapidly erode, as taxpayers would pay much more attention to the real long-range values rather than gimmicky short-term arrangements. There is evidence that a move from tax exempts to industrial stocks would emerge as one result. Such a shift would help the productive industrial sectors of society and reduce the flow to less productive municipal spending solely because of tax advantages.

Furthermore, the government would lose relatively little revenue from either this recommendation or the first; but the feedback effects would increase beneficial economic activity also. This is the underlying importance of the Kemp-Roth proposals for 10% across-the-board personal income tax cuts in rates for each of three successive years; even the promise of such ultimate cuts will alter investment behavior *now*.[35]

Finally, interest rates may under certain circumstances tend to decrease with such a tax policy change. On the other hand, if present tax rates are retained, as the investing public becomes more aware of inflation, it will increasingly demand a real return *after tax*, and this will soon lead to a significant *increase* in interest rates which would be a blow to the economy. Recently, suggestions have been floated that, coupled with such personal income tax cuts across the board, there might be some form of compulsory saving in government bonds in lieu of actual retention of the tax saving as cash by the upper income taxpayer.[36] If the maximum tax on all income is reduced to at least the levels proposed herein, if not further, the attraction of savings instruments will be sufficient to relieve any concern about the inflationary effects of additional consumer spending resulting from Kemp-Roth or equivalent, and has the other virtues described herein, including allowing the market to determine investment decisions rather than government compulsion.

Capital Losses

At present, an investor can deduct only $3000 per year of capital losses (in bad investments) from his other income. If this limit were removed altogether, or at least greatly increased, there would be a greater encouragement to invest in risky enterprises. There are always winners and losers in these types of companies, and if one can offset losses in the latter against all kinds of income from the former, there is no doubt that more capital would flow into the new equities and new venture markets. There is a narrower precedent for this in the tax code (Section 1244) for small businesses of $1 million capitalization maximum.

Stock Options

Improved taxation of stock options is badly needed. For all practical purposes, the present law, which forces a recipient to pay ordinary tax on the value of the security in excess of the option price when the option is exercised, has destroyed such options or compelled adoption of very complex alternative schemes. Yet, it is essential that young technological companies attract the brightest people to work for them, often at considerable risk to their careers. Stock options of the proper kind would serve as a tremendous incentive to these people to build their company and see it progress; it is also in the interest of the stockholders. What is needed is that the recipient be taxed on the gain, at capital gains rates, not on the exercise of the option, but when the security is sold. A long time period should be allowed between granting the option, and its exercise.[37]

One can devise numerous other tax benefits, but it is the author's thesis that the code should be ameliorated without an attempt to restructure it, which would throw everything into confusion again. These four changes would accomplish this goal, as well as encourage risk taking in socially desirable industrial directions.

Individual investors are still very much needed in innovative business, as they can act with more daring and a longer perspective than the more bureaucratized large companies which command so major a proportion of the present economic heights. Indeed, new and young companies have been the most promising growth industries. During most of the 1970s, some 6-½ million jobs were created in the private sector of the US (out of 9-½ million total). None of these 6-½ million was in the thousand biggest companies, which had no net increase in employment. All were created in smaller firms. The other three million new jobs were in government.[38]

Nevertheless, because of the very size of the large companies, they also have a crucial role to play in improving technological innovation and growth. Only they can deal with the really big projects — energy, minerals and materials, new products and systems, the military and aerospace, etc. Here, a different set of tax problems exists, and must be addressed. Much has been written recently about the excessive caution and short-term approach of the corporate sector.

Corporate Decision-Making

As stated, the great bulk of industrial capital investment is provided by existing large companies, who, because of the double taxation of dividends, reinvest far more than half of their cash flow rather than paying it all out to their shareholders. In 1979, this share reinvested was 81%.[39] If one looks at the proportion of profits retained after dividends are paid out, then the number was 69%. However, the profit is uncorrected for the effects of inflation. If such correction is made, the true profit retention would be only 25–40%, and this reveals that dividends are being paid out by borrowings and the decapitalization of enterprises.[40] Such calculations are only approximations, of course, and different sources for the base data may give slightly different numbers, but the general relationships are quite realistic.

A recent article shows the extent to which major corporations are neglecting their plant and equipment, and paying dividends with cash they don't have[41]; the investment analysts have certainly not overlooked such a major factor in today's economy!

Capital reinvestment actually permits corporations to perform a socially very useful function, because they have had to develop staffs of specialists: planning, finance, engineering, marketing, manufacturing, etc., for this purpose. Such capability gives corporations a very sophisticated mechanism for investment, one not available to the typical individual investor. Large projects demand such organizational skills.

However, in recent years real capital investment in the US has been flagging, dropping from 11% of GNP in 1974 to 10% in 1979[39]; this compares with substantially higher percentages in West Germany and Japan.[42] Much of this investment is used to replace existing capital stock and to maintain inventories; perhaps 40% of this spending, moreover, was energy- and pollution-related, not all of it of a productivity-improving character.

It is true that capacity in some industries has been expanded beyond the current recessionary needs, so that percentage of capacity utilization has been dropping, but the concomitant decline in productivity suggests, along with other indicators, that the underlying need for modernization and replacement has not been met.[43] The real addition to fixed capital stock of the US in the last five years is estimated by Dr. Martin Feldstein to be only about 2% of the GNP,[44] or somewhat over $50 billion. Whether this number is precise or not, the discussion here is intended to emphasize that gross capital investment figures do not tell enough about the real state of the American industrial machine — particularly its technological health. In this context, it is particularly important to reduce the average age of American industrial facilities, which would help increase the country's international competitiveness. At present, the average age of American plant and equipment is estimated to be 16–17 years, versus 12 years in West Germany and 10 years in Japan.[42]

Why is this so? Again, the problem is one of inflation and tax rates. In 1977, real corporate income (inflation adjusted), for example, was $139 billion, while taxes on that income, paid by corporations, bondholders and other creditors, and stockholders, were $92 billion, for a total effective tax rate of 66%.[45] Thus, the "excess" tax was $32 billion due to inflation, *i.e.,* the tax would have been $32 billion less if computed on the inflation adjusted profit at standard tax rates. This figure may have risen to $50 billion in 1980. Inflation has raised this effective rate sharply since the mid-sixties when it was closer to 50%, despite tax reductions, accelerated depreciation, and the investment tax credit. Government is thus increasingly preempting the internal cash flow of corporations (as well as of individuals), and thereby reducing the necessary funds for investment, particularly in plants incorporating newer technology.

If the corporate decision-maker expects the underlying inflation rate to continue at or around 10%, then he must, on behalf of his shareholders, expect a *real* rate of return, after tax, on his investments, of some 3–4% above this level, or 13–14%. Such a rate would apply to a relatively riskless investment. Interestingly — but not accidentally — current long-term interest rates on first class securities are at about this level. Because many of the lenders, as explained above, are tax-free institutions, they do not have to compute the effect of a tax "wedge" for their return, which to them therefore is also 3–4% above the underlying rate of inflation.

An Inadequate Return

For a corporation in the 50% tax bracket, such a return is inadequate for risk-taking new projects. It would expect a premium of 5% or more, after tax. For foreign investments, this would be greater. Thus, a prudent executive would expect something like a 20% after-tax return.

It must be remembered that cyclical or unexpected recessions, etc., usually upset such calculations over the life of the project, so that the average return for all projects in a well-diversified and well-managed company may still not match the desired 13–14% after taxes, and leveraging the equity by borrowing becomes necessary, as a study of the financial results of numerous corporations would show. (This is equivalent to a 7:1 price-earnings multiple — one frequently encountered today, being the average of the Standard and Poor's 400 Industrials. Of course, such quoted P/E multiples are based on market, not book, value, and often the former is below the latter, which reflects the investor's appraisal that the economic value of the company's physical facilities is not equal to its book value — a recognition of decapitalization, or inadequate modernization or replacement.)

With a typical 10% per year depreciation, the above example means a return of the original individual project's investment in four years (not counting construction time, or startup time, or time to reach capacity, etc.). This does not take into account the effect of the investment tax credit, if any.

The difficulty is that few large projects today show such rates of return, except perhaps energy-related investments of certain types. International price competition is one factor. Smaller plant improvement projects still do; hence, in many companies probably half the total capital budget is devoted to such projects of up to $10 million or so. These are very important in maintaining the physical plants in shape, and improving production costs. However, they do not reduce the aging of the base plant, nor do they permit, as a new plant does, the installation of the latest technology. The energy and competitive situations alone demand more such really new plants, and more scrapping of obsolete capacity. This can only be aided by removing tax disincentives, which make such large projects less attractive, and risk-taking less fashionable. Because so many of the large company securities are held by institutions such as have been described, their criteria for return on their investment are necessarily reflected in the attitudes of the managers of the companies themselves. This has resulted in shorter time horizons, and lower risk projects.

The foregoing discussion of corporate investment decision-making is, of course, quite a simplified account. Most corporations use many sophisticated analytical tools to discriminate among investment choices. A recent excellent summary of the many systems and considerations involved was published in the Winter 1981 issue of *Mergers and Acquisitions* by E. E. von Bauer of the Continental Illinois Corporation, entitled "Meaningful Risk and Return Criteria for Strategic Investment Decisions." It contains an extensive bibliography as well. But the fundamental underlying truth is not far from what is stated herein, as further amplified in the article.

Tax Measures for Corporations to Improve Technological Innovation and Capital Formation

Depreciation Rules

The one incentive on which there is a real consensus is that an accelerated depreciation of some type be adopted.[46] It was the one most favored by the Joint Economic Committee of the Congress.[47] Whether this is the 10-5-3 rule favored by industry, or the bill passed by the Senate Finance Committee in 1980, or the Jorgenson-Auerbach First Year Capital Recovery Act, as mentioned in Jorgenson's paper in this issue, or some other, they all recognize that traditional depreciation rules do not recover initial capital fast enough; therefore, when recovered, the capital is significantly reduced by the effects of inflation and is inadequate to replace that plant by more modern technology.

It does not help that the accounting profession has not yet produced a universally accepted method of accounting for inflation.[48] Thus, in the above example, if the plant could be depreciated in five years instead of 10 (an aspect of the 10-5-3 proposal), the tax-free cash flow return from this source alone would be 10% instead of 5%. In order to obtain a 25% cash flow after taxes (for a four-year payout), there would accordingly be required a profit of only 15% after tax or 30% pre-tax. This is a very much less stringent criterion than the 20% after-tax profit cited above, and would render many more initially marginal projects (but those with longer run significance), or riskier ones, feasible.

In particular, new technology would be introduced more rapidly than otherwise, to the long run benefit of the entire American economy. That is why this type of proposal is the single most important incentive for companies, and enjoys such a wide consensus. Unlike a reduction in the corporate income tax, it would probably apply only to new projects, although, of course, not of comparable value if the corporations have no earnings or are not capital-intensive. However, much new technological investment does require substantial capital, and there are carry forwards into profitable years. There is a real question here whether there would be any revenue "loss" to the Treasury of such a measure. Certainly, some of the new investment from the effective date of such a tax measure would be stimulated by considerations such as the foregoing, and hence represents new revenue to the government that would otherwise not have occurred.

Such projects would in time generate profits yielding more taxes, and when the term of accelerated depreciation has expired, business would pay a *higher* tax on that project. It is very doubtful that the static revenue losses usually employed in Treasury estimates of tax changes are applicable in a situation as clear-cut as this, which could be so stimulative of additional private investment. Again, one is dealing with dynamic effects.

Of course, the foregoing examples are simplified. In reality, corporations have many special forms of accelerated depreciation permitted under current tax law, but these are considerably less favorable than the proposed new provisions, and the Internal Revenue Service frequently disagrees with the expected life of the plant facilities proposed by the investor.

Investment Tax Credit

The present 10% tax credit is insufficient for large, risky projects. It should be raised to 15%, and for certain very important projects, such as new energy producers, perhaps as much as 25%. Such incentives are much to be preferred over direct government involvement in financing these plants, because they decentralize the decision-making, moving it closer to the market and away from bureaucracy.

There has been much discussion about making this credit refundable, *i.e.,* a direct cash payment from the Treasury if a company has no profits against which this credit can be offset. This is a very bad precedent, and would go to the weaker companies such as Chrysler.[49] If these are to be rescued, they should be treated individually and by special legislation which takes all the circumstances into account, and not by general tax provisions.

"At Risk" Rules

The investment tax credit described previously would not be useful in encouraging startup or young companies which have no profits against which to take such a credit. For these there is needed a relaxation of the "at risk" rules; this type of advantage is more deserving of such treatment than is the real estate tax treatment described above. Thus, R&D and initial capital expenditures could be written off against the investors' other income, whether organized as a partnership or a pseudocorporation (Subchapter S Corp.).

Hence, borrowed money could serve to enhance the equity capital, while the investor can write off the losses of the entire enterprise. This provision, together with the greatly eased capital loss provisions for investment in corporations, would substantially encourage new risk-taking technological ventures, while allowing the entrepreneur to retain control of his venture.[50] Because of the inherent high risk in R&D, it is very unlikely that such a shelter would fall into the abused category mentioned earlier.

Dividend Deductibility

At present, corporations can deduct interest on loans, but not dividends. This should be changed so that a corporation can decide on using either debt or equity for non-tax reasons — a truly neutral tax policy. The present system discourages paying of dividends, and has increased the temptations for acquisition activity.

There is ample need on the part of the economy to shift toward more equity investment, and toward making such investment more worthwhile; the trend has been in the reverse direction with decreasing corporate and personal liquidity.[51] Coupled with reduction of the maximum individual investment income tax mentioned above, this shift may persuade many corporations to move toward more equity, and to attract more individual stockholders rather than the heavy institutional ownership which is now characteristic of so many of the major corporations. It could also lead to greater dividend payouts in some situations, and therefore increase the value of those companies' stock.

On the other hand, as long as individuals pay lower capital gains taxes than ordinary income taxes, there will be many who will place a premium on the stocks of companies which feature strong growth by reinvesting a large proportion of their cash flow.[52] These are likely to be companies with higher technological content. Such diffusion and diversification of ownership and motivations would then result in greater risk-taking and a healthier equities market, while reducing the demand for borrowed money by the private sector. This may well result ultimately in lower overall interest rates although these are primarily influenced by the inflation rate in the long run.

Research and Development

It is evident from what has gone before that capital formation is the key issue in innovation, and that the R&D part of the cost is a lesser one. Nevertheless, it is well established that the social value of R&D far exceeds its value to the individual firm.[53] In order to induce more R&D which may become a precursor for later innovation, it seems perfectly reasonable for the general public to finance additional R&D done by firms, above some base line, measured in appropriate terms. An investment tax credit, such as proposed by Senator Danforth (S.98) and Representatives Shannon (HR1183) and Van der Jagt (HR1539), for such new R&D would help accomplish this purpose. Today's R&D portfolio may become tomorrow's capital budget, and hence an increase in the formation of both R&D *and* capital is greatly in the national interest (as Brinner also points out in his paper in this issue).

But this investment tax credit for new R&D does not necessarily — except where competition is vigorous and cash flow adequate — result in its commercialization. It is for this reason that a large investment credit and accelerated depreciation for new plants incorporating new technology offering an economic advantage, as described above, must be companion measures. Only then will improved productivity and better product quality be worth taking, and the newer plants with the latest technology will ultimately force older plants to modernize as well, thus improving the competitive situation, internally in the US and on the export market. No government planning can possibly perform this service in the US complex economy and the Japanese model of "government guidance" is simply inapplicable.

In addition, serious consideration should be given to an investment credit of 25% for *basic* R&D and engineering education equipment and teaching performed at universities but sponsored by industry, such as is proposed by Representative Shannon (HR1664). This is indeed long-range seed money, but it is necessary as a means of improving engineering research and education in US universities, where government has simply been inadequate. The declining productivity in this country is additionally due to the declining attention to appropriate engineering education, as was brought out in a recent Symposium of the National Academy of Engineering.

In the opinion of many who are close to the industrial world as well as to the educational institutions, the immediate need is for much greater and closer coupling between industry and the universities. It does no good to brag about the Nobel science winners that America has; they contribute relatively little in the short term to productivity. The Germans and the Japanese have very few Nobel prize winners, but they do much better than the US in economic performance.

Accordingly, the author has had an estimate made of the effect of a 25% type tax credit on industry-funded research carried out in academic institutions. Information has been obtained from the National Science Foundation and the Joint Tax Committee of the Congress; only the latter has really looked at this matter, and their figures are included herewith.

Table 6 presents some calculations of what the industry-supported levels might be, assuming that after-tax expenditures by industry in support of the universities would not change, thereby taking full advantage of the credit. Industry-funded/university-conducted research would grow from $160M in 1979 to $300M in 1985 without the tax credit if the recent real growth rate of 3.5%/year continues. In equivalent after-tax dollars assuming the 25% credit applies, this industry support equals $556M in 1985. Levels for other years are shown in the table. These levels compare quite closely with the Tax Committee's estimates in 1984–85. The discrepancy between the two estimates in 1981–83 is due to a more realistic assumption by the Tax Committee with respect to firms gearing up initially (*i.e.,* the lag in making arrangements) and not taking full advantage of the credit.

Industrial Basic Research

In addition, a scenario has been computed assuming that all of the incremental growth in *industrial basic research* would be channeled to universities with industry labs experiencing a zero rate of real growth. This is an extreme case on the high side. In brief, assuming a continuation of the 3.5% of historic growth rate (in real terms) for industry research funding, industry expenditures for basic research in academic institutions would grow to $760M with the 25% tax credit.

Actually, it is probable that the correct number would be in the $500–$600M range corresponding to a $200–$300M increment by 1985. Though a small amount comparable to the $4.5 billion Federally financed university research, it is almost a *doubling* of present industry support (Figure 1). This amount at the margin would carry very different constraints than Federal funding, and would likely go to selected sectors (such as engineering, molecular biology, and chemistry), and would have a profound effect there, as was said above.

The closer coupling of academic research with industrial objectives would have significant influence on students, faculty, and industry researchers out of all proportion to the funds actually spent. It is significant too that these industry funds will go to support predominantly two categories of research. One will be top research people with national or international reputations. The second will be the solution of important industrial problems. Often these faculty will be located near supporting industry, and so will be highly diverse and widely distributed throughout the states.

TABLE 6. Impact of 25% Tax Credit on Industry Funded/University Conducted Research
(M$-Of-The-Year)

Year	Trend Projection (No Tax Credit)	Danforth-Shannon-Van der Jagt Case (25% Tax Credit)	Revenue Loss to Treasury Dept.*	Joint Tax Committee Revenue Loss Estimate
1980	178	330	152	–
1981	197	367	170	116
1982	219	407	188	175
1983	243	452	209	202
1984	270	501	231	232
1985	300	556	256	255

*This is also the maximum incremental university research funded by industry due to the tax credit in equivalent after-tax $ (*i.e.*, incremental research equals the Danforth-Shannon-Van der Jagt case minus the trend projection).

Assumptions: Rate of growth of industry funded/university conducted research = 11% (*i.e.*, 3.5% real, 7.5% escalation). Corporate income tax rate = 46%; Danforth-Shannon-Van der Jagt Tax Credit = 25%; Tax credit introduced 1/1/80.

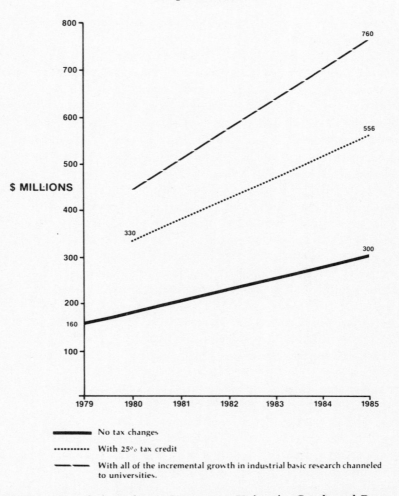

FIGURE 1. Trends in Industry Support to University-Conducted Research.

Conclusion

In this paper no effort has been made to deal with the numerous economic and political difficulties or costs of the programs outlined. The purpose is simple: this is how it is out in the real world. Indeed, the reference citations are typical of those that businessmen read regularly, rather than primary scholarly papers; of course, the businessman's specialist advisors often research these and other sources which form the basis of their counsel. However, the author has done some personal research in the more theoretical aspects of some of these topics, and has written several papers about such themes. But the world of the scholar and that of the businessman-technologist have been found to be far apart indeed, and the one seldom comprehends the other's viewpoint or parameters. The author has tried to erect a bridge of sorts, in this article. Some of the other articles in this issue are also relevant in this context. This is how and why people react to the present ground rules, and why the author predicts that his proposed changes will have certain beneficial results.

The real cost-benefit analysis for any one recommendation proposed herein is very difficult to make, particularly because of the dynamic feedback effects. The most expensive in terms of short-run effects appear at first blush, on the basis of static estimates, to be the accelerated depreciation changes, and the dividend deductibility. However, the author has already commented on the likelihood that a properly designed accelerated depreciation bill would have no real ill effects on revenue, but many positive ones. As to dividend deductibility, again the static loss calculation might have shown a loss to the Treasury of $15 billion if it had been in effect in 1980 (dividends were $51 billion, and assuming an effective corporate tax rate of 30%). However, by improving corporate liquidity and access to equity, more economic activity might well result, along with other consequences, to reduce this apparent loss significantly. The capital loss deductibility effects would depend on many factors, especially the new limit adopted. The others would not have very great initial effects, but in the long run their stimulative results would be out of all proportion to whatever modest costs there might be at first.

The conclusion reached from all this is that despite the apparent boldness of the totality of the measures proposed in this paper, the costs would be very small and the potential dynamic benefits very large indeed. The costs to the Treasury of general personal income tax rate reductions would be much greater than all of the proposals herein, but their wisdom or utility are not within the scope of this article.

It is high time to make the US technological condition the highest national priority, and commence the steps to improve it. The author does not, therefore, advocate wholesale rewriting of the tax laws, but targeted changes as specified, within the present code and decisions. Other tax cuts should also be made, but these would have different purposes, and are beyond the scope of this paper.

In writing this paper, it has been necessary to bring into peripheral discussion aspects of finance, economics, etc., inasmuch as they have impacts on tax policy and the reactions thereto by decision-makers in the technological sphere. But the problem is, of course, wider than that: it embraces the entire economy and its trends. The pressures of the moment should not blind one to the real perils of the situation. Month after month the well-regarded *Bank Credit Analyst* has been describing the underlying crises in the fiscal and monetary situation and the effects on investment and growth. Some of the papers in this special issue address the long-term perceptions of sophisticated observers and participants.

Perhaps a quotation from a speech to the Economic Club of Chicago on May 1, 1980, delivered by Henry Kaufman of Salomon Brothers and entitled "The Disregard for Capital" will serve as an apt conclusion to this presentation. (Mr. Kaufman is highly respected for his views although, like all forecasters, he is sometimes wrong on short-term trends.)

In the long historical transition from the entrepreneur to the corporate manager, the emphasis has changed from daring and risky adventures to calculated appraisals of opportunities and prudent trusteeships of corporate assets. The economy was served well by this new age of corporate management until it became embattled by inflation, government regulation, and taxation policies which were unrealistic in terms of replacement of existing plant and equipment. But, the fact remains that the links between management and stockholders have been weakened. The emphasis has been on the talents and skills of the professional manager and not his own capital resources. Consequently, most compensation has placed heavy emphasis on up-front rewards and pension and retirement benefits rather than on a manager's ability to make a capital investment. Thus, few managements have much capital risk at stake in large corporations.

It should not be surprising to find, therefore, that when tax relief is proposed, American management in the logic of its stewardship is the strong proponent for accelerated depreciation and investment tax credit and is not in the forefront in favoring reductions in the capital gains tax or eliminating the double taxation on dividends. But, in terms of reversing our disregard for capital, changing capital gains and dividend taxation policies may be as or more important than accelerated depreciation and investment tax credits. Only in this way can we revitalize the equity participation which is now a requisite for renewed economic growth.

This paper was written before Mr. Kaufman's speech came to the author's attention, but it captures the precise essence of the concerns of those who have been both entrepreneurs and managers. That is why the author recommends that the US deal with *both* types of tax treatment changes — the individual and the corporate — since existing realities must be accepted as the point of departure. In the author's opinion, there are only a few more years before the present unfavorable trend becomes irreversible. If not mastered in time, it will be the end of the American experiment in freedom with prosperity.

References

1. *Business Week,* February 10, 1981, p. 18.
2. *Business Week,* January 19, 1981, p. 85.
3. *The Economist,* January 24, 1981, p. 12.
4. *Wall Street Journal,* January 7, 1981, p. 25.
5. Penner, R.G., *New York Times,* December 7, 1980, p. 2F.
6. *Wall Street Journal,* December 18, 1980, p. 28.
7. Landau, R., "Innovation," *Chemtech,* January 1979, p. 22.
8. *New York Times,* February 8, 1981, Section 12, p. 12.
9. Mansfield, E., Congress of the International Economic Association, Tokyo, 1977; Schultze, C.L., *Regulation,* September–October 1977, pp. 10–14; Economic Report of the President, June 1977, pp. 45–48; Nordhaus, W.D., at AAAS Second Annual Colloquium on R&D in the Federal Budget, June 15, 1977.
10. *Science,* Vol. 211, February 13, 1981, p. 685.
11. "Britain's Wasted Research," *The Economist,* January 17, 1981, p. 83.
12. Galbraith, J.K., *New York Times,* January 4, 1981, p. F3.
13. Stein, H., "Curriculum for Economics, 1981," *AEI Economist,* June 1980, p. 1.
14. Kaufman, H., "The Disregard for Capital," speech May 1, 1980, Chicago Economic Club, p. 3.
15. *The Wall Street Journal,* January 30, 1981, p. 1.
16. "High Technology," *Business Week,* November 10, 1980, p. 85.
17. "Venture Capitalists Ride Again," *The Economist,* October 11, 1980, p. 110.
18. *The Wall Street Journal,* January 20, 1981, p. 6.
19. *The New York Times,* December 9, 1980, p. D2.
20. *The Wall Street Journal,* October 21, 1980, p. 34; President Reagan's interview with the press on February 2, 1981, *The New York Times,* February 3, 1981, p. A14; *The Wall Street Journal,* February 11, 1981, pp. 1 and 26, February 12, p. 24

21. "Venture Capitalists Ride Again," *The Economist*, October 11, 1980, p. 110.
22. *Business Week*, December 1, 1980, p. 104.
23. Rivlin, A.M., address at stated meeting of American Academy of Arts & Sciences, Cambridge, Massachussetts, October 8, 1980.
24. Silk, L., "Wall Street's Exuberance," *The New York Times*, November 21, 1980, p. D2.
25. *The New York Times*, February 5, 1981, p. D5.
26. Kaufman, H., "The Disregard for Capital," speech to Economic Club of Chicago, May 1, 1980.
27. *The Wall Street Journal*, February 10, 1981, p. 29.
28. *The Economist*, December 27, 1980, p. 25; see also *Business Week*, December 1, 1980, p. 23.
29. *Business Week*, December 1, 1980, p. 23; *Fortune*, February 23, 1981, p. 133; *The New York Times*, February 22, 1981, p. F3.
30. *The New York Times*, February 1, 1981, p. E1.
31. *The New York Times*, January 25, 1981, p. F13.
32. *The New York Times*, January 11, 1981, Section 12, p. 18.
33. *The Economist*, October 4, 1980, p. 85.
34. *The New York Times*, November 23, 1980, p. F3.
35. Kristol, I., *The Wall Street Journal*, December 19, 1980, p. 24.
36. Silk, L., *The New York Times*, February 6, 1981, p. 22.
37. "Taxes and Options," *The New York Times*, February 15, 1981, p. 2F.
38. *The Economist*, December 27, 1980, p. 20.
39. *Business Week*, November 3, 1980, p. 34.
40 *Newsday*, January 25, 1981, p. 74.
41. "Are More Chryslers in the Offing?" *Forbes*, February 2, 1981, p. 69.
42. *Fortune*, March 9, 1981, p. 82.
43. *Fortune*, February 9, 1981, p. 12.
44. *Nation's Business*, October 1980, p. 62.
45. *Forbes*, October 13, 1980, p. 110.
46. "Tax Cuts: First Business Wants Fast Depreciation," *The New York Times*, February 1, 1981, p. 4F.
47. Report of the Joint Economic Committee, 1980, 96th Congress, Second Session, 77.
48. Revsine, L., "Let's Stop Eating Our Seed Corn," *Harvard Business Review*, January–February, 1981, p. 128.
49. *Fortune*, September 22, 1980, p. 73.
50. "Keeping Control," *Fortune*, September 22, 1980, p. 29.
51. Carson-Parker, J., "The Capital Cloud Over Smokestack America," *Fortune*, February 23, 1981, p. 70; *The Bank Credit Analyst*, February 1981, p. 24.
52. "Stocks That Don't Pay Dividends," *The New York Times*, February 15, 1981, p. F13.
53. Mansfield, E., in *Innovation and U.S. Research*, ACS Symposium Series 129, Washington, D.C., 1980, "The Economics of Innovation," p. 95.

Technology In Society

New York / Oxford / Toronto / PERGAMON PRESS / Paris / Frankfurt / Sydney

Technology In Society, Vol. 3, pp. 241–255 (1981)
Printed in the USA. All rights reserved.

Tax Policy and Industrial Innovation in the United States

Boyd J. McKelvain and Arthur M. Bueche

A higher rate of technological innovation in industry is a key means by which the US economy can be returned to a healthy, stable rate of growth. Because of its importance to productivity growth and international competitiveness, industrial innovation is critical to the long-term control of inflation, the creation of jobs, and improved life quality.

Although the process of innovation varies among industrial sectors with regard to such things as emphasis on R&D, capital requirements, and time to payback, investment in innovation usually is more risky and longer in term than other business alternatives. Also, the investment needs in later stages of the innovation process, beyond discovery and invention, are typically much larger.

The United States continues to lead the world in scientific research output, but there is strong evidence that the rate at which it has been making use of its new technology through the introduction of new and better products and production processes has not kept pace with the needs of the economy. The rate of productivity growth has slowed to a pace lower than any of its international competitors, the balance of payments with Japan and Germany in high technology products is increasingly negative, and the US has been losing share in international markets for high-technology products as well as all other manufactured goods. These problems have contributed importantly to the condition of slow economic growth with high inflation.

Many other factors can be cited as having negatively influenced these performance measures, but it is a fact that the US rate of growth in investment in the development of new technology and its diffusion through new plant and equip-

Arthur M. Bueche is Senior Vice President for Corporate Technology of the General Electric Company. He is a member of the National Academies of Engineering and Sciences. Dr. Bueche is a past President of the Industrial Research Institute and has been an adviser on technology to many government agencies, universities, professional societies, and business organizations.

Boyd J. McKelvain is a member of the Corporate Technology Planning Staff at General Electric. He previously held policy level positions in the Federal government and management positions in a major electronics firm. Recently Mr. McKelvain served as adviser on industrial policy to the Committee for Economic Development, the National Academy of Engineering, and the Industrial Research Institute.

ment has decreased while that of its competitors has increased. And although there are no really satisfactory quantitative measures of innovation output to indicate the extent to which innovation is lagging, few would argue that increasing the rate of innovation would not make an important contribution to the long-run, permanent solution of US economic problems.

Numerous studies of industrial innovation involving hundreds of top executives from the nation's leading technology-intensive firms have been completed recently. The central conclusion that can be gleaned from all the reports is that the US is experiencing a very poor environment for longer-term, risky investments in product and process innovation. For such projects the "hurdle rate of return" — that rate required for a potential investment program to rise above the rejection line — has been increased by many factors. The most critical negative factor is uncertainty — uncertainty about the course of inflation, cost and delays of government regulation, unreliability of the patent system, antitrust actions, energy cost and availability, and so on. The importance of such uncertainties is greater for innovative investment options, and it increases almost geometrically with the projected time-to-payback.

While all these factors have served to increase the relative costs and risks of innovation, real rates of corporate cash flow and return on investment have been severely restricted by the interactive effects of inflation and the system of taxation. Here again, the relative impact on longer-term investment is most severe because capital cost recovery allowances are not geared to an inflationary economy.

Improved Federal Policies

Important and encouraging steps are being taken toward improving Federal policies in most of these areas, but immediate improvements in tax policy are especially important.

One cannot expect to overcome all the barriers and added costs of innovation that are being imposed by inflation, regulation and other constraints. Tax system modifications, however, can quickly offset these biases, restore a healthy balance between risks and rewards for innovation, and help break the inflationary spiral.

In general, the policy governing tax changes should be to move toward restructuring the system to remove the current bias toward consumption and investment in quick payback and non-productive, "hedging" assets. Also, care should be taken to provide maximum flexibility for the market system to guide investment choices as opposed to attempting to "target" the tax system to favor specific technologies, industrial sectors, or types of firms.

Of utmost urgency is to bring capital recovery allowances more in line with replacement costs for new plant and equipment. This will help to remove the tilt toward short-term, defensive types of projects, will accelerate the diffusion of new technology into productive facilities, and will pull through more new technology development activities. As product cost and quality improve, inflation will begin to come under lasting control, more stable economic growth will emerge, and the environment for further investment in innovative activities will be enhanced. In the short term, inflationary pressure from increased demand for capital goods should be minimal due to the present condition of underutilization of capacity.

What Is Industrial Innovation?

Industrial innovation is the process by which new or improved products and processes are developed and introduced into the market place. A single innovation, *i.e.*, the transistor, may progress directly from basic research through applied research, invention, product development, pilot operation, pioneer production, market development, personnel training, and so on. Others may arise from technology developed for other purposes or simply from learning-by-doing as was the case in the history of ship building.

Industrial technological innovation always involves the introduction and diffusion of new know-how or the novel application of existing technology. Conditions and requirements for innovation, however, vary among industrial sectors, types of firms, and types of innovation.

Major new product innovation is very dependent on availability of research outputs, trained people, capital availability for formation and financing of new ventures and enterprises, and a market that is willing and able to pay a premium for performance. Process innovation, on the other hand, is ordinarily aimed at achieving improved production efficiency and quality. It is often originated by the using manufacturing firm, and then improved and diffused by equipment supply firms. Process innovation, thus, is very much influenced by competitive pressures for cost and quality improvement, the availability of investment and operating capital, and in-house research and technical capabilities.

One firm's product innovation often is an element of a process innovation in another firm.

As one examines the relationships between various producer and user firms it quickly becomes apparent that in this broader sense most innovation is not product innovation at all, but contributes to productivity directly via the linkage of different firms in the physical flow of production to final demand (Utterback, 1978).

While research resources may constitute a small portion of the total cost of innovation in most sectors, the availability of research outputs, efficient technology transfer mechanisms, and competent technical manpower are essential to innovation. Basic research results — often produced in research universities — find their way into the economy through manpower trained in the university programs. Research institutions, inventors, and other sellers of new know-how offer their products in the form of patents, proprietary technology, and special equipment. The efficiency with which this market operates is very important to the rate at which innovation occurs in industry.

Why Is Innovation Important?

There is broad consensus among economic studies that technological progress in industry is a major contributor to the creation of jobs and to productivity and economic growth. On the basis of work by Denison (1962), Jorgenson (1979), Mansfield (1977) and others, there is reason to conclude that the introduction and diffusion of new technology in products and production processes has accounted for about one-third of US economic growth since the mid-1940s. Among the three major contributors, Denison ascribes about equal roles to technological innovation and labor and the smallest to capital. Jorgenson, on the other hand, ranks capital somewhat higher than technology change — with labor contributing much less.

It must be noted, however, that there is considerable interaction among these variables. New technology is diffused into the economy both through the continued upgrading of the level of technical education of the labor force and through the use of up-to-date technology as new plant and equipment are introduced. Furthermore, while an innovative new product or process usually creates the need for labor and plant and equipment, design of the new facilities typically identifies needs for additional R&D.

The impact of innovation on job creation is less well documented. It is known that high-technology businesses create employment faster than others, however. For example, from 1960 to 1976 growth in the electronics industry accounted for 700,000 of the 2.1 million jobs added in manufacturing. Employment in the semiconductor industry grew 10-fold during that period. A recent study by Data Resources Incorporated (Brinner, 1977) shows that over the past 10 years high-technology companies increased employment nine times faster than low-technology companies, and productivity growth of the former was twice the average national rate. Similar results were found in a survey by the American Electronics Association (Zschau, 1978).

The effect of employment on productivity growth can be destabilizing within a given firm or industrial sector; however, the record shows that industries with higher than average productivity growth usually increase employment faster than average (Fabricant, 1977). The indirect effects of productivity growth are often great enough to overcome the direct effects on employment, *e.g.,* increased productivity usually results in reduced selling price and the resulting demand increase calls for more output, which may offset the loss or even increase employment.

Furthermore, failure to remain technologically competitive can cost jobs. For example, the Japanese steel industry has gained worldwide technological superiority through heavy investment in automation and modern plant and equipment. A 1978 article in *Science News* reported that Japanese steelworkers are 1.8 times more productive than US steelworkers and their production costs are 10–30% less than those of the US. The article states that steel imports are resulting in the loss of 100,000 US steelmaking jobs.

International competitiveness of US industry is increasingly important to the US economic vitality. Long-term control of inflation through productivity growth is a crucial factor in the ability to compete, to pay for imports of oil and other commodities, and to maintain and improve living standards. As foreign competitors continue to catch up and surpass US industrial technology, their international marketing sophistication will allow them to gain control of more and more of the high technology markets in which the US has been most successful. Because these businesses are the ones that create jobs, the ability to meet employment needs, prevent deterioration in the payments balance and control inflation will be diminished.

Further, and even more critical to the national well-being, is the impact that these inflationary pressures have on the ability to maintain a lead in national defense technology. It has been said that, "We are not in an arms race, but in a technology race." Although the government directly supports the R&D and purchase of weapons systems, the ability of industry and university laboratories to maintain a forefront scientific research infrastructure is crucial to national security. Also critical is the industrial capability to produce the vast array of high-quality goods and services required for national defense at a cost which the nation can afford.

Where Does the US Stand Relative to the Past and to International Competition?

The status of industrial innovation can be looked at in terms of both inputs and outputs. The levels of resources invested in R&D and plant and equipment are important input measures. On the output side, one can assess productivity growth, patenting activity, technical literature production and international transactions.

Although the absolute level of R&D resources applied by the US is much larger than in other countries, the level relative to the size of the economy fell sharply in the late 1960s and early 1970s. Japan and Germany increased their effort levels rapidly during that period. Recently, however, the relative effort level in Germany has held at about the same as the US, and Japan appears to be beginning to slow its rate of increase at a point somewhere below that of the US and Germany (Figure 1).

This picture is clouded by the fact that neither the Japanese nor the Germans expend a large portion of their technical effort on national defense. Table 1 shows that the ratio of civilian R&D to GNP is lower and decreasing for the US than for Japan and Germany.

Capital investment is an important input to industrial innovation. Compared with the 1960s, the real business fixed-investment growth rate dropped significantly in the 1970s as shown by Table 2. Also, US capital investment in manufacturing as a percentage of output was far below that of the other industrialized nations during the 1970–77 time period (Table 3).

In terms of outputs, the data show a mixed picture. The US position in science appears to have remained strong according to NSF analyses of scientific and technical literature. Patent statistics are less comforting. Foreign patenting in the US increased from 20% in 1966 to 36% in 1977 with Japan and Germany taking about a third of the entire foreign share. This could indicate increased interest in commercialization of the inventions in the US as well as increased inventive capabilities of these nations. Meanwhile, US patenting in foreign countries decreased by 30% in the industrialized nations between 1966 and 1976. The

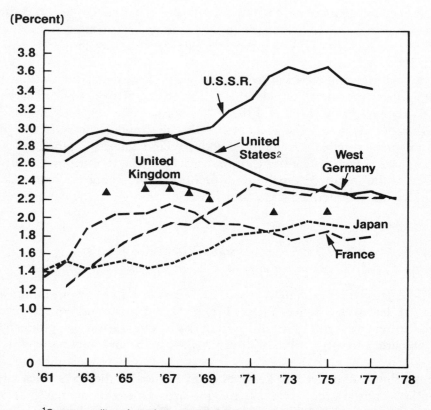

[1]Gross expenditures for performance of R&D including associated capital expenditures, except for the United States where total capital expenditure data are not available.

[2]Detailed information on capital expenditures for research and development are not available for the United States. Estimates for the period 1972-77 show that their inclusion would have an impact of less than one-tenth of one percent for each year.

NOTE: The latest data may be preliminary or estimates.

Source: National Science Board, 1979.

FIGURE 1. National Expenditures for Performance of R&D as a Percent of Gross National Product (GNP) By Country: 1961–1978.

largest drops were in Canada and the UK, perhaps due in part to low return expectations, but no increases were seen in Japan and Germany.

US aggregate productivity levels are higher than most other countries, but Figure 2 shows growth rates are the smallest among industrial nations. Furthermore, there is strong evidence that US productivity in some industrial sectors which are important to trade has fallen behind that of competitors in Japan and Germany (Jorgenson, 1979).

The US balance of trade in high-technology products was increasingly positive throughout the 1960s and until 1975. Since 1975, however, the balance has decreased by 6% (NSB, 1979). The negative balance with Japan accounts for vir-

TABLE 1. Ratio of R&D to GNP Excluding Government Funds for Defense and Space

	U.S.	Germany	Japan
1969	1.47	1.81	1.64
1974	1.46	2.27	1.91
1976	1.39	2.09	N/A

Source: National Science Board, 1979.

TABLE 2. US Capital-Spending Trend Growth
(Percent per Year)

	1960–69	1970–79
Real Business Fixed Investment	6.9	2.5
Nonresidential Structures	5.5	−0.1
Producer's Durable Equipment	8.0	3.9
Plant and Equipment Spending	7.3	1.2

Source: US Department of Commerce.

TABLE 3. Capital Investment in Manufacturing, 1970–1977

	% of Mfg. Output
Japan (1970–74)	26.5
Germany (1970–76)	15.2
Canada	15.1
UK	13.6
US	9.6

Source: US Department of Labor, Bureau of Labor Statistics.

tually all of the decline since 1975 and the balance with Germany has recently turned negative.

From a businessman's point of view, the best single measure of competitive performance and the most reliable indicator of future business success is the market share trend. Department of Commerce data shown in Table 4 indicate a decline in share levels for the more technology-intensive industry sectors, as well as for manufactures in general.

What Do Businessmen Say Are the Barriers to Innovation?

All investment decisions have certain considerations in common, primarily, the perceived risk and uncertainty compared with the potential return, and the availability of resources to invest. There are, of course, differences in the way investors analyze investment alternatives. Some have argued that US businessmen and financial analysts have become overly cautious and dependent on analytical tools that do not allow proper consideration for the dynamics of innovation and

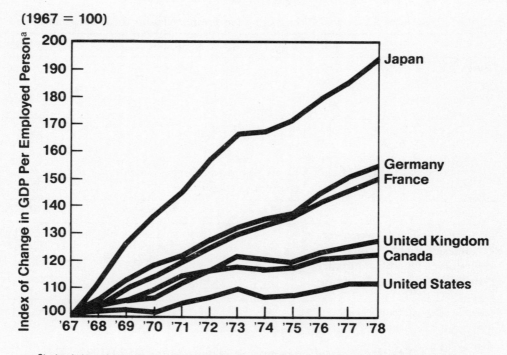

(1967 = 100)

aIndex is based on each country's own prices corrected for inflation. Consequently, the data show the trend in GDP per employed person within each country. They do not represent a comparison of the relative level of GDP per employed person among countries.

Source: U.S. Department of Labor, Bureau of Labor Statistics. (CED, 1980)

FIGURE 2. Change in GDP per Employed Person, Selected Countries, 1967 to 1978.

stifle the role of entrepreneurship and long-term perspective in investment decision-making (Abernathy and Hayes, 1980). Concern also has been expressed that financial accounting and executive incentive systems tend to bias US business toward quick-payoff, exploitative decisions in the allocation of resources (Rappaport, 1978). Differences have been noted in these areas particularly between US and Japanese business practices, and there are profound questions to be examined by US business managers and boards of directors. Within the market system, however, these issues can and will be addressed successfully by the business community if there is a national environment that is supportive and encouraging.

Top executives of the nation's leading industrial firms as well as many smaller technology-based companies recently have participated in numerous studies of national policies affecting industrial innovation. These study groups were organized by a wide range of governmental and private institutions, including the Committee for Economic Development (1980), the National Research Council (1978, 1979, 1980), the Department of Commerce (1979), the Industrial Research Institute (1980), and many others. Recently, the National Academy of Engineering (1980) published a report aimed at highlighting areas of greatest agreement and interpreting priorities for action recommended by these major studies and policy advisory statements.

TABLE 4. US Share of World Export Markets (%)

	1965	1975	1979
Chemicals	25	20	18
Electrical Machinery	24	22	19
Nonelectrical Machinery	31	28	24
Total Manufacturing	23	19	17

Source: US Department of Commerce.

The central conclusion that can be extracted from all the reports is that a wide variety of conditions have converged to produce a bias in the investment environment against the longer-term, risky activities that are required for product and process innovation.

One major area of attention has been the policies that tend to have a strong impact on the actual or potential cost of innovation. Because innovation is aimed at the introduction of new products and processes, Federal regulatory policies and practices are particularly crucial to the assessment of cost. The introduction of regulatory constraints and delays — even though in the public interest — does increase the cost to the firm of bringing the innovation into the marketplace. The increased level of regulatory action and adversarial government/industry relationship over the past few years most certainly has served to increase the cost of innovation as well as the difficulty of predicting its cost.

Many recommendations have been made for reducing and controlling the cost of achieving regulatory goals. There are some encouraging signs that improved policies and practices are being adopted and that an improved level of understanding is emerging. But, meanwhile, as benefits accrue to the public in terms of a cleaner and safer environment, the relative cost and attractiveness of alternative investments have shifted so as to decrease product and process innovation.

The US now pays for these benefits in inflated costs due to slower productivity growth (Denison, 1979), reduced competitiveness and delayed availability of better products. Since the country has not charged itself in terms of reduced money wages and salaries or government and social services, jobs are being lost to foreign competitors and the price is being paid in the marketplace.

Other cost-inducing policy issues that have been examined include the reduced reliability and inefficiency of the patent system, uncertain and sometimes punitive antitrust actions, and discouraging international trade policies.

The studies also focused on fiscal policies affecting potential return and availability of resources for innovation. The most severe negative effect of existing income tax policy on investment in innovation is that, under inflation, the tax structure creates an increasing bias against savings and longer-term investment.

One of the principal determinants of corporate investment in innovation is business cash flow (Mueller, 1967, and Grabowski, 1968). Figure 3 shows the very close relationship between corporate cash flow and investment in R&D and plant and equipment. In recent years, a variation in the relationship has developed for plant and equipment due, in part, to the increasing discrepancy between capital recovery allowances and replacement costs. Depreciation rates are based on original cost even though replacement costs are much higher as a result of inflation over the life of the asset. This results in an overstatement of corporate profits.

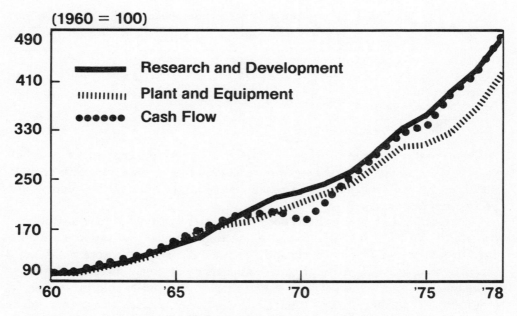

FIGURE 3. Relationship Between Expenditures on Research and Development and on Plant and Equipment and Cash Flow, US Nonfinancial Corporations, 1960 to 1978.

US Department of Commerce estimates indicate that 1978 taxes on these illusory profits amounted to $9 billion, and a National Bureau of Economic Research study suggests that indirect effects of the imbalance resulted in added taxes several times the Commerce estimate. Figure 4 compares the trend in reported and effective corporate tax rates since 1960.

Incentives for investment in innovation also are impacted by anticipated returns. The unfavorable trend in return on capital investment, after correcting for the original versus replacement cost discrepancy, is shown in Figure 5.

The close apparent relationship between after-tax return on capital and the trend in growth of real business fixed investment is shown in Figure 6a and 6b.

Other tax disincentives to savings and investment have been noted by the various studies, *i.e.*, double taxation of corporate dividends, higher tax rates on income from investment ("unearned" income), and the high rate of tax on capital gains.

The net effect of these government policies has been, on the one hand, to increase the costs and uncertainty associated with investment in innovation, and at the same time, to decrease the available resources and incentives for such investment. It is, thus, no mystery that there has been an increasingly poor savings rate and that investors have shifted their attention to quick-payback, low-risk alternatives and hedging investments.

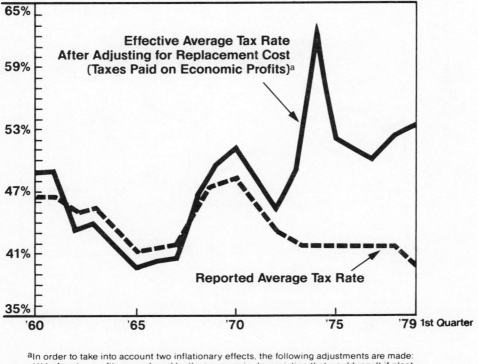

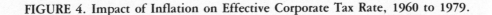

[a]In order to take into account two inflationary effects, the following adjustments are made: (1) before-tax profits are reduced by the increase in depreciation that would result if plant and equipment were valued at replacement cost rather than original cost (capital consumption allowance), and (2) the capital gain from the increase in inventory prices due to inflation is eliminated.

Source: U.S. Department of Commerce, Bureau of Economic Analysis

FIGURE 4. Impact of Inflation on Effective Corporate Tax Rate, 1960 to 1979.

What Tax Policy Changes Are Needed?

Both the National Research Council (1980) and the CED (1980) studies provide excellent documentation and evaluation of existing tax policies and recommendations for needed changes relevant to innovation.

As background, it is worth noting that Japan and Germany give considerably more favorable treatment to technological innovation than does the US (Kaplan, 1978). Japan provides special accelerated depreciation to approved new technology investments, a 20% tax credit for incremental increases in R&D expenses, and immediate write-off for contributions to capital expenditures of joint R&D associations. Germany gives special accelerated depreciation as well as a 7.5% subsidy for R&D plant and equipment. In France, special companies formed for purposes of technological innovation receive very favorable tax treatment,

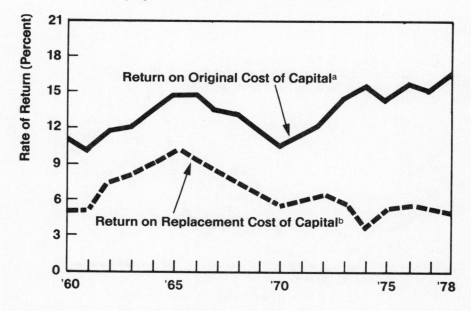

aAftertax profits plus interest divided by original cost of plant and equipment.

OAftertax profits plus interest minus capital consumption allowance and inventory gains
divided by replacement cost of capital.

Source: U.S. Department of Commerce, Bureau of Economic Analysis

FIGURE 5. Trend in Return on Total Capital Investment (Original versus Replacement
Cost Basis) for Nonfinancial Corporations, 1960 to 1978.

and sales of patent rights and other know-how are taxable only at the 15% long-
term capital gains rate. In fact, most industrial countries provide more favorable
treatment to capital gains and depreciation allowances than does the US.

The US provides no special tax incentives for depreciable structures and equipment used in R&D nor for downstream costs of innovation such as design, construction and tooling of first-of-a-kind manufacturing facilities. Also, there is no
special incentive to the exchange of patents and proprietary technology between
companies since, when purchased, they must be treated as tangible assets and
depreciated over their lifetime. Patents are not eligible for accelerated depreciation even though they typically become obsolete before their legal 17-year life is
over. Still worse, no depreciation is allowed for unpatented technology unless an
asset lifetime can be ascertained.

Certain US tax provisions do, however, provide incentives for innovation. In
addition to capital depreciation allowances, investment tax credits (ITC) encourage decisions to innovate. The value of depreciation allowances unfortunately
has been severely degraded by the effect of inflation and the ITC is limited to
equipment purchases.

Bringing capital recovery allowances for new plant and equipment more in line
with replacement costs is of first priority. This will help to restore the relative at-

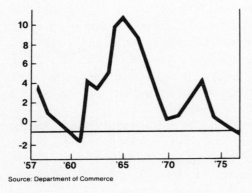

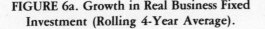

Source: Department of Commerce

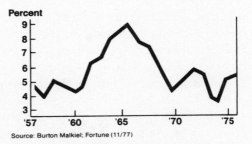

Source: Burton Malkiel; Fortune (11/77)

[1]After-tax Returns on Equity Capital represent the sum of after-tax profits (adjusted for underdepreciation and inventory gains) plus the reduction of the real value of debt due to inflation expressed as a percent of capital stock valued at replacement cost. Data pertain to non-financial corporations, not cyclically adjusted.

FIGURE 6a. Growth in Real Business Fixed Investment (Rolling 4-Year Average).

FIGURE 6b. After Tax Return on Equity Capital.

tractiveness of longer-term investments in product and process innovation by increasing their potential return, and it will begin to provide additional cash flow for further investment in R&D and capital assets.

Furthermore, since the benefit to the investor only occurs after he invests, the most immediate national benefit in terms of technology diffusion and increased employment and economic activity should accrue. These feedback effects should in turn help to offset the anticipated loss in tax revenue to the Treasury.

The case for consideration of feedback in estimating the revenue impact of a potential tax change is illustrated by experience with the recent capital gains tax change. The Treasury Department now estimates that the tax revenue loss in 1979 for the 1978 rate cut was less than $100 million instead of the $1.7 billion that had been forecast by Treasury analysts. Actually, data cited by *The Wall Street Journal* show that $1.1 billion more taxes were paid on capital gains in 1979 than in 1978. Another important concern is the potential for a short-term aggravation of inflation due to increased demand for capital goods. Since manufacturing capacity is underutilized, increased demand should not create unacceptable inflationary pressures in this sector.

Considerable attention has been given to tax treatment of R&D. Even though R&D may lead to the creation of an asset with a useful life greater than one year, US tax policy allows the option of deducting such expenses in the year they are incurred. The longer the life of the assets, the higher the cost of money, and the greater the proportion of R&D to other innovation costs, the more important this stimulus to R&D becomes. In other words, for a non-capital-intensive, high-R&D business such as pharmaceuticals, the immediate expensing of R&D is of greatest value in encouraging innovation.

Benefits to the Public

There is ample evidence that there are considerable benefits to the public from industrial R&D over and above what the investor can capture for himself. Thus, there is an argument that it is in the public interest to provide extraordinary incentives for R&D. Frequently suggested forms of such additional incentives are tax credits and flexible depreciation for R&D plant and equipment. The latter would have the effect of reducing R&D costs, and would not have the administrative difficulties associated with a further incentive for R&D expense. It can be argued, however, that given the condition of the economy and higher immediate priorities for investment in the latter stages of the innovation process, such a change should be considered as a lower priority at this time.

Two relatively low-cost tax policy changes have been suggested to improve the efficiency of the research infrastructure. First, university research programs have a critical need to upgrade their facilities and to augment their programs in certain areas of severe technical manpower shortage. Federal support for university research has grown at a commendable rate, but funds have not been made available in a way that allows the laboratories to maintain adequate, up-to-date research facilities and equipment. Furthermore, the shortage of manpower in such areas as chemical engineering, electronics and computer science is so great that universities are finding it impossible to pay competitive faculty salaries. Faculties are being drained and programs in these fields are being closed to new students for lack of capacity to teach them.

A tax credit for business contributions to university research programs has been suggested to help relieve these problems and — at the same time — create a closer working relationship between university research and its industrial users. From a tax policy point of view, however, there are good arguments for avoiding the use of tax credits to provide "uncapped subsidies" in specific areas of national need. An alternative approach to achieving these objectives would be to provide matching grants to university programs that receive industrial contributions.

Second, the rate of technology transfer could be enhanced by removing the disincentive in the tax system for the purchase of technology generated externally to the firm. A flexible depreciation allowance for patents and other technological know-how would accelerate technology diffusion and, at the same time, increase the value of technology inventories of small entrepreneurs and inventors.

Additional tax changes which have been suggested for consideration in accelerating the pace of innovation include the following:

- Further capital gains tax reduction would benefit small, technology-based firms. Tax-free treatment of reinvested gains might also be considered.
- Encouragement for pioneer plants could be provided, as in Japan, through a larger than normal first-year depreciation allowance.
- The potential negative impact on R&D resources of multinational firms could be offset by amending a recent change in Treasury Regulation Section 1.861-8. The regulation should require only directly related R&D expenses to be deducted from foreign source income.

References

W. Abernathy and R. Hayes, "Managing Our Way to Economic Decline," *Harvard Business Review*, July–August 1980.

R. Brinner and M. Alexander, *The Role of High-Technology Industries in Economic Growth* (Cambridge: Data Resources, Inc., 1977).

Commerce Technical Advisory Board, *Recommendations for Creating Jobs Through Success of Small Innovative Businesses* (Washington, DC: Department of Commerce, 1978).

Committee for Economic Development, *Stimulating Technological Progress* (Washington, DC: Committee for Economic Development, 1980).

E.F. Denison, *Sources of Economic Growth in the United States and Alternatives Before the U.S.* (New York: Committee for Economic Development, 1962).

Department of Commerce, *Final Report of the Industrial Advisory Committee on Industrial Innovation* (Washington, DC: Department of Commerce, 1979).

S. Fabricant, "Perspective on the Capital Requirements Question," *Capital for Productivity and Jobs* (New York: The American Assembly, Columbia University, 1977).

H.G. Grabowski, "The Determinants of Industrial Research and Development: A Study of the Chemical, Drug, and Petroleum Industries," *Journal of Political Economy,* March–April 1968.

Industrial Research Institute, *Position Statements of the IRI 1978–1980.* (New York: Industrial Research Institute, 1980).

D.W. Jorgenson, Testimony Before Senate Commerce Committee, November 1979.

D.W. Jorgenson and B. M. Fraumeni, "The Sectoral Sources of Aggregate U.S. Economic Growth 1948–1976," Background paper for Senate Commerce Committee Hearings, November 1979.

R.S. Kaplan, "Tax Policies of U.S. and Foreign Nations in Support of R&D and Innovation" in *Tax Policies for R&D and Technological Innovation* (Pittsburgh: Carnegie-Mellon University, 1978).

E. Mansfield, "Research and Development, Productivity Change, and Public Policy" in *Relationship Between R&D and Economic Growth/Productivity* (Washington, DC: National Science Foundation, 1977).

D.C. Mueller, "The Firm Decision Process: An Econometric Investigation," *Quarterly Journal of Economics,* February 1967.

National Academy of Engineering, *Industrial Innovation and Public Policy Options* (Washington, DC: National Academy of Engineering, 1980).

National Research Council, *The Impact of Tax and Financial Regulatory Policies on Industrial Innovation* (Washington, DC: National Academy of Sciences, 1980).

National Research Council, *Technology, Trade and the U.S. Economy* (Washington, DC: National Academy of Sciences, 1978).

National Research Council, *Antitrust, Uncertainty and Technological Innovation* (Washington, DC: National Academy of Sciences, 1980).

National Research Council, *The Impact of Regulation on Industrial Innovation* (Washington, DC: National Academy of Sciences, 1979).

National Science Board, *Science Indicators — 1978* (Washington, DC: National Science Foundation, 1979).

A. Rappaport, "Executive Incentives vs. Corporate Growth," *Harvard Business Review,* July–August 1978.

J.M. Utterback, *Dynamics of Product and Process Innovation in Industry* (Boston: MIT Center for Policy Alternatives, 1978).

E.V.W. Zschau, Statement Before Senate Select Committee on Small Business for the Capital Formation Task Force of the American Electronics Association, 1978.

Technology In Society

New York / Oxford / Toronto / PERGAMON PRESS / Paris / Frankfurt / Sydney

Technology In Society, Vol. 3, pp. 257–272 (1981)
Printed in the USA. All rights reserved.

A Tax Policy Strategy for Innovation

Kenneth McLennan and Charls E. Walker

Rapid innovation and the exploitation of economies of scale have provided a higher level of output per employee in the US economy than in any other nation. However, over the past two decades, more rapid rates of productivity growth in many other industrial nations have moved them rapidly toward the US level of output per employee. In some industries, especially within the manufacturing sector, this country's record of innovation has been surpassed by its competitors. In these industries the US no longer has a higher level of output per employee.

The extent of the decline in US innovation is partially measured by its dismal productivity record. Since 1973, US manufacturing productivity has grown at an annual rate of only 1.5%; the annual growth rate for nonmanufacturing has been well below 1%. In contrast, West Germany has maintained a high rate of annual productivity improvement in manufacturing of about 5%. Japan, like the US, experienced a sharp decline in the rate of growth of manufacturing productivity between 1973 and 1978, but in 1979 Japan's productivity growth surged to about 8%. It is hardly surprising that the consistently higher productivity growth rates of our industrial competitors have led to increased foreign competition and threatened employment in many sectors of the US economy, such as steel and automobiles.

Growth in real income and an improved quality of life have in the past depended heavily on technological innovation. Many studies attribute between one-third and one-half of the growth of real income to technological change.[1] Over the past decade lack of innovation accompanied by high rates of inflation has reduced the real after-tax income of most Americans. Real after-tax income for the median

The analyses and conclusions in this article do not necessarily represent the views of the Trustees of the Committee for Economic Development.

Kenneth McLennan is Vice President and Director of Industrial Studies at the Committee for Economic Development (CED). Before joining the Committee, he held the positions of Chairman of the Department of Economics, Temple University; Deputy Assistant Secretary for Policy Development, US Department of Labor; and Division Chief in the Manpower and Social Affairs Directorate at the Organization for Economic Cooperation and Development in Paris.

Charls E. Walker is Chairman of the Washington consulting firm which he founded in 1973 after serving for four years as Deputy Treasury Secretary. He is a graduate of the University of Texas and received his Ph.D. from The Wharton School. He has been a teacher, lecturer, writer and adviser to Presidents.

family (one full-time employed wage earner with two children) was $8,412 in 1970. This rose to slightly over $9,000 in 1972 but since then has steadily declined to its present level of about $8,000.[2] Many factors have contributed to this decline but without greater innovation it will be difficult to reverse the trend.

The unacceptably high rate of inflation is currently the most serious indicator of the weakness of the US economy. Lack of innovation and poor productivity did not cause inflation and one should not expect a reversal in the productivity trend to solve the inflation problem. Nevertheless, greater innovation can contribute to an anti-inflationary strategy since productivity gains provide an important cushion between employee compensation gains and price increases.

Tax Policy Changes as the Basis for Productivity Improvement

Some of the factors which contribute to changes in the rate of productivity growth are not easily influenced by public policy. For example, it has been found that a small part of US productivity decline is due to changes in the mix of skills in the labor force. Greater participation of women who have less experience in the labor market has been cited as a causal factor.[3] As these new entrants to the work force gain experience, one can expect that their productivity will increase without any change in public policy. In fact, it can be argued that, from a policy point of view, labor force participation should be increased because it leads to growth in the gross national product even though it can reduce the rate of productivity growth. Similarly, there has been increased emphasis on energy-conserving investments within total capital investment, but energy-conserving investments are not necessarily productivity-enhancing. However, no one would suggest that policy should try to redirect the emphasis of these investments.

Changes in the amount of paid non-work in the economy may also influence productivity. To the extent that the design of government expenditure programs encourages some workers to withdraw from paid employment and enter entitlement programs, public policy can remedy this potential influence on economic growth by removing the disincentive to stay in paid employment. But much of the increase in paid nonwork — in the form of longer vacations and other types of paid leave — is largely outside the influence of the government, since these practices emerge over time from management personnel decisions and from the collective bargaining system.

There are, in contrast, a number of other factors influencing productivity which are sensitive to changes in public policy. Larger Federal expenditures on R&D, changes in regulatory standards, modification of regulations that inhibit competition, patent policy changes that reduce the cost and delays imposed by current patent law — all are desirable. Individually, however, each of these policy changes will have only a small influence on the productivity problem.

Unless the benefits of policy changes are transformed into improved production processes there will be little measurable change in US productivity. Here tax policies are of special significance, for such policies can significantly affect the incentive to save and invest, and motivate industry to innovate.[4]

Unless tax policies are instituted which provide the environment for greater innovation, productivity growth is likely to fall far short of its potential, and it will be difficult for Americans to maintain their real standard of living in the '80s.

The Concepts of Capital Formation, Innovation, and the Distribution of the Capital Stock

A number of recent research studies confirm the importance of inadequate capital investment as a significant explanation for the slow growth of US productivity. Indeed, a low rate of investment (defined as the *physical quantity* of capital inputs) is cited as one of the most important causes of the country's poor productivity record in the 1970s.[5]

Compared to the period 1960 to 1973, the average annual rate of growth in capital investment in *equipment* has, in real terms, declined slightly for both manufacturing and the overall nonresidential sector of the economy. This in itself is reason for concern, but the decline in the rate of investment in *plant* has been even more dramatic. For example, as shown in Figure 1, the average annual increase in the net stock of overall nonresidential plant has dropped from about 4% during 1960–1973 to 2% after 1973. For manufacturing plant, the decline went from 1.6% during 1960–1973 to almost zero since 1973.

This decline in capital investment is especially significant since improved productivity depends heavily on providing workers with more and better plant and equipment with which to work. During the period 1960 to 1973 the plant and equipment provided to each US worker in the private business sector was increasing at an average annual rate of 2.32%. Since 1973, the decline in the rate of capital investment, along with rapid labor force growth caused this growth rate to decline to 0.14%.[6]

The Need for Tax Policy Changes

These capital investment trends support the need for tax policy changes which will provide business with an incentive to invest in new plant and equipment. In addition, the lack of any real growth in manufacturing plants since 1973 suggests that tax reform should also be concerned about the relative bias against investment in plant. The investment tax credit, originally introduced in 1962 and modified several times during the 1960s and 1970s, has helped prevent a major decline in the rate of growth in investment in equipment. But the credit, which is confined to equipment, has done nothing to encourage the construction of new structures. Consequently, the average age of US plants has been rising, and they have been less efficient than their industrial competitors.

An increase in the *quantity* of capital inputs contributes to productivity improvement through the benefits of increased capacity resulting from "capital deepening." An improvement in the *quality* of capital inputs results in innovations or technological change. There are difficult technical problems in separating the benefits attributable to quantity and quality change in capital inputs. It is known, however, that together an increase in capital investment and innovation are the most important determinants of productivity improvement. There is also

Type of Capital	AVERAGE ANNUAL RATE OF INCREASE					
	1960-73			1973-78		
	Structures	Equipment	Total	Structures	Equipment	Total
Manufacturing	1.6	4.0	2.8	0.2	3.9	1.9
Nonresidential	4.1	4.8	4.3	2.1	3.5	2.1
Residential	--	--	3.5	--	--	1.8

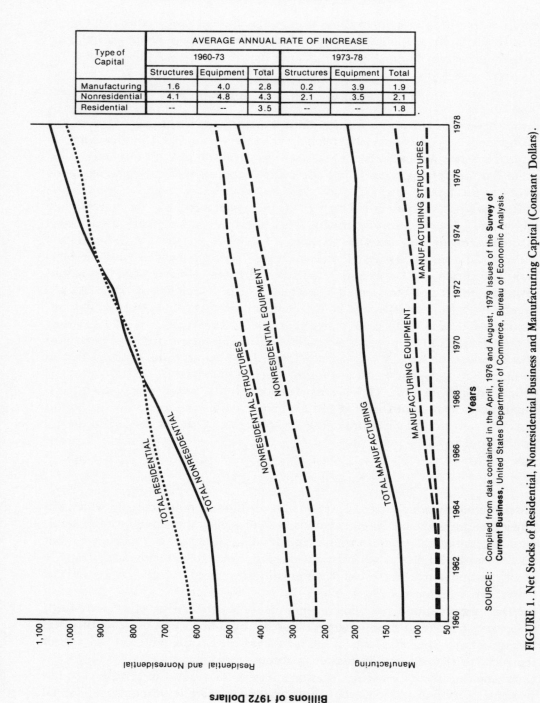

SOURCE: Compiled from data contained in the April, 1976 and August, 1979 issues of the **Survey of Current Business,** United States Department of Commerce, Bureau of Economic Analysis.

FIGURE 1. Net Stocks of Residential, Nonresidential Business and Manufacturing Capital (Constant Dollars).

evidence that the rate of innovation or technological change has declined. According to one study, technological innovation was the most important source of aggregate growth in productivity in the latter half of the 1960s. Since 1973, it has declined to its lowest level of contribution to economic growth since 1948.[7]

The distinction between "capital deepening" and innovation is not crucial since both make significant contributions to productivity improvement. There is, however, strong evidence to suggest that a technological base, in the form of successful R&D, is a necessary prerequisite to the incorporation of innovations into production processes and the development of new products. Consequently, the rapid drop in the real growth of R&D expenditures in the late 1960s and early 1970s is of some concern, especially since the distribution of R&D resources also shifted away from basic research to developmental research. Such trends are unlikely to affect productivity growth in the short run but they may have longer run adverse implications for productivity.

Research indicates that there is a complementary relationship between R&D and the capital stock of the firm.[8] This suggests that a rapid increase in capital investment is likely to "pull through" additional R&D expenditures. This does not necessarily mean, however, that the policy instruments which are most appropriate for stimulating capital investment are also optimal for insuring a strong growth in real R&D expenditures. Tax policies designed specifically to encourage greater private sector R&D as well as larger direct government expenditures on R&D may also be important to future productivity growth.

In designing tax policy changes to encourage future productivity growth, it is important to move in the direction of a tax system that is not biased in favor of investment of some types of capital assets and against others. Neutrality in the tax system would ensure that investment would flow to the most productive types of capital investment because investors are motivated to seek the highest rate of return for a given level of risk.

In practice it is almost impossible to design a tax system which is completely neutral in its incentive to invest in different sectors of the economy.[9] For example, it has long been a goal of public policy to encourage home ownership, and the interest on mortgages is deductible in calculating taxable personal income. Consequently, in a period of rapid inflation when nominal income is also rising rapidly and becoming subject to higher marginal tax rates, there is a strong incentive for individuals to invest in residential capital.

While there is no logical relationship between investment in plant and equipment and residential capital, Figure 1 shows that the absolute level and the average annual rate of growth in residential capital has been consistently higher than the level and rate of investment in manufacturing capital. It has been estimated that the existing bias against investment in plant and equipment has caused a significant shift to residential capital and away from nonresidential capital, thus retarding productivity growth.

Tax Policy Options for Stimulating Innovation

Investment in technological innovations is only the final phase in a process which starts with basic research. Typically the motive for basic research is to produce knowledge for its own sake, with only minimal consideration for its useful application. Applied research—the other part of the research phase of stimulating economic growth—strives to apply basic knowledge, through science and engineering, to the solution of a particular problem. Applied research also includes testing the technical feasibility of the results of the overall research and development (R&D) phase.

The initial innovation involves introducing the first-of-a-kind production process supported by access to raw materials; power, labor and marketing facilities to respond to demand for the output. This phase requires many times more capital resources than does R&D. Finally, if the benefits of the technical innovation are to be fully realized in the form of improved productivity, the initial innovation must be diffused throughout the economy. The rate of diffusion of innovation depends on many factors, but one of the most important is the ability of the economic system to accumulate capital.

In order to maximize the benefits of tax policy changes it is necessary to allocate the resources made available through a tax reduction among the various phases in the process of technological innovation. These resources are not necessarily confined to the resources released directly by the tax change; many of the current tax reduction proposals will also stimulate general economic growth and thereby enlarge the pool of available resources.

Indirect Incentives to Investment

Tax proposals providing an *indirect* incentive on investment include incentives to encourage individual saving. The individual saving rate in the United States, which is lower than the rate in most other nations, dropped from 8.6% of disposable income in 1973 to 5.7% in 1980. One approach to raising this rate is to provide a personal income tax credit for the "first" dollar ($200 in 1981 and in 1982) interest on savings or on dividends. The problem with this proposal is that some of the saving would have occurred without any tax incentive. Consequently, the government is trading off some revenue loss without necessarily stimulating additional savings.

This is not to say that tax credits or deductions on the "first" dollar of savings income are undesirable. There is a strong case for them on the basis of equity—*i.e.,* all savers, not just new savers, deserve special tax benefits. Still, for maximum impact on incentives, the credit should be given for the "last" rather than—or in addition to—the first dollar saved. A proposal developed by Congressmen Brown and Rousselot, along with Senator Roth, is an imaginative approach for encouraging additional individual saving. This bill would lower tax rates on savings and investment income to a maximum rate of 50%. It would also tax "earned" and "unearned" income separately, both at rates ranging from 14% to 50%. Currently, earned income is taxed at those rates, but so-called "unearned" income, such as savings interest and dividends, is added on top of the earned income amount and taxed at rates up to 70%. Under this proposal, the first dollar of unearned income would be taxed at the lowest 14% rate, rather than at the highest rate reached by the earned income.[10]

A substantial reduction in the marginal tax rate on interest income would also be beneficial in the current inflationary environment. High marginal tax rates make it more attractive for individuals to consume any discretionary income rather than invest it and have the earnings taxed at a high rate. Lower tax rates on all forms of investment income would encourage individuals to accumulate savings for investment rather than for consumption. A reduction in the consumption bias in the tax system would also help reduce inflationary pressure and contribute to innovation through investment in capital assets.

A reduction in personal income tax rates is a potentially important component in any strategy for stimulating innovation. The Kemp-Roth bill is the leading proposal designed to reduce the tax burden on individuals. The bill proposes a 10% across-the-board cut in personal income tax rates in each of the next three years. The concept of phasing-in the cut not only will permit a gradual reduction in the growth of Federal expenditures, it will also provide individuals with a continuing incentive to save and increase their work effort.

The across-the-board tax cut approach is likely to be controversial since the largest benefits of such a tax reduction will be realized by those in the upper tax brackets. However, if the goal is to stimulate investment and enhance future productivity growth, a substantial absolute tax reduction for the income groups in the higher tax brackets—those who contribute substantially to total tax revenues—will provide the greatest stimulus to savings and investment. The political debate over the Kemp-Roth proposal represents a classic illustration of the clash between those who attach considerable weight to the income distribution goal of tax policy and those who attach greater weight to using tax policy to stimulate economic growth so that the real income of everyone is raised.

The growth of the Social Security System has also affected the rate of saving and capital investment. Social Security taxes, which in 1950 were equivalent to only 0.1% of GNP, are now about 5% of GNP. In order to raise the real benefit level of Social Security payments and protect the beneficiaries' income against erosion from inflation, it has been necessary to raise Social Security taxes. During the past decade, the average American family's Social Security taxes more than tripled while its nominal income barely doubled.

There is now a significant body of research which shows that the individual's expectation of future Social Security income has resulted in a slight reduction in personal savings. However, each dollar of Social Security contribution may have reduced savings by as much as 80 cents.[11] Since the Social Security tax system will have a serious financing problem by the end of 1981, major reform of the system is necessary. The future debate over reform will provide an opportunity to make changes in the system which will not result in a further depression of savings and capital formation.

Finally, a reduction of the tax on all forms of income from capital (corporate income, capital gains, interest and dividends) would increase corporate and personal savings indirectly and encourage capital investment. Over the past decade, inflation has raised the average and marginal tax rates on income from both labor and capital. However, investment is currently discouraged because the marginal and average tax rates on capital income are higher than the corresponding rates on labor income.[12]

In addition to the straightforward rate reduction, several other tax reforms have recently been recommended to reduce the tax on capital income. These include the rollover concept, which would defer the capital gains tax on the sale of assets, provided the gains were reinvested in other capital assets. This is a politically appealing approach since under this proposal the total capital stock cannot be depleted. A similar approach has been suggested to encourage reinvestment of dividends.

The current Congressional concern with tax policy is not only motivated by concern over the increasing tax burden. Congress is deeply concerned about the trend in productivity and the decapitalization of some sectors of the economy. This concern has led to several tax proposals directly linked to increased investment designed to stimulate innovation or research and development.

Direct Tax Incentives to Increase R&D Expenditures

Research and development accounts for only a very small proportion of all the resources for the entire innovation process. The latter stages of the process — building and operating the plant and equipment which will produce the new and improved goods and services — require many more resources than the R&D phase. Nevertheless, R&D is important, and the decline in the rate of growth in real resources devoted to R&D in the late 1960s and early 1970s is of great concern. As a result, a number of tax proposals to stimulate R&D have been made.

Most of the decline in the growth of R&D expenditures is attributable to the decline in government expenditures on R&D associated with reductions in the defense and space budgets. Industry-funded R&D has continued to expand in real terms though the recent rate of growth has failed to match the rapid expansion of funding of the early 1960s.

Section 174 of the US Internal Revenue Code gives all business taxpayers the option of deducting research and experimental (development) expenditures in the year they are incurred, even though such expenditures may lead to the creation of an intangible asset (such as a patent) with a useful life in excess of one year. The definition of an R&D expenditure under Section 174 is generally favorable to businesses whose main activity is R&D rather than the commercial development of the results of R&D.

The United States has no special incentives — beyond those available for investment generally — for investment in depreciable structures and equipment used for research and experimental activities. Many of its industrial competitors provide more generous tax incentives for invention and innovation. Japan, West Germany, France, and Canada, for example, permit R&D plant and equipment to be written off much more rapidly than is possible for US firms.[13]

One of the most direct ways of providing a tax stimulus to R&D is therefore to extend Section 174 to include plant and equipment used in R&D. This would permit business to write off R&D structures and equipment in one year, or over a longer period if preferred. The rationale for providing business with this type of R&D incentive is based primarily on the rapidly increasing cost of highly sophisticated R&D plant and equipment, and on the need to give US firms roughly the same advantages currently provided in many other industrial nations.

Direct Tax Incentives to Increase Investment in New Plant and Equipment

It is now clear that high rates of inflation and the current depreciation schedule under the tax code have combined to reduce the rate of return from investment in plant and equipment and thereby raise the effective cost of investment in plant and equipment. In part, this has occurred because tax policy for capital write-off is based on the historical cost of capital assets. The result is that the effective corporate tax rate, after adjusting for replacement cost (taxes paid on economic profits) and the inflated value of inventory, is much higher than the reported tax rate. Consequently, the differential between the real rate of return (return on replacement cost of capital) and the reported rate of return, which was about six percentage points during the sixties, has now gradually widened to about 11 percentage points. The average real economic rate of return on capital investment has declined from its high of 10% in 1964 to about 5% in 1978.[14] It is therefore not surprising that, in general, new plant and equipment is not a particularly attractive type of investment.

Several proposals have been recommended to make investment in plant and equipment more attractive. Prominent among these are proposals to permit businesses to shorten the period over which capital assets are depreciated. Some form of more rapid capital recovery currently receives considerable Congressional support. This approach's major attraction is that the incentive is direct — business has to make an investment to receive the tax benefit. This type of proposal also involves simplification of the current system of depreciation and removal of some of the bias against investing in new plant.

The leading capital recovery proposal is the Capital Cost Recovery Act, introduced by Congressmen Conable and Jones. This bill would greatly simplify the existing complex schedule for depreciating capital assets and substantially shorten the write-off period.

The Conable-Jones proposal, known as "10-5-3" (and appropriately introduced as H.R. 1053) would permit vehicles to be written off in three years (up to $100,000 per year), equipment in five years and structures in ten years.[15] It therefore reduces the present 130 categories of assets to three and shortens the write-off period for all capital assets. This is a stimulus to investment in all types of capital assets and it would reduce the current bias against investment in plant since under the current tax code, on average, it takes well over 20 years, and in some cases up toward 50 years, to write off an investment in a new plant. Inasmuch as this significant reduction in asset lives would apply to R&D plant and equipment, it would reduce the need for any amendment to Section 174 as discussed earlier.

There is also Congressional support for a modificiation of the Conable-Jones approach by designating six classes of assets. This modification, voted out of the Senate Finance Committee in the last session of Congress, classified assets as follows: two-year write-off period would apply to trucks and special equipment; electronic equipment used in retail and wholesale trade and in manufacturing could be written off over four years; property which currently is written off over 11½ to 16½ years (such as primary steel products and motor vehicle manufacturing assets) would be written off over seven years; property now written off over more than 16½ could be written off in 10 years; property of public utilities would also benefit from a reduction in write-off period, and structures would be written off in 15 to 20 years.

A substantially different approach is taken in the First Year Capital Recovery (FYCR) proposal, which reduces the number of asset classes and suggests a novel approach to reducing the impact of inflation on the incentive to invest in new plant and equipment.[16] FYCR would permit taxpayers to deduct the present value of economic depreciation as an expense in arriving at income for tax purposes in the year the asset is acquired. The appropriate depreciation deduction is based on studies of used-asset prices to determine the true economic depreciation and a government-designated discount rate.

The proposal has merit in reducing the influence of inflation on capital investment, but it offers no additional incentive to invest in plant and equipment. It also involves repealing the investment tax credit. Given the current problems in many of our industries it is unlikely that this proposal will provide an adequate stimulus to the much needed investment for improving innovation. Selection of the appropriate discount rate would also run into serious practical and political problems.

In the current economic environment of high inflation and low productivity policymakers will have to determine the specific components of a tax strategy which provides the incentives for investment and at the same time stimulates personal savings. From the point of view of stimulating innovation this will probably require selecting among tax instruments which have both a direct and indirect influence on capital investment.

Selecting the Major Components of a Tax Strategy

There are several major criteria for judging which types of tax change are likely to be most effective in stimulating the investment in new plant and equipment required for innovation. The size of the expected *investment response,* in relation to the cost of the tax change, is obviously an important criterion. Secondly, the tax change should at least make the tax system *less biased against investment* in *new plants* and against investment in capital assets in general. Finally, the policy change should be *administratively* simple to implement.

Two congressional proposals ("10-5-3" and "2-4-7-10") which directly link the tax proposals are among the tax proposals which have a direct influence on investment. Studies of the impact of previous changes in the investment tax credit have shown that the stock of equipment responds rapidly to the reduction in the cost of new equipment. A similar response can be expected from both these congressional proposals. Because "10-5-3" is phased in gradually, its investment response will be slowest, though it would be much easier to accommodate within the policy constraint of reducing the current budget deficit. Both these approaches to more rapid capital recovery are administratively simple to implement and will substantially reduce the current bias against investment in new plant.

Benefits of More Rapid Capital Recovery

Conceptually, there is not much controversy over the type of benefits which some form of more rapid capital recovery would produce. As shown in Figure 2, an increase in the stock of plant and equipment is encouraged through an increase in the rate of return from the investment, coupled with the increase in cash flow. This increase either takes the form of new plant and equipment embodying the latest technical knowledge or an increase in scale of production using the same technlogy in current operations. In either case, the resulting benefits include increased productivity and the generation of greater income, output and employment. It is, of course, possible that some of the increase in productivity could be offset if greater utilization of existing plants would have resulted in a rise in the productivity of these plants.

The magnitude of these benefits is difficult to predict. This is because the decision to invest in new plant and equipment is influenced by the expected future demand as well as the reduction in the cost of capital brought about by more rapid depreciation. It is also difficult to estimate the distribution of the new investment between plant and equipment using "best practice techniques" (based on the most recent results of R&D) and the same level of technology used in firms' existing plant and equipment. This also influences the magnitude of the benefits. As a practical matter, since firms are motivated by cost reduction and the potential for gain from sales of new products, new plant and equipment are rarely introduced without incorporating the latest scientific and technical knowledge.

Investment in plant and equipment is not only essential for productivity improvement, it is also the dynamic mechanism which generates a continuous flow of research and development. This is a benefit of increased plant and equipment investment which is not generally appreciated among those who believe that increasing R&D is the most effective way to increase productivity.

The benefits in terms of improved productivity and employment growth are likely to be much greater from more rapid capital recovery than from tax incentives for R&D. Nevertheless, tax policies for stimulating plant and equipment and for encouraging industry-funded R&D are complementary. As shown in Figure 2, faster capital recovery will increase technical knowledge and encourage additional expenditures on applied R&D. As a result, the capital investment stimulus "pulls through" additional R&D.

A tax incentive to encourage a more rapid increase in industry-funded R&D

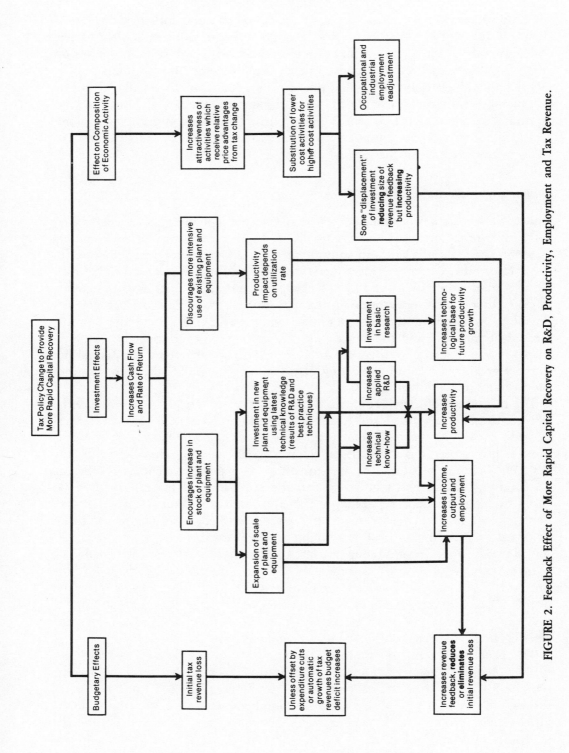

FIGURE 2. Feedback Effect of More Rapid Capital Recovery on R&D, Productivity, Employment and Tax Revenue.

would in the longer run ensure a continued increase in innovation. However, a policy change such as more rapid capital recovery, which diffuses successful innovations throughout the economy, is currently a much more important priority than any policy to stimulate R&D.

Problems in Reducing Taxes on Income and Capital

One of the problems with the tax changes being recommended is that firms which experience chronically low earnings may not be able to take advantage of the tax incentive. One suggestion to overcome this problem is to make unused credits under the investment tax credit refundable through a Federal payment in cash.

There is opposition to this approach since it may result in subsidizing inefficient businesses and therefore help keep marginal businesses alive when the market system is essentially indicating that they should fail. Tax policy should probably not provide special assistance to firms which are about to be permanently dislocated. Still, some major firms in important industries—*e.g.,* steel, automobiles, airlines, and railroads—have in recent years been unable to generate sufficient taxable earnings to utilize all of the tax credits earned through investment in equipment. One option would be to permit firms "to bank" unused investment tax credits which could be used at a later time once the firm is in a position of having large enough taxable earnings to take advantage of the credit.

The second problem is the estimated revenue cost of more rapid capital recovery and other tax proposals to stimulate investment through incentives to save. Published government estimates of these costs are almost always expressed on a static basis without taking into account the increased tax revenue generated by the income growth stimulated by the investment. Consequently, the revenue costs tend to be overestimated.

There is no dispute that revenue feedback exists, but its magnitude is extremely difficult to estimate. As shown in Figure 2, one difficulty in measuring the feedback effect is that there is a change in the composition of output due to any tax policy change. This shifts investment funds from some higher cost economic activities to lower cost activities. This is the basis for greater efficiency and higher productivity, but the shift in economic activity "displaces" investment that would have produced tax revenues in the absence of the policy change. Loss of revenue from this source, which is extremely difficult to calculate—but is probably small—should be deducted from the additional revenue generated by the increased economic activity from the investment in plant and equipment.

Even though feedback effects are difficult to measure, they should at least be taken into account in estimating the cost of the initial tax revenue loss of more rapid capital recovery. The current practice of emphasizing static revenue losses is quite misleading to policymakers, who tend to put great weight on a simple numerical cost estimate. It is also of limited assistance in making budget and general economic policy decisions. For policy decisions it is important to recognize that the feedback effect of reducing the cost of capital will at least partially—and perhaps significantly—offset the initial revenue loss.

The timing of the initial revenue loss and the rate of revenue feedback are also important considerations in estimating the real economic cost of this type of policy proposal. In the very short run the revenue loss will clearly exceed the increased revenue from the stimulation of investment. The first year net loss is likely to be relatively small, but for each specific tax proposal there are different empirical estimates of the number of years before the net loss reaches its maximum and is eventually eliminated through greater economic activity.

Offsetting the Initial Revenue Loss

There are two general ways to offset the net initial revenue loss and neither are costless economically or politically. One way is to use the projected annual growth in Federal tax revenues to meet the initial revenue loss. In 1981 this would amount to almost $80 to $90 billion, which is substantially greater than the revenue loss in the first several years for capital recovery proposals. However, since such a large proportion of government expenditure programs are open-ended and also indexed for inflation, this approach may not be feasible since such entitlements may constitute a legal right, at least in the short run. This automatic growth in spending could use up much of the projected growth in revenues.

Ideally, of course, policymakers should review the large number of evaluation studies which show that many government programs could be administered more effectively and modified in such a way as to save significant revenues but not harm the intended beneficiaries of the program. In addition, policymakers could decide to cut expenditures by eliminating or at least trimming expenditures on programs with the lowest benefit to cost ratio.

Unfortunately, there is no effective mechanism to ensure that policymakers act on evaluation studies and in the real world of policy, program reductions are highly political decisions.

Conclusions

Minor tinkering with tax rates to deal with tax bracket creep will be completely insufficient for the task of stimulating innovation in the 1980s. A sustained increase in the rate of innovation requires a much more fundamental revision of the incentive to innovate through capital investment and an increase in productive work effort.

In order to introduce a fundamental change in tax policy so that individuals have an incentive to save and businesses are motivated to construct more innovative production processes, the Administration must demonstrate that it can control Federal expenditures and gradually reduce the budget deficit. Consequently, while the tax changes to stimulate innovation should be enacted as soon as possible, their full implementation should be phased in over several years.

The first phase should include some form of more rapid capital recovery which could be introduced gradually as proposed in the original "10-5-3" proposal. Similarly, individual wage earners should get some tax relief immediately but they should know that additional reductions would be forthcoming over the next several years. If a tax incentive for saving is introduced now and also gradually increased, consumers will plan to allocate a greater share of their future income to savings. This approach will not only increase the funds for future investment, it will also assist in an anti-inflationary strategy.

The success of tax policies to encourage innovation depends heavily on whether consumers, workers and business believe that government can control the growth of Federal expenditures and reduce inflation. In the final analysis, policymakers have to decide whether greater innovation, employment growth and other net benefits of more plant and equipment investment exceed the net benefits of specific expenditure programs.

Given the current US productivity performance and the increasing threat to domestic employment from international competition, policymakers appear to have recognized the need for tax policies which increase innovation through greater investment in plant and equipment.

Notes and References

1. Edward F. Denison, *The Source of Economic Growth in the United States and the Alternatives Before U.S.* (New York: Committee for Economic Development, 1962). Many more recent studies have confirmed Denison's original findings.
2. Tax Foundation, Inc., *Monthly Tax Features*, Vol. 24, no. 8 (September 1980), p. 1.
3. See Edward F. Denison, *Explanations of Declining Productivity Growth*, Report 354 (Washington, DC: The Brookings Institution, 1979).
4. The potential of tax policy changes in fostering investment and innovation is especially great because of the widely recognized bias in the US tax system in favor of consumption and against saving and productive investment. This bias is taken as given and is not further discussed in this article.
5. J.R. Norsworthy and M.J. Harper, *The Role of Capital Formation in the Recent Slowdown in Productivity Growth*, Bureau of Labor Statistics Working Paper (Washington, DC: Bureau of Labor Statistics, January 1979); E.A. Hudson and D.W. Jorgenson, "Energy Prices and the U.S. Economy," *Data Resources U.S. Review* (September 1979). See also the testimony of Professor Jorgenson before the Committee on Commerce, Science and Transportation, United States Senate, November 14, 1979; and Peter Clark, "Capital Formation and the Recent Productivity Slowdown." *Journal of Finance*, June 1978.
6. J.R. Norsworthy, M.J. Harper and Kent Kunze, *The Slowdown in Productivity Growth: Analysis of Some Contributing Factors*, Brookings Papers on Economic Activity 2:79 (Washington, DC: The Brookings Institution, 1980).
7. Barbara M. Fraumeni and Dale W. Jorgenson, "The Role of Capital in U.S. Economic Growth, 1948–1976" in George M. von Furstenberg, ed., *Capital, Efficiency and Growth* (Cambridge, Massachusetts: Ballinger Publishing Company, 1980), p. 99.
8. Ishaq M. Nadiri, "Contributions and Determinants of Research and Development" in George M. von Furstenberg, ed., *Capital, Efficiency and Growth* (Cambridge, Massachusetts: Ballinger Publishing Company, 1980), p. 387.
9. Many experts view the consumption-based value added tax (VAT) as the most neutral tax. Although popular in Western Europe, VAT has little chance of political acceptance in the US in the foreseeable future.
10. The taxpayer could allocate his allowable deductions as he chooses between the earned and unearned income. The bill also includes provisions to discourage the use of tax shelters and encourage more productive investment.
11. N. Bulent Gultekin and Dennis E. Logue, "Social Security and Personal Saving: Survey and New Evidence" in George M. von Furstenberg, ed., *Social Security vs. Private Savings* (Cambridge, Massachusetts: Ballinger Publishing Company, 1979), p. 97.
12. See George M. von Furstenberg and Burton G. Malkiel, "The Government and Capital Formation: A Survey of Recent Issues," *Journal of Economic Literature*, Vol. 15 (September 1977), p. 839.
13. For a review of the tax treatment of R&D in other countries, see *Stimulating Technological Progress* (New York: Committee for Economic Development, January 1980), pp. 38–39.
14. See *Stimulating Technological Progress* (New York: Committee for Economic Development, January 1980), pp. 38–39.

15. The proposal will also apply a full 10% tax credit to five year assets, up from the 6-⅔% credit in existing law.

16. See Alan J. Auerbach and Dale W. Jorgenson, "The First Year Capital Recovery System," testimony before the Subcommittee on Taxation and Debt Management, Senate Finance Committee, US Senate, October 22, 1979.

Technology In Society, Vol. 3, pp. 273–280 (1981)
Printed in the USA. All rights reserved.

0160-791X/81/010273-08$02.00/0
Copyright © 1981 Pergamon Press Ltd

Capital Recovery and Economic Growth in the 1980s

Thomas A. Vanderslice

One of the classic, and possibly apocryphal, stories about Thomas Alva Edison concerns the invention of the electric lamp. After he had tried some 2,000 materials for a filament without success, a reporter asked if he were not discouraged and ready to give up because of this long history of failures. "Not at all," Edison is supposed to have replied, "I now know 2,000 substances that won't work."

Economists who have been engaged in their government's efforts to control inflation, increase productivity, stimulate employment and economic growth in recent years must feel a little bit like Thomas Edison.

Traditional methods of fighting domestic inflation have failed to cure an inflation that is worldwide. The world is now repeating—on an international scale—the mistake that the Bank of England and other central banks made on a national scale all through the trade cycles of the 19th century, the mistake which Keynes called "the most dangerous technique for the maintenance of equilibrium which can possibly be imagined," of thumping up interest rates in order to counter a boom just after it has begun to turn down.

Nevertheless, the efforts to fine-tune the US economy have not been totally unproductive, or counterproductive. A great deal of useful analytical work has been going on on the roots of modern inflation, the impact of government regulation and tax policies, and the sources of productivity advances and capital formation. If the new administration has learned these lessons the US may, in fact, be ahead in the game.

Nor are the economists wholly to blame for their failures. The problem they

Dr. Thomas A. Vanderslice has served as President, Chief Operating Officer, and a Director of General Telephone & Electronics Corporation since 1979. He is a Trustee of the Committee for Economic Development and has been Chairman of its Subcommittee on Technology Policy. Dr. Vanderslice holds a Ph.D. in chemistry and physics from Catholic University, where he was a Fulbright scholar, and is former Executive Vice President and Sector Executive of the Power Systems Sector for the General Electric Company. He is a member of numerous professional organizations, including the National Academy of Engineers and an Industry Task Force on Technology and Society.

faced is analogous to trying to tune an automobile engine when the flywheel is missing. Years of decapitalization of American industry have, in effect, removed the flywheel that balanced out the US economy. If the engine sputters and behaves erratically, whether the fuel mixture is lean or enriched, it is because more is needed than a carburetor adjustment.

One of the great strengths of American capitalism has been its balance: the balance between "equity" and debt—with each serving as a governor for the other; the balance between earnings reinvested to insure the continuation of the business, and payments to shareowners; the balance between the interests of employees, shareowners, and the public. In contrast to some other major industrial countries, whose economies might be termed bank-directed, or government-directed, the US has had a market-driven and investment-oriented economy, and this has contributed to the dynamic balance of the American economy.

But this balance has not always been sustained. The share of national income going to capital versus other sectors of the economy remained relatively constant for most of the past century and also for the post World War II years up to the mid-1960s. Since then, however, there has been a decline in the relative shares going to corporate profits which, in turn, has led to declines in capital investment as a percent of GNP, and by a like decline in research and development done by the private sector which was all the more felt since it was accompanied by governmental cutbacks in R&D at the same time.

Achieving a balanced Federal budget has become a rarity. In the past 20 years, the US government has run only one budget surplus—in 1969—while piling up deficits of $434.5 billion. Of these deficits, $371 billion or 85% of the total, were accumulated in the past ten years.

Public debt formation is not necessarily inflationary if it is balanced by real saving in the private sector. Unhappily, this is not the case. By the end of 1980, credit market debt totalled some $4 trillion—an increase of $2.4 trillion since 1970. It is particularly significant, in view of the growing need for US industry to replace its capital stock, that for much of the 1970s the household (or consuming) sector has taken down more credit in the US financial markets than the business sector itself. To restore some balance between consumption and savings—to stop "consuming our capital"—the country needs, among other steps, higher rewards for saving in the form of interest rates free of regulatory limitations and the reduction of taxation on both interest and dividend income.

Accelerated Depreciation

Of particular importance in enabling US industry to replace its capital stock in a period of high inflation and rapid technological advance is accelerated depreciation.

Depreciation and retained earnings normally generate from two-thirds to three-fourths of the cash that non-financial companies invest in plant, equipment, inventory and mineral rights. In a time of severe inflation, such as now, capital must be recovered quickly and recycled, if it is not to be seriously depleted or permanently lost.

To use an example to demonstrate this effect, assume that an asset costing $30 million was originally placed in service with an expected useful life of 30 years. The depreciation expense each year would be one-thirtieth of the original investment, or $1 million. Over the first ten years, $10 million of capital would be recovered through depreciation.

Now assume that there are changes in market structure, inflationary pressures on maintenance costs, and advances in technology—all likely occurrences today. These changes make it clear that the asset can remain cost-effective for a maximum period of only five more years. Assume the remaining five-year life is fully accepted by regulation for depreciation life.

Here is what generally happens. Utilizing an approach termed "whole life" depreciation, the five years of remaining life are added to the ten years of life already completed to produce a total, or "whole," depreciation life of 15 years. The annual depreciation expense becomes one-fifteenth of the original investment, or $2 million. During the remaining five years, this rate is used and provides another $10 million of capital recovery.

The total capital recovery over the full 15-year period was $20 million, but the original investment was $30 million! Thus, at the time the asset is retired, there remains $10 million of unrecovered capital.

A company could only avoid this failure to recover one-third of its investment by continuing to use the obsolete plant. And that is exactly what has happened.

The so-called "recovery" of 1975–77 was marked by lagging investment in new plant and equipment, common stock prices that were low relative to reported earnings, and physical assets that continued to be grossly under-valued relative to their replacement costs.

Alfred C. Neal ("Immolation of Business Capital," *Harvard Business Review*, March–April, 1978) estimates that prudent people (those who invested in blue-chip companies) lost $134 billion from 1973 through 1976 as a result of mismeasurement of the costs of productive resources. This represents the difference between "reported" versus adjusted-for-inflation profits, taxes, dividends, and retained earnings for those four years.

It is worth noting in this regard that the $90 billion that the US will pay for foreign oil in 1980 substantially exceeds the total net income of all the companies on the Fortune 500 list.

Little wonder that, from mid-1972 to mid-1979, capital outlays per worker in the US grew by only 0.6% a year, compared with a 2.9% rate over the previous 22 years.

And that productivity, which during the first two decades after World War II had grown at a very healthy 3.3% rate, faded to a 1.1% growth rate from 1973 to 1978. In 1979, there was an actual drop in the level of productivity of about a full percentage point, and it has been at a virtual standstill ever since.

Inflation was a minor problem in the 1950s. However, it began an upward trend in the 1960s, and became of serious concern in the 1970s. In fact, the US inflation rate during 1979 was higher than the average of all industrial countries for the first time in history.

As a combined result of inflation and inadequate capital formation, Department of Commerce figures badly overstate effective capital stock growth in the 1970s because of a lack of information about depreciation and obsolescence. One indication of this is the *market* valuation of the nonfinancial corporations in the economy. In 1979, it is calculated, these corporations were valued at only 65% of the computed replacement cost of their assets. As one economist writes, "It has been, in fact, a puzzle to explain why companies were investing and expanding at all in 1979, given the market's valuation of their capital in place."

The Most Serious Long-Term Problem

The more one ponders the problem of capital formation for the 1980s, the clearer it seems that inadequate capital recovery vies with the related afflictions of inflation as the most serious long-term problem.

The problem of "decapitalization" through inadequate capital recovery is not exactly new. The canal system in this country was put in place under a concept of "indefinite life." When the railroads came along, they were forced under ICC regulations to base their earnings on total investments with prescribed "long lives." Eventually, after trucks and airlines appeared—taking advantage of government-subsidized roads and airports—the railroads were left with a capital stock of undepreciated rusting rails and obsolete equipment.

The concepts and perceptions underlying current regulatory depreciation practices have been with us for many years. They were formed in the early 1900s in an era of little or no inflation and correspondingly low interest rates, slow technological change, naturally long asset lives and regulated monopoly. But they are no longer adequate—given the pace of modern technology and competition—if indeed they ever were!

Thus a recent study (September 1980) of the Committee for Economic Development on "Restoring Productivity and Real Economic Growth" concludes that, since 1973, a low rate of private investment has been a major contributor to this country's dismal productivity record. Yet the United States "is relatively more dependent on the private sector for investment in expansion and modernization of productive capacity than many of its international competitors."

This lag in capital investment has resulted in the growing obsolescence of much plant and equipment, contributing to rising inflation and US losses in international competitiveness. These high rates of inflation have, in turn, been a major force in reducing the rate of replacement of obsolete plant and equipment. This catch-22 predicament has come about, in part, because allowable depreciation of existing plant and equipment is based on historical costs, which, in a period of rapid inflation, are much lower than replacement costs.

A substantial shortening of depreciation schedules would, in CED's view, be the most practical first step toward removing major existing disincentives to capital investment.

An earlier CED study ("Technology Policy in the U.S.") last year pointed out that stepped-up investment incentives also constitute the most important measure the US can take to foster more rapid technological progress. Noting that, if the level of investment in plant and equipment can be raised, the rate of diffusion of new technology into the economy will also rise, the CED placed "the highest priority on specific changes in the tax laws to create greater investment incentives."

The CED productivity study notes that more rapid recovery allowances *do not* constitute an unconditional tax reduction for business. It is rather a tax deferral that helps to reduce the inflationary erosion of corporate funds available for replacement of plant and equiment. Such a tax deferral is, of course, valuable to the tax-paying business firm and can be extended so long as the firm achieves and maintains an accelerated rate of new capital investment that fully matches its higher level of tax deductible annual depreciation charges.

While more rapid capital recovery is essential to all industry today, accelerated depreciation is crucial to the rapidly emerging computer/telecommunications, word-processing, automation, and information-processing industries.

US productivity in the 1960–70 period benefited from the introduction of jet aircraft; the development of the interstate highway network and the consequent development of long-distance trucking; and substantial scale economies in retail trade. But with rapidly rising energy costs, more stringent environmental and safety standards, and plant and equipment rapidly becoming obsolete, sectors until now regarded as strongly innovative seem to be marking time or losing momentum. For research findings to be applied, or innovations introduced and diffused, new venture capital is needed, and this has been sharply restricted by current economic difficulties. As a result, the country finds itself increasingly dependent on imported technology for productivity improvements.

The communications industry is a spectacular exception. Today, the telecommunications industries are poised to play the same leading roles in the economy that the steel and automobile industries played decades before.

Today marks the leading edge of a revolutionary change in technology that began only a little more than a quarter century ago. This is a technology drawn from an entirely new scientific base that bears little resemblance to the science that engineers and scientists learned three or four decades ago. Today, one deals with phenomena that were both inconceivable and impossible in the old world of Newtonian mechanics. New industries are arising out of wave mechanics, quantum electronics and the new physics of solids, and their products are revolutionizing older technologies by the new order of efficiency and function they provide.

A Dazzling Pace

The pace of technical change has been dazzling. The number of circuit elements that can be held on a finger-nail-sized silicon chip has doubled every year since 1960, and the pace shows no sign of letting up. The question for these times is not how many angels can dance on the head of a pin, but how much information can be stored?

Jean-Jacques Salomon (*OECD Observer,* May 1980) has calculated that the capabilities of one of the first electronic computers (ENIAC) built in the 1940s for several million dollars could be produced in 1978 for less than $100 in a micro-computer which calculated 20 times faster, is 10,000 times more reliable, requires 56,000 times less power, and 300,000 times less space.

Twenty-five years ago it cost $1.25 to do 100,000 multiplications by computer. Today it costs less than a penny. If the costs of other things had gone down the way computing costs have, it would be possible to buy a standard-sized car for $200, and an around-the-world airline trip for $3. And if the performance gains arising from improved technology and productivity had progressed at the same rate as computer technology, an around-the-world airline flight would take 24 minutes, and the standard-sized car would get 550 miles per gallon.

The above is fantasy, but this is not a fairy tale. The marriage of computing and communication technology, though of tremendous consequence, does not mean that everyone will live happily ever after. The question remains, for instance, if the 16-year depreciation lives which are traditional in the regulated communication industries are compatible with the 5–10-year lives common in the computer industries?

Life in software, as the programmer remarked, is often hard. And the harsh reality underlying such rapid technological change is that companies have not been recovering their capital through depreciation at anywhere near the extent they need to—given the rate of inflation and the pace of technological advance.

To restore incentives for capital formation and investment several steps are needed:

First, the country must begin to move toward a removal of the bias against capital formation that exists in the economic/political system today—tax policy should at least be *neutral*—to encourage savings and investment. This type of society is seriously vulnerable to taxation on capital because it relies on private capital formation for productivity and jobs. If the government wishes to redistribute income in pursuit of a perceived greater equity, the nation must face and weigh the cost associated with the distorting effects on productivity and jobs.

Second, the country must move away from those things that divert available capital from the expenditures that can raise productivity into less productive uses—within industry and within government.

Third, the country needs tax reform. And effective capital recovery must be the centerpiece of any *meaningful* reform.

There is increasingly widespread recognition of the need to reduce the *dis*incentives and strengthen the incentives for long-term capital formation and entrepreneurial investment in innovation.

The "Steiger Amendment" capital gains tax cut of two years ago, is a case in point, and has undoubtedly contributed to the 40%–plus improvement in the stock market since that time.

And the tax cuts proposed by President Reagan contain an endorsement of the 10-5-3 depreciation bill sponsored by a majority of House and Senate members.

The significant thing about 10-5-3 is that it has been supported by a very broad coalition of business: big business, small business, capital-intensive business, labor-intensive business, and businesses involved in real estate, retail, and service of all kind.

Unfortunately, 10-5-3, in its present form, provides a stronger incentive for new factories than for new machines in existing buildings, and favors, for instance, the steel industry, which has a great deal of heavy equipment, over electronics which does not.

But the business and technical community cannot wait until the government turns the situation around. It must work hard for the changes urgently needed in government policy—in Washington, and in the state capitals—to restore the economic health of its own industries.

Aggressive Capital Recovery

A number of companies, including GTE, are taking the initiative with aggressive capital recovery actions—both internally and externally.

Last September, GTE's Chairman Theodore F. Brophy, appeared before the FCC, to urge the adoption and implementation of three changes which are needed to adapt depreciation practices to today's environment and restore the economic health of the telephone industry:

First, specific provisions should be made to permit, by the time of deregulation of terminal equipment, the full recovery of any loss of investment in terminal equipment resulting from deregulation.

Second, the present regulatory depreciation practice should be changed to provide for the full recovery of the remaining investment in *existing* plant and equipment over their remaining economic lives.

Third, the present regulatory depreciation practice should be changed to permit telephone companies to depreciate *new* plant and equipment, of all types, on a substantially accelerated basis. An appropriate basis would be that currently used for tax purposes.

The adoption of these proposals by the FCC, and, where appropriate, by state commissions is urgently needed. It is most encouraging that the FCC has subsequently taken action which will lead to substantial changes in the regulatory approach to capital recovery. It recognizes the possibility of using accelerated depreciation on existing plant and equipment, and of depreciating new plant and equipment on a substantially accelerated basis.

The adoption of these theories is, however, only a first step. Both the FCC and state commissions must quickly translate depreciation changes into rate adjustments. Until that is accomplished, there will be no improvement in capital recovery of the telephone companies. Once accomplished, it will permit telephone companies to embrace new technology, hold down the cost of telephone service, and compete in the new information retrieval and data processing marketplace on an equal footing.

At the same time, GTE has mounted a number of programs to improve the "productivity" of capital as well as people; these include companywide programs in effective cash management—not just for managers—but for all those throughout the company who have opportunities to change the *prices,* the *quantities,* the *terms,* and the *timing* of the inputs and outputs affecting cash flow.

It is also placing heavy emphasis on improving productivity company-wide. All major GTE units are engaged in at least pilot productivity programs, and a declining trend in productivity has already been turned around in some key components.

A strategic planning system is in place, and working—to effect a closer linkage of investment with corporate goals and priorities.

If GTE, or any other company, is to survive in today's inflation, the emphasis must be on costs—real costs—and revenues, not on the hope that long-term debt will somehow compensate for understated costs.

The importance of the steps described to maintaining the integrity of the investment dollar in an inflationary climate can scarcely be overrated.

The telephone industry is the third largest user of capital in the US. The telephone companies' asset base represents the investment of millions upon millions of people, and the industry's price and productivity performance is truly of national importance.

When the $90 billion the US will pay for oil in 1980 substantially exceeds the total net income of all the companies on the Fortune 500 list, it is clearly time to take action.

For these reasons, the steps that GTE and others in industry are taking to improve the use and effective "recycling" of private investment income for continued innovation and productivity growth, are not only essential, but are truly crucial for the 1980s.

Technology In Society, Vol. 3, pp. 281–289 (1981)
Printed in the USA. All rights reserved.

0160-791X/81/010281-09$02.00/0
Copyright © 1981 Pergamon Press Ltd

Advancing Technological Innovation Through Tax Policy

Edwin V. W. Zschau

During 1981, the US Congress will formulate and enact a series of changes to the existing tax laws. Many factors will be considered in the process: the amount of tax revenue generated, the impact on various income groups, the effects on business activity, fairness, and the simplicity of implementation. The purpose of this paper is to make the case that there is another factor which should be considered when formulating tax policy in the 1980s: the impact of tax policy on the rate of technological innovation in the United States.

This case is based upon the following fundamentals:

- Leadership in technology is the most valuable national resource of the United States.
- US leadership in technology has been on a steady decline over the past 20 years.
- Fostering technology advancement requires both freedom and incentives for innovators.
- Tax policy is the most powerful instrument in the hands of the Federal government for fostering technological innovation.

Here are the specifics.

Technological Leadership — The Most Valuable Resource

The quality of life of American citizens depends upon having a strong economy that is able to produce an abundance of goods and services and also provide enough well-paying jobs. The US quality of life depends upon a strong national

Edwin V. W. Zschau is Chairman of the Board and President of System Industries in Sunnyvale,California. Prior to founding System Industries in 1968, he was Assistant Professor of Management Science at the Stanford University Graduate School of Business, 1964–1968, and spent the 1967–1968 academic year at Harvard Business School as a Visiting Assistant Professor. Dr. Zschau has served on the technical staff of Bell Telephone Laboratories and as consultant to the RAND Corporation. Currently he is Lecturer in Business Policy at Stanford University. He is a former Chairman of the American Electronics Association and was Chairman of the AEA Capital Formation Task Force during 1977–78. In 1979, Dr. Zschau was elected to the Board of Directors of the American Council for Capital Formation in Washington, D.C., and in 1980 he served on the Business Advisory Panel for President Reagan and on his Task Force on Innovation and Entrepreneurship.

defense that makes any attack by foreign aggressors unthinkable. Technology is the key to both a strong economy and a strong defense.

The Economic Impact of Technology

• *Technological innovation is fundamental to economic growth.* The country is able to grow when it finds better, more efficient ways to do things and when it develops new products that meet unfulfilled consumer needs at home and abroad. Professor R. Solow of the Massachusetts Institute of Technology confirmed this in a study showing that approximately 80% of the growth in GNP of the United States between 1909 and 1949 was due to technical change; subsequent studies have reduced this number, but agree that it has been the single largest factor in such growth.

• *Technological innovation is fundamental to productivity improvements.* Through the ages, the physical capabilities of people have been enhanced by machinery, leaving more time for intellectual activities. More recently, the power of the human intellect has been extended by computers, data storage, communications systems, and visual display devices. Now the US is entering the age of robotics in which the two are combined to do certain work more effectively and efficiently than ever before. It's not surprising that a recent Brookings Institution study determined that more than one-half of the productivity increases in the United States between 1948 and 1969 were the direct result of technological innovation.

• *Technological innovation is fundamental to international trade competitiveness.* In recent years, while the export performance of the United States has produced some disturbing trends with trade deficits of $26.5 billion in 1977, $28.4 billion in 1978, and $24.7 billion in 1979, exports of R&D-intensive products (*e.g.*, high technology electronics, capital equipment and pharmaceuticals) have shown excellent growth. From 1960 to 1979, R&D-intensive manufacturing industries increased their export surplus from $5.9 billion to $29.3 billion. During the same period, the trade balance of industries without technological bases declined from near zero to a negative $16.5 billion. With the country's trading partners recognizing the importance of innovation and technology, it is becoming even more important to emphasize technology advancement as the key to competitiveness at home and abroad.

The Need for Technology in Defense

If it is assumed that maintaining a parity in weapons with the Soviet Union is essential to a strong national defense, the country must rely on technology and its implementation in weapons systems as the basis for its defense strategy. Over the past decade, the Soviet Union has eroded much of the advantage that the US used to have by improving the power and accuracy of their strategic weapons and by increasing dramatically the amount of military equipment they produce. Although the situation is not yet desperate, the trends are frightening and need to be reversed immediately.

The trends can't be reversed by trying to regain numerical superiority. That approach would be financially unfeasible and ineffective. However, they can be reversed by using US technology, which in important areas is far more advanced than that of the Russians. The US has the technology to make munitions more accurate; aircraft, submarines, and missiles more difficult to detect; and surveillance and electronic warfare systems more effective. In the 1980s, US defense must be based on the use of *finesse* through technological innovation rather than on pure *force*.

US Technological Leadership Is Declining Badly

Over the past 20 years, US technological leadership has been seriously eroded. It hasn't been squandered, as some other resources have been through overuse and waste. It has been frittered away through neglect.

The emphasis on R&D in the US has been on a steady decline over the past two decades. In the 1960s, R&D expenditures grew about 6.5% per year, but in the 1970s the annual growth of R&D was only 1.6% annually. In fact, in constant (1972) dollars US R&D expenditures in 1977 were no more than they were in 1967.

In 1964, the US spent 3% of GNP on research and development, but by 1979 it spent only 2.2%. During a comparable period, two of its most aggressive trading partners — Japan and West Germany — were increasing their R&D expenditures. Table 1 compares the trends in these nations to those in the United States and provides data which suggests the economic implications of those trends.

Given the decline in R&D expenditures in the United States, it's not surprising that US leadership in technological contributions has declined as well. In the 1950s, the United States was credited with 80% of the major inventions made during that period. However, during the 1970s, its share of major inventions had dropped to 60%. In addition, from 1964 to 1979 the US patent balance, the percentage of US patents granted to US citizens, rather than foreign inventors, dropped from 88% to 62%.

TABLE 1. Comparison of Trends

Trends	% United States	% Japan	% West Germany
R&D as a percentage of GNP			
1964	3.0	1.5	1.6
1976	2.3	1.9	2.3
Average annual rate productivity improvement 1960–78	2.6	8.5	5.4
Share of world's exports			
1960	18.0	4.0	10.3
1977	11.8	8.0	11.5

Although the statistics cited here are disturbing, the situation is not hopeless. Since technological innovation is derived from the talent of its people, it is within US control. That cannot be said for energy sources or many raw material supplies. Indeed, the growing dependence of the United States on foreign energy and raw materials makes it all the more important that America's potential for technological innovation be realized.

Fostering Technological Innovation — Freedom and Incentives

With technology so important to the national interests, yet declining in America, the Federal government must act with a sense of urgency to stimulate technological innovation. Maintaining and extending technological leadership should be a national priority.

Unfortunately, changes in the rate of technological innovation will come slowly. Innovation can't be *forced;* it can only be *fostered.* It is fostered by creating an environment that emphasizes *freedom* of scientific and industrial activities and that offers *incentives* to the innovators, entrepreneurs, and investors who have the talent and resources to advance technology. Massive government R&D programs aren't the answer. Innovation doesn't thrive in bureaucracies. Innovation takes place when an individual or a small group gets an idea, has the freedom to pursue it — perhaps to succeed but maybe to fail — and can realize some attractive reward if successful.

Most of the commercially useful breakthroughs in genetic engineering have taken place in the laboratories of small companies run by entrepreneurs, not in the huge pharmaceutical corporations. The development of the American semiconductor industry is a history of entrepreneurship and small company contributions. In fact, according to a 1967 Department of Commerce report, more than half of the major technological advances in this century originated from individual inventors and small companies.

Technology-Oriented Tax Policy Is Needed

Starting today the US must begin to recreate an environment in America that fosters innovation. It should be an environment based on free enterprise, free trade (with strict bilateral reciprocity), and freedom from unnecessary regulation. It should also be an environment with incentives that encourage investment, risk-taking, new ideas and entrepreneurship.

Eliminating ill-conceived regulations and government programs to protect and subsidize noncompetitive enterprise will go a long way toward unleashing creative forces and encouraging proper allocation of resources. However, the most powerful instrument available to the Federal government for fostering technological innovation is a tax policy that stimulates investment, entrepreneurship, and technical education and research.

Over the past two years the country has seen the powerful effect that such tax policy can have on economic growth and technological development. In 1978, the American Electronics Association, a trade association of more than 1,300 high-technology companies in the United States, presented to Congress the results of an extensive survey of the environment facing young, innovative electronics firms. That survey documented the importance of young companies in solving the nation's unemployment problem. It showed that young companies create jobs 20–115 times faster than mature companies in the electronics industry. In fact, although the mature companies in the survey average 27 times more employees than the younger companies, the younger companies were creating more new jobs per firm per year than the mature companies.

The AEA survey confirmed that risk-capital investment is essential to the start-up and growth of high-technology companies. Such companies require constant infusions of risk capital in order to finance their growth and employment increases. On the average, about $14,000 of risk capital was needed to create each job in the electronics industry since 1955.

In addition to the creation of jobs, these young companies, if adequately financed, generate other benefits to the country. For example, for each $100 invested in electronics companies founded during 1971–75, by 1976 those companies were generating $70 per year in exports, spending $33 per year on R&D, and accounting for $30 per year in Federal income taxes. In other words, the study documented the remarkable fact that the Federal government could get a 30% annual return on the risk capital invested by individual investors if only those investors had adequate incentives to make such investments!

Unfortunately, those incentives had been substantially reduced during the 1970s with the doubling of the maximum tax rate on capital gains from 25% to 49%. As a result, the risk capital needed to start and finance the growth of high-technology companies had all but dried up. In the period 1971–75, companies in the electronics industry were able to raise less capital (in constant 1972 dollars) than at any time in the prior 15-year period.

In order to rekindle the incentives for needed risk-capital investment, the AEA strongly urged in 1978 a sharp reduction in the tax on capital gains on the grounds that it would once again make risk capital available to young companies. Since such a reduction would have a stimulative effect on the economy and the stock market, the AEA predicted that this tax cut would increase Feeral tax revenues rather than decrease them.

1978 Revenue Act Highlights

The Revenue Act of 1978 contained a reduction in the maximum capital gains tax rate to 28%. The results of that new incentive have been extraordinary. Here are some of the highlights:

•Commitments of new capital to professional venture capital funds during the 18-month period between mid-1978 (when the passage of capital gains tax reduction appeared certain) and year-end 1979 totaled nearly $900 million. This increase in funds, which is now available for investment in young and growing companies, is more than double the total amount of capital committed to such funds during the seven-year period 1970–77.

•Annual investments from such venture capital funds into young companies have more than doubled since the capital gains tax rates were reduced and, more importantly, more money is now going into start-up situations.

- Young companies are now able to obtain needed capital from the public market far more easily than before the capital gains tax rates were decreased. For example, in the first quarter of 1980 the number of public offerings (31) and the funds raised by them ($139 million) were both more than double the comparable amounts for the first quarter 1979 — a year in which the number of new public offerings was greater than in any of the six previous years.
- Since the Revenue Act of 1978 was passed — despite accelerating inflation, rising interest rates and impending recession — the price appreciation of public company stocks, particularly those of small companies, has been excellent. Between November 1978 and June 1980 the NASDAQ index rose nearly 97% and the AMEX index rose 55%. Importantly, by September 16, 1980, the Standard and Poor's 500-stock index reached a level 41.6% above its close on April 13, 1978, thereby exceeding the 40% increase in stock prices that had been projected by Chase Econometric Associates, Inc., to occur by 1982 as a result of the capital gains tax reduction.
- Cutting the capital gains tax rates has not resulted in the large revenue loss that the Treasury had predicted. Instead, the Treasury collected $8.3 billion in capital gains taxes in 1979, the first year of the lower rates, *up* 14% from the $7.3 billion collected in 1977, and the $7.2 billion collected in 1978. The Treasury is collecting more at the lower rates than at the higher rates without even including the higher corporate and personal income taxes resulting from the economic stimulation that the lower capital gains tax rates are producing.

From the experience of the 1978 Revenue Act and its effect on risk capital needed to promote technological innovation, the country has seen proof of the power of tax policy in creating an environment to foster innovation. What follows are the specific proposals that must be implemented this year in order to provide further stimulus to innovation and to reverse the decline of America's technological leadership.

A Tax Policy for Fostering Technological Innovation

In order to maintain and extend its technological leadership, the US must implement a tax program that stimulates the key ingredients necessary for innovation:
- Risk capital investment;
- Entrepreneurship and individual risk taking; and
- R&D activities and education of technical personnel.

The following program would provide such stimulation and could be implemented easily.

1. *Reduce capital gains tax rates further.* So long as further reductions of capital gains tax rates have stimulative effects, they should continue to be implemented. The country has already experienced the dramatic positive impact of the 1978 reduction. Further cuts will undoubtedly result in additional stimuli to needed investment and risk taking.

It is not clear what the "optimal" capital gains tax rate is, but there are strong indications that exempting capital gains from taxation entirely would be best for our economy. Not taxing capital gains would also put the US in line with the policies of Japan and West Germany, which have had excellent records of technological advancement and economic performance in recent years.

Reductions in the capital gains tax rates should be made in phases every few years — with monitoring of the efficacy of each cut — until further reductions appear to be unjustified. As the next step, the maximum tax rate on capital gains should be reduced to about 15%. This reduction would be about the same percentage decrease as the one made in 1978.

The needed reduction of capital gains tax rates could be accomplished by one of two methods:

- Eliminate the distinction between "earned" and "unearned" income, taxing all income at the maximum rate of 50%, and increasing the excludable portion of capital gains for income tax purposes from 60% to 70%; or
- Increase the excludable portion of capital gains for income tax purposes from 60% to 80%.

In either case, capital gains should be eliminated as a preference item for calculating the minimum alternative tax.

2. *Reinstate restricted stock options.* Such stock options, which were in effect from 1950 to 1964, were a powerful tool for attracting talented scientists, engineers, technicians, and managers to risk their careers in ventures developing new technologies and products. Normally, few employees have the capital needed to become significant owners in the companies that employ them, but restricted stock options provided employees with the benefits of ownership without requiring them to make the up-front cash outlays. Instead of cash they were able to invest their time, careers, and talents.

A series of changes in the tax code from 1964 to 1976 eliminated restricted stock options entirely. Today, companies can grant only "nonqualified" options which are practically useless to most growing companies. Under the present law, when an employee exercises these "nonqualified" options, he must pay taxes — at ordinary income tax rates — on the "paper profit" between his option price and the price of the stock when he buys it. Not only is taxation at ordinary income tax rates inconsistent with what other owners pay on their capital appreciation but, in addition, the employee must pay the tax *before* he actually realizes the gain from selling the stock. It's analogous to taxing the appreciation on a homeowner's house each year even though he doesn't sell it. Employees without reserves of funds may not be able to buy the stock and also pay the tax on a "paper profit."

The terms of restricted stock options would enable an employee to purchase the stock and — if the stock is held for a suitable period — pay a capital gains tax on the difference between his selling price and his purchase price. Tax payments for restricted stock options are not made until the employee has actually realized the gain.

When they were in effect, restricted stock options were found to motivate employees to do a better job and find better ways to do the job. Since a stock option has value to the employee only if the price of the company stock increases through growth in its sales and profits, options give employees a strong incentive to find ways to expand the company's business and conduct that business more efficiently. Business growth creates more new jobs; increased efficiency results in greater productivity; and incentives to develop new ideas result in technological advancement.

In 1980, the Joint Committee on Taxation examined the revenue impact of restoring restricted stock options. The Joint Committee estimated that such a change in tax policy would result in a *net revenue gain* to the Treasury of $35 million in the first six years after the legislation is passed.

3. *Offer 25% tax credits to businesses for contributions to technical education programs, for increases (over a three-year base period) in their R&D expenditures, and for contributions to R&D programs conducted by colleges and universities.* The purpose of these tax credits would be to provide private industry with direct incentives to assist in the education of more technical personnel and to step up research and development being done in companies and in academic institutions.

It's a disgrace and a disturbing fact that Japan, with a population half as large as the United States, trains four times as many scientists and engineers per year as the US. Out of every 10,000 citizens in Japan, 400 are engineers and scientists while only one is a lawyer and three are accountants. Out of every 10,000 citizens in the US, only 70 are engineers and scientists, but 20 are lawyers and 40 are accountants. The US is becoming a society of paper-pushers, rather than producers. More money must be focused on training technical personnel and funding the research that they do if the US is to maintain its leadership in technology.

These proposed educational and R&D tax credits should be viewed both as *incentives* for private enterprise to contribute more to technological programs and as *partial funding* by the Federal government of private educational and R&D activities. Private enterprise can select and manage technical programs better than the government can, but by assisting in the funding of those well-managed programs, the government can help to produce efficiently the beneficial effects of faster technological progress.

Although detailed econometric analyses of this particular proposal have not yet been done, Data Resources, Inc., studied the effect of a 25% tax credit for all R&D expenditures (not just increases). That study concluded that during the period 1978–87 such a tax credit would:

• Increase R&D spending by an average of $5.2 billion per year;
• Add an average of $36.2 billion to the GNP per year;
• Add an average of $1.7 billion to U.S. exports per year;
• Increase productivity by an average of .28% per year;
• Reduce the annual increase in the consumer price index by .42% per year.

These estimates are indicative of the kind of impact that 25% R&D tax credits on *increases* in R&D expenditures would have, but such tax credits would be far more efficient.

Summary

Maintaining its leadership in technology should be a national priority for the United States. The most effective instrument for fostering technological advancement is tax policy. A tax program consisting of:
- Lower capital gains tax rates;
- Institution of restricted stock options; and
- Tax credits for contributions to technical education and R&D increases should be instituted in 1981. Such a program would create in this country an environment that fosters innovation and enables the US to enhance and exploit its most valuable national resource — technology.

Technology In Society

New York / Oxford / Toronto / PERGAMON PRESS / Paris / Frankfurt / Sydney